Managing Disaster

Strategies and Policy Perspectives

Edited by Louise K. Comfort

Duke Press Policy Studies
Duke University Press   Durham and London   1988

© 1988 Duke University Press
All rights reserved
Printed in the United States of America
on acid-free paper ∞

Library of Congress Cataloging-in-Publication Data
Managing disaster.
(Duke Press policy studies)
Bibliography: p.
Includes index.
1. Disaster relief—Management. 2. Disaster relief—
United States—Management. 3. Disaster relief—Government
policy—United States. I. Comfort, Louise K. (Louise
Kloos), 1935–   . II. Series.
HV555.U6M35   1988   363.3'48'0973   87-20049
ISBN 0-8223-0800-2
ISBN 0-8223-0816-9 (pbk.)

Contents

Contents

Integrating Emergency Management

Foreword

This volume is one of the major results of a "discipline building" effort that began three years ago. In 1983 the Federal Emergency Management Agency (FEMA), then under the leadership of Louis Giuffrida and Fred J. Villella, invited representatives from the National Association of Schools of Public Affairs and Administration (NASPAA) to a series of meetings at its headquarters. The meetings focused on the presence, or rather the absence, of the topic of emergency management within the curricula of university public administration programs. These meetings were later expanded to include also representatives of such practitioner groups as the International City Management Association and other state and local officials.

Following this series of meetings a national review panel on emergency management was formed to design and help implement a series of programs to introduce this field of study to the nation's public administration academic programs. I had the pleasure of chairing that panel.

The review panel prepared a series of initiatives to meet this goal. One of the major efforts focused on facilitating the development of a "critical mass" of public administration faculty who would be interested in teaching, doing research, and writing about emergency management. The primary vehicle chosen was the offering in May 1984 of a two-week intensive workshop on emergency management at FEMA's Emmitsburg, Maryland, training center. It was to be followed by three more workshops in succeeding years.

I served as director of that workshop, with the able assistance of Dr. William Petak of the University of Southern California. Thirty-three faculty members were chosen to attend on a competitive basis from the nation's public administration programs.

This new book on disaster management is the third published product of participants of the program begun in 1984. The other works involve a special edition of the *Public Administration Review* (1985), and a case analysis book now in the process of publication.

It has been a distinct personal and professional privilege for me to have been involved in this pioneering effort. I am very proud of the productivity of the individuals who were part of the Emmitsburg workshop, and particularly congratulate Dr. Louise Comfort for her ingenuity and perseverance in conceptualizing and editing this new contribution to the literature of the field. I am honored to have been asked to write the foreword to this book. It will be an outstanding addition to the "discipline" of emergency management.

Charles F. Bonser, Dean,
School of Public and Environmental Affairs,
Indiana University

Preface

This book marks an important shift in the definition of responsibility for disaster. For centuries, catastrophic events have been considered "acts of God" and beyond the control of human decisionmakers. The important tradition of sociological research developed by the National Academy of Sciences/National Research Council and by the internationally recognized Disaster Research Center, formerly of Ohio State University and now at the University of Delaware, looked first at the response of individuals and communities to disasters as sudden, unplanned disruptions of the social order. More recently, other university-based centers for hazard studies have focused on the interdisciplinary aspects of disastrous events, acknowledging the interaction between natural hazards and human systems.

Two factors have prompted a systematic effort to reexamine the roles and limits of public service agencies in disaster management. These factors are, first, an increased acceptance of public responsibility for the burden of costs engendered by disasters, exemplified by the Disaster Relief Act of 1974, and, second, the continuing movement of civilian populations into hazard-prone areas. While public service agencies have the legally mandated responsibility to protect life and property of citizens in events of disaster, attention and interest have largely shifted from a focus on collective response after the event to the responsible mitigation of hazard vulnerability and reduction of risk through pre-paredness activities in order to minimize the catastrophic effects of such events upon civilian populations.

The successful reduction of risk, however, requires both more informed public policy and more systematic education in disaster miti-gation and management for public service personnel. New technolo-gies in communications, information-gathering, processing, and moni-toring of hazardous events now allow the conception of mitigation and management strategies previously not undertaken by public service agencies. Reformulation of the parameters regarding what governmen-tal agencies can and cannot do for civilian populations requires redraw-ing the relationships between public and private organizations, gov-ernmental agencies, and citizens. In this process increasing the accuracy and relevance of information, the timeliness of communication, and the systematic review of actions taken among the set of organizations involved in disaster management offers powerful means of reducing uncertainty for participating decisionmakers, thereby improving pro-fessional performance in disaster mitigation and management. This book offers a reconsideration of strategies and policy perspectives for managing disaster in an increasingly professional public service.

This book represents a collection of original essays by twenty-one active scholars in the field of public policy and administration focusing on the set of current issues in disaster management. Two basic ques-tions serve as the organizing focus of the book: what are the primary issues confronting public managers in event of disaster; and what actions can public agencies responsibly take to protect the lives and property of citizens. This collection of essays is unusual in that it brings together in one volume a range of perspectives from authors who have had experience, through study and observation, with disasters from Alaska to Florida, California to Maine in the United States, and from Peru through the Netherlands to Israel in international settings.

The book is organized in seven parts. In part one, two essays exam-ine the central tasks that public managers face in designing policy and structuring problems for action in the uncertain environment of disas-ter mitigation and management. Parts two through five review the classic phases of mitigation, preparedness, response, recovery, and reconstruction in the disaster process. Each of these parts begins with a lead essay that reviews current issues confronting public managers for that phase of the process. Other essays follow that examine in greater depth particular issues generating concern for public managers in that phase of the disaster management process. These four parts draw largely upon observation and experience with disaster management in the United States. Increasingly important in an interdependent world is the international perspective in disaster management. Part six presents two essays on issues of disaster management in international settings. In part seven a final set of essays examines critical aspects involved in the development of professional judgment, central to effective performance, in emergency management.

While this book represents a systematic effort to reconsider policy and organizational requirements for improving professional performance in disaster management, it is a beginning step in what will necessarily be a continuing process of organizational learning through trial, error, and reflective adaptation of present capabilities to changing demands for public service. Yet this book is written with sober awareness of the complexity of that process, and it is offered as a contribution to the ongoing task of professional inquiry in the field of disaster management.

Many people have contributed to the development and production of this book. We thank them all, but several people deserve particular mention. The book had its origins in the Senior Executive Seminar on Emergency Management held at Emmitsburg, Maryland, May 20–June 2, 1984. Charles Bonser and William Petak gave both direction and inspiration to the group of professors of public administration and policy in a manner that generated lasting interest in, and professional commitment to, the problems of disaster management. The seminar was cosponsored by the Federal Emergency Management Agency and the National Association of Schools of Public Administration and Affairs, and we are grateful to these organizations and their staff members for making this opportunity available to us. Staff members at the National Emergency Training Center at Emmitsburg contributed time, energy, and effort to make the seminar a valuable learning experience for us. Paul Watson, in particular, has followed this project and actively supported its development and completion. Richard Rowson, director of Duke University Press, has offered continued guidance and encouragement for the development of this project in its effort to reach both the academic and practicing audiences in public administration who are interested in disaster management.

As editor of the book, I owe a special debt of gratitude to the Graduate School of Public and International Affairs for supporting this project over two years from its inception to completion. This project has had the unusual experience of benefiting from the active support of four deans of GSPIA: John Funari, Leon Haley, Edison Montgomery, and Lawrence Korb. Each has contributed encouragement and institutional support for the continuing work of the project. Barbara Wells has managed the details of cross-continental telephone calls and repeated mailings to participating authors with grace and good humor. Kathy Rud and Joyce Valiquette typed the major portion of the manuscript with professional skill and patience, managing to cope with multiple changes and to convert the footnote styles from twenty-one authors into a common format. Ruth Buncher, Willadean Bailey, and Amy Jacob assisted with the final typing of the manuscript and the continuing tasks of correspondence and production over the two-year period of the project.

Finally, I wish to express my warm thanks and appreciation to the other twenty authors contributing to this book. A sense of common professional commitment and shared discovery has developed in our collective work on this project. Each author has contributed a distinctive perspective, a particular kind of experience with disaster management. The collection of essays is richer for the diversity, more comprehensive and complete in its portrayal of the disaster management process than would be possible for any single author to produce. It has been my privilege as editor to observe the development of the project into a coherent whole and to recognize the special contribution of each author to the volume. The project has indeed reinforced the development of a national and international network among scholars who are doing research and teaching in the field of disaster management.

Louise K. Comfort
Pittsburgh, Pennsylvania
July 1987

The Policy Problem

Designing Policy for Action:
The Emergency Management System
⚡ Louise K. Comfort

"Design like science is a tool for understanding as well as acting."—Herbert
A. Simon

The Policy Question: Requiem . . . Or Responsible Action?

The devastation is sudden, swift, and catastrophic. On November 13,
1985, a river of mud from the Nevada del Ruiz volcano flowed through
the town of Armero, Colombia, leaving over 22,000 people dead. On
September 19 and 20, 1985, two massive earthquakes collapsed apart-
ment buildings, hotels, hospitals, schools, businesses, and government office buildings in Mexico City, leaving over 7,000 dead reported
by official sources; other sources estimated over 11,000 dead. On May
31, 1985, a swath of twenty-four tornadoes swept through eastern Ohio,
western Pennsylvania, and into Canada, twisting towns, farms, and
lives, killing 66 people in western Pennsylvania alone. On December
4, 1984, a leak in a methyl isocyanate tank released a cloud of poison
gas over Bhopal, India, causing over 2,000 deaths and uncounted
injuries. To public policymakers and administrators the question is
reframed afresh with each event. What is the public interest? What
should the government do? Are there alternatives for public action that
are more effective in protecting lives and property?

The sobering fact is that such events are not unexpected in a complex, interdependent world. As the numbers of people, structures, and technologies increase and interact in vulnerable physical environments, particularly in metropolitan areas, the likelihood of natural hazards or technological failures becoming catastrophic events in these environments escalates rapidly.[1] The traditional explanation that such events are "acts of God" and therefore beyond human control is decreasingly plausible when sophisticated technologies, communications networks, and organizational capacities offer new possibilities for mobilizing public action in response to the multiple demands of a disaster.

In policy terms, the government has three basic strategies that it can mix and vary to create the desired organizational and social action in event of disaster. First, it can assist individuals and organizations to improve their capacity to achieve policy goals, that is, to protect lives and property within their own homes, workplaces, and communities. Second, it can allocate resources, tasks, and time to establish continuity in organizational structures and procedures across changing budget years, personnel assignments, and administrative regions. Third, it can establish integrating patterns of communication to link individuals and organizations engaged in emergency activities to one another as well as to relevant clientele and resources in the environment. These strategies, taken together, allow the conscious design of an organizational network[2] that can mobilize the relevant resources, knowledge, and personnel to take appropriate and timely action under emergency conditions.

Such an action network is necessarily interorganizational and interdisciplinary.[3] It links jurisdictional levels of government—city, county, state, federal, and, with growing frequency, international—in emergency operations. Within each jurisdictional level the action network connects the organizations that have emergency responsibilities —police, fire, public works, emergency medical services, and others—in coordinated response to disaster. The design for an integrated emergency management system has been actively promoted by policymakers and analysts for a number of years.[4] Yet management systems devised to improve integrated agency performance have been overwhelmed repeatedly in actual disaster operations.[5] The chief obstacle to improved performance is the enormous complexity of the disaster environment, given the limitations of human cognitive capacity and routine administrative procedures.[6] Based upon observed performance, standard administrative planning and practices alone are inadequate in major disasters. Creating the appropriate mix of organizational learning, command, and control structures, and integrating patterns of communication to achieve effective performance in the dynamic emergency environment is the continuing challenge to emergency managers at all levels of government.

Sustaining an organizational network in emergency management requires continuing inquiry into recurring problems in actual jurisdictions, assessing the constraints imposed by geography, resources, and time against the essential tasks for performance under emergency conditions. What are the requisite elements of emergency management for a given jurisdiction, and how do these elements interact with other segments of the emergency management system? How do people learn to assess risk and cope with life-threatening events? What kinds of knowledge and skills are needed to inform responsible public action under catastrophic conditions? The network depends upon the ability of its participants to generate valid information, facilitate informed choice, and foster timely commitment to action.[7] Further, the network is strengthened when the participants reflect upon actions taken, retain the procedures that proved effective, and discard those that were not.[8] Such a network is necessarily a learning system.

The policy question also changes in this complex, dynamic environment. Policymakers indeed have options now that were not available to them earlier. The focus of the policy question is critical. Do we allocate our attention and resources to repairing damage after the catastrophe has occurred, or do we direct our efforts to discovering new means of reducing the likelihood and/or costs of disaster occurring in our cities and communities? For public policymakers and administrators, the task becomes how to transform the continuing requiem for the dead into responsible action for the living.

Three conditions that characterize emergency environments serve to limit the effectiveness of standard means of policy formulation and implementation. These conditions are uncertainty, interaction, and complexity. Inherent in the problem of disaster management policy is the uncertainty of events to which public service agencies must respond. The ordinary instruments of planning are regrettably inadequate when the magnitude, scope, and timing of the response required by the emergency are unknown. Yet it is precisely the conditions of uncertainty and the interactive effects of emergencies upon civilian populations and infrastructure that require serious governmental focus. Intrinsic to emergency management, uncertainty needs to be incorporated into the policy process as a fundamental component.

Interaction, or the sequence of reciprocal events that may be triggered between a disaster and affected civilian populations and infrastructure, needs to be anticipated by responsible policymakers. Complexity is the product of uncertainty and interaction which together compound the possible issues for public action involved in emergency planning nearly beyond human calculation. For example, what impact would a major earthquake have upon the water and gas mains of a given metropolitan area? What effect would breaks in the water mains, in turn, have upon the capacity of the fire department of that jurisdiction to suppress fires erupting from broken gas mains? The measurement of uncertainty and interaction relies upon no known equation in public management. The number of possible risks—and public actions —ensuing from their reciprocal effects makes emergency planning immensely complex. Nonetheless, estimating the degree of uncertainty and the extent of interaction involved in probable emergency events is a task faced by every emergency manager responsible for public operations. This responsibility warrants careful attention to the concept of design in the formulation and implementation of emergency management policy.

Toward a Model of Professional Design in Emergency Management

Coping with the complexity involved in emergency management requires a clear conceptualization of the policy process in this context. The tasks involved in determining responsible public action in emergency management may be represented by a preliminary model of professional design, as shown in figure 1. Illustrating Simon's concept of design, the emergency management system is portrayed as operating at the interface between the policy goal and the emergency environment. It represents the conscious effort to create the appropriate mix of change through developmental learning processes, continuity through organizational structure, and integration through interactive communication patterns needed to sustain a functioning emergency management system in a complex, dynamic environment.

Design, to Herbert Simon, is the conscious effort to create a rational or "artificial" system to facilitate the accomplishment of a specific social goal.[9] Given the dynamic, interactive nature of the social environ-

Figure 1. A Model of Professional Design in Emergency Management

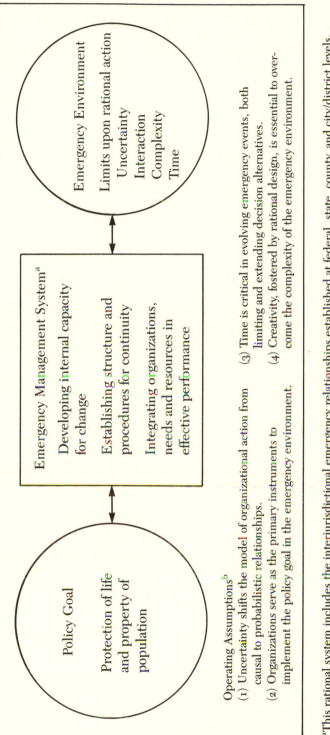

Policy Goal

Protection of life and property of population

Emergency Management System[a]

Developing internal capacity for change

Establishing structure and procedures for continuity

Integrating organizations, needs and resources in effective performance

Emergency Environment

Limits upon rational action
Uncertainty
Interaction
Complexity
Time

Operating Assumptions[b]
(1) Uncertainty shifts the model of organizational action from causal to probabilistic relationships.
(2) Organizations serve as the primary instruments to implement the policy goal in the emergency environment.

(3) Time is critical in evolving emergency events, both limiting and extending decision alternatives.
(4) Creativity, fostered by rational design, is essential to overcome the complexity of the emergency environment.

[a]This rational system includes the interjurisdictional emergency relationships established at federal, state, county, and city/district levels.
[b]This model draws upon the concept of professional design stated by H. A. Simon (1969, 1981) and the discussion of organizational behavior in L. B. Mohr (1982).

ment, specific goals tend to go astray in the ordinary course of events without continuing effort to focus attention, action, and resources for their accomplishment.[10] Design serves to focus the rational actions of human participants in the natural environment with its full range of uncertainty, variability, and complexity.

The policy goal in emergency management is the protection of life and property of citizens from known and unknown hazards.[11] The rational system designed to serve this goal in the United States is the Federal Emergency Management Agency and its counterpart organizations at state and local levels with emergency responsibilities. The environment represents the entire range of hazards—natural or man-made—that could conceivably threaten the American people. From a design perspective, effective action by the emergency management system depends upon the capacity of its internal units and operational processes to meet the demands that emerge from the environment in terms of the stated policy goal. Design offers the means of consciously determining rational action to achieve intended goals in the continual flux of the social environment.

Operating Assumptions of the Emergency
Management System

Through design, responsible personnel can simplify the complexity of emergency environments in order to facilitate action. Four assumptions regarding this environment are central to determining the components and operating conditions of emergency management. First, uncertainty characterizes the operating environment, influencing the effectiveness of organizational procedures and task assignments designed to guide emergency actions. For example, after the May 31, 1985, tornadoes swept through ten counties in western Pennsylvania, the Volunteer Fire Department of Jackson Center in Mercer County assembled in their fire hall, prepared to offer assistance to their neighboring town of Atlantic in Crawford County, badly hit in the disaster. As specified in their mutual assistance agreement with the Town of Atlantic, the fire chief waited for the formal request for assistance from the Atlantic Fire Department. The telephone call never came, and, consistent with the prearranged rules, the Jackson Center Fire Department did not go to Atlantic during that long, traumatic night. Later, the Jackson Center fire chief learned that the telephone lines had been ripped out by the tornado, and the Atlantic Fire Department had no means to communicate its urgent need for assistance to Jackson Center.[12]

The uncertainty in communications capacity created by the tornado invalidated the rules specified in the mutual aid agreement between the two communities. Ironically, the rules were drawn precisely to reduce uncertainty in management decisions under disaster conditions. The emergency management system may be viewed more accurately as a dynamic process in which organizations and jurisdictions interact to increase the likelihood of accomplishing expected goals for performance in a disaster, rather than as an authoritative set of rules that ensures a certain outcome.[13]

Second, organizations, as mechanisms for coordinating individual actions, are the primary actors in the emergency management system. Using the same example of the tornado disaster in western Pennsylvania, the fire chief of Jackson Center acted in his organizational role, not as an individual, in determining his response to the disaster. As an individual, he might have simply driven over to Atlantic to see if people needed help. As fire chief, he was responsible for upholding a set of previous agreements and marshaling his resources for mutual assistance accordingly. This example illustrates the importance of institutional arrangements in structuring the emergency management process by specifying the range and order of probable actions in reference to emergency events.[14] While organizational structure is not sufficient to achieve effective emergency management, it is a necessary mechanism for coordinating individual actions under the complex conditions of a disaster.

Third, time plays a critical role in the design of effective emergency management. In the 1985 Pennsylvania tornado disaster, a major factor in the high rate of damage ($262 million) and the high number of victims (66 deaths) was the lack of warning to the citizens.[15] In a survey of citizens affected by the tornado, 71.3 percent of those interviewed reported they had less than five minutes' warning before the tornado struck.[16] Time is especially critical in the interdependent emergency environment, as the consequences of failure to take appropriate action in preparation for an emergency are multiplied many times over during the actual event. Further, in the context of disaster events, time measures both the degeneration of response capacity as resources are expended and the improvement of the emergency situation as services are restored and recovery activities are implemented. Balancing needs against available resources over time is a classic paradox for emergency managers. Design in emergency management policy can facilitate the sequential ordering of interactive choices toward the intended goal by estimating the cumulative effects of time upon actors and conditions involved in emergency events.

Fourth, creativity is an essential component of the emergency management process. Emergency conditions inherently pose ill-structured problems that stubbornly defy prior expectations for action.[17] In the September 19, 1985, earthquake disaster in Mexico City, for example, the U.S. disaster assistance teams were stymied by the lack of communication and coordination with other international teams who were working toward the same goal. There were no previous policies to guide international search and rescue operations. Given the obvious need for better coordination in international search and rescue operations, the leaders of several international teams began to meet each evening to report on the day's activities, to share information, and to outline coordinated activities for the next day's work. This nightly meeting of team leaders, created by the respective teams after they arrived in Mexico City, facilitated the search and rescue work of the participating international teams.[18] Yet vital to their capacity to invent a better solution to the problems of international coordination was the fact that most international teams were staying in downtown hotels within relatively easy access to one another. Searching for means to improve the quality of decisionmaking in emergency management, therefore, includes the design of rational procedures to enrich the information context of decisionmaking for organizations with emergency responsibilities.[19] While creativity cannot be ordered on demand, rational procedures such as information search, retrieval, and feedback processes among participating organizations with emergency responsibilities may be designed to enhance creativity under certain conditions.[20] Creativity necessarily complements and extends rational procedures to fit the dynamic conditions of emergency.

These four assumptions constitute a set of guiding premises that underly a concept of professional design in emergency management. This concept assumes that effective performance depends upon the learning capacity of the individuals and organizations involved. With respect to each assumption, the means of solving the problems posed for effective emergency management is a process of learning—both individually and organizationally. None of the conditions addressed by the assumptions can be compelled through an authoritative declaration of power or money. Uncertainty, for example, can only be reduced through wider information search and generation of feasible alternatives for action. Organizations are effective units of operation in the emergency management process only to the extent that they can mobilize individuals to act with requisite skills and at appropriate times, which implies a coordinated learning process. Time allows observation of the environment that generates emergencies as well as actions to manage them, and reflection upon the effectiveness of those actions in terms of achieving policy goals, a learning process. Creativity includes the synthesis of diverse types of information and ideas to invent a more effective action or explanation of events that contribute to managing the disaster, intrinsically a learning process. Professional performance, therefore, is developmental. A primary task of design in emergency management policy becomes ordering that learning process in constructive, rational ways at the multiple levels of governmental action.

The informed and deliberate selection of strategies for action, based upon evidence subject to public disconfirmation and correction, constitutes a professional orientation to public action. Design becomes a distinguishing characteristic of a professional emergency management system. It combines rational with creative processes to facilitate organizational learning and uses the results of that process to correct and improve the performance of the functioning emergency management system. The proposed model represents an iterative process that uses the strategies of change, continuity, and integration to adapt the emergency management system to its task of achieving the stated policy goal in a dynamic environment.

The Strategy for Change: Developing Learning Capacity in Emergency Organizations

Three rational processes—assessment of risk, feedback of information to decisionmakers, and adjustment of performance based upon current information—are essential to the development of a learning capacity among organizations in the emergency management system. Operating interactively, these processes result in a powerful clarification of goals for action at the respective jurisdictional levels of emergency operations and the sequential phases of emergency management. Given the bounded rationality of human decisionmakers,[21] design specifies the information search, feedback, and decision processes within the complex emergency management system in a manner that refocuses the goals for action at each succeeding level of organizational decision.

In the complex emergency operating environment, the continuing clarification of goals for action is essential at successive jurisdictional levels, between multiple organizations, and at differing time periods within the emergency management process.[22] Although the overall goal is clear—preservation of life and protection of property—the specification of appropriate actions and the rational ordering of priorities vary in at least three ways: (1) over time during the emergency management cycle; (2) by jurisdiction and organization in emergency operations; and (3) with particular disaster agents. Using design concepts, emergency service personnel assess the degree of risk presented by a given emergency event and review periodically the appropriateness of their planned actions against the evolving requirements of the emergency situation. The feedback from this careful assessment process allows the emergency organizations to refocus their actions as the conditions of the environment change. Like a gyroscope seeking its balance under shifting conditions, the effective emergency management system continually assesses the changing profile of its environment and reinterprets its goal in that new reality.

Design structures the search for new information, altered levels of performance, or marked discrepancies between observed and expected conditions that signal the need for action in a goalseeking organization. Design facilitates the process of discovering practical solutions to actual problems, as in architecture or engineering. However, the solutions involve not only the efficient use of physical resources and space, but also the effective use of time and information. Goal clarification, fostered by design, drives the learning process in the emergency management system.

In the western Pennsylvania tornado disaster, for example, action by citizens and by local, state, and federal officials was hindered by breakdowns in communication, inadequate perception of risk, and difficulty in reciprocally adjusting actions to meet the changing needs of the situation.[23] Although all participants shared the same macrolevel goal in this disaster, the goal needed to be specified appropriately at the mid- and microlevels of decisionmaking in the interorganizational emergency management system to facilitate timely and informed choices. Without continual clarification of goals from macro- to microlevels of organizational action and back again, the interorganizational system fails to learn.

Risk Assessment in Emergency Management

Risk assessment plays a critical role in the function of goal clarification, essential to a strategy of change. Since there are differing levels of perceived risk, a major task of design in the emergency management process is to specify assessment criteria that recognize variation in degree of risk but commonality in meanings of risk across organizations and jurisdictions. To calibrate action appropriate to perceived risk across the complex emergency management system requires clearly understood and accepted criteria for risk assessment at multiple jurisdictional and organizational decision centers. Clarity of goals in the complex net of intergovernmental emergency operations follows most reliably from a finely tuned risk assessment process in emergency management.

Feedback in Emergency Management
Decision Processes

Designing procedures for action in a changing environment requires a continual monitoring of the discrepancy between intent and outcome of the action. In engineering problems this need for information on observed performance is met through feedback systems. In professional emergency management practices, feedback procedures can be designed to serve this same function of systematic return of information on observed performance to decisionmakers on a timely basis. Such procedures, operating between multiple organizations, require a network of interactive communications processes and a set of commonly understood criteria for assessing emergency conditions. For the feedback procedures to have the desired effect, the technical means of assessing and reporting risk, or changes in environmental conditions, need to be established at critical points of observation in the system. Determining what those points are, and what levels of skill are required for satisfactory assessment of emergency conditions, are questions of design. Decisions on these issues can be considered rationally and used to structure the learning process within and between the participating organizations.

Feedback systems also become a rational means of incorporating the effects of time upon emergency operating conditions into the decision process. Feedback systems serve as valuable mechanisms for scheduling successive actions in the evolving pattern of interorganizational emergency management. Individuals and organizations change their behavior only when they consciously discover a discrepancy between their intended action and actual practice. This discrepancy leads individuals and organizations to reconsider the basic premises for their actions, a process that organizational theorists term "double loop" learning.[24] While feedback systems do not guarantee "double loop" learning within or between organizations, they do enrich the information available to decisionmakers within those organizations and increase the likelihood that organizational learning will occur.

Adjusting Performance in Emergency Operations

The content of information gained from interorganizational feedback processes, coupled with clear understanding of policy goals at the successive levels of emergency operations, allows the generation of alternative solutions that may offer a closer fit between intent and outcome in actions taken. In the continual search for effective performance, feedback systems provide a rationally ordered flow of information between the dynamic emergency environment and organizational decisionmakers, and back again. While informal feedback mechanisms exist via communications patterns among friends and coworkers in most complex organizations, significant improvement in the identification of error and consequent adjustment of performance on the basis of current interaction is achieved when the feedback is designed on a systematic basis.[25]

Establishing carefully sequenced feedback processes within and between organizations, and within and between jurisdictional levels of the emergency management system, is a rational task accomplished with systematic planning and practice. Once in place, such systems perform the vital function of linking the set of emergency organizations into a flexible network that is capable of operating effectively at the municipal level to manage a local emergency or expanding to a national disaster management system, drawing information, technical assistance, and resources from a nationwide base. Such a national emergency management system, viewed as a set of organizational ecologies that simultaneously inform and support one another, is likely to provide a more timely and appropriate response than an organization directed from a single centralized source of authority.[26] Feedback systems, operating simultaneously at multiple levels in the successive stages of the emergency cycle, create a productive synergism among decisionmakers operating within their particular organizations at their respective jurisdictional levels. The power of feedback processes in the interorganizational emergency management system is that they improve the capacity for double-loop learning among decisionmakers, which allows the decisionmakers, in turn, to redesign their performance in more effective ways.

In summary, three subprocesses—assessment of risk, feedback of information to relevant decisionmakers, and correction of error —together offer a powerful mechanism for the reciprocal adjustment of goals and means in the operating emergency management system. This continuing adjustment involves a vital process of learning within the emergency management system and, consciously designed, represents a strategy for change. This strategy is essential throughout all four phases of the emergency management cycle—mitigation, preparedness, response, and recovery—but it is most effective when used to reduce the risk of loss to communities in the mitigation and preparedness phases.

The Strategy for Continuity: Establishing Structures and Procedures to Ensure Stability in Changing Environments

As rational instruments for action, the multiple organizations involved in the emergency management system represent conscious allocations of resources, attention, and responsibilities directed toward the achievement of policy goals. Once established, these organizations represent an explicit conception of appropriate public action under emergency conditions. The recurring dilemma in designing emergency organizations is how to utilize effectively known resources and personnel under unknown conditions. The organizations need to provide continuity in operating procedures while allowing flexibility to adapt to sudden demands for change.

The concept of a national emergency network recognizes that no single agency or jurisdiction has the resources, technical skills, or operational capacity to cope with a major disaster alone. The multiple organizations involved share the responsibility for effective performance in event of emergency. This shared responsibility for professional performance drives the design of the emergency network and further identifies the points of needed development and redesign in professional practice. The limitations of human capacity to function in the overwhelmingly complex environment of disaster are precisely the problem addressed by design in emergency organizations and procedures. Maximizing limited human capacity, in any given emergency event, becomes the organizational task. Three primary focuses in emergency organizations and procedures serve to structure the human capacity to act under emergency conditions: (1) decisionmaking processes; (2) priority setting; and (3) management of information. Each of these warrants careful consideration in the design of an intergovernmental emergency management system.

Decisionmaking Processes

Given the assumptions listed above, the decisionmaking process for emergency organizations is distinctly different under emergency conditions than in routine operations. In an emergency, problems are ill-structured. Environmental conditions are changing and dynamic. Numbers of clientele involved expand and contract dramatically. Time is critical, and complexity increases geometrically with the degree of interaction among participants and conditions. Systematic methods of decisionmaking, based upon orderly search of all possible alternatives for action, prove less effective in complex environments than "rules of thumb" or heuristic decision processes.[27] Observation of emergency decisionmakers in action, in both simulated and actual emergency events, documents this statement.[28] In the uncertain environment of an emergency, heuristic search and problem-solving practices acknowledge the element of innovation involved in decisionmaking. The function of design in emergency decisionmaking processes is to structure the elements of decision—information, timing, known constraints, interaction among participants—in a process that is likely to yield the most appropriate choice in the most timely fashion. This process, while not rejecting systematic decision procedures, does not require them for decisions to be taken given the operating constraints of the emergency management cycle.

Organization and representation of relevant information in a sequence and format that boundedly rational decisionmakers can access and accept is a product of design. Yet the escalating complexity of emergency environments tends to invalidate previously defined rules of decision if they are too precisely specified. In the parlance of artificial intelligence, the logic of decisionmaking in emergency environments is "fuzzy"[29] or imprecise, and wisely so, as it recognizes the necessity for innovative problem-solving in unforeseen situations.

Priority Setting in Dynamic Emergency Environments

Decisionmaking in emergency management necessarily involves priority setting, or the ordering of tasks according to perceived importance for achieving the policy goal. Established priorities, critical in emergency management because they involve the specification of resources, tasks, and time to cope with unknown hazards, structure options for action within the units of the emergency management system over the four phases of the emergency management cycle. Further, the decision processes by which these priorities are set become instrumental in ordering the resources, attention, and activities of the multiple participants in the emergency management process.

For example, emergency managers in California, confronting a major vulnerability to earthquakes in the coastal cities over the next twenty years, struggle with the problem of limited resources, massive risk to millions of people, and an unknown probability of occurrence of an earthquake. The problem crosses all phases of emergency management —mitigation, preparedness, response, and recovery. Yet the practical choices for action to reduce the risk in one phase limit the resources, attention, and energies available to reduce the risk in other phases. If resources and time are expended in structural mitigation efforts such as the reinforcement of masonry buildings, will there be enough money, time, and resources for preparedness activities such as the design and dissemination of earthquake education programs for the public schools or the conduct of simulated operations exercises for city and county public service personnel? Or, anticipating massive destruction, should emergency managers pool scarce resources in a statewide disaster fund to be used for relief and recovery immediately following the disaster, leaving less money available for mitigation and preparedness activities prior to the event? At what level of governmental jurisdiction do the respective responsibilities for disaster management fall? If, under the Disaster Relief Act of 1974, the federal government has the responsibility for providing disaster relief, do California emergency managers need to be concerned about the allocation of monies to relief efforts at the state and local levels of governmental operations? How the resources and responsibilities are distributed within the interjurisdictional emergency management system orders the sequence of actions among the multiple participants in the implementation of emergency management policy. Consciously developed, this structural design represents a means of establishing continuity in the operations of the emergency management system.

Institutional structure, used in this way, becomes a mechanism for reducing complexity and increasing consistency in action in complex environments. March and Olsen define structure as "a collection of institutions, rules of behavior, norms, roles, physical arrangements, buildings and archives that are relatively invariant in the face of turnover of individuals and relatively resilient to the idiosyncratic preferences and expectations of individuals."[30]

In emergency management policy, structure, introduced into operations by design, is both a means of limiting error and of clarifying choices for action by multiple participants over time in complex environments. The challenge to emergency managers lies in designing this structure in ways that achieve the stability desired for effective performance of the emergency management system, without restricting the flexibility required for adaptation to changing conditions.

Management of Information

In organizations operating under conditions of uncertainty and complexity, the management of information is critical to their capacity to act effectively. The organization and flow of information regarding the conditions and demands for action from the environment activate the participants in the interdependent emergency management system. Designing procedures for regulating the amount, kind, and sources of information transmitted within and between organizations engaged in emergency management is central to timely, informed choice by organizational decisionmakers. The skilled use of external memory devices, such as computerized decision support systems, resource lists, and maps, increases the likelihood that the relevant information is available to the respective decisionmakers at the appropriate time. Under conditions of uncertainty, the types of information search, processing, and dissemination procedures determine both the degree of organizational learning and the degree of organizational control in interdependent action.[31] Creating the appropriate balance is a task facilitated, but not guaranteed, by design.[32]

In summary, the design of processes for making decisions, setting priorities, and managing information for the interjurisdictional emergency management system orders the sequence of choice opportunities for managers as they strive to achieve the stated policy goal of protection of life and property for their respective communities. This set of subprocesses, operating interactively, becomes a strategy for maintaining stability, despite changing conditions, for the emergency management system. The resulting continuity, combined with the benefit of change, represents the combination of creative insight within rational bounds that marks professional performance in emergency management.

The Strategy for Integration: Linking Individuals, Organizations, and Resources through Effective Communication Patterns

Integrating the multiple components of the emergency management system into a coherent action agency is perhaps the most difficult task confronting public managers with emergency responsibilities. For most of the organizations involved, participation in emergency management activities is only one of many responsibilities that they carry. Every municipal police or fire department, every state transportation or health agency, every federal agency such as the Army Corps of Engineers or the Department of Transportation involved in a given emergency operation has primary responsibilities in other areas. For these agencies, participation in emergency management activities is necessarily part-time, and other daily demands compete for their attention, resources, and time.[33]

Only the Federal Emergency Management Agency and its state and local counterparts are engaged full-time in emergency management policy formulation and implementation at their respective levels of government. These full-time agencies do not engage in actual emergency operations. Their task is the indirect but difficult one of coordinating the response agencies and assisting the vulnerable populations in developing their capacity to take informed action in all phases of the emergency management cycle: mitigation, preparedness, response, and recovery. Their principal means of accomplishing this task is through communications. Critical to performance, the establishment of an effective multiway network of professional communications in emergency management requires conscious design.

Full-time emergency management personnel represent a core group in designing and maintaining a professional network of communications in emergency management. Their primary task is to interpret the emergency environment intelligently to the response agencies in order to facilitate action. This task involves a continuing inquiry into the substantive problems involved in all phases of emergency management, production of valid information about those problems, communication of that information to relevant professionals and organizations with emergency responsibilities, and feedback from those organizations into the redesign of emergency management policy and procedures.

In performing this two-way function of interpreting policy goals to participants in the emergency environment and gathering information from the environment in order to redefine the policy goals, full-time emergency management personnel screen, select, and synthesize information that circulates among other organizations and individuals interested in emergency management. To the extent that this information base is shared and understood by all participating organizations and individuals involved in the emergency management network, it fosters the evolution of shared values, cooperation, and commitment to action.[34] Yet this process involves the exercise of judgmental criteria in the selection, interpretation, and communication of information between the emergency environment and relevant organizational actors, and back again.

Three criteria, characteristic of professional practice, enhance the quality of judgments made in the selection and synthesis of information disseminated through the emergency management network. These criteria are: (1) focus, (2) discipline, and (3) an ethical commitment to public purpose. Each criterion plays an essential role in selecting information from the environment relevant to emergency management. Together the set constitutes a recognizable heuristic that can be used to synthesize information from diverse sources to support informed commitment to action among the multiple participants in the emergency system. This heuristic, or set of criteria informing professional judgment in emergency management policy and practice, serves to integrate the different individuals and organizations with emergency responsibilities in a coherent program of action. Combining elements of both continuity and change, the development of professional judgment by the individuals and organizations of the emergency management system constitutes a strategy of integration. It is fundamentally a learning process, with the product of such judgments subject to professional review and testing in actual practice.

Translating Design into Professional Practice in Emergency Management

Returning to the task of determining responsible public action in emergency management, the test of design is to observe the actual mix of governmental strategies in emergency management policy and practice. Observation and analysis of governmental policy and practice in emergency management is presented in the sequence of essays that follow in this volume. The essays also demonstrate the three strategies of change, continuity, and integration. While most essays encompass elements of all three strategies, each focuses on one strategy more than the others. The strategy of change is illustrated especially in the essays by Ruchelman, Ender and Kim, Kartez and Kelley, Sylves, Rosenthal, and Podesta and Olson. The strategy of continuity is discussed particularly in the analyses by Mittler, Mitchell, May, Comfort, and Cahill. The strategy of integration is central in the essays by Pavlak, Elmore, Partridge, and the final essay by Comfort. The essays by Cigler, Waugh, Lewis, and LaPlante identify current issues confronting public managers with emergency responsibilities in the respective phases of the emergency management cycle within the United States' experience. The essay by Dror examines issues in all three strategies in a global context. All essays are directed toward a reexamination of the policy question of what the government can do to improve performance in the uncertain, interactive, complex environment of emergency management. Such a reexamination, undertaken by policymakers, public managers, and citizens alike, is fundamental to responsible performance in emergency management. As we become more aware of costs in practice and alternatives in policy, there is no choice but action.

Structuring Problems for Policy Action
⚡ Thomas J. Pavlak

"To know the world, one must construct it." — Pavese

The scene was nineteenth-century Paris during a wave of rioting that threatened to engulf the city. The commander of an army detachment had been ordered to clear a city square by firing on the *canaille* (rabble) massed there. On reaching the square, the officer found himself confronted by a menacing crowd. He immediately commanded his troops to assume the firing position, their rifles aimed at the crowd. As a deadly silence fell upon the crowd, the officer drew his sword, raised it, and shouted as loudly as he could: "Mesdames, m'sieurs, I have orders to fire at the *canaille*. But as I see a number of honest, respectable citizens before me, I request that they leave so that I can safely shoot the *canaille*." Within a few minutes the square was empty.[1]

On July 13, 1977, two bolts of lightning struck two power transmission towers in Westchester County within twenty minutes of each other, triggering a massive and costly blackout in New York City. A key contributor to the blackout was the system operator's misreading of a default signal for current flowing over a particular feeder line. The operator expected to see a zero reading, as the line normally carried little or no current. That evening, however, there had been two relay failures, creating an unusual set of circumstances. The first relay failure led automatically to a high flow of current over that line, while the second failure blocked the flow over the line. Unaware of the dual relay failures, the operator treated the zero reading as normal when, in this particular instance, it was in fact an abnormal reading. As additional problems began to show up in the system this misperception led to a logical, systematic, "by the book" sequence of erroneous corrective actions that ended in the system being brought to a halt: a blackout.[2]

What do these seemingly disparate incidents, a century and an ocean apart, have in common? First, they typify problematic situations in the emergency environment. The decisionmakers in both settings faced a highly complex, ambiguous, and uncertain decision problem. Immediate action was required, yet the nature of the problem was unclear. Information was incomplete, the probable outcome of alternative actions was unknown, and the costs of error were great. Both decisionmakers had a prescribed set of routines to follow which, given the uniqueness of the situation, would exacerbate rather than solve the problem. What each situation required was creative and insightful judgment.

These two examples of decisionmaking in emergency situations also serve to illustrate the central theme of this chapter: the importance of problem structuring in emergency management. In the first example, the army commander correctly sensed that his superiors' proposed solution to the problem of clearing the city square—using violence to counter the threat of violence—would succeed in dispersing the crowd, but almost certainly would provoke an escalation of the rioting as word of the troops' action spread. By creatively reframing the problem the commander was able to remove both the original threat and the greater danger posed by his superiors' "solution."

The New York City blackout example illustrates the harmful consequences that can result when emergency response actions are based on erroneous assumptions—that is, when the wrong problem is solved. The operator's initial determination that the feeder line was operating normally created a frame of reference for interpreting new information regarding additional problems that began showing up in the system. Left unchallenged, this reference frame led to a sequence of corrective actions that was logical, systematic, "by the book,"—and incorrect. Ironically, the corrective actions taken only helped to bring about the blackout that they were designed to prevent.

The Importance of Problem Structuring

Perhaps the most difficult task for managers seeking to improve their problem-solving capability is accepting the notion that policy problems need to be framed or structured. Many people believe that policy problems are objective entities that exist "out there" waiting to be detected; all that is required is to determine the facts of the situation.[3] But the "facts" of a given problematic situation may be in dispute, or interpreted differently by different observers, or simply unknown. The same objective conditions may yield a variety of formulations of the problems requiring policy action. These competing conceptualizations of policy problems are rooted in the varying backgrounds, experiences, beliefs, and values that collectively make up each decisionmaker's frame of reference toward the problematic situation. Thus, rather than being objectively given, policy problems are socially constructed or defined, the products of decisionmakers imposing their frames of reference on problematic situations.[4] As Lindblom and Cohen put it, "We do not discover a problem 'out there,' we make a choice about how we want to formulate a problem."[5]

Constructing appropriate formulations of policy problems is especially difficult in the emergency management system, where problems typically are ill-structured rather than well-structured. Ill-structured means that there is considerable complexity, ambiguity, and uncertainty in the problematic situation. While no clear formulation of the problem is available, proposed policy alternatives abound. There is no consensus on a course of action, however, or even on a method for developing one. Information needed for informed decisionmaking is inadequate and costly or even impossible to obtain; conversely, there may be information overload, with decisionmakers receiving streams of overlapping, ambiguous, and contradictory information. The decision process is likely to be influenced by a number of key policy stakeholders whose objectives or value preferences may conflict or are unknown. The probable outcomes of policy alternatives are unknown, so that estimates of uncertainty and risk cannot be made with any degree of confidence. Finally, policy problems in the emergency management system also are what Russell Ackoff terms "messes"—that is, parts of whole systems of problems that cannot be formulated, let alone solved, independently of one another.[6]

When faced with ill-structured, messy decision situations the initial task for emergency managers is to clarify the nature of the problem. This is a critical step in problem-solving, for faulty specification of the problem is likely to produce inappropriate policy solutions.[7] Russell Ackoff has observed, "We fail more often because we solve the wrong problem than because we get the wrong solution to the right problem."[8] Howard Raiffa terms this a "Type III" error.[9] The danger of committing a Type III error is particularly acute for emergency managers given the high complexity, ambiguity, and uncertainty of emergency situations —and the potential in many instances for truly disastrous outcomes when policies fail.

Conventional decision analytic techniques are not likely to be very useful for emergency managers, for they assume the existence of a well-structured problem to be solved.[10] Programmed decision routines such as standard operating procedures may even be counterproductive, particularly when decisionmakers experience a completely novel emergency situation. In such cases, as illustrated by the New York City blackout example, reliance on standard operating procedures actually may create barriers to solving the problem. In an important sense the solution is the problem to be solved.

Successful problem structuring requires that emergency managers be able to transform ill-defined, messy problems into more tractable problems that are able to be acted upon within the restrictions imposed by decisionmakers' bounded rationality. This difficult task is further complicated by what Norman Maier has termed "solution-mindedness," the tendency for decisionmakers to evaluate solutions to problems prematurely, before the nature of the problem is understood.[11] This inhibits exploration of novel formulations of the problem, restricting choice to a narrow set of given alternatives serving preexisting goals. The result is an increased likelihood of an inappropriate policy solution being chosen. To counter this tendency decisionmakers need to develop what David Dery has called a "problem-mindedness" orientation, one that focuses on exploring the nature of the problem, seeking to clarify and define it before searching for a solution.[12]

There are a number of problem-structuring techniques that can help to foster a problem-minded decision process, increase decisionmakers' skills in formulating policy problems, and promote what Chris Argyris calls "double-loop" learning.[13] In the sections that follow we introduce two problem-structuring techniques that have been used successfully in a wide variety of decision settings: stakeholder analysis and assumption surfacing (SAAS) and the analytic hierarchy process

(AHP). These techniques have been designed explicitly for dealing with the type of ill-structured problems that characterize the emergency environment. They enable decisionmakers to employ rational decision-making processes in ambiguous, dynamic settings by transforming ill-structured problems into more manageable ones. This helps to avoid decision responses that are likely to be ineffective, such as the tendency toward uncritical continuity of existing decision paths; uncritical change toward completely new directions; defensive avoidance or delay of a decision; and panic and frantic search for more and better options.[14] Each technique can be effective in all phases of emergency management, but they are most likely to be beneficial in the mitigation and recovery phases, where they can be employed most fully.

A Dialectical Approach to Problem-solving

Ian Mitroff and James Emshoff offer a methodology for solving ill-structured problems that focuses on the key assumptions underlying conflicting perceptions of the problematic situation.[15] Their approach represents a formalized version of Hegelian dialectical inquiry that seeks to make creative use of the conflict inherent in ill-structured problem settings. It involves specifying stakeholder assumptions about the problematic situation, engaging in dialectical analysis of these assumptions, and then integrating what emerges from the dialectics to create a new formulation of the problem.

There are three basic steps or phases in the process that Mitroff and Richard Mason call stakeholder analysis and assumption surfacing (SAAS): group formation, assumption surfacing, and dialectical debate and synthesis.[16] The first step in SAAS consists of identifying key policy stakeholders—those individuals and groups who influence and are influenced by the policy decision. In identifying key stakeholders particular attention is given to obtaining maximally different perspectives on the problematic situation.

The next step is to uncover and analyze the critical assumptions upon which stakeholders' perceptions of the policy problem rest. Here the decisionmakers are asked to work backward from stakeholders' proposed policy solutions to the assumptions underlying their recommended course of action. These assumptions are then ranked according to stakeholders' assessment of their relative importance and uncertainty, the critical assumptions being those that are important but uncertain. Mitroff and Mason have found that it is possible to reduce the generated assumptions to a few really critical or key assumptions, making dialectical analysis more manageable and productive.[17]

During the dialectical debate phase, each critical assumption is challenged by a counterassumption. Implausible counterassumptions are discarded and the remaining assumptions are pooled in an attempt to negotiate a compromise among them. This is done by asking stakeholders to relax their assumptions or to restate them in ways that incorporate differences between their critical assumptions and those held by others. In this way a "zone of compromise" is sought from which can be drawn a set of compromise assumptions or even a synthesis of accepted assumptions. These then form the basis for a new and more integrated, holistic formulation of the problem and preferred policy choice.

Applying SAAS to Hazard Mitigation Policy

The mitigation phase of emergency management includes those activities that reduce the degree of long-term risk to human life and property from natural and technological hazards. This includes land use regulation, building and safety codes, disaster insurance programs, and tax incentives and disincentives.[18] Given that the economic and political stakes are likely to be high, mitigation policy decisions typically emerge only after protracted community debate. The policy debate often takes place in an atmosphere that is charged with conflict, as a result of multiple actors having a stake in the outcome, differing views of the mitigation problem facing the community, and strong preferences for specific policy solutions. Whatever the policy choice, there is likely to be controversy surrounding the policy action taken.

Consider the following policy debate concerning the problem of a flood hazard facing a small community. The community is considering adopting a flood hazard mitigation plan that includes a proposal for construction of levees to protect the village center. The Army Corps of Engineers has estimated the cost of levee construction to be about $7.5 million, not including annual maintenance and operating costs for the levees and pumps. Federal funds would cover most of the cost of construction, but operating and maintenance costs would be borne by the village. Owing to the generally dilapidated condition of the central business district, the total value of the sixty floodplain buildings is only about $1.5 million.

The hazard mitigation plan is met with considerable skepticism by many villagers. Homeowners in particular are concerned that they will have to shoulder the burden of increased taxes to provide flood protection for a declining business district. Business owners in the central business district (CBD), in contrast, fear that they cannot survive the economic losses that another flood will bring. Facing a potentially divisive community conflict over the hazard mitigation plan, the mayor decides to bring representatives of the various community groups together to discuss their differences. In doing so, she is seeking to reconcile the groups' differences in perspectives on the problem so that an alternative can be found that will win community support and provide adequate flood protection. She also is eager to apply a problem-solving tool she learned while participating in a strategic planning session of the executive board of the state association of Women Business Executives.

The mayor has identified six key stakeholder groups: homeowners; CBD property owners, primarily businessmen; the head of the planning department, who prepared the hazard mitigation plan; the county's emergency management office; the Corps of Engineers District Office; and the municipal departments responsible for dealing with the flood threat and response to a flood (police, fire, public works). She begins the session by asking each group's representatives to comment on the flood hazard mitigation plan.

As the discussion of the hazard mitigation plan unfolds, it becomes apparent that each stakeholder group's position relies heavily on a small set of critical assumptions. These assumptions relate to the costs of the levee construction proposal, the relative burden that would be placed on different taxpayer groups under the proposed plan, operation of the levee and pump system, the economic viability of the village's central business district, and the commitment of community segments to revitalization of the CBD.

For example, the CBD business owners' support for the levee proposal is based on their assumptions that (1) the central business district can be made economically viable, provided that adequate protection from future flooding is assured; (2) costs of operating and maintaining the levee and pump system will be shared fairly by all segments of the community; and (3) there is general community interest in maintaining the village center, given its historical significance to the community.

The principal opposition to the levee proposal comes from a group of concerned homeowners whose opposition rests on three critical assumptions: (1) the CBD is no longer economically viable, given movement of the town's population away from the village center and its general image as a "run-down" area; (2) homeowners will be asked to bear a disproportionate share of the tax burden for the levee proposal; and (3) CBD business owners have little commitment to the community, as evidenced by their unwillingness to invest in the village center, allowing it to decline into its current run-down state.

Having brought to the surface the critical assumptions held by key stakeholders, the mayor now engages the group in a closer examination of them. She begins by pointing out the contradictory assumptions on cost burden held by the homeowners and business owners. She presents a detailed estimate of the costs to the community of operating and maintaining the levee and pump system. Included is her proposal for financing the costs, a general property tax increase and an increase in the merchants' license fees. The mayor notes that the tax burden will be shared by business owners, who will bear the added costs of bringing their properties into compliance with building code standards. While there are questions about the cost estimates, the group treats them seriously. In particular, the mayor notices the homeowners' group showing a willingness to agree that the cost burden will be distributed equitably.

Discussion shifts to the question of investing in the flood protection plan, given the economic decline of the CBD. The business owners' assumption that the CBD can be revitalized is challenged by the counterassumption that it simply is no longer viable. Most community residents have taken to shopping at a regional mall located fifteen miles north of town. Committing the community to a flood protection system for a dying business district is a waste of scarce community resources, it is argued, especially since the business owners have been unwilling to make a commitment to preserving the CBD. The business owners attempt to rebut this counterassumption, pointing out the uncertainty surrounding investment in a flood-prone area, the lack of investment capital due to the economic decline of the CBD, and their willingness to support the flood protection plan with its associated tax increases.

As the debate progresses, both stakeholder groups become more sensitive to the assumptions underlying each other's positions on the flood protection issue. At one point a homeowner half-jokingly remarks that for the cost of the Corps of Engineers project the community could build a new downtown area, outside the flood zone. The thought of relocating the CBD had occurred to others, but had not been pursued seriously, as it had not seemed politically or economically feasible. It now appears to be worth exploring, given the likelihood of impasse on the CBD flood protection plan. Initial cost estimates are quickly developed, including the cost of preparing a new site for the CBD. The figures look promising—the relocation alternative is estimated to be about $6 million, significantly less than the levee construction proposal.

Some initial information on federal/state grant and loan programs that are potential sources of funding for CBD relocation is presented to the group. Discussion of possible federal Community Development Block Grant and Economic Development Administration funding for the relocation proposal raises the question of the business owners' willingness to invest in the proposed new CBD. The community debate proceeds in this way, with additional information being presented, additional assumptions being brought out and tested, and compromises and syntheses being sought. As this occurs, the focus of the debate shifts from stakeholder groups' defense of their positions regarding the original perceived problem of protecting the CBD from flooding to a concern for economic revitalization of the community and the plausibility of assumptions underlying the relocation proposal. While no clear vote of endorsement emerges from the debate, the consensus of those present is that relocation is a viable option, provided that federal and state assistance can be obtained and CBD business owners whose floodplain properties are purchased make a commitment to rebuild in the new business district.

While greatly simplified for purposes of presentation, the flood protection problem illustrated here nevertheless does identify three salient features of assumption analysis. First, SAAS seeks to uncover and make explicit key assumptions about the problem that frequently are "hidden," even to those holding them. Second, it focuses stakeholders' attention on a common body of data or information about the policy problem. In doing so, it recognizes that different stakeholder groups may have conflicting interpretations of the same information, based on their different assumptions about the problematic situation. Assumption analysis aims to move the policy debate beyond these conflicts by systematically surfacing, challenging, pooling, and then synthesizing the most plausible of these conflicting assumptions. Finally, SAAS recognizes the inevitability of conflict in problem solving and seeks to incorporate it into the policy debate in a constructive and creative manner.

As a decisionmaking tool, SAAS promotes creative problem solving and helps to reduce the probability of Type III error in policy decisionmaking. The second problem-structuring technique that we will examine is particularly useful in decision settings where a primary concern is to determine priorities for action.

The Analytic Hierarchy Process

The analytic hierarchy process is an approach to problem-solving developed by Thomas A. Saaty as a general tool for decisionmaking.[19] In the analytic hierarchy process, a problem is structured by constructing a hierarchic representation of its major elements, then assigning relative priorities to each element at each level of the hierarchy. In constructing the hierarchy, the top level usually is assigned to the overall goal or objective of the decision exercise. The intermediate levels are composed of factors that may affect the attainment of the primary goal or objective. These include environmental factors (for example, political and economic considerations), performance criteria (such as acceptable levels of risk to public safety), and key actors (for instance, a citizens' group or business owners). At the lowest level of the hierarchy usually is found the set of specific policy alternatives under consideration.

Figure 1 illustrates the hierarchic structure that might be constructed by the group of community representatives dealing with the flood hazard mitigation problem in the previous example. The group is debating the development of a flood protection plan for the community. The hazard mitigation plan's proposal to construct a levee and pump system is the primary option under consideration. Other options for the municipality include developing a partial levee system at a lower cost, but with greater assumed risk of flood damage; the CBD relocation proposal; and doing nothing for the time being, until the community is in a better financial position to assume the burden of the "start-up" costs of one of the first three options.

As shown in figure 1, the municipal officials' overall objective is to

Figure 1. The Decision Problem

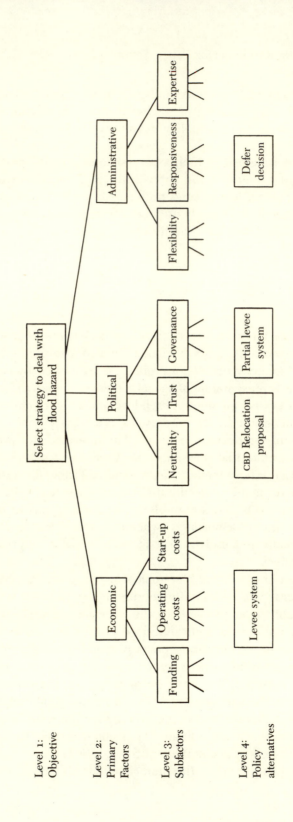

Level 1:
Objective

Level 2:
Primary
Factors

Level 3:
Subfactors

Level 4:
Policy
alternatives

select a strategy that will best provide for the development of a flood protection system to serve the community. In their view, three primary factors have a substantial impact on the development of the flood control system for the community: economic, political, and administrative factors. These broad factors in turn may be broken down into a group of subfactors, each likely to affect the development of the flood protection system in some meaningful way. For example, given the community's current problem of fiscal stress, start-up and operating costs should be kept as low as possible. Finally, at the lowest level of the hierarchy are found the four policy alternatives being considered by the municipality.

Having constructed a hierarchic representation of the problem, the municipal decisionmakers now must determine the relative importance of each problem element in attaining the municipality's objective. Using a nine-point scale of relative importance, paired comparisons are made for each set of elements at each level of the hierarchy. At level 2, the following comparisons are made: economic vs. political; political vs. administrative; and economic vs. administrative. At level 3, the subfactors under each set of primary factors are considered in paired comparisons.

Once numerical values are established for the relative importance of each factor and subfactor, overall priorities are determined by multiplying each subfactor's priority by the priority of its corresponding higher-order factor. In this way the primary factors of political, economic, and administrative considerations influence the relative importance of each of their specific subfactors. As a final step in the AHP, each subfactor is matched against the policy alternatives. The decisionmaker is asking: "With respect to the subfactor 'flexibility,' what is the desirability of the CBD relocation plan relative to the other alternatives?" When the process of paired comparisons is complete, a matrix of priority values is produced that reflects the relative impact of each primary factor and subfactor on each policy alternative. A simplified decision outcome matrix is shown in table 1.

As seen in the table, the municipal officials' expressed preference is for policy option 2: the CBD relocation proposal. Despite their concerns about start-up costs and the economic risk in creating a new CBD, three factors lead to preference for the relocation plan: the removal of the CBD flood threat, the opportunity for economic growth and new jobs, and the avoidance of operating costs of the levee and pump system.

Table 1. Decision Preferences

Policy alter- natives	Subfactors						Global priori- ties
	Fund- ing (.165)	Costs (.200)	Trust (.150)	Gover- nance (.150)	Flexi- bility (.160)	Respon- sive- ness (.175)	
Levee system	.05	.05	.35	.35	.40	.35	.248
CBD relocation proposal	.50	.45	.35	.30	.30	.35	.381
Partial levee System	.40	.30	.15	.10	.10	.20	.214
Defer decision	.05	.20	.15	.25	.20	.10	.157

The hierarchic structure and priority ratings assigned to problem elements represent the perceptions of this group of municipal officials only; that is, the same decision problem considered by another group might result in a very different hierarchic structuring of the problem and different priority weightings. For this reason, it is desirable to include in the decision analysis the perspectives of different stakeholders, to ensure that a variety of frames of reference are elicited. Used in this way the AHP can help to structure a decision problem so that it is amenable to systematic analysis while taking into account differing values and preferences of the decisionmakers.

SAAS and AHP are just two of several very useful tools for structuring complex policy problems. Others include Social Judgment Analysis, Toulmin's argumentation model, and Shalit's wheel technique.[20] These are highly flexible tools that can be used in combination, wholly, or in part; with decisionmaker groups or by an individual analyst; and, depending on the decision setting, in considerable depth or as a "quick cut" at the problem. They represent a way of approaching or looking at policy problems rather than a set of rigidly prescribed procedures that are guaranteed to produce a correct "solution" to a problem. For these reasons they represent a useful and very flexible set of tools for problem structuring.

Problem Structuring and Organizational Paradox

The organizational requisites for effective policy action in the emergency environment are well documented in the chapters in this volume, particularly in the cogent essays by Louise Comfort and Ralph Lewis. These organizational requisites include the capacity to adapt to rapidly changing emergency conditions, particularly during the response phase of a disaster event; creativity and innovation in organizational decisionmaking; and organizational self-reflection, particularly the willingness to challenge assumptions and the ability to learn from feedback on organizational performance. These requisites for responsive action also illustrate the paradoxical nature of organizational effectiveness in the emergency environment. For example, Ralph Lewis notes that disaster preparedness may help to reduce the potential for harmful consequences of a disaster event, but also may restrict creativity and innovativeness in responding to the event.[21]

Kim Cameron argues persuasively that the presence of such paradoxes, and maintenance of a balance among them, are a paramount attribute of organizations that can adapt successfully to turbulent environments.[22] By paradox Cameron refers to the simultaneous existence of opposites or contradictions within the organizational system. For example, Cameron notes that effective organizations are both loosely and tightly coupled; they show both high specialization and high generality of roles; they are marked by continuity of leadership as well as the infusion of new leaders; they possess deviation-amplifying as well as deviation-reducing processes; they expand information search in decisionmaking while also creating barriers to information overload; and they promote disengagement and disidentification with past organizational strategies while fostering reintegration and reinforcement of organizational roots.[23] According to Cameron the key to success for organizations does not lie in resolving these paradoxes but rather in maintaining them in a state of creative tension. In Cameron's terms, it is the presence of balanced paradoxes that "energizes and empowers" organizational systems to be effective in responding to environmental demands.[24]

Loose coupling, for example, encourages wide search in decisionmaking, initiation, and functional autonomy, all of which are necessary for creativity and flexibility in organizational response to emergency situations. Also needed, however, is rapid execution of decisions, implementation of innovations, and functional reciprocity, which are fostered by tight coupling. Similarly, a high degree of role specialization reinforces expertise and efficiency, while role generalization reinforces flexibility and interdependence. Continuity of leadership is essential for stability, long-term planning, and institutional memory while increased innovation, adaptability, and currency requires an infusion of new leaders. Organizational processes that amplify deviation encourage productive conflict and challenging of assumptions, while processes that reduce deviation encourage the harmony and consensus needed to engender trust and the smooth flow of communication. Expanded search in decisionmaking results in wider environmental scanning, access to more information, and greater diversity of input into the decision process, while the creation of inhibitors to information overload is essential for simplifying the decision process and fostering convergence in decisionmaking. Finally, new perspectives and innovation are stimulated by disengagement and disidentification, while reintegration and reinforcement are important for fostering commitment to a special sense of organizational identity and mission.[25]

In Cameron's view the organization need not resolve these paradoxes to be effective. Rather, the maintenance of a creative tension or balance among the elements of paradox serves to energize and empower the organization to respond effectively to environmental demands. Imbalance, or too great an emphasis on one element in a paradox, can be dysfunctional. For example, overemphasis on managerial control through routinization of decision rules can reduce capability to respond to unique situations. The presence of "balanced paradox," on the other hand, produces creative tensions that can promote organizational excellence.

Recognition that paradoxes are inherent in emergency organizations is central to effective problem-solving. Structuring policy problems to include an awareness of the need to balance paradoxes can help emergency managers to avoid Type III error, particularly in situations where organizational design has produced an imbalance that may be dysfunctional (for example, an overreliance on routinized decision rules). Finally, the ongoing effort to maintain balanced paradoxes can further the development of the self-reflective, problem-solving organization.

Mitigation

Current Policy Issues in Mitigation ⚡ Beverly A. Cigler

The field of emergency management historically has focused on the immediate and urgent aspects of a disaster—the response function of police, fire, emergency medical services, and civil defense personnel; the advance planning and training necessary for emergency operations; and the postdisaster recovery period in which damage is repaired. There is, however, a growing awareness that emergency management is much more complex and comprehensive than traditionally perceived. The primary function of government is to protect life and property. This involves not just crisis-reactive responses to emergencies, but also finding ways to avoid problems in the first place and preparing for those that will undoubtedly occur. An inclusive approach to emergency management considers a four-stage cyclical process, centered on a disaster or other emergency event.[1] These stages include: predisaster mitigation/prevention; predisaster preparedness; disaster response; and postdisaster response or recovery.

This chapter focuses on the phase of emergency management most often neglected by researchers and society—mitigation. It examines long-term planning, engineering, economics, and policy development and implementation concerns related to predisaster events. The chapter will (1) introduce basic concepts related to hazard mitigation; (2)

explore the key factors in effecting adjustments to natural and technological hazards; (3) review the various mitigation strategies for coping
with natural and technological hazards, drawing on the research literature to assess the state of mitigation practice; and (4) conclude by
exploring the benefits and costs of mitigation.

Hazard Mitigation

Hazards are defined here as threats to life, well-being, material goods,
and environment from the extremes of natural processes or technology.[2]
Extremes in the natural environment include floods, earthquakes,
tornadoes, volcanic eruptions, landslides, tsunami, and drought. Technological extremes include chemical spills, accumulated exposure to
chemicals, nuclear accidents, and other events caused directly by
human activity.

The challenges of nature and technology in increasing the exposure
of people and property to risk pose a dilemma for any government
seeking the fullest protection for its people and their property. New
technologies, for example, make economic development possible but
also create new hazards that pose costly trade-offs in terms of environmental quality and social and economic benefits and costs. There is
little agreement about what risks are involved, their costs, and what to
do about them. Under normal circumstances few citizens place a high
priority on any phase of emergency management. However, these
same individuals expect their government leaders to manage effectively disasters that occur, but rarely link long-term planning with
crisis events.

Natural disasters demonstrate the societal dilemma. The fatalistic
assumption that natural disasters will happen and all we can do is cope
is slowly being altered, leading to increased reliance on governmental
action. Advancements in science, engineering, and planning show
that we can often prevent natural disasters and/or lessen the impacts of
those that occur. Doing so is increasingly recognized as our social
responsibility.[3] Floods, for example, are the most serious natural disaster in the United States, in terms of lives lost, people affected, property damaged, and frequency. Yet floods are killing more people and
destroying or damaging more property each year.[4] It is not nature that
is changing. "Natural disaster" may be a misnomer since people are

responsible for the increased problems as they make their environment more prone to disasters and themselves more vulnerable to those
hazards. After a flood, for example, people almost invariably move
back into hazard zones, and sometimes in greater numbers.[5]

Technology has emerged as society's major source of hazard. Such
man-made emergencies stimulate great public reliance on government
for aid, largely because of our general unfamiliarity with such relatively new hazards. Citizens perceive that effective public management can decrease risks from such threats as the transportation of
hazardous substances and explosions at fixed facilities. The random
nature of these threats, and the fact that accidents can occur quickly
and without warning highlights the importance of planning. The chemical revolution and other created hazard potentials are assumed to be
amenable to "fixes" of various kinds, and it is believed that effects of
such hazards can be substantially reduced. A wide variety of environmental laws, incorporating strong regulatory and nonregulatory programs, exists to prevent technological disasters.[6]

Hazards, then, are a consequence of both the physical and social
systems and the interaction between them.[7] They can be averted or
lessened by adoption and implementation of policies to mitigate risk
and the negative effects of natural and technological extremes. Mitigation of technological disasters can range from altering expectations and
the choices of technology to preventing or lessening the consequences
of a hazard.[8] Mitigation of natural hazards can occur through a variety
of structural measures, the protective engineering works such as dams,
levees, and sea walls, and nonstructural options including land use
regulations, zoning laws, building codes, and economic programs (such
as tax and insurance incentives) designed to keep vulnerable structures and activities out of the most hazard-prone areas or to minimize
the likelihood of structural damage. Postdisaster actions such as rebuilding damaged structures in hazard-resistant ways or relocating structures and people are also mitigation strategies due to their concerns
with the long-term reduction of the effects of hazards.

While there are many commonalities among hazards,[9] the many
differences between technological and natural hazards structure the
mitigation options available. Both kinds of hazards involve highly specialized but different scientific and technical bases, as well as distinctive public issues. Natural hazards sometimes do cause failures of
technological systems and the two hazard types clearly interact. Landslides and earthquakes, for example, damage roads, pipelines, and

railways. While technological hazards create havoc on the natural environment, such hazards rarely trigger natural disasters. (One exception
is the so-called "greenhouse effect," whereby the release of pollutants
into the earth's atmosphere warms the earth and increases the potential for flooding due to the melting of the polar ice caps.) In addition,
unlike natural hazards, technological hazards (1) stem directly from
human causes, (2) generally occur at known locations, and (3) pose new
experiences for society.

A recent trend in dealing with hazards is multiple hazard management, an integrated or coordinated approach addressing the full range
of hazards to which communities are prone. Multiple hazard mitigation is the component of multiple hazard management concerned with
reducing the long-term adverse impacts of the full range of hazards
within a community, state, region, or the nation as a whole.[10] Such an
approach is appealing since it focuses attention on the full range of
hazards, allows for consideration of the interaction among hazards, and
offers increased opportunities for greater efficiency in the use of
finances, personnel, and other resources.

While some disaster response functions, such as communications,
are ideal candidates for multiple hazard management, an integrated
approach toward mitigation is more problematic due to the complexity
within and between the two major hazard types—natural and technological. The challenges to multiple hazard mitigation include the facts
that (1) most existing programs are based on legislation addressing
specific hazards; (2) hazards officials are a diverse group, with planners, developers, and builders, for example, rarely working with other
officials such as police, fire, and other first-responder emergency management personnel; (3) most hazards officials devote only part-time
effort to hazard mitigation, complicating opportunities for coordination; (4) the engineering, scientific, and economic expertise involving
hazards is limited; and (5) interaction among technical staff and public
decisionmakers is not well established.

In summary, the risks associated with disaster are a consequence of
the character of both physical and social systems and their interaction.
A variety of mitigation strategies can reduce risk and the negative
effects of hazard extremes. The practice of mitigation measures developed on a hazard-by-hazard basis by diverse groups of specialists and
bureaucracies dominates, although integrated approaches for such
generic mitigation activities as risk assessment and mapping, as well as

the estimation of economic losses, are receiving widespread attention. These integrated approaches offer an ability to focus attention on a full range of hazards and interaction among them, in addition to greater efficiency in the use of finances, personnel, and other agency resources.

The next section examines three interrelated categories of factors affecting adjustment to natural and technological hazards that have been shown to be especially important: (1) individual assumption of risk;[11] (2) governmental assumptions of risk that influence the formulation and/or implementation of mitigation strategies;[12] and (3) intergovernmental and other intersystem incentives such as interest groups and technical assistance.[13]

Factors Affecting Adjustment to Hazards

Individual Assumption of Risk

The adoption and implementation of mitigation strategies by individuals, organizations, and communities is influenced by people's perceptions and interpretations of risk. This includes knowledge or belief about the seriousness of threats as well as the subjective probability of experiencing a damaging loss. If people simply discount the probability of loss from infrequently occurring events, there will be little concern with hazards.[14] A key characteristic of environmental hazards, for example, is that exposure does not necessarily result in loss of life, injury, or illness. Rather, the probability of suffering adverse effects is rather low. Thus many people ignore warning information about the location of hazards when deciding where to live.

A variety of factors can contribute to the formation of risk perception, including the ability to estimate risk, perceived causes of hazard extremes, and experience.[15] Intellectual limitations and the need to reduce anxiety often lead to the denial of risk and to unrealistic oversimplifications of complex problems.[16] Inferential or judgmental rules (that is, heuristics) are often used by people to simplify risk problems. Examples are: (1) information availability—the tendency to view a hazard as more frequent if instances of it are easy to envision or recall; and (2) representativeness—the tendency to assume that roughly similar activities and events (nuclear power and nuclear war, for example) have the same characteristics and risks. While such judgmental operations appear to simplify individual risk assessment, serious biases and error may result.

One bias associated with information availability is the difficulty of imagining low probability/high consequence events happening to one-self. Floodplain residents are reluctant to buy low cost flood insurance, for example.[17] Individuals really believe that lightning never strikes the same place twice, just as those experiencing a serious flood think another will not occur soon. Overconfidence has been shown to be still another problem with individual risk estimates.[18]

The high tolerance levels for risks held by most individuals histori-cally has made restrictive policies politically unfeasible. As a result, one of the most frequently practiced hazard mitigation strategies is simply to inform those at risk of the risk and leave it to their own calculations of costs and benefits as to how to adjust. Labeling and advertising are offered to consumers on products they use; the hurri-cane threat is known to coastal residents.

Reliance on the information-based mitigation strategy is becoming politically unfeasible also, however. The costs of exposure to hazards are not borne solely by individuals who often knowingly subject them-selves to the risk. The costs of rescue, cleanup, and rehabilitation, for example, are shifted to society as a whole. Similarly, some health care and other costs are not borne solely by individuals.[19]

These external diseconomies have led to some recent shifts in public policy. For natural hazards, governments are turning to a wider variety of mitigation techniques, often regulatory in nature. Second, less emphasis is placed on the costly and questionably effective construc-tion projects dominated in the past by federal "pork barrel" funding, with more emphasis placed on land use planning and management. Third, even with construction projects, the national government is encouraging greater state and local involvement in mitigation by requir-ing greater cost-sharing. In addition, the national government has become aggressive in demanding local compliance with the National Flood Insurance Program (NFIP), the major incentive for local land use planning. The national government has made it clear to local governments that skyrocketing insurance claims being made against government require serious floodplain management and that repeated flooding in communities is related to inadequate enforcement of regulations.[20]

A similar pattern of increased and more stringent governmental involvement affects technological hazards. Persuasion, incentives, and/or

penalties are in greater use than in the past.[21] Government can penalize
—through indemnifying those harmed by way of the market (wages),
the courts (awarding damages), and transfer payments (taxes). Incentives (for example, credits or subsidies) can be offered, especially if
persuasive pleas for voluntary compliance are not successful. Finally, a
regulatory approach can be used to ban or regulate both products and
processes.

A final trend affecting increased governmental attempts to deal with
high tolerance for risk is legal in nature. Prevailing American attitudes
toward property owners' rights to develop their land unrestrained by
government regulations offer disincentives for strong local political
leadership in natural hazard mitigation and in dealing with such concerns as the location of hazardous waste sites. Local governments are
in jeopardy of lawsuits if they tightly regulate land uses in flood,
avalanche, erosion, or natural hazard areas, or attempt other mitigation strategies. However, those same officials may also be sued if they
issue permits for hazard-causing uses, increase natural or technological hazards, or fail to design or maintain mitigation measures such as
flood control works.[22] In sum, local public officials are experiencing a
variety of threats of litigation from individuals and the national government and are increasingly concerned about liability issues whether
they take action or choose no action.

Mitigation strategies are a local responsibility, despite individuals'
low risk perceptions of threats from natural and technological extremes.
Care is taken not to operate landfills, for example, in areas of high
groundwater. Compliance with state and federal statutory requirements is important. Better data bases are being developed for designing
and enforcing regulations. Officials are likely to win suits that challenge regulations or other mitigation measures, and lose lawsuits by
those who are damaged by uncontrolled development.[23]

Governmental Assumption of Risk

The high tolerance for risk by individuals is linked to increased governmental concern for the costs of individual risk assumption borne by
society, the second category of factors related to possibilities for adjustment to natural and technological extremes. Disasters are low
probability/high consequence events. From the perspective of the
national government, hazard mitigation is a "national" problem, potentially affecting any individual and his or her material possessions, as

well as the land, water, and air in the environment. From the national vantage point natural and technological hazards are a serious national problem, presenting staggering economic losses in property each year as well as significant losses of human life.[24] As one moves to lower levels of government the damages experienced become fewer from that level of government's vantage point (for example, the national government is impacted by all disasters in the United States, and each state is concerned with the aggregate of disasters in that state). Local governments may be the least likely to perceive hazards as important problems if such hazards are not in their immediate environment or experience.

Ways to deal with the national emergency management problem that appear rational and effective at the national level may be perceived as unwieldy, irrational, and inefficient from the perspective of a single community. Perceived risk, then, is a factor that shifts according to which level of government is being examined. The paradox for mitigation effectiveness is that local governments, though least likely to perceive emergency management in general as a key priority, are at center stage in terms of responsibility for overall emergency management. Although the Tenth Amendment reserves to the states the power to conduct their internal affairs, the major responsibilities, such as land use planning for natural hazard mitigation, have been delegated to local governments.

Mitigation strategies for technological hazards are necessarily dominated by federal environmental legislation (toxic substances laws, clean air and water laws), but the lack of a single national agency dealing with technological hazards makes coordination difficult. Programs are scattered among several categorical environmental laws and agencies, as well as those at the state and local levels. Federal laws are not self-implementing, however, and subnational governments play the critical role in the policy implementation process in our decentralized governmental system. Mitigation is included among the Federal Emergency Management Agency's (FEMA) responsibilities, although this umbrella agency for emergency management has devoted most of its efforts toward disaster preparedness and response to major events. The exception is FEMA's National Flood Insurance Program (NFIP) which offers regulations, executive orders, and interagency agreements as strong encouragement of local land use regulations.

The states carry key integrative and informational responsibilities in dealing with all levels of governments, agencies, and the private sector (usually volunteers). Moreover, the trend with federal postdisaster assistance is to decrease levels of federal subsidies and encourage more regulation in the mitigation phase by state and local governments.

Intergovernmental and Other
Intersystem Incentives

The perceived costs of policy implementation, based on social values and the interplay of groups in society, and the capacity of governmental units to design and implement policies comprise a final category of key factors affecting adjustments to natural and technological hazards.

Prevailing American attitudes toward personal property and government regulation work against adoption of many mitigation strategies. Highly developed political coalitions promoting mitigation are rare, due to the low probability of disaster events and the human tendency to discount their probability. Interest groups opposing mitigation strategies (some developers, builders, real estate interests, etc.) are well organized, as are chemical producers and others directly involved in increasing the threats of technological hazards.

The positive aspects of mitigation receive low political visibility, leading to low political salience. Many infrastructure disasters occur, for example, because few people notice maintenance of sewer or water lines. Officials perceive no political awards for their efforts and have little incentive to be concerned with issues of maintenance and rehabilitation. With the existing system of political awards, few officials accept the social responsibility to come forward in rallying concern for the adoption or enforcement of strong mitigation measures.

One way to increase state and local investment in mitigation is an increase in federal regulations. Another is increased federal cost-sharing requirements for state and local governments in the construction of public works as well as for postdisaster relief and assistance. State involvement can increase local investment in emergency management through direct regulations, mandating the adoption of local regulations, setting standards for local program performance, and building the capacity of local governments to manage their own programs more effectively. The states, however, have been slow to respond to these potential roles and increased state effort adds to the complexity involved in planning and coordinating among levels of government and among agencies.[25]

The vast differences across communities in the degree and kind of hazards complicates the adoption and implementation of mitigation strategies. Local communities differ greatly in their management capacity to plan and implement emergency management policies, especially the long-range planning expertise required for mitigation.[26] Local mitigation plans are likely to proceed at slower than optimal rates in the absence of an integrated multiple hazard approach, technical knowledge, adequate staffing, personnel, and other resources that enhance general management capacity.

With over 82,000 separate governmental units in the United States, the fragmentation complicates planning and implementing mitigation techniques. No single agency for dealing with disasters is practical by itself at any level. Yet the lack of a single agency in charge can lead to lost responsibility, especially when finances, staffing, information, authority, and facilities are also lacking. Intergovernmental coordination and cooperation and inter- and intraorganizational decisionmaking play pivotal roles in designing and implementing mitigation options. Regulations passed by one level of government necessitate promulgation and enforcement of compliance by other levels. Deficiencies in resources can be avoided by actions at other levels. Joint action among levels of government and across agency types requires communication, coordination, and other organizational management skills.[27]

State of Mitigation Practice

Mitigation policies have recently shifted from almost exclusive concern with structural options to nonstructural options in the form of social regulation and land use planning. This section reviews (1) the major drawbacks of structural options; (2) the trend toward regulatory and planning approaches; and (3) the problems with such alternatives. It shows that the trend away from costly engineering options has meant that information, not just money, has become a major vehicle for policy change.

Structural Options

Engineering solutions have traditionally dominated hazard mitigation. Flooding is controlled by the construction of dams, levees, channel alterations, and other devices. Care is given to the proper collection, treatment, and disposal of hazardous wastes. Stacks are constructed and emission control equipment used to treat air pollutants. Drinking water is purified and waste water is collected and treated.

While structural options clearly have benefits, they also have a number of weaknesses. First, they are very costly, both for government and the private sector. Federal flood control construction, for example, has exceeded $14 billion to date. Compliance with current federal air pollution control regulations may cost the private sector in excess of $24 billion.[28] Some economists have argued that the benefit-cost procedures used at the federal level exaggerate benefits and understate the costs of such structural projects as flood control.[29]

Second, despite massive federal and private expenditures, property losses and potential health problems continue to rise. One reason is that hazards grow at a faster rate than the structural solutions can be put in place. A good example is the population at risk from hurricanes, which is increasing rapidly. Another example is that federal hazardous waste and drinking water standards cannot keep pace with the one to two thousand new chemicals introduced each year that join an estimated seventy thousand chemicals already in general use. Structural solutions are useful in dealing with existing hazards but not as useful in preventing new hazards from emerging or people from exposing themselves further to any type of hazards. In addition, many structural solutions were designed before the nature of many hazards was understood, especially chemical hazards.[30] Also, hazardous events sometimes exceed the design limitation of structural works in place. Two-thirds of this nation's flood losses are attributable to catastrophic floods that exceed commonly accepted design criteria. Moreover, the construction of dams, levees, and other structural measures produces changes in the hydrological structures of streams, modifying their hazard characteristics. While channelization, for example, will relieve flood problems in one area, it may create them in unprotected, downstream areas as the stream seeks to dissipate its energy at flood stage. A final reason that property losses and potential health problems continue to rise is that structural works can fail. An example is a dam break.

Third, structural alternatives have traditionally worked to the disadvantage of nonstructural measures. Dams to prevent floods actually induce urban development in floodplains and stimulate a false sense of security among floodplain occupants. Flood damages may well increase, not in spite of mitigation policies but because of them.

The failure of the federal government to require extensive cost-sharing by state and local governments, the fourth drawback of structural options, has affected both the incidence of benefits and the costs from structural approaches. (Recent changes in federal policy have dramatically increased cost-sharing.) A lack of cost-sharing raised questions of equity and distribution of costs across society, as well as about the efficient level and mix of structural and nonstructural mitigation measures.

Regulatory Approaches

Regulatory strategies have moved to a dominant role for both natural and technological hazard mitigation. Land use management aims to modify human behavior, a recognition that "natural hazard" damages are often induced by human behavior. Rather than keeping flood waters away from people (by a dam), the nonstructural alternative attempts to keep people away from the flood waters through zoning, subdivision, and other regulations, highlighting the need to devise informational strategies to inform citizens and develop regulations.

Similarly, land use planning and management can attempt to prevent the generation of pollutants at specific locations where they pose a hazard, and to separate people from pollution spatially. In addition, public health regulations determine the design and operation of water and waste water systems and facilities for disposal of solid and hazardous wastes. A particularly important alternative relies on engineering and structural design options. This is the building code which sets standards for construction materials, design, and procedures to protect life and property.[31]

There are a number of problems with implementation of the land use planning and management mitigation options. First, the national government's approach to the encouragement of land use planning objectives for hazard management has often ignored other local objectives, confusing local governments' planning.

Second, without strong federal or state mandates, or sanctions, local officials have not demonstrated the political will to adopt and/or enforce land use measures. Even when regulations do exist they have not been vigorously implemented by local officials, largely due to the strength of landowner and developer opposition. The low salience for both individuals and government of low probability/high consequence events, coupled with devotion to individual property rights, makes the necessary stringent regulatory approach difficult. The adoption and implementation phases of the policy process are problematic for local governments, not just because of interest groups but because of inadequate local planning and management capacity in the form of personnel, finances, and other resources. In addition, most threats from hazards involve spillovers among governmental jurisdictions, and interlocal cooperation is rarely adequate in any policy area.

Third, most nonstructural measures focus on new construction and are not as useful for mitigating hazards faced by existing development.[32] It is economically and politically unlikely, for example, that all existing buildings in an earthquake-prone city will be strengthened or that all existing buildings in a floodplain will be floodproofed.

For many technological hazards, especially those of a chemical nature, the difficulties with the regulatory approach are staggering. Our decentralized political system forces the lowest administrative levels to carry enormous enforcement burdens but without adequate administrative capacity.

Benefits and Costs of Mitigation

Despite the myriad of mitigation measures used in dealing with natural and technological hazards, damages continue to mount. The usual response is to call for even more mitigation. Yet the existence of actual or potential damage is not proof that there is too little mitigation. Economists have argued that we should first turn to other questions: How much should we spend on mitigation? What is the efficient level of risk we wish to tolerate? What is a socially acceptable level of risk? Is the aggregate risk or the distribution of the risk more important? Should ecological risk receive lower priority than human health risks? What are the true costs and benefits of mitigation?[33]

These questions suggest that damage costs must be compared to the costs of adjustment. Yet we know very little about the total costs of mitigation.[34] We do know that adjustments to mitigate the extremes of natural and technological threats are not totally successful. In addition, given the rare probabilities of some types of extremes—for example, an earthquake devastating Los Angeles—total adjustment to the threat is impracticable and may be unwise from a cost-benefit perspective. Few would argue that we relocate Los Angeles or that every existing (not future) building be earthquake-resistant, whatever that may require in each successive time period.

In addition to the difficult questions involved with deciding on the costs and types of mitigation, some benefits can be measured from disasters and from occupying hazard zones. The economic productivity from occupying many earthquake-prone areas far outweighs the costs of a potential earthquake. When dry agricultural lands are irrigated by flooding, the water is a benefit. After a disaster, human response generally enhances social cohesion.[35]

The mitigation of natural and technological hazards poses the classic problem of social regulation. How should the costs of the problems be distributed? How much avoidance is necessary, given the enormous costs of unperfected solutions, whether large-scale facilities such as dams or mapping for land use regulations? What are the most effective ways of altering current practice? Who should bear the costs of remedying undesirable consequences of past practices?

Social decisionmaking relating to natural and technological hazards is especially complicated due to the high consequence/low probability nature of such disasters. It is difficult to aggregate preferences, especially in light of limited knowledge. The uncertainty derived from lack of knowledge and the probabilistic nature of many problems further complicate decisionmaking. The ethical character of the dilemma demands debate regarding the present generation's right to impose on future generations the uncertainties associated with their decisions, as well as consideration of the distributional impacts of decisions.

The irreversibility of certain decisions regarding low probability/ high consequence events and the inability to reverse catastrophic events with any large degree of success raise significant questions about using an efficiency criterion for evaluating social decisions or other economic justifications.[36] Given the high stakes, the struggle over policy decisions for hazard mitigation will continue to be intense as information development and dissemination provide the major ingredients for successful solutions.

Natural Hazard Mitigation and Development: An Exploration of the Roles of the Public and Private Sectors ✒ Leonard I. Ruchelman

The Problem: Mitigating Natural Hazards

In the United States as in most societies, the concept of mitigating natural hazards through nonstructural means is relatively new. It was not until the late 1960s that the federal government began to focus on methods of preventing hazardous events other than by such costly means as dams, levees, and other large-scale projects.[1] Because this concept is new, much remains to be done in developing ideas on which to base workable solutions.

Of special interest in any discussion of natural hazard mitigation is the role of the private sector as it interfaces with government on questions of preventing or reducing risk. This is because natural hazards are often linked with the activities of government and business.[2] For example, with the endorsement of government regulatory agencies several California nuclear reactors were allowed to locate near active fault lines; and offshore oil rigs in the Gulf of Mexico were allowed to be built in the path of tropical storms. Similarly, overdependence on government projects to eliminate the hazards of extreme natural events may serve to entice people into settling areas that would be best devoted to less intensive uses. In 1983 flooding on the Colorado River quickly filled up several reservoirs, requiring the release of water before they overflowed. Downstream, floodplains were inundated along with their residents who felt safe living there because they believed public technology had brought the Colorado "under control."

A lesson to be learned from such incidents is that hazard planning and prevention at the local, state, and national levels should address the interaction of the public and private sectors whenever feasible. This chapter views public-private relations in the area of land development and human settlement patterns as being especially critical to hazard mitigation policy. Looking at the record of development in the United States and other parts of the world, there is evidence that methods of reducing exposure to risk have been largely ignored and that human settlements have been experiencing growing exposure to natural catastrophe. A recent assessment of the United States shows that the national aggregate annual expected value of dollar losses caused by exposure of people and property to nine types of hazardous natural events currently exceeds $22.3 billion per year and that these annual expected losses will rise to a level of about $37.7 billion (measured in 1980 dollars) in the year 2000.[3] The anticipated loss of life from such exposures will rise from 1,183 to 1,790 over the same period.[4] Viewing worldwide data, a 1984 report by the Swedish Red Cross found a sharp increase in natural disasters from the 1960s to the 1970s, and from the 1970s to the 1980s.[5] Many more people died per year in disasters in the 1970s (142,820) than in the 1960s (22,570). The difference is far too great to be explained by population growth alone.

Viewing such trends, the purpose of the present work is to examine the following questions: What is the role of private development in increasing vulnerability to natural hazards? To what extent does government encourage development in high-risk areas through the unintentional effects of existing policies? How can the public and private sectors work together for upgrading and expanding hazard mitigation standards?

An Overview of Public-Private Interactions

In order to account for patterns of interaction between public and private institutions in the area of land development, five possible forms have been identified in the literature.[6] A basic interest in each of the models presented below is to compare the public and private sectors on the question of who benefits from land development and who bears the costs of catastrophe that may result from such development.

Laissez-faire. In this form of interaction the public sector permits the private sector to engage in development with little or no government control. This arrangement is based on the premise that the prime obligation of business is to satisfy the demands of the marketplace through the pursuit of profits and that government takes responsibility for any unintended consequences that could affect the public such as disasters. (Economists call these externalities.) A basic assumption of the laissez-faire approach is that over the long run it will produce the greatest net benefits for society.

Promotion. Here the public sector encourages private sector development by providing the preconditions for development through provision of public infrastructure, advertising, and work force education. These preconditions are established under the rationale that they will attract economic investment which ultimately benefits the entire community through increased tax revenue. Promotional activities involve no prior agreement with representatives of the business community. In addition to assuming the costs of promotional activities, government is also expected to bear the costs of unintended consequences that may be caused by increased vulnerability to natural hazards.

Cooperation. In this form the public and private sectors cooperate or act in partnership to achieve mutually shared goals. One example would be agreement between government and developers stipulating that if government establishes certain preconditions such as public infrastructure, the developers will respond in a specified manner to mitigate the potential effects of hazards. If this approach is to work, representatives of both the public and private sectors must see clear gains for themselves.

Inducement. In this arrangement government provides incentives to developers in the form of tax abatements or loans to induce private sector behavior that will accomplish the public goal of reducing exposure to hazards. This relationship differs from cooperation because it does not assume that the public and private sectors share mutual goals. Instead, it recognizes that the private sector's primary goal is profit and attempts to structure circumstances by which the private sector, in pursuing its profit objectives, will at the same time accomplish public ends. In this model the private sector gains through public subsidies while the public sector expects to reduce long-run costs.

Regulation. Here the public sector controls development so that it is consistent with public objectives. Private development may be limited as to where it may locate, its size, materials that can be used, and certain aspects of structural design. In some instances the developer may even be required to provide certain public amenities as a condition for building. Where the regulatory model prevails, private profits are likely to be less at the same time that public costs are reduced.

As we shall see, these models are not necessarily exclusive of one another but more or less overlap depending on circumstances.

The Role of the Private Sector

Consideration of the role of the private sector in natural hazard mitigation acknowledges that while business shares responsibility with government for the protection of lives and property, the priorities of business are different from those of government. While government is expected to establish policy for the health, welfare, and safety of the people, business as an economic entity acts to satisfy the demands of the marketplace as a higher priority.[7]

This can be seen in the area of land development in the United States. Historian Sam Bass Warner explains that as persons who escaped the deprivations of European feudal society, the early settlers cherished land as a civil right.[8] Land ownership meant not only freedom from the meddling of feudal lords or town officials but also freedom for even the poorest family to profit from rising values in a country absorbing ever greater numbers of settlers.

Over the years the special importance accorded property rights has been supplemented by the growth ethic.[9] In communities all over America, business groups allied with election officials and other local interests have carried out aggressive campaigns of industrial and commercial expansion. By 1960 scarcely a large city in the United States lacked a well-organized program to promote economic development. Examples are numerous.[10] In Pittsburgh the Allegheny Conference on Community Development was formed under the leadership of R. K. Mellon to promote revitalization of Pittsburgh's Golden Triangle. Chicago's Mayor Richard J. Daley was able to build the strength of the Chicago Democratic party by changing the skyline of Chicago's Loop and lakefront. In San Francisco Mayor Joseph Alioto became the center of a redevelopment coalition composed of big labor, important corporations, real estate interests, and the city's major newspapers. Subsequently, San Francisco's skyline has been dramatically changed with the building of several huge skyscrapers.[11]

More recently, in the 1970s and 1980s, economic development has been diffusing out into the suburbs to a greater extent than ever before. This can be seen in table 1, which shows employment changes as a measure of economic growth. Such diffusion is largely attributable to changing technology which makes it possible for more companies to locate in outlying areas where land, rents, utilities, and taxes are less expensive than in cities. Consequently competition between central city and suburban jurisdictions has become more intense than ever before.

Promotional strategies include national advertising proclaiming the special advantages of a community, preparing large "industrial parks" prior to receiving new industries, and, with the concurrence of local government, providing special tax incentives. Progress is equated with the number of buildings constructed, the number of jobs created, and increases in local spending. Attitudes that support community development are usually stated as follows:[12]

- ☐ Growth broadens the tax base and reduces per capita tax burdens;
- ☐ Growth brings job opportunities to residents;
- ☐ Community development eventually results in improved community services such as fire and health services, roads, and schools;
- ☐ Even though growth may have costs that exceed new tax revenues, the overall benefits more than counterbalance the direct costs.

Unfortunately, where the pursuit of growth is not carefully planned, the environment begins to suffer as measured by air and water pollution, loss of open space, increased highway congestion, and destruction of wetlands and other ecologically sensitive areas. While the public has been showing a growing awareness of environmental problems, the issue of increasing exposure to natural hazards that also results from haphazard growth has received very little attention.[13]

This can be illustrated in the case of Los Angeles, which is often referred to as "Hazard City." No other American city exhibits an environment in which the highest quality of urban life can be achieved at the same time that it is threatened with the greatest number of physi-

Table 1. Employment Changes in Central Cities and
Surrounding Suburban Counties of Nine Metropolitan Areas,
1982–1985 (in percentages)

	City	Suburban
Atlanta	+ 10.2	+ 22.6
Chicago	+ 4.0	+ 20.0
Detroit	+ 2.1	+ 14.4
Washington	+ 3.4	+ 17.1
St. Louis	− 4.1	+ 14.8
San Francisco	+ 2.1	+ 9.7
Baltimore	+ 0.1	+ 8.9
Philadelphia	− 0.2	+ 8.5
New York	+ 3.5	+ 5.5

Note: Figures for Atlanta, Chicago, Detroit, and San Francisco are for the counties
in which they are located.
Source: U.S. News and World Report, November 18, 1985, p. 84.

cal hazards. What makes Los Angeles so attractive is its semidesert
climate of rainless summers and mild winters combined with enticing
beaches and tropical vegetation. Snow-capped mountain peaks serve
as backdrop. Yet the area is vulnerable to catastrophe because the very
same features have attracted so many inhabitants. As more and more
people settle in the area seeking a leisure-oriented good life, they have
inadvertently exacerbated the potential for disaster through thought-
less development and indiscriminate use of natural resources. Of thirteen potential hazards that can affect communities, the greater Los
Angeles area is vulnerable to eight. Only avalanches, hurricanes, vol-
canoes, tornadoes, and blizzards are missing from this list.

The most serious threat is seismic disturbance as manifested by
earthquakes. In fact the whole of Los Angeles is underlain by a fault
mosaic that periodically causes tremors in the earth.[14] The last severe
earthquake (magnitude 6.7 on the Richter scale) occurred in the San
Fernando Valley, the city's northern suburbs, in 1971. In a mere ten
seconds tremors demolished or severely damaged more than one thousand buildings, brought down several overpasses in the city's freeway
system, and ultimately claimed 65 lives. Total damage exceeded $500
million.[15] Despite gloomy predictions by scientists of even more severe
earthquakes in the future (possibly as high as 8.1 on the Richter scale),
many Los Angeles inhabitants are fatalistic. Although awareness of risk

is increasing slowly through concentrated public education efforts, the general attitude of the residents is represented by the businessman who considered erecting spectator stands to the northeast of the San Andreas Fault so that interested persons could witness the event when it happened.

Other natural hazards that threaten this region are giant sea waves generated by submarine earthquakes (tsunamis), sinking coastlines caused by crustal subsidence resulting from the extraction of oil, landslides, brush fires, floods, drought, and smog. In search of scenic beauty and appreciating land values in "unique" settings, Angelenos have built on top of cliffs, near ravines, along the coastline, in arid brush land, and next to earth faults. Though Los Angeles represents an extreme example because of the multiplicity of natural hazards to which it is exposed, other American communities similarly court danger through development in dangerous areas without forethought on questions of prevention.

In this light an argument can be made that the traditional or common view of "natural disasters" should be changed. Because human beings are now playing so great a role in natural disasters, such disasters are no longer "natural." A distinction could be made between the "trigger events" (rain, earth tremors, hurricanes) that are natural, and the resulting disasters that may be largely man-made. For example, a severe storm over a densely settled housing development on a coastal island may prove to be a major disaster in terms of property damage and human deaths. Is the disaster the result of the storm or of the fact that people are inhabiting such a dangerous area?

In addition to the physical aspects of disasters, it is necessary to focus on social and economic aspects as guided by development interests. Two long-time observers of natural disasters, Anders Wijkman and Lloyd Timberlake, argue that because researchers have tended to study only the physical events of disasters, natural hazards have been isolated from the rest of man-environment relations.[16] An important consequence of this is that governments have been encouraged to put their trust in large-scale prevention measures such as dams, early warning systems, and satellite monitoring. While such measures provide real benefits to society, it is also necessary to consider patterns of land development and usage if vulnerability to the forces of nature is to be reduced or eliminated.

Figure 1 illustrates how various factors are likely to contribute to disaster. Where households are established in drought-prone areas, in flood plains, near geographic fault lines, and on steep hillsides, storms, dry spells, or modest earthquakes can cause more damage than was possible prior to such settlement. According to ecologists the degradation of forests, pastures, and soils contributes to the frequency of floods and droughtlike conditions. Deforestation of hillsides means that stormwater rushes off slopes and is not absorbed for percolation. This results in flash floods as well as water shortages in summer months as streams dry up. In semiarid areas the elimination of plant cover in the soil because of tree-cutting or overgrazing can contribute to a decline in the efficient use of rainwater. This, in turn, leads to drier soils that only exacerbate the effects of a dry spell.

The Role of the Public Sector

What are the responsibilities of the public sector in mitigating hazards that are caused by development and human settlements? As the following listing shows, different types of approaches are available to government to protect communities and their residents.[17]

1 Approaches that are intended to minimize the probability of hazard occurrence and/or that protect specific locations. For example, reforestation to decrease water runoff with regard to the former, or construction of dams and levees with regard to the latter.
2 Reinforcement of buildings exposed to hazards. For example, anchoring structures or reinforcing beams of buildings.
3 Site development to protect structures from hazards. For example, slope stabilization or drainage improvement.
4 Identification of hazard-prone sites through mapping and preventing or restricting their development or use. For example, floodplain zoning.
5 Approaches that focus on loss recovery, relief, and community rehabilitation. Examples include insurance programs and low-interest loans authorized by government.
6 Hazard warning and evacuation strategies such as those used to deal with approaching hurricanes or floods.
7 Establishment of standards for building construction and performance through building and fire codes.

Figure 1. The Evolution of Natural Hazards

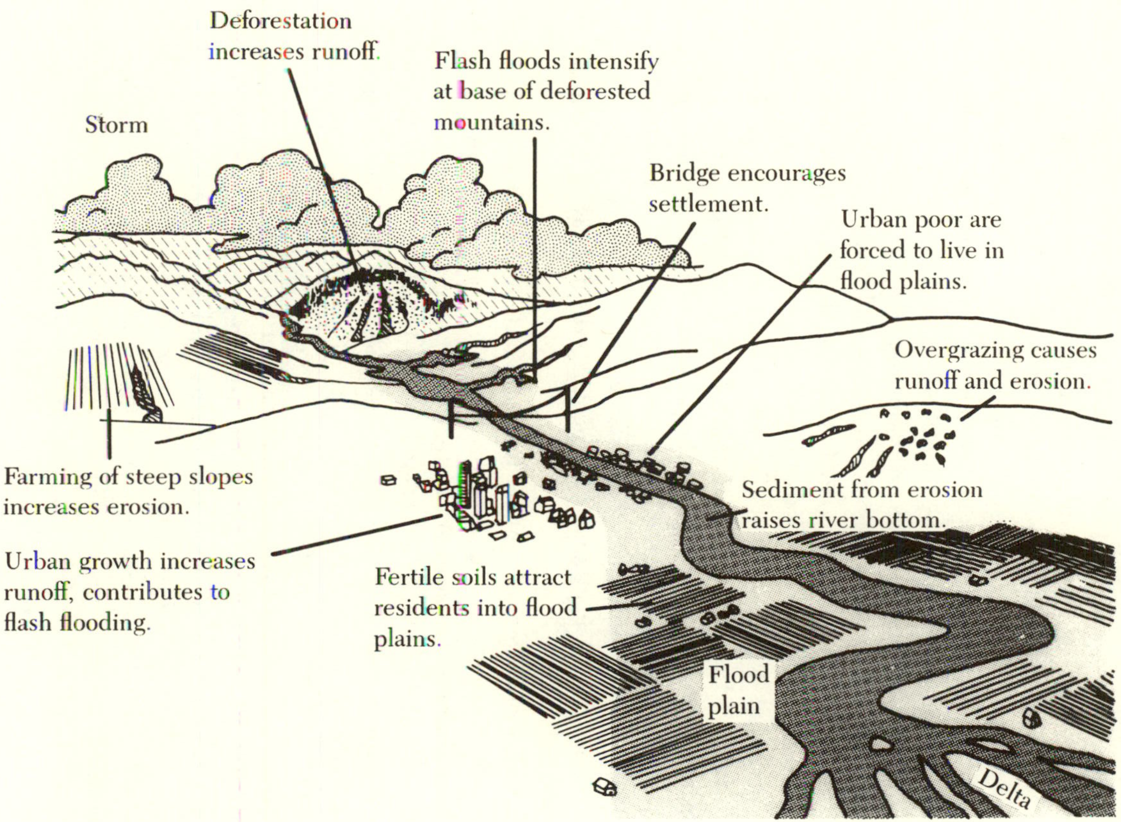

Storm

Deforestation increases runoff.

Flash floods intensify at base of deforested mountains.

Bridge encourages settlement.

Urban poor are forced to live in flood plains.

Overgrazing causes runoff and erosion.

Sediment from erosion raises river bottom.

Flood plain

Delta

Farming of steep slopes increases erosion.

Urban growth increases runoff, contributes to flash flooding.

Fertile soils attract residents into flood plains.

The National Flood Insurance Act of 1968 is an example of how
government has relied on a combination of approaches to prevent
natural hazards and/or to reduce their effects. While the act provides
flood insurance for individual property owners, eligibility is linked to
whether a jurisdiction has met certain planning requirements; namely,
flood hazard areas must be identified, a hazard map prepared, and a
floodplain management plan established. By 1982 approximately two
million policies were in effect covering $100 billion in property. Never-
theless, a study by Raymond J. Burby and Steven P. French of over
1,200 communities enrolled in the National Flood Insurance Program
shows that it has not been effective in reducing the rate of floodplain
invasion.[18] In fact, the findings illustrate an interesting paradox; namely,
factors that stimulate the adoption of land use management programs
on the local level also stimulate encroachment on the hazard area
which in turn limits program effectiveness. Thus government provision of low-cost insurance has encouraged rather than restricted private risk taking.

Other government policies have similarly contributed to the movement of population into high-risk areas. A study sponsored by the
United States Department of Interior of some 300 barrier islands off
the Atlantic and Gulf Coasts found that, despite warnings, at least half
of the seventeen or more federal agencies that have jurisdiction have
actually encouraged development on these islands.[19] The development, in turn, has made the islands more hazardous places in which to
live. Such agencies as the Department of Energy, the Army Corps of
Engineers, the Federal Insurance Administration, the Federal Highway Administration, the Coast Guard, and the Department of Housing and Urban Development are authorized to build power plants,
build highways and bridges, erect groins and jetties, provide low-cost
housing projects, give low-interest business loans for barrier island
investment and provide low-cost storm insurance. All of these actions
are taken with little or no control over the size or environmental
impacts of the projects.

The Department of Interior study states that although about one-
fourth of the agencies administer programs which directly or indirectly
provide protection for the barrier islands, more than one-half of the
agencies administer grant, loan, permit, or construction programs that
have had adverse impacts on the islands. The remainder administer
property, insurance, and relief programs that have actually made the
islands more vulnerable to hazards. Population growth in coastal coun-

ties has resulted in increased demand for recreation, housing, and business facilities on the relatively fragile foundations offered by the barrier islands. As a result, 175 of the 300 seacoast isles now have direct vehicular access by road, bridge, or causeway, 9 have airports, and 24 have regular ferry-boat service. Paradoxically, the government's efforts to stabilize the islands by building groins and jetties that extend out to sea to prevent sand from drifting away have caused damage. Scientists explain that such construction causes erosion of the beach on the downcurrent side and can harm adjacent islands.

The structural approach to hazard mitigation has also been subject to criticism on the grounds that this, too, produces unintended hazardous effects.[20] The Army Corps of Engineers program of building dams, levees, and structures to prevent floods also creates them by channeling floodwaters to unprotected areas. Dams also encourage development in floodplains by creating the false assumption that a flood cannot occur. Where the design limitations of a dam are exceeded, however, flooding will occur. As previously noted, this happened to the Colorado River in the summer of 1983.[21]

An important aspect of federal natural hazard policy is that major responsibility for implementation rests with state and local government through such tools as land-use plans, zoning ordinances, and building and health codes. Thus the general ineffectiveness of federal mitigation policies raises questions about the capacity of state and local government. Of special concern is the willingness of state and local government jurisdictions to bear the costs of carrying out strong measures where such actions may constrain economic development. According to Bruce B. Clary, "Strong pressures are often present in communities that militate against effective mitigation practices. Studies of disasters indicate that the marketplace is the usual determinant of locational decisions, frequently leading to rebuilding in a hazard area."[22]

Where building codes and zoning laws to reduce hazards are strictly enforced, communities are likely to become less vulnerable; but where planning departments and building departments lack the necessary expertise, developers are allowed to encroach on hazardous areas through variances and exceptions to development regulations. In many instances, also, state laws and regulations are successfully challenged in the courts because of inconsistencies in application.[23]

Problems of Public-Private Interaction

One reason for the lack of success in achieving an effective natural hazard mitigation posture in the United States is that the private sector must relate to government on more than one level. Business that is interstate in scope must deal primarily with federal agencies. Insurance and banking companies deal with state government. Builders and developers deal with local government. Thus the intergovernmental system contributes to a confusion of responsibility in the making and implementation of emergency management policy. In many instances, moreover, states and localities are in competition with each other to attract new industry and promote development. Such conditions tend to limit and diffuse predisaster mitigation planning and help to explain why government policies have tended to exacerbate exposure to hazardous events; this occurs even where the intent of government has been to reduce exposure to natural hazards.

As a first step in remedying this situation, counterproductive policies involving government relations with private economic interests must be identified through a carefully structured monitoring process. This requires a broad analytical assessment of the entire process of hazard mitigation throughout the country rather than the present piecemeal approach. Especially important is the involvement of appropriate business interests in the planning process so that they may discover their interests in making the plan work. Similarly, others who use the land on a large scale, such as corporate farmers and lumber interests, must also be involved.

A second reason for the lack of success in making and implementing hazard mitigation policy is that private decisionmaking has tended to focus on immediate benefits, namely profits, and has tended to ignore long-term costs that result from natural catastrophes. This is especially problematic in land development where the developer is usually interested primarily in constructing and selling structures as quickly as possible, avoiding long-term concerns. Where this happens, it is usually the owner of the structure who must face the consequences of hazards. Yet in land development as in all areas of business and industry, banks and investment institutions quite obviously have long-term stakes in avoiding disasters that may interfere with expected returns on investments. Similarly, public utilities, transportation firms, and realty firms also have a vested interest in preventing costly disruptions caused by hazards. The task ahead is to make a more concerted effort in targeting the risk management practices of such businesses and relating them to the goals of natural hazard mitigation programs.

A third aspect to the problem of natural hazard mitigation is the general lack of knowledge or awareness of man's role in causing natural catastrophes. Both the public and private sectors of society need to be educated on the value of predisaster prevention rather than postdisaster relief. This necessarily involves educational institutions as well as mass media such as television, radio, newspapers, and magazines. On the international level relief organizations are beginning to educate the public on the need to link disaster relief to preventive strategies. Anders Wijkman, secretary general of the Swedish Red Cross, and Lloyd Timberlake, editorial director of Earthscan, elaborate as follows: "The public—in both the industrialized and the developing countries —must come to see disasters not simply as 'acts of God' striking helpless people, but as the results of the complex ways in which people operate within their environment. They must come to understand that charity and concern are most effective when they begin before, not after, the disaster."[24]

Conclusions

In viewing the record of public-private relations in land development in the United States, it is evident that the prevailing pattern of interaction has been a combination of the laissez-faire and promotional forms. The underlying rationale to this approach is that the community will ultimately benefit to the greatest degree where the private sector is allowed to pursue its development goals with little or no regulation from government. Proponents contend that development leads to increased jobs and an increased tax base and this, in turn, raises the incomes of city residents and improves the public services that can be provided by government.

Following the logic of this model, it is easy to understand its broad appeal. Attempts by government to impose restraints or to guide development in order to reduce risks of natural hazards have for the most part been ineffective. There is evidence, furthermore, that government programs intended to mitigate natural hazards have been coopted by development interests and used to promote growth. As we noted, construction of flood control facilities has served to encourage migration into flood zones and has thereby increased the real costs of floods. Government programs for disaster relief, low-cost loans, and subsidized insurance have, at times, encouraged rather than inhibited private risk-taking activity. Contrary to their intended purpose, such programs lend credence to the widespread belief that wherever people go, government will somehow protect them. Thus people continue to move into such high-hazard areas as the hurricane flood-prone areas along the Gulf Coast and south Atlantic. Similarly, people continue to be attracted into seismically active areas such as Los Angeles and its surroundings. Consequently, according to William Petak and Arthur Atkisson, "the United States now faces the probability that one or more major community catastrophes, each far greater in loss of life and property than any previous one, may occur during the next several decades."[25]

Another approach that remains to be tested and that may contribute real payoffs in the area of natural hazard mitigation is public-private cooperation. This model recognizes that developers and investors are citizens as well as business persons. An appeal for cooperation to achieve public goals in the reduction of hazards may succeed if these individuals are allowed to get personally involved in the planning process. Second, businesses and corporations require and seek a certain degree of public acceptance. Widely publicized actions to cooperate with public sector goals provide evidence of their social responsibility and good citizenship. Third, the private sector may cooperate with the public sector because one or more of its subgoals may coincide with public sector purposes. Social and economic stability or a safe environment may be subgoals of portions of the private sector because they encourage investment.

There are, of course, pitfalls in the cooperative approach. Without serious analysis, cooperation becomes a mere rhetorical device, an exhortation to both sectors to act in a way that may contravene the interests of one or both sectors. Any form of cooperation that implies reduced profits for business is unlikely to occur except in symbolic ways. However, only the cooperative model is likely to be able to sell the idea that the net benefits of predisaster mitigation are greater than those for postdisaster recovery. This is a concept that has yet to be accepted and no less successfully implemented.

The Design and Implementation of Disaster Mitigation Policy

⚡ Richard L. Ender and John Choon K. Kim, with Lidia L. Selkregg and Stephan F. Johnson

Mitigation can be defined as a management strategy to balance current action and expenditures with potential losses from future disaster occurrences.[1]

In terms of the number of people, the amount of property, and the critical economic facilities exposed to natural hazards risk, many areas in the United States are more vulnerable today than they were two decades ago. Growth in the economy and population are not the only factors in this increased risk. Measures which might have been taken to reduce the dangers from earthquakes, tsunamis, and other hazards have not been taken or have been only partially or imperfectly instituted. Lands designated high-risk have been developed for industrial, commercial, and residential use.

This chapter examines the key elements of and obstacles to implementation related to hazard mitigation policy, introduces a design for disaster mitigation planning, and recommends measures designed to overcome systemic obstacles to policy implementation.

A National Science Foundation-sponsored study of the 1964 Great Alaska Earthquake and subsequent mitigation policies in southcentral Alaska form the context in which hazards response and implementation issues were analyzed.[2] However, the findings are applicable to a broad range of low probability/high consequence events associated with natural hazards.

Key Elements and Obstacles in
the Implementation of Risk Mitigation

However well a risk mitigation policy is designed, many problems are associated with implementation. Research on general problems of policy implementation[3] is only partially applicable to risk mitigation. Case studies have focused on failed implementation of Great Society programs involving continuously visible and defined groups of people such as the poor, the unemployed, or a minority group. Natural hazard mitigation presents different implementation problems compared to many other government programs designed to attack social and environmental ills. The threat from natural disasters is largely invisible and of low probability, though of great potential consequence. Additionally, the actual effect of implementation measures to deal with such disasters cannot be easily evaluated in the short run and at low cost. The following discussion will review factors critical to establishing conditions for and identifying primary obstacles to successful policy implementation.

Implementation within the Organizational Context

Organizational structures should be designed to facilitate the attainment of goals and objectives. The structure of organizations has a significant influence on implementation. One structural feature that significantly influences policy implementation is organizational fragmentation. Responsibility for a policy area is frequently dispersed among several organizations, often radically decentralizing the power to accomplish policy goals. These are buttressed by state constitutions and city charters that mandate a fragmented administrative structure, and by federal grant programs that allow state and local governments to mirror fragmented national efforts. Such diffusion complicates policy coordination because it inhibits changes in policy, wastes resources, generates undesired actions, confuses officials at lower level jurisdictions, and results in conflicting policies and responsibilities that fall into the cracks of organizational boundaries. The more actors and agencies involved and the more interdependent their decisions, the greater the ambiguity and the less the probability of successful implementation.[4]

The lack of interagency coordination has a particularly debilitating effect on policy implementation. Priorities of agencies differ, and bureaucrats tend to avoid communication with their counterparts in other agencies, even when their responsibilities clearly overlap or interface. Federal agencies operate independently and often pursue or encourage policies different from those of other agencies.[5] In general, the more coordination required to implement a policy, the less its chances of success.[6]

Charges of inadequate coordination have often been leveled at past hazard management attempts. A California study noted, "The real problem in implementation is that too much decentralization in response to prediction may lead to nonpreparedness, as well as pre-paredness. There has been more fragmentation than cohesion around this interest. The agencies have tended to go their own way. Each local jurisdiction looks after itself."[7] Due to fragmentation the narrow respon-sibilities of many agencies sometimes mean that certain functions sim-ply get overlooked and fall between the cracks of organizational structure.

A second problem in successful implementation is operational rules of administrative agencies that skirt or neglect geophysical risk mitiga-tion. The process of building plan approval and inspection focuses on structural and design requirements, and virtually ignores siting con-siderations. Except in the more complex projects in Alaska, neither a licensed engineer nor a building official is required to consider siting in relation to geophysical risk, nor does geophysical risk mitigation appear prominently in land use regulations. Design codes when imple-mented are seen as maximums, not minimums that require strength-ening under higher risk circumstances. Formal and informal standard operating procedures generally do not include any regular incorpora-tion of geophysical risk. An Alaskan borough planning commissioner noted, "We have never denied anybody anything because they were in a high-risk area."

Notable exceptions are found in California, where cities ranging in size from Portola Valley (population 4,500) to Los Angeles (population 2,902,000) have introduced zoning regulations along active faults. A larger number of communities throughout the country control con-struction in landslide-prone areas, where earthquakes might trigger

renewed movement, either through stipulations pertaining to grading
in the UBC (for example, requiring additional information on soil and
geological conditions) or through individually adopted drainage and
grading ordinances.[8]

A significant design and land use problem is that critical facilities,
such as lifelines, high-occupancy buildings, emergency facilities, unique
and large structures where failure might be catastrophic, underdesigned
structures, and other nonresistive developments exist and continue to
be constructed in high-hazard areas. Additionally, new construction
commonly takes place in hazardous areas after earthquake damage and
after existing structures are identified in high-hazard areas.

A third structural obstacle relates to how an organization is viewed.
Many people assume that decisionmakers and governmental entities
will act rationally when faced with hazard-risk information. This suggests that when officials receive information on risks, new measures to
reduce risks, or recommended reforms to the planning and implementation process, they will proceed with certain rational steps implicit in
the new information. The rational actor will "value maximize," or
attempt to gain the most from a desired goal. In relation to natural
hazards, value maximization can be seen as acting to reduce dangers to
lives and property. The concepts of such rational behavior are predominant in planning and policy analysis because they explain or anticipate
human and organizational behavior in logical and predictable ways.
However, human beings and human organizations are powerfully
affected by nonrational factors.[9] One result of the dominance of rational
actor assumptions in addressing risk mitigation is that scientists may
assume that geophysical facts need only to be made clear to policymakers for appropriate action to occur. Planners may believe that the
presentation of well-developed and logically consistent land use plans
will lead to their adoption, and policy analysts often think that authoritative and well-developed policies will be implemented. Frequently,
and particularly in the case of geophysical hazard mitigation, these
types of assumptions are faulty and frustrate implementation.

Intergovernmental Relations

Reducing natural disaster risk is obviously the responsibility of a great
many agencies at all levels of government. Each level of government
(federal, state, and local) has a crucial role to play in the quest for
public safety in seismic regions. A number of studies encourage

significant improvement in the federal, state, and local capabilities and in partnerships for the implementation of seismic safety plans.[10]

The Working Group on Earthquake Hazards Reduction notes that federal, state, and local governmental units and the private sector generally have inadequate understanding of earthquake hazards and how to avoid the hazards or mitigate the damage. Coordination of federal land use planning and development programs to avoid earthquake hazards and mitigate damage is virtually nonexistent.

Despite Alaska's unique institutionalized history of coordination among federal, state, and local agencies, it has little to show in the area of risk mitigation. Though joint federal/state efforts began the development of criteria to evaluate resources and land use subsequent to the 1964 earthquake, seismic risks were seldom evaluated and policies for their mitigation were never recommended.

While local government, through its planning, zoning, and code enforcement powers, has substantial jurisdiction in risk mitigation, mitigation in Alaska has largely involved the federal government. The factors that limit local government interest in and capacity for response also weaken its incentive to take strong mitigation measures. While each level of agreement needs the others' contributions in an intergovernmental partnership, researchers agree that the state governments are clearly in a pivotal position in evaluating hazards and determining levels of protection and safety standards for all kinds of structures —taking ultimate, direct responsibility for important types of facilities, identifying and evaluating major fault zones and areas of earthquake hazard, and preparing guidelines for land use regulations and construction in these zones.

In recognition of the political realities of land use planning for seismic safety of thirteen local communities in California, Wyner suggested that initiatives to utilize land use planning as an approach to earthquake risk mitigation probably must come from some place other than the local government.[11] Another study points out the incongruity of local jurisdictions finding themselves in the lead in the hazardous structure abatement program. The cost and the technical complexity of a hazardous structure abatement program simply dwarfs the resources of most local jurisdictions. Olson and Nilson suggested a carefully coordinated and large-scale intergovernmental effort involving the federal, state, and local governments as well as important private sector interests.[12]

One way to approach earthquake risk mitigation would be to assess the nature of hazards in terms of the level of government which will cope with the aftermath of a severe event. From this perspective, natural disasters clearly vary from a local, to state, to federal problem.

Implementation of Support Systems

If necessary resources are inadequate, implementation likely will be ineffective. Important resources include finances, adequate staff, and the information, authority, and facilities necessary to translate proposals into functioning public services.

The accuracy, reliability, and availability of scientific geotechnical information has been a major obstacle to implementation. More scientific and technical information is usually needed. However, weaknesses in information also are used as an excuse to throw out policy implementation. Existing technical information is not used adequately. In 1959 a geological study of the Anchorage area warned of the potential for earthquake-triggered landslides in areas where they actually occurred in 1964 with loss of life and property.[13] This unwanted insight led an Anchorage newspaper editorial shortly after the earthquake to state, "Alaskans are learning there are some things worse than the aftershocks that follow an earthquake. Among them are scientists."[14] The claim of imperfect scientific information is often used as an excuse for inaction.

A study of seismic safety policies in thirteen California communities indicated that allocation of monetary resources reflects the priorities of land use objectives.[15] The study found that no community had added new staff specifically to implement land use goals. Virtually all had adopted Seismic Safety Elements (SSE) that recommend gathering more data about geologic conditions in areas that might be susceptible to earthquake damage. Yet with a few exceptions involving construction of public facilities, no jurisdiction had allocated funds for this kind of research. New data relevant to land use planning came only from reports submitted by private developers as part of the permit approval process for new buildings.

Shortage of funds is an obvious problem for public programs. Since hazard mitigation has little institutional presence and no constituency, it has difficulty making claims on resources. This fact increases its vulnerability to funding cuts or underfunding during periods of revenue shortfall. This is particularly true in smaller communities where the cost of hazards studies and other measures may be the same as for large cities. Also, many officials see the results of such studies leading to expensive requirements for funding of politically unpopular risk mitigation measures.

A crucial weakness in local seismic safety policy is enforcement of seismic design regulations. Comparatively low salaries and inadequate inspection and design review staff are important obstacles to good performance. State governments should do what they can to make available specialized personnel who are competent in seismic design problems and familiar with sophisticated forms of earthquake-resistant construction.[16]

Planning and technical staff hired by federal, state, and local agencies rarely are trained to deal with seismic risk as part of the assessment process. Many consider mapping, storing, and displaying physical data to be the end product rather than the process leading to assessment and implementation of mitigation measures. When communities seek outside assistance for studies and maps or turn to state and federal data bases for information they often lack the necessary expertise to translate it into planning recommendations and administrative regulations and policies. The result is an increasing stack of studies, model codes, and research. Inadequacies in technical and policy staff and simple lack of political will combine to frustrate implementation.

Seismic data have rarely been included as part of the baseline used in preparing comprehensive or special development project plans. In fact, the research agenda for continued studies of earthquake issues in urban and regional planning, developed by the American Planning Association and submitted to the National Science Foundation, reflects the need for development of natural hazard education curricula for planners. Along with this they suggest training on how to use seismic data, how to reinforce and develop knowledgeable constituencies, and how to evaluate "societal impacts of living with natural hazards and how social systems adjust to such impacts."[17] Moreover, when planners are knowledgeable, statutes do not provide a meaningful and effective way for seismic experts to be involved in the process of approving development construction in areas of geophysical risk. Even when recognition of experts is institutionalized, the role is generally advisory rather than regulatory.

FEMA found that adequate staffing and resources at all levels of government determine the efficiency of an agency's programs and initiatives. In many agencies earthquake preparedness has been accorded low priority. Only recently did FEMA recommend that additional resources be provided to accelerate earthquake hazard mitigation and preparedness activities under the National Earthquake Hazards Reduction Program.[18]

Leadership

Where the implementors' attitudes or perspectives differ from the decisionmakers', the policy implementation process becomes more complicated. Because implementors generally have discretion, their attitudes toward policies may be obstacles to effective policy implementation. Communications from superiors are often unclear or inconsistent, and most implementors enjoy substantial independence. Some policies fall within the "zone of indifference" of administrators; others elicit strong feelings. These policies may conflict with implementors' substantive policy views or their personal or organizational interests. Here is where dispositions pose obstacles to implementation. The attitudes of staff and elected officials toward seismic safety's role in land use planning have an important bearing on how it and other seismic safety policies will be implemented. Engineers may see any seismic-related problem posed by a development proposal as technically solvable, thus limiting mitigation options. At the same time planning department personnel may not see land use-related seismic safety matters as very important to them.

Given the virtual absence of resources allocated to implementing land use recommendations in related seismic risk, personal dispositions of key individuals take on added importance. Without money or official incentives, only the strong personal commitment of individual leaders will make seismic safety an important factor in land use planning. With very few exceptions such attitudes have been absent, and seismic safety has become just another item on a long list of factors involved in land development.

These findings are consistent with other studies. Planners operate in the political world. Seismic safety is not a popular political issue, and most local elected officials do not want to hear about it. It is much easier for a politician to deal with the problem of a street that is too narrow to accommodate traffic or an undersized culvert than it is to define an acceptable level of natural hazard risk.[19]

A comparative study in long-term recovery from natural disasters found that perceptual or attitudinal characteristics affect a locality's inclination to mitigate hazards.[20] What mitigation involves, particularly the specific techniques and processes, is not clear to all decision-makers. A local official may fully support the concept and process of recovery but be unable to push for mitigation measures because of perceived cost-benefit ratios for different mitigation options. The study found that the availability of experienced professional leadership at the local level, such as a city manager, county executive, mayor, or other elected official, made a very positive contribution to recovery. The effective use of local governmental power was, in fact, more important than the form of local government. In the final analysis, however, when economic and development pressures outweigh the perceived benefits of mitigation, the former win over the latter.[21]

The lack of statutory support for geotechnical hazard mitigation measures reduces the probability that leaders in government and the bureaucracy will take hazards into account. Beyond these limitations, agency heads and local government leaders often lack the managerial and political skills to do what can be done within existing law. Medium-sized cities in Alaska and other locations have high turnover rates in city managers and other professional staff, making it unlikely that such officials will obtain the necessary knowledge and political support needed to promote risk mitigation measures. More important, however, is that leaders lack commitment to geophysical risk mitigation. It takes an exceptional leader who, in the face of the other obstacles and the pressure of daily responsibilities, can develop and sustain a personal commitment to protect his community against geophysical hazards. Studies suggest that effective leadership at all governmental levels in developing, adopting, and implementing the earthquake hazard mitigation measures is the single most important factor.[22]

Political Environment

Planners, engineers, building officials, and others asked to explain failures of geophysical risk mitigation efforts in Alaska have often responded with one word: "Politics." When the Anchorage Municipal Assembly allowed reconstruction to resume in the Turnagain slide area, a building official said that construction was allowed for "political reasons rather than construction safety reasons." Another official said with respect to the same area, "We get a lot of calls by people to report violations, but money in this town and the attorneys they buy overpower our concerned guy."

Specifying just what "earthquake politics" is and how it affects risk mitigation is difficult. Elected officials blame deficiencies on technical information and the absence of direction and assistance from staff and other levels of government. Staff point to these explanations as excuses to mask "political" resistance to mitigation measures, but also fail to pursue the "rational" policy options for reasons that have to be judged as expedient rather than logical.

The political environment in which earthquake hazard mitigation implementation takes place has an important bearing on the likelihood of success. Three aspects of the political environment of seismic safety policy seem particularly relevant in a discussion of land use, building structure, site planning, and critical facilities—interest group support, mass public support, and the political benefits or incentives for office holders.

Earthquake hazard mitigation is not an issue that has stimulated the creation of new interest groups, nor for the most part has it attracted the support of already established local interest groups. Local interest groups do not initiate requests for new and stricter land use policies. While no group represents earthquake hazard mitigation, realtors, property owners, bankers, environmentalists, land developers, neighborhood community councils, and other organizations are all heavily represented on legislative, planning, zoning, and platting bodies as well as providing public feedback to these same groups.

Private development interests argue for reduction in seismic safety standards in already adopted policies, or homeowner groups argue that seismic safety should be one of many reasons used to reject or modify a development proposal. Usually earthquake risk reduction does not carry the day. Wyner's study concluded that seismic safety was in no case the primary or sole justification for political behavior.[23]

If a planning and zoning board allows construction in a high-hazard zone, who complains? However, if the same body attempts to enforce mitigation against local interests there is a strong and immediate response. To political scientists who consider pluralism the dominant philosophy of American government, earthquake hazard mitigation represents part of the "general interest" which gets submerged in the face of the power of specialized interests.[24]

The interest group process is also strongly supported by elements of the political culture, particularly the emphasis on individual and property rights. Earthquake hazard mitigation is an approach that focuses on the protection and the needs of the community. In the inevitable weighing of the relative strengths of claims by community groups, risk mitigation is too diffuse and lacks the critical support of a financially active or otherwise motivated constituency. Thus mitigation efforts are weakened by an inability to "countervail" in the political process. Public recognition of these risks is transitory, tied strongly to the ongoing occurrence of seismic events.

Though mass public support for seismic safety policy and its implementation remains latent and has not been translated into overt political behavior, research suggests that the public believes that local government should actively pursue seismic safety goals.[25] Those attitudes, however, have not been sufficient to generate any significant political response,[26] but reactivation of this latent support has begun to surface—even in "the absence of earthquake-oriented political constituencies."[27]

Most local officials do not perceive earthquake hazard mitigation and implementation of land use policy as providing any political benefits to them. They tend to believe that the public does not know much about seismic safety, ranks it very low on any priority list of community problems, and does not engage in any sustained activity to organize support for mitigation policy in "the absence of earthquake-oriented political constituency." Political incentives in the form of punishments or rewards are almost entirely lacking, at least as perceived by those who must adopt and implement seismic hazards mitigation policy at the local level.

Power can cause things to happen or prevent things from happening.[28] Where mitigation measures do come up, the decisionmaking process presents access points for veto groups to "replay the match" endlessly until a solution emerges which reflects the realities of local political power. The result of earthquake politics is that geophysical hazard mitigation has not so much been defeated as denied an opportunity for a fair open hearing in the decision process.

A considerable absence of "inside" advocates has also been found in recent studies of seismic hazards mitigation.[29] Public problems, political issues, and policy proposals tend to be "owned" by specific legislators, committees, or institutional entities. Like stray dogs, "unowned" problems, issues, and policy proposals swiftly become undernourished and have a way of disappearing into the night. The sustained interests of a few policymakers can make a difference. When problems are "institutionalized" the interests and energies of individual policy influentials are linked to the fate of such problems and issues, and the probability that these matters will be heard and acted upon by the policy system is considerably increased.

Public Education and Communication

Before a population can respond effectively to the threat of an earthquake it needs information. People must know the nature of the threat and what can be done to minimize it. Information and its dissemination through the communications process play a key role in reducing the impact of earthquakes and other hazards.

There is an expanding body of knowledge based on the geological, engineering, and socioeconomic aspects of natural hazards, but a gap always exists between what is being learned through research and what is being applied. The challenge is to improve and increase the use and application of existing knowledge on earthquakes, despite its inadequacy and incompleteness.

Scientists and planners need to build communication skills to inform the public and the policymakers of their findings. Uncertainty makes communications between the technical expert, the planner, and the layman citizen or public official difficult. A U.S. Geological Survey geologist brought to Alaska after the 1964 earthquake noted that the value systems of scientists, which include careful emphasis on areas of doubt, possible weaknesses in the data, and at times excessive modesty, can convey ambiguity and uncertainty to the layman even when general conclusions are clear.[30] Considerations of seismic risk in land use planning, building structures, site planning, critical facilities, and other areas will gain greater prominence only if scientists and researchers promote understanding of their work, learn how to communicate and evaluate their needs and the needs of planners and policymakers, and design their products and recommendations to be of greatest use. This broadening of scientific responsibility would enhance public understanding and support of research needed to assist policymakers in setting guidelines for public safety.

While the public currently appears to lack knowledge about earthquake safety measures, several studies[31] have concluded that while the public recognizes the dangers posed by earthquakes and believes that specific actions can and should be taken to lessen these dangers, it is not organized and mobilized to provide concrete and politically relevant support for policy innovations. The public wants to know more about both the earthquake threat and the current status of preparedness, and such receptivity obviously provides opportunities for policy-makers to "cultivate" public opinion. If the media are willing to cooperate on a sustained basis, the impacts of a public education campaign can be significant. Communication plays a key role in disseminating the knowledge and information on earthquake hazards and mitigation measures between researchers (producers), policymakers (users), and planners (users).[32] Since researchers and users tend to have divergent motivations, it may be necessary to use intermediaries to interpret research results and to create products that clearly will be helpful to the users.

Such mechanisms as disclosure provisions on land transfers, enhancing technical proficiencies of practitioners, education programs aimed at such key groups as builders and developers, and long-term consistent coverage by the media would ameliorate obstacles to public education and information. Education is needed at the elementary school level through higher education.[33]

Design for Disaster Mitigation Plan and Recommendation for Action

The implementation of risk mitigation systems depends on the effectiveness of the administration charged with its management. Mitigating life and property losses which may result from some future natural disaster has historically been a difficult task largely eluding public policymakers. Many public and private officials interviewed were pessimistic about the prospects of improved risk mitigation efforts. The reasons cited include fragmentation of policy responsibility; lack of public and interest group support for political action; inadequate commitment of financial and human resources relative to the magnitude of the problem; ingrained sociocultural beliefs about property and personal rights; government subsidy of risk-taking; uncertainty about the level of risk and potential for economic loss from any one disaster scenario; general weaknesses in the implementation process; and the power of local economic elites to prevent measures perceived to be counter to their financial interests.

These obstacles require an approach that recognizes the existing inherent systemic impediments. Altering a system that rewards failure to act would mean a number of changes in how risk is dealt with in the policymaking process. Depoliticizing disaster recovery and making federal assistance correspond to need and efforts in mitigation would begin the process of political accountability and development of local and state leadership willing to address the issues of natural hazards risk.

Designing a comprehensive disaster mitigation plan can provide a framework in which hazards risks are evaluated just as economics and other factors are. There is less need to alter the level of responsibility or create revolutionary changes in processes than to implement the systematic inclusion of hazards risk into the ongoing decisionmaking processes. Just as policymakers are held accountable for the economic and more recently the social consequences of their decisions, so must this accountability extend to physical risk.

In risk management, design serves as a means of defining carefully the desired set of government actions under emergency conditions and identifying the resources, personnel, and practices necessary to accomplish a stated goal.[34] Effective risk mitigation planning must take place before disaster strikes. Only then can community participation and education of policymakers be effective. This will ensure that both groups understand the multitude of topics involved in the planning process and the responsibilities that each has in promoting public safety. To date, in the field of seismic risk, mitigation is reflected in the application of building codes to avoidance of structural failure of individual buildings or to development of land use restriction for areas of proven instability. Less attention is given to the disruption that may result from failure of the whole urban infrastructure. Because the city or region functions as an integrated network, the failure of one element can affect the function of the entire system. Moreover, when disruption occurs in the major components of a city or regional infrastructure—transportation, communication, utilities, land use, or social services—the whole economy is affected. Weakening of the economic base in turn affects recovery.

Damage to a community's infrastructure also affects the economic infrastructure of the region and state. Evaluating the social and economic impact of a future seismic event would help identify potential infrastructure disruption and allow for preparation of long-range plans that would consider the effects of seismic risk. An analysis of transportation, utilities, communication, production centers, and other systems could guide the application of hazard mitigation regulations in

Figure 1. Risk Mitigation and Implementation Process

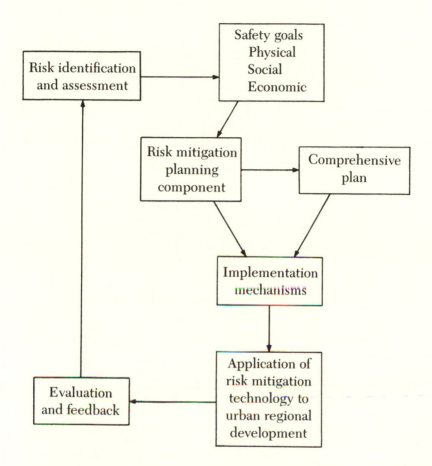

Source: Lidia L. Selkregg et al., *Earthquake Hazard Mitigation: Planning and Policy Implementation—The Alaska Case*, National Science Foundation Grant CEE8112632, 1984.

plans for future economies and public needs.

A region or city exists as a function of its socioeconomic base and environmental assets and limitations. The relationships of people and their environments change after a major disaster. New relationships may be necessary. Preplanning for postdisaster reconstruction is needed to ensure that an effective and rapid recovery occurs within the frame-

Figure 2. Comprehensive Planning Model

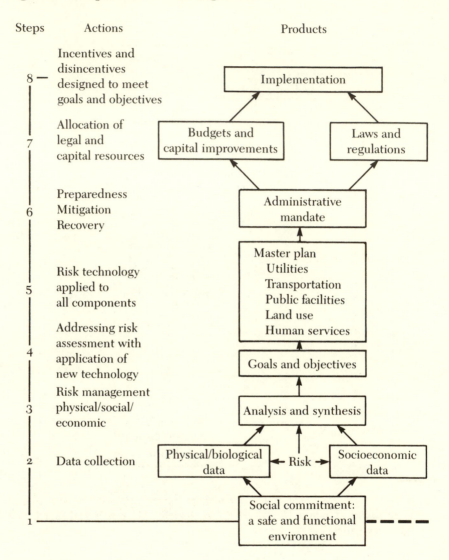

Source: Lidia L. Selkregg et al., *Earthquake Hazard Mitigation: Planning and Policy Implementation—The Alaska Case*, National Science Foundation Grant CEE8112632, 1984.

Actors

Public sector
Private sector

Legislators
Administrators
Public

Legislators
Administrators
Planners
Public

Inter-, intragovernment
participation and coordination
Engineers, planners,
sociologists, economists,
architects, etc.

Public
Legislators
Planners and policymakers
Planners
Policy analysts
Scientists

Scientists

Feedback—update data base and
process based on change,
new technology, and experience

work of the reestablishment of strong socioeconomic systems.

A comprehensive regional or city development plan tying together more specific plans that focus on various planning components is needed to assess the impact of seismic risk (see figure 1). Risk evaluation and safety goals currently remain isolated in "special studies" rather than being incorporated into comprehensive planning and implementation processes. After a risk analysis is made the manmade environment should reflect awareness and application of risk mitigation components and should include an economic evaluation of costs and benefits and a comparison of alternatives when changes in established patterns are recommended. Moreover, implementation of mitigation strategies for development in high-risk areas has been uneven. While progress has been made in such fields as engineering and geology, effective administrative implementation has been lacking. Although development is taking place on steep slopes, wetlands, and on manmade fills, comprehensive development plans or zoning of new development districts do not include geotechnical evaluation and seismic risk mitigation measures.

Identification is insufficient without application of knowledge obtained through scientific studies. Present methodologies do not seem to ensure the successful application of technology directed to disaster prevention and mitigation, and have resulted in sporadic and inconsistent application of technology directed to risk mitigation. As shown in figure 2, designing successful planning and administrative processes for mitigation must include (1) development of comprehensive goals and objectives based on the understanding of the physical, social, and economic makeup of the regional or urban system; and (2) development of a master plan for implementation through team building that relates all components to the urban or regional structure; that is, where people work, where they live, where they play, how they move throughout the areas, and how and where they are cared for. The result is a combination of traditional planning focusing on civic design and municipal order with emphasis on a product, and the newer outlook emphasizing development of general goal statements, implementation plans, and recognition of interactions and feedback throughout the process.

Knowledge of risks should apply to all components, and implementation of goals and objectives should be adjusted in response to increased technical knowledge and to changes in the socioeconomic makeup of the area. To accomplish this, coordination and cooperation is indispensable. The current goal-setting process without a defined implementation mechanism does not provide the guidelines needed to express the true intent of the goals.

Agenda-setting in Nonstructural Hazard Mitigation Policy
⚡ Elliott Mittler

Natural disasters strike communities in a probabilistic fashion, that is, randomly, at a rate of occurrence based on historical record, and generally without warning. People in a community may know they are at risk, but local decisionmakers must weigh the expected negative consequences associated with disasters against the cost of mitigating and/or responding to disasters, especially given the uncertainty of accurate prediction and the knowledge that major disasters rarely occur in a prespecified location. The consequences of inaction may be devastating; on the other hand, considerable effort and expense may be expended in mitigation activities that are later perceived as unnecessary when the anticipated event fails to materialize.

The natural disaster mitigation issue has been placed on the agenda of many local and state governments, and case studies have been written to describe how some communities have dealt with this issue.[1] These case studies indicate that communities facing similar hazard risks have chosen to confront potential disasters with a wide range of responses, from doing nothing to enacting legislation. Observing and documenting these mixed results, researchers have not yet concluded what are the necessary and sufficient conditions needed to enact legislation.

In order for legislation to be enacted an issue must first get on a decision agenda. Qualitatively, it should also be amenable to political solutions, so that a high probability exists that feasible legislation can be formulated and then enacted. It is the intent of this chapter to describe the public policy agenda-setting process and, using Kingdon's model, explain why some Gulf and Atlantic Coast states enacted nonstructural mitigation laws for hurricanes and resultant floods following Hurricanes Agnes and Eloise in the 1970s while others with similar risks levels did not.[2]

Compared with other aspects of the policy process, little is known about the dynamics of agenda-setting.[3] However, there are points on which those that study agenda-setting appear to agree. Most basic is the notion that "social problems," that is, objective conditions that have negative impacts on society or some significant segment of the population, are not automatically considered to be political issues.[4] Rather, such risks appear to be selected in reference more to cultural goals than to rational analysis.[5] Another important idea is that crises or disasters do not inevitably result in ameliorative actions by policymakers; it is also necessary that some individual or group be on the scene that can translate the crisis into a policy issue.[6] A third notion prominent in the literature is that agenda-setting is a nonlinear, nonadditive product of several elements: social networks (such as elected officials, members of the bureaucracy, legislative staffs, members of the scientific community); activists or entrepreneurs; resources; and opportunities. A fourth concept presents agenda-setting as part of a set of political choices, representing a strategic balance of environmental demands and constraints—fiscal limits, institutional constellations of procedures and power, the capacity of relevant governmental agencies to act upon alternative policies.[7] Much of the recent work on the topic of agenda-setting under conditions of uncertainty emphasizes the complex interactive nature of the process and the emergent nature of the decisions that are made.[8]

The public policy agenda-setting process described by Kingdon is an example of this kind of approach that seems particularly appropriate for analyzing how community political leaders respond to natural disasters. First, as Brodkin notes, Kingdon is concerned specifically with the "institutional" agenda that government officials are actively considering and not with the wide range of issues and policy alternatives that exist throughout society.[9] This concern is consistent with the focus of this analysis on legislative activity in a single problem area. Second, his approach seems particularly well-suited to hazard mitigation policy, which, unlike many other items on the decision agenda, tends to follow what Cobb, Ross, and Ross term the "inside initiative" model of agenda-setting.[10] Inside initiative is said to occur when individuals and groups within government take the lead in policy development without the extensive involvement of, or much knowledge on the part of, the public. Third, although developed to analyze agenda-setting at the federal level, Kingdon's model has demonstrated applicability at the state level.[11]

In this chapter four topics will be discussed to describe what ten states have done in response to hurricane and concomitant flood threats in order to determine if a similar pattern of action was followed by those states that enacted nonstructural mitigation laws. These topics include (1) a brief summary of Kingdon's public policy schema; (2) a description of the risk the ten states face from hurricanes and the damage caused them by Agnes and Eloise; (3) a history of major laws passed in the ten states to mitigate the hurricane and flood disasters; and (4) attitudes held by key influentials in the ten states concerning hurricanes and nonstructural mitigation legislation. For the purposes of this chapter nonstructural mitigation will refer to land use controls, zoning, building codes, and broader laws that encompass these elements.

Public Policymaking

Before public policies with a high probability of being enacted can be considered by a legislature, Kingdon claims that three independent developments must already have occurred. A first condition is that policymakers, generally specialists in the bureaucracy and the professional communities, must have developed politically expedient alternatives that meet the following criteria: (1) they are technically feasible; (2) they are politically acceptable, that is, they are consistent with notions of what is proper for this government body to enact, as well as being equitable and efficient; and (3) they must have anticipated opposition and constraints such as budget, public reaction, and other proposals and have the potential for being altered to gain a wider acceptance and ultimately the approval of elected officials. In other words, having a viable alternative ready for adoption increases the probability that it will be placed on a decision agenda.[12]

As a second condition it must be generally recognized that a problem exists. According to Kingdon this normally happens in a discontinuous fashion. What is on today's decision agenda may not have been on yesterday and may not be an indicator of what will be on tomorrow. A problem may suddenly appear and vanish just as quickly or, once upon the scene, persist for years.

A third condition is that politicians must decide that the problem is worthy of their consideration in order to place the problem on the decision agenda. "If any one set of participants in the policy process is important in the shaping of the agenda," Kingdon emphasizes, "it is the elected officials and their appointees, rather than career bureaucrats or nongovernmental actors."[13]

If the outcomes of these three processes come together at the same time and "couple," then legislation is possible. This outcome is most likely when a policy window—or opportunity to get on the decision agenda—opens. In the field of natural disasters a policy window may open at the state government level when a major disaster strikes, causing significant damage and/or loss of life, or when a federal law is passed that encourages states to act. If Kingdon is correct, when disaster strikes or when enabling legislation passes, the state-level proponents of mitigation laws must have a politically feasible alternative ready for legislative debate which already has wide professional support. Policy entrepreneurs[14]—people who push for their ideas but are willing to negotiate and compromise to get their alternative accepted —must also be in place to influence legislative action.

To test Kingdon's model it is necessary to show that policy windows have opened following the occurrence of disasters that led to the passage of legislation to mitigate future ones. In the next section hurricanes and their effects on state legislatures will be explored.

Hurricanes and States

Within the United States hurricanes are a threat to the Gulf states from Texas to Florida and the Atlantic states from Florida to Maine. A sample of these states was selected by Rossi et al. to be included in their national study of the politics of hazard mitigation.[15] Key politically influential people in the public and private sectors were interviewed in the summer of 1977 to determine their attitudes toward natural hazard mitigation. A further analysis of their data was conducted by this author to determine which of these key figures supported, were neutral to, and opposed natural hazards legislation.[16]

Ten hurricane-prone states included in those analyses were selected to investigate the policymaking process. Six states, Connecticut, Florida, New Jersey, New York, Pennsylvania, and Virginia, were selected because they had suffered damage from Hurricanes Agnes (1972) and Eloise (1975), which created what would appear to be policy windows subsequent to those years (see table 1).

The other four states, Louisiana, New Hampshire, North Carolina, and South Carolina, were selected as control states because they were not affected by either hurricane but still face moderate to high objective risks associated with hurricane winds, storm surges, and floods. There are no clear research results linking objective risk and legislative action. Besides applying Kingdon's propositions, the selection of these four states permits an exploration of the influence of objective risk on legislation.[17]

State Legislation

Between 1972 and 1979 six states passed major modifications of existing laws or enacted new legislation that dealt with hurricane and flood mitigation (see table 2). Of that group, five states—Florida, New Jersey, New York, Pennsylvania, and Virginia—were among those that had experienced damage from Agnes and Eloise. Connecticut was the only state that did not alter its laws after being struck by the hurricanes. Of the four control states that were not affected by the hurricanes, only one, North Carolina, passed important legislation with hurricane and flood mitigation elements.

At first glance it does seem that a policy window was created by the hurricane events and that feasible plans were available to be enacted by states affected by Agnes and Eloise. It also seems that objective risk alone is not a good predictor of passed legislation because the objective risks noted in table 1 are approximately the same for the six states that passed legislation and the four that did not. However, recall that a

Table 1. Objective Risk and Hurricane Flood Damage

	Objective risk			Hurricane flood damage	
State	Hurricane wind	Storm surge	Flood	Agnes (1972)	Eloise (1975)
Connecticut	High	Medium	Low	Low	Low
Florida	High	High	Medium	Medium	Medium
Louisiana	High	High	Medium	—	—
New Hampshire	High	—	Medium	—	—
New Jersey	High	Medium	Low	Medium	Medium
New York	High	Medium	Low	High	Medium
North Carolina	High	Medium	Medium	—	—
Pennsylvania	Low	—	Low	High	High
South Carolina	High	High	Medium	—	—
Virginia	High	Medium	Medium	High	Low

Key: Objective risks for hurricane wind, storm surge, and flood are derived from Petak and Atkisson, *Natural Hazard Risk Assessment and Public Policy*, table 5-14, pp. 212–14, where "high" refers to states with expected hazard-induced building damage over 1.5 times the national average; "medium" refers to states with 0.75 to 1.5 times the national average; "low" refers to states with less than 0.75 times the national average; "—" refers to states with no objective risk. Hurricane flood damage from Agnes and Eloise is derived from Petak and Atkisson, table 3-2, p. 69, where "high" refers to damage over $40 million; "medium" refers to damage between $10 million and $40 million; "low" refers to damage under $10 million; "—" refers to no damage.

policy window can also be opened if *federal* legislation is passed that enables states to enact suggested or mandatory laws of their own. During the late 1960s and 1970s two federal laws, the National Flood Insurance Act of 1968 and the Coastal Zone Management Act of 1972, and subsequent amendments were enacted that prompted several of the states to pass some of the laws listed in table 2.

The National Flood Insurance Act created the National Flood Insurance Program (NFIP) as a voluntary program in which flood-prone local communities could subscribe to purchase flood insurance.[18] After Hurricane Agnes Congress moved to make the NFIP mandatory through the passage of the Flood Disaster Protection Act of 1973, making this the first mandatory federal land use control act. Following its passage some states enacted legislation of their own to help local governments meet the NFIP requirements, draw up required floodplain maps, and

Table 2. Major State Laws and Amendments with
Hurricane and Flood Mitigation Elements
Enacted from 1972 to 1979

State	Laws and Amendments
Connecticut	None
Florida	Revision, Beach and Shore Preservation Act, Part 1. Regulation of Construction, Reconstruction, and Other Physical Activity, 1978
Louisiana	None
New Hampshire	None
New Jersey	Amendment, State Flood Control Facilities Act, 1972 Emergency Services Act of 1972 Coastal Area Facility Review Act of 1973 Amendment, State Flood Control Facilities Act, 1979
New York	Tidal Wetlands Act, 1973 Participation in Flood Insurance Programs, 1974 Freshwater Wetlands Act of 1975 Flood Control, 1978
North Carolina	Coastal Area Management Act of 1974
Pennsylvania	Flood Plain Management Act of 1978 Storm Water Management Act of 1978
South Carolina	None
Virginia	The New Virginia Wetlands Act of 1972 Flood Damage Reduction Act of 1977 Virginia Farmer Major Drought, Flood and Hurricane Disaster Act, 1978

set up minimum standards that each local government has to meet.

The Coastal Zone Management Act (CZMA) had a similar effect on states. It set up "an incentive-based voluntary participation arrangement aimed at encouraging coastal states to design and manage their own individual coastal programs."[19] CZMA was designed to provide state grants for planning and implementation of state programs. Although it was passed in 1972, funding was not authorized by Congress until 1974. However, some states reacted as early as 1972 and began to formulate coastal management programs.

Each state is to a large degree enmeshed in its own complex legal history and dealings with past natural disasters. States are also impinged upon both by unique disaster experience and by federal statutes. Thus it is not possible to make generalizations about how the ten hurricane-prone states as a bloc performed legislatively in the natural disaster mitigation arena. Instead, what follows is a state-by-state analysis of legislation to clarify what each state did and why.

Connecticut. During the 1950s Connecticut pioneered floodplain zoning and management, passing the Flood Control and Beach Erosion Act in 1955.[20] During the 1960s and 1970s only minor modifications were enacted. Apparently state officials felt those laws were adequate to deal with the aftermath of Agnes and Eloise, which caused relatively "low" damage to the state. By the early 1980s, however, the NFIP state coordinator felt that Connecticut's floodplain management program needed "updating to bring it into line with state-of-the-art methods and philosophies."[21] This was accomplished with the passage of the Flood Management Act in 1984.[22]

Florida. Since 1965 Florida had on its books the Beach and Shore Protection Act, with land use and construction elements to mitigate the hazards of floods and hurricanes.[23] No major revision was enacted until 1978, when part one, "Regulation of Construction, Reconstruction and Other Physical Activity," was strengthened by the inclusion of more rigorous nonstructural mitigation elements. The 1978 revisions specifically mentioned that the new amendments were designed to protect against hurricanes and floods. Coastal zone management was added to the 1965 statute as part three after the passage of the Florida Coastal Zone Protection Act of 1985.[24]

Louisiana. Since the early nineteenth century Louisiana has engaged in flood control through the construction and maintenance of levees. Laws passed as recently as 1985 continue to link flood control to levee construction.[25] Non-structural mitigation laws and regulations are not found among Louisiana statutes. The state authorized its parishes and municipalities in 1971 to comply with NFIP requirements, thereby maintaining the tradition of home rule laws that give local governments the power to enact zoning laws, building codes, and subdivision regulations in flood-prone areas.[26]

New Hampshire. No nonstructural mitigation laws are to be found in the state statutes.

New Jersey. This state seems to be very responsive to disasters, having both a long history of mitigation laws and a record of enacting legislation following major disasters. In 1948 New Jersey passed the State Flood Control Facilities Act,[27] added to that in 1962 with the Flood Hazard Area Control Act,[28] and amended both with major changes in 1972 following Agnes and in 1979. The state regulates the floodplain and mandates local governments to comply with state standards. After hurricane Agnes New Jersey also passed the Emergency Services Act of 1972 to provide a state postdisaster plan.[29]

Nonstructural mitigation laws have been included in New Jersey's coastal management program. The Wetlands Act of 1970,[30] set up in response to the Federal Wetlands Act, gave the state a broad mandate in the field and was followed by the Coastal Area Facility Review Act of 1973,[31] a compatible state program to the federal CZMA.

New York. The Tidal Wetlands Act of 1973[32] and Fresh Water Wetlands Act of 1975[33] are statutes that incorporate nonstructural mitigation elements enforceable by the state to balance environmental concerns with economic, social, and agricultural development and simultaneously provide flood control measures. In 1974 the state added Article 36: Participation in Flood Insurance Programs to the state's Environmental Conservation Law statutes mandating that any federally designated flood-prone community must participate in the NFIP.[34] If local governments failed to do so, the state was authorized to regulate the floodplain directly. New York passed a comprehensive flood control bill in 1978 that allowed state participation in the federal flood control program and extended state control over the floodplain.[35]

North Carolina. State floodplain management was enacted in 1971 with the passage of the Floodway Regulation Act.[36] Following hurricane Agnes in 1972 the Coastal Area Management Act of 1974[37] was passed and since has been widely heralded as one of the premier acts of this nature passed by a state legislature.[38] Nonstructural mitigation elements are key provisions of the act.

Pennsylvania. Although Pennsylvania suffered major damage from both Agnes in 1972 and Eloise in 1975, the state was unable to pass statewide flood control and storm water runoff management laws until 1978. Prior to this time Pennsylvania had been a strong home rule state in which local governments had jurisdiction over flood control. In 1936 the state passed the Prevention and Control of Floods statute giving municipalities the power to construct flood control works.[39] The only state control over floods was specifically granted by the Water Obstruction Act in 1913 which allowed the state to control obstruction (such as dams, piers, and bridges) of flood flows in order to protect the public's right to navigation.[40]

In 1978 Pennsylvania passed the Flood Plain Management Act[41] and the Storm Water Management Act,[42] both of which required participation at the municipal level with assistance and enforcement from the state. The Flood Plain Management Act required municipal participation in the NFIP while the Storm Water Management Act required a municipal watershed plan to protect local communities from floods and stormwater runoff. Combined, these two laws were considered comprehensive, so the Water Obstruction Act was repealed in 1979.

South Carolina. South Carolina has passed no laws that specifically address the use of nonstructural mitigations to deal with flood and hurricane control. The state did pass the South Carolina Coastal Zone Act in 1977; however, that law is basically an environmental statute to protect tidelands and wetlands and does not mention either floods or hurricanes.[43]

Virginia. In 1966 Virginia enacted the Open-Space Land Act to limit the spread of urban growth and to protect the natural environment.[44] That act was strengthened by the passage of the New Virginia Wetlands Act of 1972.[45]

Because the responsibility and authority for zoning rests with local governing bodies, the Flood Damage Reduction Act of 1977 gave local governments the responsibility for floodplain management in compliance with the NFIP, with the state administering a floodplain management plan and providing assistance to the local communities to meet federal standards.[46] Although not part of flood control legislation, a 1978 agricultural law—the Virginia Farmer Major Drought, Flood, and Hurricane Disaster Act—provides farmers with financial assistance in those areas devastated by a major disaster and proclaimed by the governor to be state disaster areas.[47]

Inferences

Of the six states affected by Hurricanes Agnes and Eloise, it appears that policy windows were created in five states that allowed for the passage of nonstructural mitigation laws to protect against future hurricanes and floods. The Connecticut legislature, which did not enact new legislation, seems to have believed that current state laws were adequate, so no problem was perceived to exist in the state to warrant new laws. In terms of Kingdon's schema, condition two—recognition that there is a problem—was not met in the case of Connecticut.

North Carolina, the one state that enacted laws but was unaffected by either Agnes or Eloise, passed its legislation in response to a federal law, the CZMA.

The coincidental passage of laws following the presumed creation of policy windows seems on the surface to support the contentions of Kingdon. However, states such as Pennsylvania and Florida waited until 1978 to enact new laws even though Hurricanes Agnes and Eloise occurred in 1972 and 1975. Kingdon's model suggests a probable explanation for this weak linkage. To increase the probability of successfully getting laws enacted, it is not sufficient to have an "open" policy window; there also must be a viable alternative solution available that can be supported by the bureaucratic structure and policy entrepreneurs.

In Pennsylvania, for example, the state was presumably unprepared for a disaster the size of Agnes, and at that time had no active group promoting statewide nonstructural mitigation policies. With a historically low objective risk and municipalities empowered to deal with flood control, it is reasonable to assume hurricane and flood mitigation was not part of the state's decision agenda in 1972. It is also reasonable to argue that it would take five or six years for a support group to form and then develop a policy alternative that could be endorsed by the state legislature.[48] The occurrence of Eloise in 1975 could have kept the policy window open and encouraged the support group because it gave evidence that Agnes was not a fluke. If this is a reasonable explanation, then one would expect to find strong support in 1977 for nonstructural mitigation among the state agency heads who deal with disasters and also among legislators who would presumably have placed this issue on their decision agenda.

Like Pennsylvania four other states, Florida, New Jersey, New York, and Virginia, enacted major nonstructural mitigation statutes during or shortly after 1977. Thus, if all three of Kingdon's conditions are necessary and sufficient, one would expect to find strong support for such policies among elected and appointed state officials in these five states in 1977 and not among officials in the five states that did not enact legislation during those times. In the next section the attitudes of key political figures of the ten states surveyed in the summer of 1977 will be discussed to test this hypothesis.

Attitudes of Key Political Figures

Background

The original Rossi et al. study interviewed key persons from twenty states in order to determine their attitudes toward natural disaster public policies. From each state a sample population was drawn from twenty-five possible positions including the governor and eight elected legislators, heads of five state agencies dealing with natural hazards, three federal agency officials in the state, and eight private partisans likely to be involved in natural hazards issues. In all, 461 usable interviews were secured. Of those, 21 were from Connecticut, 26 from Florida, 20 from Louisiana, 21 from New Hampshire, 23 from New Jersey, 23 from New York, 25 from North Carolina, 24 from Pennsylvania, 24 from South Carolina, and 24 from Virginia.

The study results presented by Rossi and his colleagues indicated the majority of the respondents did not favor or actually opposed nonstructural mitigation policies.[49] These researchers used mainly descriptive statistics, which revealed the generally negative orientation of the entire sample and specific subsets such as individual states and job categories. Rossi and his colleagues did find a small but significant minority of respondents who were in favor of legislation. However, they did not perform separate analyses on this group to determine their characteristics or hypothesize about the reasons for their positive attitudes.

In order to identify the specific attitudes and attributes of those who supported, were neutral toward, and opposed nonstructural mitigation policies, a block-clustering algorithm developed by Hartigan was employed.[50] Block-clustering was performed on the entire sample of respondents and 132 variables, yielding twenty-nine clusters from the variable-respondent matrix. An iterative algorithm is used to cluster both respondents and variables simultaneously to reveal the identity of each cluster member and their shared set of attitudes and attributes. From the twenty-nine clusters it was then possible to aggregate the respondents according to their attitudes and determine the amount of support for nonstructural mitigation policies within each state.

Results

The attitudes held by key respondents in the five states that enacted major nonstructural mitigation statutes during or shortly after 1977

Table 3. Attitudes Held by Key State Figures
concerning Hurricanes

State	Key figures	Estimated probability of a serious hurricane occurring in the next 10 years
Connecticut	Elected officials	Low
	State agency heads	Very high
	Federal officials	High
Florida	Elected officials	High
	State agency heads	High
	Federal officials	Very high
Louisiana	Elected officials	Very high
	State agency heads	Very high
	Federal officials	Very high
New Hampshire	Elected officials	Low
	State agency heads	Medium
	Federal officials	Low
New Jersey	Elected officials	Very high
	State agency heads	Very high
	Federal officials	Very high
New York	Elected officials	Very high
	State agency heads	Very high
	Federal officials	Very high
North Carolina	Elected officials	High
	State agency heads	High
	Federal officials	High
Pennsylvania	Elected officials	Very high
	State agency heads	Very high
	Federal officials	Very high
South Carolina	Elected officials	Low
	State agency heads	Low
	Federal officials	Low

Respondents have personally experienced a hurricane	State has experienced a serious hurricane in the last 10 years	State public policy has changed due to a natural disaster in the last 10 years
Yes	Disagree	Disagree
Yes	Agree	Agree
Yes	Agree	Agree
Yes	Agree	Disagree
Yes	Agree	Agree
Yes	Agree	Agree
Yes	Agree	Agree
Yes	Agree	Agree
No	Agree	Agree
No	Disagree	Disagree
Yes	Disagree	Disagree
No	Disagree	Disagree
Yes	Disagree	Disagree
Yes	Agree	Agree
Yes	Agree	Agree
Yes	Agree	Agree
Yes	Agree	Agree
No	Agree	Agree
No	Disagree	Disagree
Yes	Agree	Disagree
No	Disagree	Disagree
Yes	Agree	Agree
Yes	Agree	Agree
Yes	Agree	Agree
No	Disagree	Disagree
No	Disagree	Disagree
Yes	Agree	Agree

Table 3. (continued)

State	Key figures	Estimated probability of a serious hurricane occurring in the next 10 years
Virginia	Elected officials	High
	State agency heads	High
	Federal officials	High

Key: Hurricane probabilities are the approximate averages of the three categories of officials, where: "Very High" = 90–100 percent; "High" = 60–89 percent; "Medium" = 50–59 percent; "Low" = 1–49 percent.

(Florida, New Jersey, New York, Pennsylvania, and Virginia) are remarkably similar (see tables 3 and 4). A majority of elected officials, state agency heads, and federal officials believe that their states have experienced a serious hurricane in the past ten years and that the chances of experiencing a serious hurricane in the next ten years are "high" or "very high." Although they were not asked directly by Rossi and his colleagues one could conclude that these officials believe that their subjective or perceived risk from hurricanes is high. The data indicate these same officials have personally experienced a hurricane and believe that public policy has changed as a result of a natural disaster in the past ten years.

Most important, officials in these five states generally favor state legislation regulating land use or tightening up building codes to lower the risk from natural disasters. Except for elected officials in Florida and Virginia, they also support similar legislation at the federal level. A majority of elected officials in Florida, New Jersey, and New York have identified themselves as being important in the legislative process to enact laws pertaining to natural disasters.

Based on the evidence shown in tables 3 and 4, it appears that the key elected officials and pertinent bureaucratic personnel in the five states that passed nonstructural mitigation statutes have the supportive attitudes that Kingdon postulated. They view their situations as being high-ris (identify hurricanes as a problem) and broadly support the use of nonstructural mitigation to reduce the risk (share a feasible alternative solution). Several elected officials also have identified themselves as important in the legislative process—presumably as policy entrepreneurs.

Respondents have personally experienced a hurricane	State has experienced a serious hurricane in the last 10 years	State public policy has changed due to a natural disaster in the last 10 years
Yes	Agree	Agree
Yes	Agree	Agree
Yes	Agree	Disagree

A group of officials is considered to hold an attitude if at least a majority of that group are in clusters that contain the attitude.

Among the other five states, there are some contradictory attitudes that indicate that one or more of Kingdon's conditions have not been met. Specifically, in Connecticut a majority of the elected officials perceive the threat from hurricanes as low and believe that the state has not experienced a serious hurricane in the past ten years, implying that both Agnes and Eloise were not serious. These elected officials also did not support either state or federal nonstructural mitigation and did not consider themselves to be important in the legislative process concerning natural disasters. Therefore two of Kingdon's conditions apparently were not met. First, hurricanes were not identified as a problem by elected officials. Second, a nonstructural mitigation alternative supported by bureaucrats was not acceptable to the elected officials.

Because there is bureaucratic support for statewide nonstructural mitigation measures in Connecticut, it appears that a support group exists but has not yet found a way to get elected officials to perceive that a problem exists or to accept their alternative for the decision agenda. One might predict that if a policy window "opened" for elected officials, there would be a chance for new legislation. Since Connecticut did in fact pass a Flood Management Act in 1984, that scenario may have developed.

A majority of all respondents in Louisiana recognize that hurricanes are a very serious problem in the state and that the state has experienced serious hurricanes in the past ten years. However, elected officials do not support the creation of statewide nonstructural mitigation measures to reduce the risk from natural disasters. Most elected officials

Table 4. Attitudes Held by Key State Figures concerning
Nonstructural Mitigation Legislation

State	Key figures	Supports federal nonstructural mitigation legislation
Connecticut	Elected officials	No
	State agency heads	Yes
	Federal officials	No
Florida	Elected officials	No
	State agency heads	Yes
	Federal officials	Yes
Louisiana	Elected officials	No
	State agency heads	Yes
	Federal officials	Yes
New Hampshire	Elected officials	No
	State agency heads	No
	Federal officials	Yes
New Jersey	Elected officials	Yes
	State agency heads	Yes
	Federal officials	Yes
New York	Elected officials	Yes
	State agency heads	Yes
	Federal officials	Yes
North Carolina	Elected officials	No
	State agency heads	Yes
	Federal officials	Yes
Pennsylvania	Elected officials	Yes
	State agency heads	Yes
	Federal officials	Yes
South Carolina	Elected officials	No
	State agency heads	No
	Federal officials	Yes

Supports state nonstructural mitigation legislation	Opposes state-wide non-structural mitigation legislation in flood plains	Considers self important in natural disaster legislation process	Considers self inactive in natural disaster legislation process
No	No	No	No
Yes	No	No	No
Yes	No	No	No
Yes	No	Yes	No
Yes	No	No	No
Yes	No	No	No
No	No	No	Yes
Yes	No	No	No
No	No	No	No
No	No	No	No
No	No	No	No
No	No	No	No
Yes	No	Yes	No
Yes	No	No	No
Yes	No	No	No
Yes	No	Yes	No
Yes	No	No	No
Yes	No	No	No
No	No	No	No
No	No	No	No
No	No	No	No
Yes	No	No	No
Yes	No	No	No
Yes	No	No	No
No	Yes	No	Yes
No	No	No	No
No	No	No	No

Table 4. (continued)

State	Key figures	Supports federal nonstructural mitigation legislation
Virginia	Elected officials	No
	State agency heads	Yes
	Federal officials	Yes

Key: A group of officials is considered to hold an attitude if at least a majority

consider themselves to be not active in state natural disaster legislation or regulation. As indicated in its legal history, Louisiana has traditionally empowered local governments to deal with nonstructural mitigation issues and has combated floods with levees. Thus it appears that Louisiana has not met Kingdon's first condition: nonstructural mitigation alternatives are not politically acceptable at the state level.

It appears obvious, given the data in tables 3 and 4, that among key New Hampshire figures the risk from hurricanes is considered low and that support for nonstructural mitigation laws is virtually nonexistent. At this time there does not appear to be organized support at the bureaucratic levels, so New Hampshire does not meet any of Kingdon's three conditions.

The situation in North Carolina is somewhat more complex than in New Hampshire and less so than in Connecticut. Although, like their New Hampshire counterparts, key political figures do not support state-level nonstructural mitigation laws, they do recognize that the hurricane risk in North Carolina is high. Because North Carolina had developed a strong coastal zone management law in 1974, these attitudes may reflect a perceived hurricane threat. However, unlike Connecticut, elected officials and bureaucrats in North Carolina consider current laws sufficient to mitigate the potential danger. If this is plausible, then key figures perceive neither a problem nor the need for a solution.

South Carolina's key figures resemble New Hampshire respondents in their views of the hurricane threat. No one expects a serious hurricane to strike the state in the next ten years, and aside from federal

Supports state nonstructural mitigation legislation	Opposes state-wide non-structural mitigation legislation in flood plains	Considers self important in natural disaster legislation process	Considers self inactive in natural disaster legislation process
Yes	No	No	Yes
Yes	No	No	No
No	No	No	No

of that group are in clusters that contain the attitude.

officials there is no support for nonstructural mitigation laws. Unlike all other states, elected officials in South Carolina expressed their opposition to statewide land-use laws and building codes that would restrict the usage of land or strengthen buildings in floodplains or earthquake-prone areas. It thus appears that none of Kingdon's conditions have been met in South Carolina.

Conclusions

The combined results from the analysis of attitudes of key influentials and the discussion of state legal histories appear to support Kingdon's public policy propositions. The five states that passed nonstructural mitigation laws from 1977 to 1979 were the only ones in the ten-state sample that met all three of the conditions Kingdon considers necessary to put an issue on the state decision agenda. First, the bureaucratic machine had apparently devised feasible flood and hurricane nonstructural mitigation alternatives that could be endorsed by the elected officials. Second, the elected officials perceived hurricanes and floods as a problem. Third, nonstructural mitigation was determined by the elected officials to be in their action domain.

Conversely, when one or more of Kingdon's conditions were not met, legislation was not enacted. This helps to confirm Kingdon's claims that the three conditions are necessary and sufficient for getting an issue on the decision agenda and that any single condition alone, no matter how strong, will not lead to legislative action.

Examples from Connecticut and Louisiana indicate how and why all three of Kingdon's conditions need to be present if legislation is to be considered. Because elected officials in Connecticut thought that their current laws were adequate to mitigate the hurricane and flood threats, they apparently did not conclude that the hurricane threat was a problem. Therefore, despite the damage caused by Agnes and Eloise and the support for nonstructural mitigation laws by state and federal bureaucrats, elected officials did not believe that there was any need for new legislation or bureaucratic advice.

The case of Louisiana highlights why issue salience alone is not sufficient for an issue to be put on the decision agenda. All respondents believed that hurricanes are a potential cause of major disasters in the state. In the original study by Rossi and colleagues, Louisiana's key figures were the only ones to rate hurricane effects as the most serious problem that faced the state in the past ten years.[51] Yet they showed no support for statewide nonmitigation policies. Only by understanding Louisiana legal history did it become apparent why. The state legislature had consistently viewed hurricane and flood control to be local problems ameliorated by the construction of levees. Thus issue salience was high, but it did not lead to nonstructural mitigation legislation because structural approaches had historically been more prominent.

Coalitions in Nonstructural Mitigation Policy

Although Kingdon claims that the three conditions are independent, circumstances surrounding natural disaster legislation indicate that legislation is more likely when the three processes are achieved in a specific order.[52] This finding illustrates Kirlin's characterization of the policy process as a set of strategic interactive political choices.[53] Major hurricanes and floods are regional in scope and normally strike geographical areas larger than one state. Because of the regional nature of disasters, knowledge of the risks involved and potential mitigation strategies historically have been determined at the wider federal level, and several federal acts have mandated state and local responses.

Hypothetically, given these conditions, a coalition forms that supports statewide nonstructural mitigation. Such a coalition would consist of federal agencies charged with assessing the disaster risk and making that knowledge available to state officials. Federal programs such as the NFIP create a federal bureaucracy to dispense information and potential solutions to states to mitigate disasters. Even in states that are indifferent to or opposed to mitigation—for example, New Hampshire and South Carolina—federal agency heads are committed to keep the issue alive (see table 4).

Next, the coalition incorporates state agency heads when the latter are convinced that a problem exists and that a statewide solution is feasible. Along with securing the involvement of professional communities to supplement federal knowledge and assistance, state agencies can take the lead to develop appropriate solutions capable of legislative acceptance and can begin to lobby for their support. This step was apparently under way in Connecticut and failed in Louisiana where new nonstructural mitigation alternatives could not overcome the traditional legislative support of structural mitigation measures.

The coalition is complete when the support of key legislators has been secured and policy entrepreneurs have been developed. The coalition now waits for an appropriate time to push for legislation, when a policy window opens. After a policy window opens, full legislative support is sought to enact mitigation laws. In 1977 Florida, New Jersey, New York, and Pennsylvania appeared to be at this stage.

After legislation is enacted, the need to retain the mitigation coalition is not strong, and the group may disband until a new set of circumstances causes mitigation proponents to reform. North Carolina seemed to have an acceptable nonstructural mitigation public policy, and thus no coalition was actively promoting further legislation along those lines.

If Kingdon's model and this refinement above are correct interpretations of how nonstructural mitigation measures have been passed at the state level, a blueprint may be available for others to follow to enact similar legislation.[54] However, further research is needed to determine the universality of the model and its applications.

Preparedness

Current Policy and Implementation Issues in Disaster Preparedness
⚡ William L. Waugh, Jr.

The Problem: Preparing for Uncertain Events

Recent technological and natural disasters have increased public and official consciousness of real and potential hazards and the need to prepare for possible disasters. That attention to disaster preparedness may be fleeting, however, despite the magnitudes of the tragedies. To paraphrase Joseph Stalin, large numbers of deaths are mere statistics; public and media attention seldom lingers when events are distant and the statistics are not easy to translate into human lives. It is also uncertain that the events will stimulate significant and effective policy initiatives. The lessons, then, may be lost.

Issue salience, policy design, and implementation problems have been continuing impediments to disaster preparedness efforts. Disaster response mechanisms, by and large, are inadequate for most potential hazards due to difficulties in identifying hazards, defining risks, and communicating that information to policymakers and the public in a clear and compelling manner. Emergency managers are expected to develop a variety of policy and program options that can provide minimal standards of preparedness capabilities. The difficulty of those technical tasks is compounded by political considerations as program budgets are products of political competition and accommodation. Action may be dependent upon the support of "attentive" and influential publics, and the allocation of fiscal and other resources may be influenced crucially by geographic or economic or partisan interests, as well as by the personalities of the policymakers and the political milieu itself.

This essay addresses the broad policy issues involved in the design and implementation of preparedness programs, rather than specific programmatic concerns. Why have the problems of low issue salience and policy implementation inhibited effective preparedness efforts? What is it about the disaster preparedness function that makes it difficult to provide response mechanisms for the myriad of hazards in an advanced industrialized society? Why have preparedness efforts to date been less than adequate? And what can be done to provide better disaster planning and preparation?

The need for more and better disaster preparedness efforts is manifest. Technological advances present new hazards, require different emergency response mechanisms, and necessitate dynamic planning processes to assure that preparedness programs keep pace with change. The more "modern" a society grows, the more fragile it becomes.[1] That fragility, moreover, may also be the result of the accumulated risks presented by "old technologies."

What can government do to prepare for those potential disasters? Emergency preparedness needs do not compete well for either public attention or public resources. Without a recent history of catastrophic, mass casualty, or high property loss events, communities, states, and nations feel little imperative to prepare for the next disaster. Voters and policymakers have to be persuaded on the basis of probabilities. However, even when recognition exists of the need to design and implement disaster response procedures and to allocate sufficient resources, there is no certainty that the preparedness efforts will be adequate. The very uncertainty of the events and their intensities mitigates against the development of adequate programs.

The worst-case scenarios on which plans and preparations may be based are matters of conjecture and subject to error. Credibility is also a factor and even timely warnings may go unheeded by threatened communities;[2] evacuation planning may fail to take into account some critical factors; essential medical services may not survive catastrophic events; scarce resources may be misallocated during the confusion of an emergency response; or any number of other unanticipated eventualities may lessen the effectiveness of the best-laid plans. Testing and evaluation of plans and procedures will lessen the likelihood of such failures and shortcomings, but without actual and recent crisis applications, there is no way of assuring that preparedness efforts have been adequate. The best that can be done is to respond reasonably to the best estimates of the experts and to build flexibility and slack resources into the plans. The effectiveness of that effort is dependent upon how well we can deal with the unpredictability of events and with the planning and policymaking problems raised by the low salience of disaster preparedness concerns, the fragmented policymaking and administrative structure, and the problems of implementing workable programs once the legislative foundation is laid.

The Preparedness Function

As an emergency management function, preparedness entails those "activities closest to the onset of a disaster which minimize damage and enhance disaster response operations."[3] Functionally, disaster preparedness overlaps somewhat with disaster mitigation and is perhaps most closely associated with disaster planning, although it includes a number of other activities involved in implementing and testing emergency plans and preparing for disaster response.

A broader view of the preparedness function can be found in the Federal Emergency Management Agency's (FEMA) Integrated Emergency Management System (IEMS) operational model. That model identifies preparedness as "any activity that develops operational capabilities for responding to an emergency," including the development of (1) emergency management organization; (2) emergency operations planning; (3) resource management; (4) direction and control; (5) emergency communication; (6) alerting and warning; (7) emergency public information; (8) continuity of government; (9) shelter protection; (10) evacuation; (11) protective measures; (12) emergency support services; (13) emergency reporting; (14) training and education; and (15) exercises and drills.[4]

More broadly, the FEMA approach includes hazard analyses to determine the type, probability, and probable intensity of potential disasters; capability assessment to ascertain what resources exist for disaster response, to determine needed capability enhancements, and to upgrade response capabilities; emergency planning, to include formalization and evaluation of plans; and capability maintenance and improvement, including the training of emergency personnel and the education of administrators, policymakers, and the public concerning potential hazards and response procedures. The FEMA approach as it is now being developed is functional rather than disaster-specific; that is, the procedures and organizational structures would be useful for a number of disaster types.

The IEMS model, however, is based on questionable assumptions. It assumes unambiguous preparedness objectives, identifiable and measurable risk factors, adequately defined causal relationships to guide policy design, and the existence of organizations legally and administratively capable of acting and politically inclined to do so. The model further assumes that there is a substantial capacity to assess hazards, to learn from disasters, and to provide the resources necessary to maintain and upgrade response and recovery capabilities and to perfect mitigation strategies. The model in other words is a guide for policy design and implementation, rather than a mechanism for action. The nature of the preparedness function, particularly in terms of the variety of hazards and risks that may threaten a society, mitigates against the development of a single effective mechanism for managing disasters, although in policy terms the same design and implementation strategies may be operative under a wide variety of circumstances.

The policy implementation literature suggests strongly that successful efforts may depend upon a variety of factors. Daniel Mazmanian and Paul Sabatier's tests of implementation success,[5] for example, are based on (1) the tractability of the problem to be addressed—for example, the technical difficulties involved and the extent of the behavioral change required; (2) the ability of the implementing statute to provide clear guidance (particularly in terms of objectives and causal relationships), ample resources (ranging from fiscal, personnel, and material to information and technical expertise), and "hierarchical integration or clear lines of responsibility and authority"; (3) such nonstatutory variables as the socioeconomic conditions, public support, constituency support, and the commitment of leadership skills of the implementing officials.

Given the evolution and the uncertain nature of the emergency management effort, one would expect implementation problems. Natural and man-made hazards are not generally "tractable" problems, to use Mazmanian and Sabatier's term. While there is a high level of public awareness of, say, earthquake risks in California and technical information on why that risk exists, not to mention the likelihood of a major quake in the near future, there is little real information on the vulnerability of California communities. The recent major earthquakes near Mexico City are necessitating a reevaluation of California's preparedness and mitigation efforts. The point is not that Californians will be unprepared, but that they do not quite understand what they are preparing for and how to do it effectively because the requisite information is not available. The inadequacy of information is even more evident when one considers the earthquake hazards around the New Madrid fault and Charleston, South Carolina.[6]

In addition to the informational and expertise problems encountered in disaster preparedness efforts, programs at all levels generally also lack clear and measurable objectives, ample resource allocations, and adequate levels of public and official commitment. While the IEMS model may serve as a goal for policy design and program development, the capacities and capabilities that it requires should be the strategic objectives of disaster preparedness efforts. As the Mazmanian and Sabatier tests indicate, the principal policy problems to be addressed are (1) the acquisition of information on the nature of potential hazards and the risks that they present; (2) the kinds of mitigation and preparedness actions that are technically, as well as economically and politically, feasible and effective; (3) the development of clear preparedness program objectives and the allocation of ample resources to meet those objectives; (4) the designation of appropriate lead agencies, coordinating bodies, and responsible authorities; and (5) the cultivation of public and official support for disaster preparedness programs. For the most part those objectives are consistent with those of the IEMS model. The implementation of the system, however, has met with considerable difficulty and it is important to know why that has happened.

The disaster preparedness programs of state and local governments indicate that other considerations may guide the development of effective policies and the implementation of effective programs. State and local efforts have often done little more than monitoring and surveillance of potentially hazardous conditions without formal response or other contingency plans.[7] The lack of central control or guidance by state or federal authorities in most cases has meant that local governments have little real expertise in emergency management and have not invested the necessary resources to develop adequate programs.[8] The first question or issue in disaster preparedness is, then, who has or should have responsibility for initiating disaster response plans, implementing and testing the plans, and providing the necessary financial and technical support to assure adequate program capacity. Preparedness efforts in general and current programs in particular have suffered from a number of major policy design and implementation problems, as well as from problems related to hazard identification and definition. As a result, disaster preparedness efforts have been characterized by (1) low levels of official and public support; (2) fragmented decision processes and uncoordinated policymaking; and (3) poor and/or incomplete program implementation strategies and procedures.

Issue Salience and Political Support

Disaster planners have had to contend with the fundamental distrust with which citizens and business interests view central planning, particularly when increased expense due to higher taxes or the cost of compliance with regulations, or decreased discretion in how property can be used, is at issue. Disaster planners have also had to deal with the low priority given disaster plans and policy among decisionmakers at all levels of government and by the public as a whole. Relative to other concerns—both competing programmatic goals and competing interests in the budgetary process—emergency management is not a compelling issue. Low-probability events, high-probability but low-intensity events, and distant events simply do not exert much influence on public perceptions or public policy.

After the disaster in Bhopal, India, citizens in West Virginia and Georgia questioned the use of methyl isocyanate in their communities. Disclosures of leaks from Union Carbide plants in the United States caused some public reaction, but many communities judged that the plants' value to local economies outweighed the risks. Similar reactions followed the 1985 explosion of a liquified natural gas storage facility near Mexico City that cost hundreds of lives.

To some extent those events and their attendant publicity had spillover effects in terms of increased concern about the transportation and storage of hazardous materials and other hazards. Public and official attention, however, was fleeting and media attention quickly turned to the next disaster. That is not to say, however, that the public is unconcerned about the potential destructiveness of natural and man-made hazards. Certainly public awareness of earthquake hazards in California, hurricane potential in the littoral states, tornado and high wind dangers in the plains and southeastern states, and flash flood threats in the mountain and desert areas remains high. Frequent disaster occurrences and high levels of damage and injury attract and keep public attention. The relatively high salience of specific hazard issues also is generally reflected in government preparedness and mitigation efforts.[9] "Hundred-year" floods and other infrequent occurrences do not excite enough interest in planning efforts or encourage the commitment of public resources to preparedness.

Public and official support for preparedness efforts may also be influenced greatly by the perceived obtrusiveness of the mitigation and response programs. Land-use planning is one of the most intensely political issues in state and local government. To the extent that preparedness efforts will require greater government control over the use and development of land, including the design and construction of buildings, public support for those programs will be minimal. Citizens and officials are more responsive to programs that require only passive participation and do not have obvious economic costs. Public officials, moreover, have short tenures and frequent election concerns; thus they may not be willing to commit scarce political and fiscal resources to programs that may or may not be needed during their terms of office.

The interest that the federal government has shown in civil defense-related disaster preparedness has increased the salience of the issue but has also politicized it to the point where it may be difficult to implement workable programs. The "policy windows"[10] created by President Reagan's strong support for defense-related programs and the "budgetary window" created by his willingness to fund such programs have meant that emergency managers may expect more support for their programs now than they have found in the past, although that support may be restricted to crisis relocation and shelter programs with clear civil defense applications. This may explain the relative success of FEMA and its constituent programs in the last several federal budget cycles. The "coupling"[11] of issues can be a successful policymaking strategy and, it would seem, a successful budgetary strategy. Increased funding for non-civil defense programs may also be attributed to the presence of so many Californians, including the president, in influential administration roles. The dangers associated with earthquakes, in particular, are of high salience in California due to the long history of destructive events, the large number of affected people, the large amount of damage caused by past earthquakes, and, perhaps, the recent prediction by the U.S. Geological Survey of a major earthquake within the next few years.

Notwithstanding the reasons for the policy window for disaster preparedness programs at the federal level, the milieu itself mitigates against strong fiscal support for such programs. Fiscal resources are scarce. There is strong pressure to rely on state and local policymakers to address issues like disaster planning and preparation.

The salience question is important because the problem of getting disaster preparedness, even emergency management in general, on the agendas of public officials at any level is particularly difficult at this time. Low political priority translates into low or nonexistent funding and, without the commitment of monies and personnel, not to mention simply attention, the programs have few prospects for success. That is perhaps the most limiting aspect of disaster preparedness programs.

Fragmented Decisionmaking
and Intergovernmental Relations

The federal system itself acts to inhibit coherent and comprehensive disaster preparedness efforts.[12] Vertical fragmentation due to the division of powers between the federal and state governments and the limited powers given local governments by states make decisionmaking and program coordination awkward at best and ineffective at worst. Horizontal fragmentation due to the jurisdictional prerogatives of a multitude of agencies adds to the difficulties. The unwillingness of the federal government to assume the role of "lead government" in disaster preparedness has already been noted. The willingness of state governments to assume those roles is questionable.[13]

Most disasters produce very localized damage without mass casualties or high levels of property damage. Therefore, principal responsibility for planning and preparing for disasters belongs to local authorities who most often have neither the expertise nor the resources to support adequate preparedness programs. In some cases the local

officials may not have the authority to implement adequate preparedness and mitigation programs. That means that local governments may
have to rely on state officials for technical expertise and resources. The
political reality is that in many cases it is easier by far to find fiscal
resources and political support for recovery efforts than it is to find
them for predisaster programs.

The horizontal fragmentation inherent in our system of state and
local governments also has been a continuing impediment when policy
problems and issues extend beyond the boundaries of a single state or
local jurisdiction. In large measure the development of the intergovernmental system of fiscal transfers—from grants-in-aid to block grants
to revenue sharing in its several forms—and technical assistance was
due to the scarcity of expertise and other resources at the local level,
the lack of responsiveness of state governments to local concerns, and
the perception that the federal government could provide better guidance in certain policy areas than could state governments, including
providing for minimum levels of support for programs and minimum
standards of operation. If it increased its role, the federal government
could increase the capacity of state and local governments to mitigate
and prepare for potential hazards, could act as a coordinator and facili-
tator of state and local programs, or, in the extreme case, could sup-
plant the state and local agencies engaged in disaster preparedness.

Conversely, the arguments against greater federal involvement in
local policymaking include concerns that federal "guidance" means
"control." Local policymakers and emergency managers, it is argued,
distrust their counterparts at the state and federal levels and object to
the setting of priorities by distant bureaucrats.[14] In terms of the preparedness programs now in existence in the United States, much concern has been expressed by local emergency management officials that
the federal role has been inconsistent, that priorities and programmatic concerns have tended to change frequently depending upon the
mood of the "feds" or the particular hazard enjoying popularity at that
moment. Federal support and guidance, they believe, have been unde-
pendable and inadequate to the task of designing and implementing
effective preparedness programs. Federal commitment to disaster preparedness appears weak at best.[15]

At the same time local officials have argued the existence of a hidden
agenda in federal involvement, particularly in terms of FEMA's IEMS.
They fear that the interest in a functionally integrated response mechanism is due to its utility as a crisis response and relocation program for

civil defense. Certainly that expectation of dual use is clear in the legislative debate concerning civil defense since Congress's explicit intention was to use the civil defense crisis relocation program for nonwar-related mass evacuations.[16] Peter May has attributed the negative response of many communities to the federal preparedness efforts to the "contamination effect" of crisis relocation planning.[17] Whether the fears are justified or not, twenty to thirty communities have refused to engage in mass evacuation planning because their plans may become variables in the calculus of strategic nuclear planning. Those communities have elected to be unprepared for mass evacuations to avoid earthquakes, flooding, or other potential disasters rather than let their plans encourage rash action by nuclear arms strategists.[18]

Political conflicts and distrust among governments are also compounded by conflicts and distrust among agencies within the same governments. The fragmentation of preparedness efforts due to agency or program "turf" battles or mandate prerogatives also produces some difficulty in emergency management policymaking and program implementation. FEMA's constituent programs exemplify the difficulties inherent in efforts to coordinate and/or consolidate dissimilar disaster planning and preparedness programs. Even within an agency like FEMA, there may be major territorial conflicts—and, the likelihood of similar conflicts among disaster-specific agencies (such as civil defense and tornado watch/warning) and functionally differentiated emergency response agencies (such as fire protection and emergency medical services) is even greater in the absence of a single, responsible higher authority. That is, in fact, the finding of the General Accounting Office (GAO) in its recent studies of the implementation of federal disaster preparedness programs under the organizational mantle of FEMA.

Policy Implementation Problems

Certainly the difficulty in designing workable preparedness programs is exacerbated by low levels of interest and commitment on the parts of officials and the public. Further, the fragmented decisionmaking processes created by the federal system of government and the profusion of emergency response and planning agencies within and among state and local jurisdictions inhibit the implementation of emergency preparedness programs. Other factors have also inhibited effective policy implementation, and many of those factors are evident in implementation problems at the federal level.

Between 1980 and 1984 a series of GAO studies addressed the questions raised by the poor implementation of FEMA programs in such areas as hurricane preparedness, earthquake mitigation and preparedness, and civil defense, as well as in preparedness and mitigation efforts in general. In virtually every case the GAO found a lack of leadership and direction. The "supplemental role" assumed by FEMA, despite its designation as the lead agency for most major disaster or emergency programs, did not provide necessary guidance and leadership for state and local policymakers and emergency managers.[19] Notwithstanding the organizational problems encountered by FEMA during the early months of its existence, the agency had not taken a proactive role in the development of emergency management and disaster relief capabilities at state and local levels.

The GAO also pointed to a number of major difficulties encountered by FEMA in the implementation of multiagency plans and responses to disasters. For example, the hurricane preparedness efforts demonstrated a lack of interagency cooperation. FEMA's Hurricane Preparedness Planning Program provided some monies to local governments to finance the development of response plans for twenty-two high-risk locations. At the same time, the National Weather Service (NWS), National Oceanic and Atmospheric Administration, was providing assistance to a similar list of high-risk areas utilizing information generated by its SLOSH (Sea, Lake, and Overland Surges from Hurricanes) and SPLASH (Special Program to List the Amplitude of Surges of Hurricanes) computer simulations. The Army Corps of Engineers, moreover, had been involved in the development of state and local government emergency planning capabilities and was instrumental in the development of three evacuation studies for the state of Florida. The high-risk areas selected by each agency overlapped significantly but there was no effort to coordinate the programs. Funding for the NWS and Corps of Engineers programs was discontinued in fiscal year 1984 even though both agencies had technical expertise in hurricane planning and response that FEMA lacked.[20]

Disaster preparedness policymaking, then, has suffered from the lack of strong leadership and centralized decisionmaking. By opting for a "supplemental" role the federal government, through FEMA, has left it up to state and local authorities to develop adequate preparedness programs. By and large that failure to provide leadership is consistent with the current philosophy of local self-reliance and autonomy. The federal role is seen as being one of facilitating the development of state and local programs and the dissemination of information. To a lesser extent, that has meant the provision of seed money for experimental and model programs and for basic research through the National Science Foundation and presumably through FEMA, although that willingness to contribute funds also seems to be eroding. The questions, then, are whether state governments have the resources and expertise to support disaster preparedness efforts and whether, even with resources and expertise, they are willing to do so.

Even when there has been a relatively firm commitment to develop preparedness programs, the implementation of those programs has not always produced effective organizational arrangements and processes and the efficient use of available resources. For example, the National Earthquake Hazards Reduction Act in 1977 addresses a broad spectrum of concerns. FEMA was designated as the lead agency by Executive Order 12148, signed July 20, 1979, and was given even greater responsibilities as lead agency by Executive Order 12381, signed September 8, 1982. Under the act, the responsible agencies are required to address the issues of building codes, design and construction methods and standards, earthquake prediction, public education and training for state and local officials, and research to increase the repertoire of mitigation techniques. Although designated the lead agency, FEMA was not the agency with the necessary technical expertise. The U.S. Geological Survey and the National Bureau of Standards provided the technical knowledge. The National Science Foundation provided funds for mitigation and earthquake prediction research. The latter three agencies were also responsible for funding or at least controlling the funds for earthquake preparedness programs and research. The GAO found that poor coordination and the lack of a strong, concerted policymaking effort inhibited the implementation of the act's provisions. The GAO recommended the development of an interagency coordinating body and a comprehensive, consolidated program budget. Implementation difficulties were explained by staffing problems within FEMA (particularly high turnover), limited technical expertise, and uncertainty concerning FEMA's authority under the act. The problems identified were essentially the same as those found in other disaster preparedness programs.[21]

In fairness to FEMA, the same kinds of criticisms were made of the

Nuclear Regulatory Agency and its role in the events leading up to and following the near disastrous Three Mile Island accident in 1979, particularly in terms of the agency's failure to implement safety procedures mandated by Congress.[22] The GAO also has indicated that some of the problems encountered by FEMA are common to designated lead agencies in multiagency response programs. Indeed, programmatic shortcomings such as FEMA's may be endemic to agencies created through reorganizations involving consolidation of organizationally dissimilar programs and may be indicative more of poor planning preceding the reorganization than of the capabilities of the new agency. Agencies created under the Reorganization Act of 1977 have had particular problems according to the GAO.[23]

Looking back at the Mazmanian and Sabatier tests of implementation success, the problems that FEMA encountered are understandable in many cases. The technical problems involved in disaster preparedness are considerable. The accuracy of earthquake predictions or hurricane landfall estimates has been illusive, although the first formal prediction of a California earthquake was made during the spring of 1985. In most cases, emergency managers and policymakers have to deal with risk factors, probabilities, and estimated intensities that diminish high issue salience. The tractability of problems or disasters is also difficult because of the extent of the behavioral change that might be required to prepare for or to mitigate the effects of potential disasters. Land-use regulations and mass evacuation plan simulations or drills can be very intrusive and very costly policy actions.

In terms of the other tests, statutory and nonstatutory, one would expect severe implementation problems at the federal level. The programs established under the nominal direction of FEMA were not set up with clear objectives, have not been given ample resources, and do not have strong public or constituent support. As lead agency, FEMA has not been given or has not chosen to assume responsibility for the implementation and operation of the aforementioned programs. Current socioeconomic conditions, moreover, are not conducive to a strong federal role in disaster preparedness, except in the area of civil defense.

Much the same can be said of the state and local roles in disaster preparedness policymaking, with the further complication that decentralized policymaking hinders coordination of efforts and standardization of everything from program criteria to resource measures to jargon. The largest impediments to effective state and local efforts seem to be the lack of fiscal resources and technical expertise. Those problems may be less severe in states and localities that have had considerable experience with disasters, but they are severe in other areas.

Conclusions

Disaster preparedness presents some unusual and some familiar policy problems. Some communities are consciously choosing to accept the risks represented by real and potential hazards and making minimal preparations. Other communities are simply ignoring hazards. Issue salience is a major obstacle to effective policymaking and implementation.

The fragmented policymaking process does not help. Individual states are trying to sensitize their citizens to well-known hazards, but the commitment of resources is seldom made. In terms of the major hazards, like earthquakes and hurricanes, there is little or no national leadership or guidance, resources remain inadequate, and program goals and standards are uneven. Present national policies mitigate against concerted, coordinated efforts and encourage piecemeal responses by individual communities. Budget cuts have reduced capacities to plan and prepare for disasters. Reductions in revenue-sharing and other largely discretionary spending programs will also have their effects. If the role of the federal government is effectively reduced, the policy question will be whether state and local governments will choose to fund disaster preparedness efforts over other programs. The question of whether sufficient technical expertise can be brought to bear will be secondary to the funding question.

What needs to be done to have effective disaster preparedness programs? Certainly the dynamic model represented by the IEMS framework offers some guidance. To develop the capacity to acquire information and expertise, to translate that information into an action plan addressing the major hazards that society faces, to design an organization with the responsibility and capacity to act in accord with those causal determinations, and to secure the necessary commitment of resources and investment of effort requires much more, however. The problems of low issue salience, fragmented and uncoordinated decisionmaking, and ineffective policy design and program implementation have been addressed here. Informational and perceptual problems, as well as the salience, decisionmaking, and program implementation issues, will be addressed in the chapters to follow. Jack D. Kartez and William J. Kelley address the questions of how to use research to prepare for the "next disaster," rather than simply engaging in crisis management, and how to eliminate the organizational and attitudinal hurdles encountered in past disasters before the next one occurs. Richard T. Sylves provides an overview of the threats posed by hazardous substances and analyzes the political, organizational, and technical problems that arise in such technological disasters. These chapters, in other words, address the questions of what should we be preparing for and how should we do it organizationally. In essence, how can the preparedness model be made dynamic, a learning and adapting model?

Research-based Disaster Planning: Conditions for Implementation ⚡ Jack D. Kartez and William J. Kelley

Few studies of local government response to disaster ever fault public managers for failing to make heroic efforts to save lives and restore essential services. A long history of investigations repeatedly criticizes managers for not anticipating the social and organizational demands of the disaster environment. Local managers are exhorted to plan for the near inevitable appearance of citizen volunteers, inquiries from the general public seeking information, the arrival of large numbers of radio and TV news personnel, as well as the sudden involvement of external agencies and other levels of government. Not to plan for these demands can result in emergency operation centers crowded by newsmen,[1] a confused public trying to sort out inaccurate information and rumors from vital public instructions,[2] groups of volunteers who are viewed as a crowd control problem rather than a valuable resource,[3] and conflicts in communication and coordination between agencies and governments that have never worked together.[4] After conducting case studies of rescue operations in six major disasters, Drabek and his colleagues concluded, "Emergency managers must recognize that disaster response in American society is multiorganizational, emergent and frequently requires improvisation."[5]

But is improvisation the only alternative for coping with the nonroutine response demands stemming from individual and group behavior in a disaster? Do local administrators always have to apply on-the-spot adaptive learning to find strategies for managing these demands? The situational nature of each disaster may always create the need for adaptation, but there is also ample research evidence that many disaster demands requiring adaptive response are predictable. Most local governments *do* engage in formal disaster planning. The 1982 nationwide study of local emergency management conducted by the International City Management Association (ICMA) reported that a large majority (80 percent) of jurisdictions have adopted disaster plans.[6] But these plans seldom reflect the full range of disaster demands likely to be encountered. One remark by the director of the ICMA study highlights this issue: "What is puzzling is that after years of disaster research on organizational behavior in major emergencies, local government continues to be surprised when their standard operating procedures in their lengthy, detailed response plans are found irrelevant in the disaster event."[7] What are the lessons of past disasters? What do researchers expect managers to plan for? Part one of this chapter addresses these questions by briefly outlining lessons learned from postdisaster research. Part two focuses on what stands between this useful body of knowledge and organizational willingness *to prepare* for such demands.

Research-based Disaster Planning

Social scientists' studies of disasters date back to the National Academy of Sciences' formation of a Disaster Studies Committee in 1952, and the ambitious research program of the Ohio State University Disaster Research Center begun in 1963. Early research focused on dispelling "myths" about people's behavior in disasters.[8] On-site studies also began to identify some frequent problems in managing disaster response. More recent work has identified recurrent problems that result from not anticipating the need to expand organizational boundaries to accommodate both official and unofficial resources.

Given urbanization and growth, the media have come to play a dominant role in providing a lifeline of communication from local government to citizens in major disasters. The media can also create problems by triggering the convergence of people on disaster scenes, creating rumors, or simply failing to use accurate information.[9]

After several decades of research on disaster response, the accumulated body of knowledge represents a potential tool for local government administrators. Anticipating the task-demand structures in a disaster, above and beyond those normally required, involves the use of these insights. Ronald W. Perry has argued that administratively devised strategies working against people's expected reaction patterns create more problems than they solve. For example, the jammed telephone lines and rumors that occur when people try to confirm warnings or lifesaving instructions could be avoided and positively managed by providing accessible lines of communication, such as phone-in centers. Perry has called predisaster strategies to meet such needs "research-based community emergency planning."[10]

The administrative problems in disaster response addressed by Perry and others may be considered demands that are caused by the behavior of the larger social system under stress. Thus they are different from the functional demands caused by the physical impacts of the disaster agent itself (firefighting, emergency medical care, structural damage control).[11] The "external" demands go beyond the mere extension of each agency's routine "internal" tasks. Such external demands are not necessarily in the domain of responsibility of any one service-providing local agency. They usually cut across the activities of many agencies in a major emergency response. It is these external demands that researchers believe are underemphasized in current public agency approaches to preparedness.

The Utility of Research to Practice

If local administrators were unwilling to use such techniques in disasters because they were impractical, there would be little reason to pursue the question of why localities do not plan for social demands of disaster management. However, recent research[12] and accounts by local administrators[13] show that managers do adopt strategies to meet these demands in disasters. For example, when phones were restored after the Wichita Falls tornado of 1979, a "rumor control line" was set up and operated by city personnel. Because of the need for and presence of volunteers, one manager was delegated to address the cascade of questions about how and where to use them in overall efforts.

Similar strategies of using volunteers extensively and overcoming communication difficulties with citizens were adapted by communities in
Washington State following the 1980 Mount St. Helens eruption.[14]

In the Kansas and Washington State cases managerial strategies added
up to responses that actively accommodated behavior in the disaster
environment. However, none of these actions was planned and each
took valuable time to organize and implement. Furthermore, as the
city manager in Wichita Falls later observed, some potential resources
went overlooked. For example, traffic control for clearing debris-choked
streets might have been solved by using already organized community
groups.[15] Drabek's study of the search-and-rescue effort alone found
twenty separate local and state agencies, organized volunteer groups
(Red Cross, amateur radio), and military units involved.[16]

The focal issue here is the feasibility of local planning to meet these
external demands. The fact that local managers and agencies have
adapted in the event is not evidence of preparedness, only of ingenuity
and fortune. A large element of the disaster research community argues
that there is a better way. While we agree, there is also a need to
identify what obstacles may be in the way. The pilot study described in
part two pursues this issue. Little systemic information exists on how
managers do view the issues. A challenge for disaster planning theory
is to move understanding from the unique setting of the disaster event
to the context of local public administration in "normal times." This
essay concludes with a framework for investigating these issues further
in research, training, and practice.

Managerial Views of Research-based
Disaster Planning

Toward this modest end of exploration, we conducted a pilot study of
the views among forty-two individual managers of department head
rank in six cities and counties of Washington's metropolitan Puget
Sound region. The setting has some desirable characteristics for studying views of preparedness in normal times. The Seattle-King County
and Tacoma-Pierce County metropolitan areas are subject to long-term
earthquake risks and experienced two minor earthquakes in 1949 and
1965. The eruption of Mount St. Helens in 1980 heightened the reality of seismic activity in the Cascade Mountains, but never affected the

study jurisdictions. Except for a presidentially declared flood disaster in 1977, affecting unincorporated areas of the two counties, no major hazards have befallen the bulk of the area's urban population. To include views of managers in smaller satellite communities, the cities of Puyallup (Pierce County) and Renton (King County) were also chosen for the pilot study.

Exploratory Study Design

Finding a method to uncover managerial assumptions about disaster demands presents some dilemmas. Academic studies of local commitment to preparedness (and mitigation) often result in the frustrated conclusion that the problem is "motivating officials to participate in such a process when there is no crisis."[17] When the California Seismic Safety Commission surveyed local managers' attitudes towards preparedness in 1979, they were equally frustrated to find that chief administrators unrealistically rated their response capabilities far above that of independent state, federal, and research agency assessments.[18] This result may reflect unrealistic optimism or indifference or perhaps both. The point is that separating apathy from complacency is difficult, and global questions about the "salience" of preparedness usually yield ambiguous results.

The pilot study attempted to move beyond these ambiguities toward identifying managerial views on planning for specific demands. To accomplish this we developed compact descriptions of the disaster environment and three types of generic social and organizational demands. The three demands were (1) managing citizen volunteers as a resource in disaster; (2) providing the public and media with disaster information; and (3) preparing to work in multiorganizational networks spanning departmental and jurisdictional boundaries. For each demand we identified two or three "strategies" for preparedness from the burgeoning literature of disaster theory and practice. Neither the demands nor strategies are exhaustive statements of the social response issues, but we believe they are representative. These research-based strategies and background information were then brought directly to study participants for their evaluation.

This process of exploring managerial contingencies for accepting hypothetical task decisions has been used in a variety of organizational settings.[19] In this case the objective was to have managers verbally model their reasons for accepting or rejecting each of the seven pre-

Table 1. Selected "Lessons Learned": Social Response
Demands and Preparedness Strategies

Demands	Potential characteristics	Strategies evaluated
Volunteer utilization	Large numbers of individuals and groups converge on disaster scene offering assistance.	Untrained volunteer plan: predesignated agency to coordinate and supervise nonorganized volunteers in the event
	Sheer volume of volunteers can obstruct response.	
	Volunteers with special skills may go unrecognized or not used in area of training.	
	Effective utilization of volunteers may be hampered due to lack of familiarity with procedures.	Citizen education training: predisaster education and training of volunteer groups and individuals
Public information	Demand for information can last for several days and require hourly updates.	Phone hotline: citizen phone-in center for disaster public information
	Citizens may aggressively seek information from multiple agencies, thus tying up phones and personnel.	Neighborhood networks: use of previously organized community groups (e.g., Crime Watch) to help disseminate information and confirm warnings
	Normal communication systems may be temporarily inoperative, creating a need for alternative approaches.	Media information centers: single location with adequate space and designated liaison for news media
	While media can play an important role in providing	

Table 1. (continued)

Demands	Potential characteristics	Strategies evaluated
	public information, large numbers of nonlocal media can cause management problems.	
Multiorgan-izational response	Multiple organizations from various jurisdictions will be at the scene. These organizations will represent levels of govern-ment and private agencies that have never worked together before.	Interjurisdictional forum: task force to examine regional issues and foster familiarity and trust

Interdepartmental meetings: periodic manager meetings to keep preparedness on the agenda and to work out details of interdependent task responsibilities |

paredness strategies shown in table 1. Each of the strategies is briefly described below.

Volunteer Strategies

Specialized civil defense programs for registering volunteers before a disaster (for example, developing local "cadres" or citizen groups will-ing to assist with disaster responsibilities) and training for radiological defense (RADEF) were once widely funded by federal government. These programs have declined with reduced funding and movement of local programs away from exclusive civil defense concerns. Some juris-dictions (mainly counties) promote and support search-and-rescue vol-unteer programs and local chapters of the Amateur Radio Emergency System (ARES). These programs are often oriented towards more fre-quent emergencies such as a lost hunter, missing aircraft, or boating accident.[20]

We generalized the concept of unofficial and official volunteer resources (including the convergence of helpers) by defining two strategies. An Untrained Volunteer Plan involves designating one local government agency to anticipate the influx of citizen volunteers in a disaster and assume the role of directing those resources to remove the burden from other overtaxed units. Citizen Education/Training is an extension of the more traditional practice of maintaining a core of organized citizens who can augment agency resources in a disaster (for example, radio operators, volunteer monitors, hotline operators, etc.).

Public Information Strategies

Public demand for vital instructions, warnings, and plain reassurance, and the secondary impacts of media crowding emergency operations and citizens jamming telephone lines have been discussed. Both researchers[21] and the U.S. Mayors' Conference[22] have suggested making positive use of the telephone in major emergencies by preparing equipment and personnel to operate phone hotlines.

A second strategy is to make use of the block watch, crime watch, and neighborhood planning groups that have developed in recent years. Maintaining agreed-upon procedures with the citizen coordinators of these groups can provide one means to pass vital information to citizens or to locate senior citizens and homebound populations needing special attention. Because many of these groups are neighborhood based, we called this strategy neighborhood networks.

The central media role in disasters is well established, but a frequent complaint of media personnel is that no provision is ever made for their inevitable presence. One approach is to establish "one focal point, with officials selected in advance to handle these tasks" of keeping the media informed but out of the way of essential operations.[23] We called this third strategy a media information center.

Multiorganizational Response Preparations

The final two strategies used in this pilot investigation address the demand placed on local government departments to work with each other and with neighboring localities in disaster. Much has been made of the need to develop rapport before a disaster strikes. The U.S. Mayors' Conference *Emergency Manual* suggests that jurisdictions maintain an emergency planning committee meeting once a month. Efforts to meet similar needs between jurisdictions have been suggested by the National Governors' Association.[24] Thus two strategies for building multiorganizational response abilities are to maintain monthly interdepartmental meetings of a standing staff committee and, perhaps less frequently, holding meetings of an interjurisdictional forum.

Interview Format

Interviews lasting an average of three hours were conducted with heads of seven key departments in each jurisdiction. Each manager was asked to rate the seven strategies (after hearing descriptions of the disaster demands). Following the closed-end responses, managers were asked to comment on their rationale for rating each strategy, using three criteria. The three criteria were: (1) Would this strategy have any benefit to your jurisdiction's capabilities? (2) How much effort will it take to develop support for organizationally maintaining this strategy as an accepted procedure? and (3) How likely is it that your jurisdiction will ever adopt this strategy? Four-point scales were used ranging from 1 (no benefit, no effort required, and no chance of adoption) to 4 (great benefit, great effort to adopt, and almost certain chances of adoption).[25]

Analysis of Results

Managers' ratings of the preparedness strategies showed consistent rank-orders of preference on all three criteria of benefit, effort, and likelihood of adoption (see table 2). Casual inspection of these rankings shows a consistent positive relationship between mean scores for benefit and likelihood of adoption, while a consistent inverse relationship exists between mean effort required and likelihood.

Managers from diverse settings all expressed highest support for planning to work with the media in disaster, and viewed this as requiring little effort. Yet only one jurisdiction actually had such arrangements in place; and the two key departments involved (executive and emergency services) pointed to completely different locations and staff responsible as constituting preparations for the media!

Clear doubts were expressed about hotlines, neighborhood networks, and citizen education/training. All were viewed as having "some benefits" on average, but requiring great effort. Presumably this is why all three ranked lowest in likelihood of adoption. Similarly,

Table 2. Managers' Rankings of the Suggested Strategies
on Three Evaluative Criteria

Strategy	Perceived likelihood of adopting	Perceived benefits of strategy	Perceived effort to adopt
Media information center	1[a](2.84)[b]	1 (3.96)	6 (2.46)
Interdepartmental meetings	2 (2.71)	4 (3.23)	7 (2.36)
Untrained volunteer plan	3 (2.60)	3 (3.37)	2 (2.93)
Interjurisdictional forum	4 (2.52)	2 (3.43)	3 (2.88)
Phone hotlines	5 (2.48)	5 (3.07)	4 (2.86)
Neighborhood networks	6 (2.38)	7 (2.78)	5 (2.77)
Citizen education and training	7 (2.15)	6 (3.02)	1 (3.46)

a. Rank of strategy on this criteria.
b. Mean scores shown in parentheses.
N = 41

interjurisdictional forums ranked very high in benefit but also in effort, and thus ranked relatively low in adoption prospects.

The consistency of these rank orders suggests that managers judge the prospects of adoption along the path of least resistance. The only major anomaly in this pattern was for untrained volunteer plans, where there was a sharp division of opinion between agencies maintaining volunteer programs or procedures (mainly emergency services staff) and most other departments. For the most part departments not specializing in emergency services (including public safety agencies) were unaware of the volunteer plans already being maintained in their jurisdictions. As table 2 shows, citizen education/training received particularly dismal prospects for adoption by most managers, yet the two counties and one large city all maintained some predisaster cadre or search-and-rescue programs through emergency services units or departments.

Why do these preferences between strategies exist, for the most part crossing disciplinary lines? Why do managers view arrangements with the media as so desirable and feasible, for example, compared to other possible measures? What if any factors distinguish differences in managerial opinions for each strategy and across all strategies?

Use of Free Response Data

To answer some of these questions, the specific comments each participant made were evaluated to uncover reasons for these preferences. To utilize these comments the two researchers first independently summarized over two hundred pages of interview notes into specific groups of statements that had been made about the pros and cons of each strategy. This initial classification of managers' comments was based on the actual language used, but intersubjective agreement was tested as each comment was assigned to a category. The use of free response data is similar to Paul Anderson's study of "decisionmaking by objection."[26] Considerable overlap existed between these preliminary categories. A second round of classification involved aggregating ninety-seven initial statements into more inclusive conceptual categories.

While this procedure yielded a total of nineteen types of conceptual issues, only seven of these categories were identified repeatedly in discussing the different strategies. Table 3 provides a brief description of these seven categories, or, as we began to call them, managerial conditions for adoption. Table 4 identifies the frequency with which managers noted these "conditions" for each strategy. The left-hand column of table 4 lists each condition and the top row of the table identifies the strategies in order of mean likelihood of adoption, from highest (media information centers) to lowest. Each cell of table 4 shows (1) the percentage of managers who made the comment; and (2) the difference in likelihood scores given by all managers who voiced that particular issue versus those that did not.

Therefore table 4 shows a verbal lexicon of considerations that managers raised during the discussions and also reports the actual differences in judgment associated with each consideration.

Low priority for disaster planning, a need for top management support, lack of resources, and doubts about the strategy's usefulness were

Table 3. Key Conditions Influencing Management
Views on Preparedness

Condition	Description
Low priority	Disaster planning itself has low priority
Normative support	To give sufficient attention to disaster planning requires the support and leadership of key department heads in general, and the CAO in particular.
Reliability of strategy	For some strategies, managers viewed the lengthening of lines of communication, whether by people or additional phone systems, as likely to produce unreliable results.
Coordination obstacles	Too difficult to contact and coordinate with all who need to be involved in planning (e.g., external groups and agencies)
Lack of resources	Two issues: One being the cost (in dollars or level of effort) of developing and maintaining strategy exceeds available resources; the other being the benefit of the strategy does not warrant the resources required
Experience with demand	A clear recognition of the demand stemming from two sources: direct experience with similar type problem (emergency rather than major disaster); or "lessons learned" vicariously from colleague with major disaster experience
Experience with strategy	Prior experience with similar technique or existing program produced higher level of confidence in the proposed strategy.

Table 4. How Conditions Influenced Evaluation of Strategies

Condition	Media information center		Inter-departmental meetings		Untrained volunteer plan	
	a	b	a	b	a	b
Low priority	17	−.76	22	−.28	27	−.40
Normative support	22	−.30	42	−.29	17	−.13
Reliability of strategy	17	−.76	0		17	−.90
Coordination obstacles	20	.00				
Lack of resources	7	.00	0		37	−.33
Experience with demand	55	+.36	17	+.61	0	
Experience with strategy	.0		10	+.45	49	+.37

a. Percentage of 41 managers who identified this condition.

all associated, for the most part, with lower ratings of adoption likelihood. On the other hand, we found that those managers who expressed familiarity with either the need for or routine usefulness of the strategy always expressed higher opinions of the likelihood of adoption. Each of these issues is discussed in further detail below.

Priority and Top Management Support (Conditions 1 and 2)

Somewhat to our frustration, managers often made little distinction between planning for specific demands and the overall perceived importance of disaster planning to their organization. The data in table 4 only partly reflect the pervasiveness of this issue in all the interviews. Raising the priority of disaster planning was almost always seen as being dependent on the normative support attached to emergency

| | | (ranging from most feasible to least feasible) | | | | | |
| Inter-jurisdictional forum | | Phone hotline | | Neighborhood network | | Citizen education training | |
a	b	a	b	a	b	a	b
22	−.46	12	−.33	12	−.00	46	−.50
29	−.46	0		17	+.43	17	+.50
0		37	−.72	29	−.38	0	
17	−.55	0		34	−.82	0	
0		24	−.98	39	−.29	63	−.07
39	+.23	32	+.70	0		0	
29	+.39	29	+.43	24	+.69	24	+.78

b. Difference in mean likelihood scores between managers who made comment and all others.

preparedness functions by the chief administrative officer. A common view was expressed by the head of one large public safety department: "My number one priority is getting the uniforms out in response to calls. The public judges me on that performance, not whether I'm sitting around planning for an earthquake that may never happen. If left alone, disaster planning would get even less priority from my office. It requires that the executive clearly make this a priority."

The lowest likelihood ratings for all strategies came from departments in the jurisdiction whose chief administrator expressed the following philosophy: "There are people whose job is to worry about disasters. If they [emergency services] asked me to assign someone from my office, I'd say sorry, that's your job. . . . It doesn't make much sense to reach all the way to the top to get someone to come down and do your job." Another instance of the importance of top management's role came from the city of Seattle, where emergency services is an established function within the large and powerful Fire Department.

The fire chief emphasized the role of the mayor's office in gaining multidepartment involvement in ongoing planning. The mayor's office was asked to charge key departments with assigning staff to the planning process and monthly interagency meetings. According to the fire department, "The Mayor's Office got results. If we'd [asked] we'd still be waiting." Seattle was the only one of the study jurisdictions maintaining regular interdepartmental meetings.

These and many similar instances underscore the critical role of the CAO in initiating and maintaining disaster planning as more than a paper exercise. Managers were most interested by far in discussing the general climate for disaster planning in their jursidictions rather than specific demands of the disaster environment. To many the salient issue is whether disaster planning has any priority at all. The overall context for considering specific planning practices is set by this condition.

Strategy Reliability (Condition 3)

Specific doubts *were* expressed about the usefulness of some strategies. Lengthening lines of communication is a concern that surfaced in discussing the role of emergent volunteer groups. One manager commented, "The more volunteers, the more fractured the structure, the more other departments are involved, the more difficult the management problem. You need people you know and trust with whom you have instant communications. The next layer of people, whether the Army or the Kiwanis Club, creates as many problems as it solves." Municipal law enforcement in particular, tended to view volunteer emergence as a crowd control problem.

There were similar concerns about the reliability of communication systems in the hotline and neighborhood network strategies. Doubts were expressed that the phone system would survive to support a hotline, although experience shows (as in Mexico City's catastrophic 1985 earthquake) that major portions of local phone networks survive. A number expressed fears that hotline operators would increase rather than decrease rumors and conflicting information, a different kind of complaint. By contrast only a small number (17 percent) expressed concerns about the reliability of the media. However, the problem was often defined in narrow terms, as in the case of the emergency manager who said, "Our media are all right, I know them all, but those other media are the problem." The probability of very large numbers of media personnel converging on the scene often seemed to be thought quite low.

Difficulty of Coordination and
Lack of Resources (Conditions 4 and 5)

Unease was also voiced over the difficulty of maintaining liaison with all those who need to be involved before a disaster strikes. Frequent comments were that community groups are neither well-organized enough nor cover enough precincts of a jurisdiction to provide a useful framework for planned collaboration with public agencies. Although one-fifth of managers also expressed concerns about the difficulty of planning cooperation with the highly independent media, this viewpoint had no association with lower ratings as it did for other strategies.

Lack of staff resources to implement strategies requiring extensive coordination in normal times was also always associated with low likelihood of adoption. Many law enforcement agencies committed to the crime and block watch programs feel they are hard-pressed to muster enough resources to meet that routine demand. We found no jurisdictions systematically using the community crime prevention networks as a vehicle for even general public education about emergency preparedness.

Experience: Familiarity and Images of
Disaster Demands (Conditions 6 and 7)

So far we have discussed only negative influences on the perceived prospects for adopting each of the strategies. Most of these influences involve a litany of organizational constraints against giving much attention to these issues, not the disaster environment. One illuminating finding, though, was the positive influence that experience, even from normal times, can have on preparedness.

To interpret this finding, an analogy to management motivation theory is useful. According to expectancy theory, performance can be conceived as having two antecedents; expectancy and instrumentality.[27] Instrumentality is the perception of whether the performance of a task addresses a valued need or goal. Expectancy is the perception of whether the effort (in doing the task) will lead to the needed level of performance. The analogous issues in disaster preparedness are whether managers perceive the external demands as real and consequential enough to warrant preparation and secondly, whether the suggested strategies appear to be the most effective means of preparation. In the study, managers with either some level of familiarity with the demand or with the strategy both viewed adoption more favorably. Familiarity with the demand typically stemmed from involvement with a similar situation during a more routine emergency (as opposed to major disaster) or from hearing a professional colleague report his or her disaster experience (vicarious learning). Familiarity with a strategy stemmed from the manager's knowledge about an accepted routine program or task environment that was comparable to the disaster preparedness strategy being proposed.

As table 4 shows, both factors were consistently associated with higher feasibility ratings for each strategy with which managers had some kind of familiarity. Significantly, these instances of familiarity all come from "normal times" contexts of public management rather than disaster environments. Only a few managers (10 percent) had experienced a major disaster. For example, those managers who were familiar with the availability of municipal electric utility phone banks for power blackouts viewed disaster hotlines as significantly more feasible than their colleagues did. Managers in the same jurisdiction were often unaware of these existing resources, and their ratings were lower. Over half of all managers volunteered explicit statements about the need to work with the media because of routine experience, in part explaining the very high feasibility given to the media information centers. Managers thus have less trouble *visualizing* the media's demand for public information in a disaster.

By comparison, no managers reported recognizing a special demand to work with volunteers and community groups in disaster because of their routine experience or that of colleagues. But about one-quarter could relate routine experience with ongoing programs to the usefulness of neighborhood networks and citizen education/training. As in the case of those familiar with utility hotlines, these managers rated feasibility much higher ($+.69$ and $+.78$, respectively).

Managers who have never been in a disaster can also draw erroneous conclusions from routine experiences they have had. When we described the need to give direction to citizen helpers in disaster to prevent crowds or overwhelming of trained personnel, the reply of one highly competent executive was, "What's the problem? You're only talking about a few blocks, and we'll rope it off." The underlying problem here was well expressed by one public works head with disaster experience, who said: "Somehow we need to create those images for our [staff] people, so they'll have some perspective."

So while normal experience is not a panacea, these attempts by managers to relate disaster demands to "normal times," in the absence of direct experience, point to a lesson for those who want research prescriptions implemented. Since March and Simon's exposition of the bounded rationality of decisionmaking, researchers in management and applied psychology have tried to identify the heuristics or rules of thumb that are inherent in human judgment. One of these heuristics is *availability*. Availability refers to the tendency to make choices among uncertain or unfamiliar alternatives by making analogies to the most memorable (often the most frequent) past situation that appears similar.[28] This practice can also lead to errors in problem sensing, or bias.

Such simplifying assumptions about the world pervade all management decisions but are particularly relevant to disaster preparedness. As Simon points out it is the unfamiliar, risky events that are hardest to anticipate correctly.[29] Not surprisingly, there were only a few instances of any agencies in our pilot study sample having even minimal plans for the external demands covered. The frequency of daily routine task environments exerts a powerful influence on what key managers will notice or anticipate about their domain of possible responsibility in a disaster. Furthermore, unusual and extreme past events have a persistent influence even though they lack the frequency of routine. For example, the tendency of municipal police to view the prospect of mass community emergency involvement in terms of their riot experiences in the 1960s has often been noted in Disaster Research Center work. This heuristic persists among personnel in the larger jurisdictions we studied here even many years later.

Need for More Sensitivity to
Managerial Contexts

The research literature has created an atmosphere of criticism of local government. Local managers are dunned for failing to relinquish their everyday roles and assume new roles and tasks in a community crisis.[30] The growing prescriptions rightly call for more frequent interdisciplinary collaboration in public agency disaster planning.

Even under optimal conditions there may be unforeseen cognitive

Figure 1. Adaptive Planning Antecedents and Outcomes

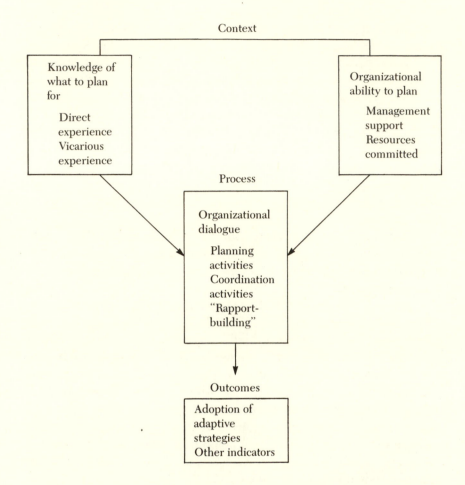

barriers in planning for unfamiliar community crisis environments. The networking ideas dominating sociological disaster research are appealing but only tap part of the problem. For example, Caplow's study for FEMA of key official emergency planning networks found that "even the most effective communication networks did not avail themselves of the resources offered by the voluntary and private sectors."[31] Indeed, only one of the fifteen networks studied involved contacts with the media. Although emergency exercises are perhaps the most crucial planning activity for any locality, Drabek had to conclude that even where the communities he studied fortuitously had held annual exercises shortly before disaster, they were still "surprised by the complexity of the real event."[32] These findings indicate cognitive barriers that are not amenable to change through "social networking" alone.

Before castigating public administrators for failing to plan for the subtle external demands of disaster response, more attention needs to be paid to insights on decisionmaking from the mainstream of management studies and psychology. Notably, the most recent summary of the Disaster Research Center's findings on organizational behavior[33] has given sharper focus to this issue. Quarantelli notes that managerial expectations of community behavior in disaster are too often "arbitrarily included in disaster plans" based on incorrect common-sense assumptions. He recognizes, though, that these tacit biases in assumptions are deeply rooted, and asserts that even actual experience that conflicts with prior views is often dismissed as a fluke. This cognitive immunity suggests an important lesson for researchers and trainers. Simply lecturing managers on what they have failed to anticipate is unlikely to change perceptions.

Conclusion: Integrating Research and Practice

Beyond focusing only on the failures of local practice, much could be learned by examining exactly what factors are antecedents of better planning efforts. As our pilot study shows—even among localities with little history of disasters to motivate them—there are cases where adaptive planning strategies have been adopted. What is needed is systematic study of local practice that relates the context, process, and outcomes of disaster planning to each other (figure 1).

The context for planning includes both (1) knowing what to plan for and (2) organizational support to use that knowledge. Whether the process is called planning, coordination, or rapport-building is a problem. All these terms have been used with much ambiguity. In whatever mode, the process must stimulate dialogue about what is known and what problems exist for which there is an inadequate planning base. As the pilot study suggests, much knowledge within a city or county's own agencies does not get brought to the surface and applied because such dialogue does not exist. The point is that improvements in disaster planning are dependent on both individual and organizational factors that jointly influence outcomes.

The fundamental problem, however, remains the disagreement over what constitutes a desirable outcome of disaster planning. Researchers and practitioners often talk past each other. Since 1952 scholars have argued that local officials should view disasters "as a precipitant for innovative, planned change." Local officials usually do not understand or relate to this argument. Meanwhile, institutional guidelines for local plans promote a traditional military-style command and control approach with its voluminous books of procedure. Yet research on experience in actual disasters repeatedly shows the shortcomings of this model.

In our work we will continue to experiment with planning assessment tools such as the adaptive planning inventory used in the pilot study. Its practical advantage is that it translates the essence of social science arguments into a language that relates to operational realities of planning and management. At the same time it also affects practice by allowing local participants to assess their own attitudes towards and preparations for disaster response needs. Our particular approach simulates the dialogue that is often missing in practice. Other indicators of good local practice should be developed, as should reliable measures of the context and process concepts proposed here. The alternative is to continue to rely only on broad normative statements of what local governments should do that often have no specific meaning for practitioners.

Federal Preparedness for Hazardous and Toxic Waste Disaster ⚡ Richard T. Sylves

In manufacture, storage, transport, and disposal, hazardous chemicals exist as potential disaster agents. Yet people are reluctant to perceive hazardous chemicals dumped as waste products on the land as potential disaster agents, even though there continues to be a regular succession of hazardous chemical accidents stemming from improper storage and disposal of wastes. For example, on April 21, 1980, a fire of unknown origin broke out at Chemical Control Warehouse company's inactive waste treatment facility in Elizabeth, New Jersey. The site was littered with some 20,000 leaking and corroded drums containing pesticides, explosives, radioactive wastes, acids, and other hazardous substances. A cloud of heavily toxic gases rose from the site and for a period threatened to blow over lower Manhattan. Fire fighters who fought to extinguish the blaze were exposed to the gases but people in the vicinity of the burning dump were fortunate to have experienced only minimal exposures. Nevertheless, significant quantities of contaminated water flowed into the Elizabeth River during the incident.[1]

The most horrifying chemical disaster to date occurred on December 3, 1984, in Bhopal, India. In the predawn hours of that day an accident on the grounds of Union Carbide released a huge cloud of methyl isocyanate, a substance used in the manufacture of pesticides.

Virtually no warnings were issued to alert the people of Bhopal, a city of 700,000 residents. Within hours of the release, well over 2,000 people died and an estimated 200,000 people were injured. The effects of this disaster will be felt for many years as those exposed to the gas fight to overcome vision and respiratory problems as well as a host of other physiological and mutagenic problems. The Bhopal accident is now classified as "the worst industrial accident in history."[2]

How has the United States prepared itself to address the problems of disaster mitigation, emergency preparedness, emergency response and alert warning, evacuation, and recovery from disaster, in the context of chemical accidents?[3] Furthermore, is the United States prepared to address hazardous and toxic waste disposal as a new hazard in the field of emergency management?

This essay presents an overview of federal preparedness for chemical disasters, particularly those stemming from toxic wastes. It examines policy instruments currently available to federal officials who must respond to chemical emergencies. Not addressed is the matter of state and local emergency preparedness for chemical accidents, nor is there an analysis of the record of governmental response to domestic chemical accidents or disasters.

The general public sees chemical disasters as triggered by accidents that occur during the manufacture, storage, or transportation of hazardous and toxic substances. Few individuals perceive toxic waste sites as potential agents of disaster, unless they live adjacent to a toxic waste site. Waugh is correct in his assertion that "there is a lack of attentive issue publics in disaster preparedness" and the area of toxic substance disaster is no exception.[4] Hazardous and toxic waste sites contain substances that alone or in combination with other substances present threats that are often poorly understood on a scientific, medical, and technical basis; the speed of onset of such hazard agents is difficult if not impossible to calculate; and the parties that should be liable for damages may be unidentifiable or incapable of making even limited restitution.

To understand how the United States is prepared for chemical disasters one needs to appreciate that much of the national government's capacity to plan against and respond to chemical accidents is a product of toxic waste management and regulation. This essay will demonstrate that the federal government is likely to respond to a hazardous or toxic substance disaster situation as a function of federal environmental emergency response. The evidence suggests that the federal response to any toxic substance disaster threat will be predicated on federal agency experience learned in toxic waste management.

Toxic Waste Dumps as Disaster Agents

In 1940 the annual production of synthetic organic chemicals was less than 10 billion pounds per year. There are an estimated two million chemical compounds in existence, 70,000 of which are in substantial use. Of this latter number approximately a thousand chemicals are suspected of being carcinogenic. While worker safety, consumer protection, public health, and transportation regulations have been applied to many toxic and hazardous substances, the cleanup of toxic and hazardous substances deposited into land environments as waste by-products is a relatively new federal, state, and local government responsibility. Most of this regulation did not begin until the mid-1970s.

Hazardous waste has been defined as any by-product that poses a substantial present or potential threat to humans, animals, or plants because it is harmful, nondegradable, and may produce effects that are biologically magnified.[5] For decades large industrial companies as well as municipalities have been depositing millions of tons of toxic substances at inadequate and inappropriate storage sites. Despite a number of early tragedies, the public and their elected representatives did not seriously address the problem, or possibility, of toxic waste disaster until the revelations of contamination at Love Canal in Niagara Falls in 1979.

There is a growing recognition that toxic waste dumps that are either unregulated, mismanaged, or both exist as potential disaster agents that threaten health and property. Hazardous and toxic waste storage poses hazards no less serious than those posed in hazardous and toxic substance manufacture and transport. In at least one sense, toxic waste dumps are a special category of technological hazard. Presumably private corporations assume responsibility and liability for accidents encountered in the manufacture, storage, and transportation of dangerous substances. These firms often lead cleanup efforts when an accident occurs. This is usually not so in the case of hazardous waste sites. When a toxic waste site is privately owned, the owner is usually incapable of responding to disaster situations created by chemicals escaping in some form from his property. Frequently illegal dumping of toxic wastes has been done on leased land, or on unoccupied land, without the owner's knowledge. In other instances, previous owners have sanctioned dumping of toxic materials on land which they later sold to an unsuspecting new owner. When public authorities assume ownership of toxic waste sites, either due to tax delinquency or through use of condemnatory powers, these authorities are often ill-equipped and unprepared to address the toxic chemical problems they inherit.

Substances found in toxic waste dumps pose multiple threats. Surface contaminants can be air pollution sources that carry poisonous or noxious gases. These releases can cause a variety of human ailments, or they can cause the death of exposed victims through major tissue damage or asphyxiation. Toxic substance accidents have drawn increased media attention in recent years because many toxic substances "are linked to cancer, a disease that Americans not unreasonably have come to fear more than any other."[6] Surface contaminants may be ignitable or explosive, thus posing a fire hazard. Substances manifesting high reactivity may explode under normal conditions or when mixed with rain or groundwater. Surface dangers may exist for those individuals who either deliberately or inadvertently traverse unfenced toxic waste sites. Many of these abandoned dumps are unsecured and have no warning signs. Where only warning signs are in place, small children may be unable to see, read, or understand the warnings.

Toxic substances that flow into subterranean environments pose another hazard. When toxic substances migrate into groundwater, they can be carried as leachate back to the surface, polluting streams and rivers adjacent to the site. If groundwater or surface water near the site is used as a source of potable water, public and private water supplies may be imperiled. This poses a threat of contamination not only to homes and commercial establishments adjacent to the site but also to unsuspecting water consumers along water pipelines extending many miles from the site. If toxic materials despoil rivers or aquifers, thousands of people living miles from the dump site could ingest toxic or bacteriological contaminants. Abandonment of polluted surface or underground water supplies will pose serious problems if there are no replacement water supplies or if provision for new supplies requires major new and expensive capital construction projects. The threat of potential disaster from toxic waste sites may continue years into the future, so that unsuspecting and innocent later generations may be put at risk by the lethal and mutagenic substances hiding underground. This raises the issue of intergenerational justice.[7]

Part of what constitutes disaster is major property loss or damage. When a hurricane or tornado devastates public or private property, public and private insurance agencies go into action to settle claims that make possible the financing needed to rebuild homes, businesses, and public facilities that are, in effect, impoverished by the disaster. Toxic waste dumps impoverish property owners in an insidious manner. Homes, commercial establishments, and public facilities undergo rapid devaluation in the real estate market when contaminated, or when perceived as being vulnerable to contamination, by toxic wastes. Douglas and Wildavsky argue, "What makes them [people] understandably angry is damage that they feel they should have been warned against, that they might have avoided had they known, damage caused by other people, particularly people profiting from their innocence."[8] Many unfortunate people continue to live in residences adjacent to high-danger toxic waste sites because they are unable or unwilling to absorb the huge financial loss incurred in selling a virtually worthless property. Private businesses as well as municipalities confront similar property devaluation problems when their land and structures are discovered to be near a toxic waste site.

Federal Laws Governing Chemical Emergencies

The Federal Disaster Relief Act is a very powerful law, but in spite of the catastrophic characteristics of chemical disaster, "very few disaster declarations have ever been made for chemical emergencies in the United States, under the Federal Disaster Relief Act, or under its state and local counterparts."[9] The 1979 presidential disaster declaration invoked by President Carter for Love Canal was one of the first for a chemical emergency in United States history.

The history of the national government's assault on hazardous substances discloses that early laws addressing the problem were weak and tentative. Many laws enacted to address environmental problems contained selected provisions that referred to toxic substances, but toxics were usually relegated to a subset of concerns under laws with other central purposes. For example, the Federal Water Pollution Control Act Amendments of 1972 contain reference to toxic wastes, but only with respect to water pollution control and abatement. Section 311 of this law authorizes the U.S. Environmental Protection Agency

(EPA) to respond to releases of oil and hazardous substances discharged into the nation's navigable waters, while the U.S. Coast Guard is authorized to handle spills in the coastal zone.[10]

The Toxic Substances Control Act of 1976 (TOSCA) was one of the first federal laws specifically directed to toxic substance regulation. TOSCA filled a number of gaps in federal toxic substance regulation and promoted interagency coordination of toxic substance regulation. This laid the foundation for regulating toxic substances at each point in the use cycle. Nevertheless, TOSCA mandates that EPA screen about 70,000 or more chemical substances used in commerce and a thousand or so more that enter the market each year.[11] The magnitude of the task virtually ensures that the agency will only be partially successful in its implementation of the statute.

The Resource Conservation and Recovery Act of 1976 (RCRA) was enacted into law as a companion to TOSCA. RCRA undertook the monumental task of regulating the generation, transportation, and disposal of hazardous wastes. This statute directs the EPA to track hazardous materials "from cradle to grave." Only a fraction of the materials labeled "hazardous," are in fact "toxic" in a physical and legal sense. Moreover, the waste disposal phase is only one of a number of phases in the use cycle of hazardous materials. Nevertheless, RCRA helped to shift responsibility for disposal of hazardous and toxic materials back to the corporations that produce them in the first place.

The Resource Conservation and Recovery Act posed difficulties for the Environmental Protection Agency. The agency was unable to develop regulations applicable to hazardous materials and at the same time investigate potential hazardous waste areas preliminary to enforcement actions. Opting to concentrate on development of regulations, EPA officials relinquished authority to investigate "imminent hazard" areas to the U.S. Department of Justice in the mid-1970s.

There was little high-profile action against firms illegally disposing of toxic materials until 1978. Early in that year the media brought increased public attention to a variety of hazardous waste incidents and a new phase of governmental activism began. The Justice Department filed suit in the first hazardous waste enforcement action since passage of the original RCRA in 1976. The Kin-Buc company was cited for mismanaging toxic waste disposal at its Raritan River landfill located near Scotch Plains, New Jersey.[12] The Justice Department managed to initiate thirty-one cases against alleged RCRA violators by November 1980. The attorney general's prosecutors were able to win eight of these cases. Winning usually meant that the perpetrator promised to discontinue discharges, provided for some acceptable means of alternate discharge, and made some kind of commitment to furnish compensation for cleanup costs. Government officials responsible for RCRA enforcement have made headway in identifying hazardous waste sites and in filing suit against dumpers and landowners who polluted the land with hazardous substances. However, until 1980 there was no federal law that supplied the legal authority or funds to actually clean up a contaminated hazardous or toxic waste site.

These cases set the stage for enactment of the Comprehensive Environmental Response, Compensation, and Liability Act of 1980, referred to as Superfund. President Carter signed Superfund into law on December 11, 1980. The act provided for a $1.6 billion fund to be accumulated over a five-year period. About 86 percent of Superfund's resources were to come through a tax paid by manufacturers, producers, exporters, and importers of oil and forty-two chemical substances. The remaining 14 percent of the funding was to be paid from the federal government's general revenue.

Superfund authorizes EPA to clean up spilled toxic wastes and hazardous waste sites even before recovering cleanup costs from the parties responsible for dumping at the sites. EPA can identify and investigate alleged sites of illegal dumping.[13] EPA is expected to work with state and local governments to provide "an immediate and comprehensive response to accidental release of hazardous substances."[14]

Superfund imposes liability for spills on the dumpers, but it does not set forth amounts of insurance coverage to be carried by parties handling hazardous substances, nor does it require creation of a victim compensation fund. However, EPA officials were able to use Superfund authority for property buy-outs. In 1982 Times Beach, Missouri, was determined to be contaminated with significant quantities of dioxin that could not be easily or inexpensively removed. Then-EPA Administrator Ann Gorsuch (Burford) authorized the purchase of all homes in Times Beach under terms of fair market value.

Federal Agency Powers in Chemical Emergency Situations

In 1968 the National Contingency Plan (NCP) was to be developed in order to specify how the federal government would respond to emergencies resulting from oil spills and from release of hazardous substances into navigable waters. With the enactment of Superfund in 1980, EPA was expected to revise and republish the NCP. The plan details the responsibilities of fourteen federal agencies, as well as the obligations of state and local governments in cleaning up releases of hazardous substances and oil spills to all media. In other words, revision of NCP extended federal emergency response beyond mere cleanup of discharges or spills to surface water. Land, air, and groundwater media were now domains of federal chemical emergency jurisdiction as well.

The National Contingency Plan basically encourages coordination of federal, state, and local government involvement in response actions; allows state and local governments to be reimbursed by the federal government for reasonable response costs; and authorizes the federal government to undertake cleanup when the responsible party or the state cannot or will not do so.[15]

There continues to be a division of labor between the EPA and the Coast Guard in emergency response to chemical spills. When a chemical accident occurs near coastal waters or on the Great Lakes, the Coast Guard has the lead responsibility. Accidents occurring inland or in inland waters make EPA the lead federal response agency. Within EPA the Emergency Response Division, assisted by the Hazardous Response Support Division, carries out the emergency response.

The EPA emergency response program outlines two types of removal actions: immediate removals and planned removals. Immediate removals encompass actions that EPA must take when a significant hazardous substance emergency exists. The disaster may be either imminent or ongoing. When there is direct human contact with a hazardous substance or when exposure to a hazardous substance threatens humans, animals, or the food chain, a hazardous substance emergency exists. In the event of fires and explosions involving hazardous material, EPA emergency response is again necessary, as it is also when hazardous substances pose an immediate threat to drinking water supply.

EPA directives refer to immediate removal as "a first aid approach to emergency."[16] This means that EPA goes about cleaning up the accident site to stop the hazardous release and to minimize damage or threat of damage to human health or to the environment. Most spills that occur in chemical transportation accidents fall into the immediate removal category. However, EPA imposes special conditions on emergencies resulting from inactive hazardous waste sites, also referred to as toxic waste dumps. EPA reports, "Inactive hazardous waste sites will be stabilized but the cleanup may continue beyond stabilization if this course appears less expensive than stopping and returning later for final cleanup or remedial action."[17]

Consequently, EPA officials working at the scene of a hazardous waste emergency site must determine when an emergency situation at the site no longer exists. This calculation is apparently a function of the cost of the immediate cleanup versus the cost of long-term remedial cleanup. When a site is "stabilized" it is presumably no longer an immediate danger to humans or local ecology. However, it is extremely difficult to decide when a hazardous waste site is stabilized, especially if contaminants are either wholly or partially buried beneath the ground. It is conceivable that hazardous waste sites in the "planned removal" category could result in disasters or emergency situations before they are actually cleaned up. Given the complexity, uncertainty, and dangers that surround toxic waste site cleanup, conventional economic rationality may not necessarily be applicable or appropriate in this realm of emergency management. Public health and environmental protection are not easily "valuated" in such circumstances.

When EPA undertakes an immediate removal, its emergency response includes collecting and analyzing samples; controlling the release of the hazardous substance or substances; removing hazardous substances from the site and storing, treating, or destroying them; providing alternate water supplies; installing security fencing; deterring the spread of pollutants; and evacuating threatened citizens.[18]

EPA is not the only federal agency involved in responding to a hazardous materials emergency. Other federal agencies participating in the National Contingency Plan work through a National Response Team (NRT) chaired by an EPA official. NRT policies are implemented on a day-to-day basis by Regional Response Teams located in each of the ten standard federal regions. Under the plan the Federal Emergency Management Agency (FEMA) is responsible for preparation, maintenance, and testing of evacuation plans. FEMA also assists in carrying out actual civil evacuations that may become necessary during hazardous substance accident events. Hazardous substance damage to aquatic and terrestrial life is researched by either the Marine Fisheries Service of the Commerce Department or the Fish and Wildlife Service of the Interior Department. The Public Health Service of the Depart-

ment of Health and Human Services investigates cases of human exposure to hazardous substances and assesses the threat to public welfare
posed by an imminent or ongoing hazardous substance disaster.[19]

When a responsible party contacts the toll-free number of the
National Response Center in Washington in order to report a hazardous materials incident, lead responsibility is then assigned to either
the Coast Guard or the EPA. The location and nature of the emergency
determines which agency is assigned the lead. Lead agency officials
then appoint an On-Scene Coordinator (OSC) who manages and super-
vises the emergency response activities deemed necessary to protect
public health and the environment. The OSC also interacts with EPA
officials in disseminating information to the media and to citizen
organizations.

Training and Research and Development
for Hazardous Substance Accidents

EPA must perform considerable research and development work to
engineer and perfect, with private industrial assistance, the technologies needed to respond to hazardous substance accidents. Given that
no two chemical accidents are likely to be identical, and given that
many involve exotic chemicals or combinations of chemicals reacting
in a variety of media, it is extremely difficult to prepare probable
scenarios through which to simulate chemical disasters.

Much of EPA's research and development on hazardous substance
emergency preparedness is performed by the agency's Environmental
Emergency Response Unit (EERU) in Edison, New Jersey. The Edison
facility brings together emergency response personnel, EPA's Environmental Response Team, and contractors from private industry. EERU
equipment is tested in actual emergencies and is used in training
courses. The unit has a fully operational physical-chemical treatment
unit mounted on a flatbed trailer truck, which can be dispatched to
chemical accident sites. It is developing a mobile hazardous waste
incineration system, capable of detoxifying PCBs, kepone, malathion,
and TCDD. EERU also has a mature program of research and development directed to cleaning up oil spills as well. Some hazardous substance identification research is conducted at EPA's Environmental
Monitoring Systems Laboratory in Las Vegas, Nevada. This lab devel-

ops sampling, analysis, and classification procedures, and also works to improve monitoring procedures at hazardous waste disposal and cleanup sites.[20]

When a chemical emergency is in progress, EERU technicians and equipment are used to evaluate the severity and extent of contamination. EPA has special emergency response teams based in Edison, New Jersey, and Cincinnati, Ohio. On-site analytical support teams help emergency response authorities determine safe and effective treatment and disposal options. Most of EERU's experience has been in the realm of hazardous substance and oil spill contamination of groundwater, drinking water, and surface water.

EERU promotes hazardous substance accident preparedness through training programs, evaluation of emergency technologies, and publication of technical manuals and procedural guides. EERU researchers, in cooperation with FEMA personnel, published a manual in 1981 on contingency planning for hazardous materials spills. Moreover, several hundred emergency response personnel from federal, state, local, or private organizations have completed EERU coursework since the hazardous substance emergency training program was inaugurated in 1981.[21] FEMA's National Emergency Training Center plans to design a comprehensive hazardous materials curriculum through a workshop involving hazardous materials emergency officials.

Building from experience in civil defense and radiological emergency response planning, FEMA officials are beginning to assume new and expanded responsibilities in emergency preparedness for hazardous materials accidents. The agency's newsletter reports, "The knowledge and experience developed in these radiological emergency preparedness activities will serve as a bridge in the new program to develop a comprehensive, generic hazardous materials preparedness capability that integrates emergency management of hazardous materials by the public and private sectors."[22]

The National Response Team's new Emergency Preparedness Committee, chaired by FEMA, should give the agency an enhanced role in formulation of hazardous materials emergency preparedness and response plans. FEMA officials are contemplating use of emergency planning zones for potential hazardous substance emergency sites. Emergency planning zones have long been used in off-site radiological emergency response planning around commercial nuclear power plants by FEMA and the Nuclear Regulatory Commission.

Concluding Observations

Given the Bhopal accident and the Love Canal tragedy, few would argue that toxic substances do not carry with them the potential to create disaster. This overview has demonstrated that the national government's capacity to address chemical accidents is largely a function of how it manages and regulates toxic waste. Admittedly, the Department of Transportation, the Occupational Safety and Health Administration of the Department of Labor, as well as other federal agencies besides EPA and FEMA, play a role in federal chemical emergency preparedness. However, DOT, OSHA, PHS, and other federal agencies participate in chemical emergency response through the National Contingency Plan and through the National Response Team. EPA chairs the NRT and has held the lead responsibility in formulating the NCP.

The Superfund law of 1980 set the foundation for the federal government's handling of chemical or toxic substance emergencies. Under this law the EPA holds major authority and responsibility in toxic waste management and in toxic substance emergency response. Because toxic waste sites are potential causes of disaster, it is appropriate that federal emergency action in toxic substance events flow from federal toxic waste management. Toxic substances are approached fundamentally from the waste and disposal perspective because industrial accountability is lowest at this point in the toxic substance use cycle. Moreover, the magnitude of the problems posed by toxic wastes is often so great that municipal and sometimes state governments are unable to respond appropriately.

This essay has examined formal institutional relationships that are intended to maintain federal preparedness for toxic substance emergencies. Whether these relationships ensure a coordinated and effective federal response to chemical disaster can only be determined from experience in disaster situations. Part of the success of this preparedness depends upon the smooth vertical integration of federal agencies with state and local agencies that must respond to hazardous substance threats. Clearly there is a need to better educate the public about the hazards of toxic substances. This will require a significant degree of behavioral and social change. In some areas drills and warning signals need to be recognized so that appropriate safety measures can be taken. Hazardous waste storage or disposal imposes a special obligation upon public authorities to protect the public health and welfare from the hazards presented by toxic waste facilities and toxic burial grounds. These hazards carry disaster potential due to the physiological and mutagenic damage that can be inflicted. The ecological damage could be irreversible in its consequences. Hazardous and toxic wastes compel a reconceptualization of the definition of disaster. Such a redefinition needs to be carried out by policymakers at the national level so that emergency management can play an appropriate part in the nation's program of hazardous and toxic substance control and cleanup.

Response

Management Issues in Emergency Response ⚡ Ralph G. Lewis

Order in Emerging Events

This chapter might be subtitled "Order Out of Chaos." That is the English title of a book by the physicist Ilya Prigogine in which he argues that order may emerge out of chaos.[1] Some may feel that the use of the term *chaos* is too extreme to describe the type of events in which we are interested. However, the phrase emphasizes the point that the response period in emergency events is characterized by discontinuity with the normal and the routine, but that emergency events are manageable and order will emerge.

The Concept of Emergency Response

Efforts to deal with policy issues related to the response stage of emergency management are complicated by at least two definitional problems. The first involves the use of the terms *disaster* and *emergency*. These terms have different definitions although they are used inter-

changeably by some authors. In this essay the term emergency refers
to an entire event and the term disaster describes events that have
resulted in extensive negative consequences. Emergency conveys a
sense of urgency but it also emphasizes the freedom and responsibility
of decisionmaking generally associated with the term management. In
fact, our concern is with the management of emergency events in
order to avoid or at least to minimize the negative consequences associated with disasters.

The second factor involves the identification of the types of activities
associated with the response phase in an emergency event. Numerous
models are used to describe the developmental sequences—identifiable
time periods—associated with emergency events. In turn, the number and character of event phases influences the identification and
characterization of associated emergency management activities.

From a management perspective the model shown in figure 1 is
appropriate for at least two reasons. It recognizes that management
activities in response to an emergency are initiated as soon as some
form of specific warning occurs (pre-impact) and that they continue on
through to an emergency/short-term recovery period. It also demonstrates the fact that any rigid attempt to place activities in a time-
related developmental sequence is limited by the overlap between
categories. For example, efforts to inform a population that it lives
near a geological fault that may cause an earthquake some day is
certainly a pre-event activity and should be considered as emergency
preparedness. On the other hand, efforts to warn a population about
the existence of a hurricane that has already formed probably should
be considered an emergency response event though it is clearly pre-
event in terms of impact.

Within this time perspective there are a number of specific need-
related activities that are generally associated with the response stage.
As shown in table 1, these activities can be divided into two major
categories based upon the source that generates the need for the
activity: event-culture generated and response-management generated.
These categories and the associated activities are adapted from work
done at the Ohio State Disaster Research Center.[2] The event-culture
category includes those types of activities generated by the event itself
—its nature, scope, and intensity—and are essentially dictated by the
values, norms, and available technology of the general society. For
example, there is social consensus that if possible individuals should
be warned about the potential of an event such as a hurricane. There is

Figure 1. Emergency Event Phases

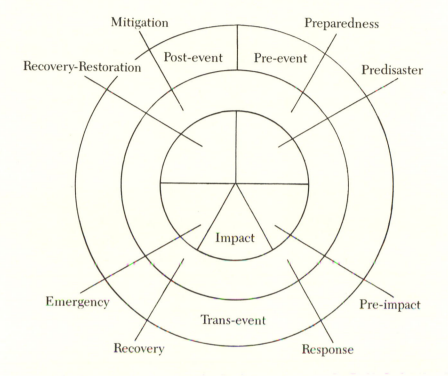

also general agreement that efforts should be initiated to search for and rescue the victims of such an event. As shown in table 1 it is possible to associate specific activities with different stages in the response period.

On the other hand, response-management generated activities are required during all three stages of the response period. For example, communications are required to (1) provide notification or warnings during the pre-impact stage, (2) maintain an organization during the actual impact of an event, (3) aid in search-and-rescue missions or conduct a damage assessment during the emergency stage. Although specifically associated with the response period of an emergency event for the purposes of this essay, it should be noted that, with the exception of planning, these activities basically encompass the traditional activities associated with administration: planning, organizing, staffing, leadership, and control.

Table 1. Response Period Activities by Source and Stage

Source of demand/need	Pre-impact	Impact	Postimpact emergency
Event/ culture generated	1 Activate-prepare 2 Notify-warn 3 Evacuate		1 Search and rescue 2 Care of injured and dead 3 Welfare-shelter, etc. 4 Restoration of essential services 5 Protection against continued threats 6 Community order
Response/ management generated		1 Develop and maintain communica-tions 2 Situation assessment-intelligence 3 Mobilization and utilization 4 Coordination 5 Authority and control	

Source: Adapted from Russell R. Dynes, Enrico L. Quarantelli, Gary A. Kreps, *A Perspective on Disaster Planning* (Columbus: Disaster Research Center, Ohio State University Report, series 2, 1972).

The Response Context

Emergency events and disasters generate extraordinary conditions among individuals and the social systems they affect. Briefly, emergency events are difficult to anticipate, thereby inhibiting planning. Moreover, when they do occur they place unique burdens—new or expanded—on existing decisionmaking and service delivery systems. Because emergency events have the potential for negative consequences, they tend to generate a feeling of crisis, that is, a sense of urgency and concern about emergency actions. Yet potential negative consequences may be mitigated (if not avoided) or exacerbated during emergencies, depending upon the decisions that are made and how they are carried out. Although the characteristics vary with the nature of the triggering incident and the degree of experience and response capability, these conditions start during the pre-impact stage and continue through the emergency stage and into the recovery period. From a management standpoint, the major characteristics of emergency events include:

1 Risk—in terms of the potential negative consequences (economic costs, physical destruction, personal injury, and death) associated with the event
2 Uncertainty—high degrees of uncertainty concerning the occurrence of events and their outcomes and/or the probabilities associated with different policy alternatives
3 Fluidity—changes in the character of the event, the information available concerning the character of events, the response demands placed upon the system, the identity and objectives of participants
4 Competition/Conflict—tensions between the vested interests, value systems, goals, and needs of different segments of the population, organizations, and individual participants in the event
5 Action Orientation—the need and/or the desire on the part of participants to take action that will affect the outcome(s) of the event in a positive way
6 Timing—limitations in the time available that create a sense of urgency for the officials who must analyze the problem and act to influence the event
7 Communications—limitations if not breakdowns in the normal communication systems
8 Data/Information—variations in the quantity and quality of data

concerning the event and event participants and in the ability to turn data into information

9 Consequences—the realization of postevent consequences and the political implications associated with all decisions made by public officials

In short, the response phase represents a period in time in which new needs are generated, leading to new demands for services. Because the demands are unique, the traditional or routine ways in which a system—individual, organization, or society—has coped with service demands may no longer be appropriate. Thus new coping techniques must be developed and utilized in the midst of the event.

It is also necessary to dispel some myths concerning human behavior during emergency events. According to the best available research from several decades of study:

1 Panic and breakdown are not common forms of behavior. Rather, there is a basic tendency for individuals and systems to behave in the manner to which they have become accustomed.

2 People are not immobilized nor are major psychological problems common. Rather, large numbers of individuals are available and capable of providing assistance to others.

3 The response capabilities of local communities or even smaller systems generally are not overwhelmed but continue to operate.

4 Antisocial behavior—looting, etc.—is not common. In fact, the emergence of altruistic behavior is significantly more common.

5 Postevent morale is not necessarily low despite the negative experience of many individuals. In fact, the heightened sense of mutual need and support help to enhance morale.

6 The coping abilities of systems do not collapse, although there may be major changes in the manner in which they cope with changed needs and demands.[3]

Caveats

Three assumptions underlie the organization of this essay. First, emergency events and their impact can be analyzed on at least five different levels depending upon the inclusiveness of the system involved. These levels include (1) individuals, (2) small groups such as families, (3)

formal organizations—ranging from subdivisions to a total organization such as a city or county government, (4) total communities, and (5) societies and/or national governments.

This essay focuses on systems that can be characterized as organizations and/or communities. These levels were chosen for several reasons. The individual level of analysis is not addressed here because public policies are developed by individuals only as they occupy positions in more inclusive systems. This is true even though individuals are affected by emergency events and the manner in which more inclusive systems respond to such events. Further, the primary responsibility for responding to emergency events is formally allocated to local systems—primarily local governments and their subunits—and/or specific agencies within the state and federal governments. Finally, the total society has been excluded because we, at least in the United States, have had limited experience with national-level emergency events. Both the impact of emergency events and the sense of urgency associated with them tend to decrease as one moves from less to more inclusive systems. Thus as a nation we have not really experienced a national emergency, with the possible exceptions of war-related events and perhaps the 1973 "oil crisis."

The significance and response implications of an emergency event will vary with the system level affected. In general the significance of an event and its impact decreases as we move from less to more inclusive levels. For example, a fire may destroy the home of a family and exhaust their immediate ability to deal with its consequences. However, from the perspective of the larger community this event may be relatively common and fall within the range of an emergency—or less—that can be managed, using existing resources and routine procedures.

Second, the model of emergency response employed in this essay assumes the existence of an emergency event with the potential for significant negative consequences. For example, in discussing the pre-impact period it is assumed that an event with the potential for significant negative impacts may occur. In terms of the postimpact stage, it is assumed that the negative consequences, physical and/or social, are significant enough to impair the system. These assumptions are made to facilitate discussion, even though the object of successful emergency management efforts is to avoid or at least to minimize negative consequences.

Third, the triggering incidents for emergency events can vary across a number of dimensions. The exact nature of these variations will have significant implications for their negative consequences and system responses. Thus great care should be exercised in even trying to identify a typical event. For example, prior research on "natural disasters" has revealed a tendency for goal-value consensus to increase, for community conflict to decrease, and for community integration to increase during and after an event such as a hurricane. It is not clear, however, that such developments take place during and after conflict-generated events such as civil disorders or even man-made events such as toxic waste spills.

Policy and the Response Period

Policy issues related to the response period of an emergency may be placed in two major categories. The first involves activities that actually take place during the preparedness phase and the relationship between preparedness and response. Although not the major focus of this essay, these issues are important because how they are managed will affect response capabilities during an emergency event and will help to determine the success or failure of such efforts. The second involves the capacity of organizations to cope with the discontinuity and crisis associated with emergency response.

Preparedness and Response

Macrolevel policy may not be an issue in the response period. In fact, the ideal scenario is one in which policies adopted in the pre-event period anticipate all contingencies and are implemented so well that policy decisions do not have to be made during the response period. In short, the better we prepare, the more routine and successful the response period should be.

However, this ideal condition is not always going to occur. No matter how carefully we plan, we could never develop specific policies to deal with all of the variations in the types and magnitudes of triggering events, anticipate all of the things that could go wrong or foresee all of the different demands placed upon organizations and communities during the response period of emergency events.

Operational Strategies and Policy Issues

The policy issues related to emergency response are the same as those related to other public policy issues. That is, they involve concepts of the general good; the question of who will benefit; the nature, scope, and cost of services; and the adequacy and degree of equity in the services provided. A community may address the issue of whether to establish "special care shelters" for the elderly and individuals with chronic medical problems who are ordered to evacuate because of a hurricane. If the community wants adequate and equitable emergency response services, these issues must be addressed during the pre-event "preparedness" phase. Moreover, the decisionmaking mechanism for these issues is likely to involve the same political and interorganizational considerations as any other public policy issue. At most, the same level of adequacy and equity will be achieved as is usually achieved by the system(s) making the decisions.

As shown in table 1, there are a number of major service activities specifically associated with the response period. For each of these activities, there is a body of current knowledge concerning appropriate response strategies. For example, issues associated with warnings and evacuations are addressed by Quarantelli[4] and by Perry, Lindell, and Greene.[5] Search-and-rescue issues are addressed by Drabek et al.[6] There are also a number of sources such as the U.S. Council of Mayors, the International City Management Association, and the Federal Emergency Management Agency which provide operational guidelines for responding to emergency events. For example, the U.S. Council of Mayors emphasizes the importance of an Emergency Operations Center to help ensure the rapid and accurate communications flow—both internal and external—needed to provide the basis of coordination and command. They also stress the importance of mutual aid agreements between political jurisdictions as a means of expanding the resource base available to any given community. All three sources also stress the importance of clear-cut role definitions and lines of authority in helping to maintain control and coordinate activities during the response period. Great care should be taken, however, in generalizing about the types of needs that will be generated during events or the appropriate policies for dealing with them, because both the needs and appropriate policies will vary with differences in factors such as the nature of the triggering event.

Response as Implementation

Emergency preparedness and response are connected because response represents the policy implementation stage. In fact, implementation distinguishes the response phase from the other activity phases of emergency events. Over the years issues related to policy implementation have been ignored. The apparent assumption was that legislators and/or administrators had only to adopt policy and it would be systematically and faithfully carried out by the individuals responsible for implementation. During the past decade increased attention has been focused on the policy implementation phase.[7] It is now clear to everyone who pays attention that successful policy implementation is dependent upon a number of factors in the policy development and adoption phases. These factors include (1) the extent to which the policy and related activities are viewed as a high priority effort within the organization; (2) the degree to which consensus agreement and support were achieved concerning the goals and operational activities specified in the emergency; and (3) the degree to which policies were communicated to and understood by the individuals and/or organizations responsible for their implementation.

If actually carried out, the efforts required to maximize the potential for implementation compliance would require considerable resources in both time and money. Thus a major policy issue in emergency response is whether we are willing or should be willing to spend money in the pre-event period preparing for events that have a low probability of occurring, even if these events have the potential for significant negative consequences if they do occur. To date the de facto answer to this question appears to have been a resounding no. A recent study conducted by the International City Management Association (ICMA) confirms this conclusion.[8]

Coping with Crisis

Assuming that emergency events will not always be avoided by perfect planning and implementation, policy issues are generated by the crisis context of the response period. These are management and organizational issues that ultimately affect organizational capacities to respond to emergency events.

Programmed versus Nonprogrammed Decisions

In general the types of decision problems faced by administrators during emergency events are similar to those which Herbert Simon has identified as nonprogrammed as opposed to programmed decisions.[9] That is, they are decisions about nonroutine issues which have to be made under crisis conditions that have been forced by the external environment. These problems tend to be complicated in that they involve a number of interrelated factors. They also tend to be problems that are ill-structured—not amenable to routine analysis and procedures. Thus they are ultimately problems characterized by high degrees of uncertainty. Finally, decisions about these problems have to be made in limited time periods because they involve significant issues that could have serious consequences.

Simon and others have argued that the skills required to deal with nonprogrammed decisions are different than those needed to deal with routine matters. These skills are often described by terms such as judgment and intuition as opposed to terms such as scientific analysis. McKenney and Keen,[10] for example, report that programmed problems were preferred by people they described as "systematics"—that is, individuals who tend to approach a problem by structuring it in terms of a method known to lead to a solution. On the other hand, nonprogrammed problems were preferred by individuals comfortable with trial-and-error approaches.[11] Mintzberg[12] has suggested that individuals who deal effectively with this type of decisionmaking problem may be characterized by right-brained rather than left-brained thinking styles.

An important policy issue emerges from this shift in the type of decisionmaking problem faced in emergency events. How do we ensure that individuals with the requisite skills are available when needed in organizations that tend to choose staff for making routine rather than nonroutine decisions?

Mechanistic versus Organic Structures

Over time, organizations develop structures and routine patterns of dealing with the recurring events and problems in their normal environment. For most formal organizations these structures can usually be characterized as multiple-level hierarchies in which authority is centralized at the top and with functional divisions of labor that emphasize specialization among subcomponents and individuals. Within this framework, data usually flow toward the top at a deliberate pace; there individual administrators make carefully considered decisions which then flow back down to the individuals responsible for action.

In contrast, the environment associated with the response period of emergency events is not normal. It is characterized by change, uncertainty, and a sense of urgency in which communications and decision-making systems may break down and standard operating procedures may not apply. Research on the relationships among variations in the external environments of organizations, their structures, and operational effectiveness has shown that no single structural arrangement is necessarily the most effective in dealing with all types of environments.[13]

The work of Burns and Stalker has particular significance for understanding the potential effects of organizational structure on response capabilities during emergency events. Burns and Stalker found differences between the organizations that performed well in changing environments and those that performed well in stable environments. Those that performed well in changing environments were identified as "organic" in contrast to "mechanistic" organizations. According to Burns and Stalker, organically structured organizations tend to have the following organizational characteristics:

1 Organizational structures that include the possibility of matrix or task force approaches to the division of labor
2 Job (task) assignments that are not rigidly defined in advance and that allow for readjustment to the emerging situation
3 A network or matrix communication structure and an emphasis on maximizing the flow of communications

4 An emphasis on consultation and coordination rather than instruction and command

5 An emphasis on self-control and discretion as opposed to direct system control

6 Limited preoccupation with adhering to the chain of command[14]

These organizational characteristics are valuable in dealing with uncertainty associated with nonprogrammed decisions and with the need for speed in decisionmaking. They create a flatter organizational structure that facilitates communications flow, participatory (team) decisionmaking, and mutual support. More recent works specifically focused on crisis management emphasize the importance of similar organizational characteristics, particularly in reference to the highest-level emergency management team.[15] Littlejohn, for example, describes the crisis management team as a matrix organization that is characterized by high levels of (1) open communications—both vertical and horizontal, (2) trust among members, (3) involvement and participation, (4) commitment or goal consensus, and (5) delegation.

Organic organizations may also be valuable in dealing with the problems caused by breakdowns in communications and the need for on-site decisions by lower-level personnel. Crozier has described this type of problem: "Those who have the necessary information do not have the power to decide, and those who have the power to decide cannot get the necessary information."[16]

Some portion of this problem can be overcome through improved communication systems and the creation of emergency operation centers staffed by the highest levels of the management team. Nevertheless there will still be situations—particularly in the postimpact emergency period—in which lower-level personnel are faced with on-site decisions that have to be made in order to ensure effective response but for which there are no clear preexisting policies or standard operating procedures. In fact, some situations may involve "bending the rules" and some may even require actions that violate existing policies and procedures. In order to facilitate such actions, an internal climate is needed that encourages individuals to make independent decisions when necessary and enhances their ability to make them in a creative manner. Such climates are associated with organizations that are characterized by (1) goal versus process control, (2) self-control (autonomy, loose control) versus imposed control (tight, rigid), (3) open and free-flowing communications, (4) the ability to consult outside of the normal chain of command, and (5) encouragement of experimentation and innovation rather than sticking to the rules.[17]

Unfortunately, most organizations—certainly most large governmental organizations—cannot be characterized as organic organizations nor do they have the internal environments that encourage independent and creative thinking. Rather, the opposite tends to be true. That is, most organizations tend to be mechanistic in nature and to discourage rather than encourage independent or innovative thinking in terms of rigid standard operating procedures. That such conditions exist is not particularly surprising when we consider that these organizations, their structures, policies, and procedures have evolved out of long experience in dealing with routine problems in a relatively successful manner. However, these characteristics present difficulties in coping with nonroutine events and problems.

Overall, emergency policy issues involve organizational and individual dilemmas. How do organizations that have apparently been successful in dealing with routine problems in a stable environment create the capability to deal with nonroutine problems in a crisis environment? Further, how do individuals who have been programmed to follow bureaucratic rules and standard operating procedures become independent and innovative thinkers when faced with nonroutine problems that do not conform to standard operating procedures?

Administration vs. Leadership

The response period of emergency events may also generate new demands on the individuals who occupy management positions within an organization. Under normal circumstances most formal organizations are characterized by a centralized hierarchical decisionmaking arrangement in which the chief executive officer—mayor, manager, chief—and other high-level administrators depend upon their formal positions in the organization to provide most of the authority or power needed to administer the organization. This approach tends to work because these administrators are usually dealing with their internal organization and the identity of participants and the lines of authority are fairly well known. In contrast the response period of emergency events may involve situations where roles and the lines of authority are ambiguous; new individuals and organizations may emerge on the scene; and new relationships, agreements, and divisions of labor need to be established. Efforts to expand the resources available for response activities may require contacts with persons outside the organization such as the heads of volunteer groups or private contractors. Such a situation requires individual leadership—the personal ability to influence others—as well as a formal administrative position in the organization.

Littlejohn identifies the following characteristics as vital to the crisis team manager:

1 The ability to adopt and support the team management philosophy
2 The capacity to be strong "team players"
3 The ability to delegate (coordinate and facilitate rather than direct and order)
4 The ability to be a strong, effective communicator
5 A high degree of salesmanship talent (persuasiveness) in order to enhance informal authority where formal authority may be limited
6 The ability to make decisions under conditions of uncertainty and ambiguity
7 The ability to synthesize facts and to make decisions by the comparison of facts and ideas
8 The ability to establish priorities and follow through in a timely order[18]

There is some evidence that higher-level managers and executives are more likely to possess these skills—good judgment and tolerance for ambiguity—than middle- and lower-level managers.[19] This finding is encouraging because chief executives usually assume command in crisis situations. Yet there is no evidence that higher-level administrators are more likely to follow a team management philosophy or to have the ability to coordinate rather than direct. In fact, in many organizations such characteristics would be contrary to centralized approaches which at least appear to be effective in dealing with the routine activities of the organization.

Thus the policy issue involves both designing a means to overcome the discontinuities between the ongoing routine needs of the organization and developing the leadership potential needed to respond to emergency events.

Going with the Flow

As a result of years of empirical studies a substantial knowledge base has been created concerning some of the common organizational and community changes associated with emergency events. According to researchers affiliated with the Disaster Research Center, these changes include (1) the development of an emergency consensus concerning the types of goals and activities that should be given priority; (2) the expansion of the citizenship role to include more emphasis on involvement, mutual support, and altruistic behaviors; (3) citizen convergence on the event site; (4) deemphasis of formal, contractual rules and impersonal relationships and increased emphasis on personal, spontaneous activities and personal relationships; (5) extension and expansion of organizational tasks and relationships and the emergence of new organizations in response to the emergency demands.[20]

These developments appear to emerge naturally and therefore represent policy issues in terms of managing their impact upon disaster events, activities, if not actually finding means to utilize them in disaster response. For example, the expansion of citizenship roles and site convergence provide a pool of volunteer workers who can be used to extend the human resources available for response activities such as search and rescue. In a similar manner the deemphasis on formal, contractual relationships can facilitate the "bending of rules" needed to obtain resources and get things done during the emergency period.

Contradiction and Paradox

Finally there are a number of contradictions and paradoxes that should not be overlooked when considering policy issues related to managing the response period of emergency events. These include the following:

1 Preparedness planning activities may help reduce the potential for negative consequences by removing hazards, training staff, and providing standard operational procedures, but they may also restrict the independent and innovative thinking needed during major emergency events.
2 Increased emphasis on command and control as part of the coordination process may also produce unintended negative effects such as ambiguity of roles and the disruption of communication.
3 Increased emphasis on centralization as part of the coordination process may produce unintended negative effects such as loss of expertise, decision-action delay, data overload, and dysfunctional distances between points of decision and action.
4 The emphasis on the return to normalcy and "present-time" ori-

entation facilitates consensus development in the postimpact emergency period but may hinder long-term mitigation efforts by avoiding conflict and returning to inappropriate practices.

5 The better managed the event—that is, the fewer the negative consequences—the less is the likelihood of external support for recovery and mitigation and the lower are the internal concern and activities designed to prepare for future events.

There are no simple solutions to issues such as these. But these issues illustrate uncertainty as one of the distinguishing characteristics of the response period.

Increasing Problem-solving Capacity between Organizations: The Role of Information in Managing the May 31, 1985, Tornado Disaster in Western Pennsylvania ⚡ Louise K. Comfort and Anthony G. Cahill

The Problem: Improving Problem-solving Capacity between Organizations in Disaster Management

Problem-solving among multiple organizations committed to the same public goal is difficult under stable conditions. In the dynamic, uncertain environment of an emergency, complexity in problem-solving escalates in direct proportion to the scale of the emergency. No single organization can meet the massive, urgent demands of a disaster. Yet interorganizational coordination requires a conceptual framework that extends beyond the routine experience of any single organization. The recurring dilemma in the interjurisdictional disaster management process is how to extend problem-solving capacity between organizations in the complex, uncertain environment of an actual disaster.

Difficulties in interorganizational problem-solving under disaster conditions are compounded by significant differences in training, facilities, experience, and conceptual grasp of the requirements for action among organizations at the diverse levels of government involved in the disaster management process. As the locus of decisionmaking shifts among the jurisdictional levels of governmental response in a major disaster, public personnel unfamiliar with the working environments and cultural mores of other governmental organizations or jurisdictions are expected to work together smoothly and efficiently according to a rationally designed organizational plan. In practice, problem-solving capacity drops repeatedly as public service personnel move from familiar operating conditions across organizational boundaries into more complex, uncertain, and dynamic settings.[1]

This problem, documented in actual emergency operations settings,[2] challenges established plans for interorganizational command and control.[3] Emergency planning is supported by legal requirements at federal, state, and county levels, but the discrepancy between formal plans for interjurisdictional coordination in disaster management and the capacity of the participating organizations to act upon those plans in an actual disaster is serious and significant.

Previous research on multiorganizational emergency response[4] has focused not on the complexity of the interjurisdictional environment in which contemporary disaster response and recovery operations occur, but on discrete phases of the emergency response process (such as search and rescue), often in remote areas. These studies report that "natural networks" of citizens, public officials, and voluntary organizations emerge to cope with small-scale disasters. These indigenous and self-initiating networks in disaster response and recovery operations, as in other domains, exhibit high levels of intragroup communication, highly similar sets of values and goals, and often unarticulated but effective systems for feedback and evaluation of performance. Such "self-evident natural networks," frequently based on geography or self-expressed membership in a group, are found to be effective mechanisms for disseminating information, catalysts for untried innovations, and important vehicles for socialization and group learning processes among members.[5] Given such characteristics, the paradox is that multiple organizations involved in disaster response and recovery operations often demonstrate high levels of cooperation and mutual assistance in tasks with clearly defined goals and limited alternatives for action over a short period of time. However, organizations have difficulty in developing or sustaining high levels of continuing coordination in tasks that are complex, uncertain, and extend over a prolonged period of time. The difficulty of marshaling and sequencing concurrent problem-solving activities is exacerbated by breakdowns in formally established communications channels and inadequate information at interdependent decision centers to support timely and appropriate action.

The complexity of the disaster environment taxes our present knowledge and methods of management. Neither the allocation of specific mission responsibilities across jurisdictional boundaries by the Federal Emergency Management Agency nor the identification of emergent processes between organizations[6] sufficiently addresses the problem of how multiple organizations, within and between jurisdictions, can collectively increase their problem-solving capacities in dynamic, uncertain conditions.

The Interorganizational Problem-solving Process

Discovering solutions to complex problems in an interorganizational environment is a dynamic process. Subject to the same constraints of human cognition and memory that characterize individual problem-solving, interorganizational problem-solving additionally requires a reconceptualization of the goals of common action and a sufficiently specific body of shared knowledge among the participating organizations to allow the concurrent formulation of constructive alternatives for coordination.[7]

Problem-solving between organizations, as for individuals, is essentially a process of discovering "what works" under specific conditions with particular resources and constraints. Herbert Simon describes problem-solving as "a process of selective trial and error, using heuristic rules derived from previous experience, that are sometimes successful in discovering means that are more or less efficacious in attaining some end. It is legitimate to regard the imperatives embodying the means as 'derived' in some sense from the imperatives embodying the ends, but the process of derivation is not a deductive process, it is one of discovery."[8]

Central to this process of discovery are the elements of information, communication, goals and norms, and reflective feedback on actions taken. Present knowledge does not allow us to specify the order, direction, and rate of flow of these elements within or between the participating organizations that lead reliably to effective interorganizational problem-solving, especially in the uncertain environment of disaster. Although it is easier to identify where the interorganizational problem-solving process breaks down in disaster management than to explain

what elements produce effective results, previous research and observation do allow the formulation of a modest set of explanatory hypotheses. The capacity for interorganizational problem-solving tends to
increase within the emergency management system as the following
four factors increase:

- □ open and continual flow of information within and between
  organizations
- □ interpersonal communication and trust between individuals across
  organizational and jurisdictional lines
- □ articulation and acknowledgement of professional values, goals,
  and norms used by participating organizations to select, assess,
  and interpret information from the disaster environment
- □ reflection and feedback among the participating organizations to
  detect and correct error and to adjust performance to the changing demands of the disaster environment

These subprocesses are interactive and dynamic. As one increases, it is
likely to activate others. As one is blocked, it tends to block others.

The challenge of disaster management is to create the working balance among the four subprocesses that results in timely and appropriate action at multiple points within the system toward the common
goal of protection of life and property. Achieving the desired balance
may be facilitated by conscious design, informed by a clear understanding of the contribution of each element to the larger process of
interorganizational problem-solving.

Open Flow of Information

Information is the basic element for increasing problem-solving capacity within the disaster management system. The flow of information
within and between participating organizations is essential to determining the existence and nature of a problem. The style, content, and
direction of this information flow is critical to eliciting the attention
and cooperation of participant organizations in the problem search.[9]
Flowing through open and two-way processes among the participating
organizations, information creates a basis of shared understanding of
emergency requirements and supports norms for collective action in
the emergency management system. The ability to gather, process,
and disseminate information quickly and accurately through the
multijurisdictional emergency management system reduces uncertainty

at each level of government, thereby increasing the effectiveness of performance for the system as a whole. Information processes, carefully designed and implemented, play an integrative role in the disaster management system.

Interpersonal Communication and Trust

Interpersonal communication drives the dynamic of the process. In mobilizing the attention, commitment, and coordinated action of multiple participants in a complex problem-solving process, the quality and style of interpersonal communication is vital.[10] Motivating participants to overcome the initial doubt, incomplete understanding, and resistance to change inherent in any problem-solving process is indeed more art than science, and the task is complicated even more by the involvement of multiple organizations. In environments of relative stability, the "personal factor"[11] contributes substantially to creating the common understanding and trust among individuals necessary for joint action. In environments of high uncertainty, this quality of interpersonal trust is essential for collective action. Building that trust in a multiorganizational operating environment is a complex process, perhaps the most difficult task involved in creating an integrated emergency management system. Extending trust is inherently a voluntary act, and withholding trust despite executive orders, administrative regulations, or policy statements is a time-honored mechanism of resistance to change. Recognizing that effective problem-solving in environments of high uncertainty requires building a set of relationships among the participants based on a common objective and shared commitments, rather than on external requirements, is a crucial first step in generating this trust.[12] Authority among the participants shifts from a base of force to one of "wisdom or spirit,"[13] and incentives for individual action within the group shift from maximizing control through increasing one's power over others to maximizing effectiveness by increasing one's understanding of the problem and acting accordingly.

Creating such a basis for collective action between organizations involves extending the reciprocal, binding relationships characteristic of community or *gemeinschaft* into the larger, more complex relationships characteristic of society or *gesellschaft*. Tönnies referred to the distinctive common bond among the members of a community as "consensus" or "the special social force and sympathy which keeps human beings together as members of a totality." To Tönnies, consensus or understanding was built through language.[14] Even in large complex organizations, such as the Emergency Management System, the style of communications within and among participants may either invite expression of differing perceptions of a given problem and encourage active engagement in responsible common action, or it may discourage such reciprocal problem-solving activity.

Articulation of Professional Norms

The explicit articulation of professional norms serves the vital function of screening the flow of information by a commonly accepted set of criteria to sort essential from extraneous information and to allocate scarce attention and resources for action. How individuals structure and label new information and measure this information against constantly changing sets of often unarticulated criteria—the "deep structure" of organizations[15]—is critically important to effective problem-solving.

Without some means of understanding the potentially divergent sets of values and goals held by multiple sets of actors, the "highly complex webs of relationships between and among individuals and groups"[16] may overwhelm rather than facilitate decisionmaking capacity between organizations.[17] This tendency is magnified under conditions of uncertainty, when information processing requirements for decisionmaking in organizations tend to increase.[18]

Systematic Feedback Mechanisms

Regular opportunities for reflection on actual performance and redesign of actions based upon incoming information complete the learning cycle, within as well as among organizations.[19] Establishing a clear connection between actions and their consequences allows individuals to assess those consequences, determine the utility of their actions, and discard ineffective actions in favor of an alternative.[20]

While such opportunities may develop spontaneously among individuals and in small, naturally occurring networks,[21] they require deliberate design in larger, more complex organizational environments.[22] In moving from individual to intraorganizational to interorganizational action, the feedback linkage becomes less direct. It is less certain what actions produce what consequences. Problem-solving performance drops as trials made in error are not corrected. Information essential to appropriate action is not transmitted to relevant participants. Uncertainty regarding the outcome of proposed actions increases, and learning among the participants decreases.

Competing demands for attention from many participants engaged in diverse activities tend to diffuse the common focus on a single problem,[23] and the problem-solving capacity of both individuals and organizations drops. The effectiveness of coordinated action depends upon the extent to which multiple organizations can concurrently identify problems in their respective performances and adjust their actions accordingly in order to accomplish their shared goal.[24]

In summary, the concept of interorganizational problem-solving moves the level of interaction among individuals to a magnitude of abstraction that exceeds the limits of human short-term memory and information-processing capacity. The model of an integrated emergency management system, based upon this concept, simply exceeds the cognitive abilities of human decisionmakers, without technical assistance or external memory devices. The problems generated by a massive disaster are so large and so complex that they strain the problem-solving capacity of managers relying upon traditional administrative practices of command and control.

In the dynamic environment of a disaster, the four principal components—information, communication, goals and norms, and reflective feedback—of interorganizational problem-solving operate with varying levels of intensity and influence upon the participating organizations over the differing time phases of the disaster management process. Yet the desired coordination in interorganizational performance is not likely to occur without deliberate design, especially in large-scale disaster and recovery operations involving multiple organizations interacting across jurisdictional boundaries.[25] This recurring strain upon interorganizational problem-solving capacity was vividly illustrated in the emergency management process activated in response to the May 31, 1985, tornado disaster in western Pennsylvania.

Interorganizational Problem-solving
in the May 31, 1985, Tornado Disaster
in Western Pennsylvania

Early in the evening of May 31, 1985, a series of tornadoes struck western Pennsylvania with devastating force. In less than five hours, four separate sets of tornadoes ripped through thirteen counties, destroying virtually everything in their paths. The tornadoes left sixty-six people dead and caused an estimated $260 million in property damage.[26] Confronted with massive destruction, local and state officials requested a presidential declaration of disaster in order to implement federal policies on disaster relief and recovery. On June 3 President Reagan declared ten counties in western Pennsylvania a disaster area.[27] The president's declaration activated the federal government's policies in the recovery and reconstruction phases of the disaster, and at that point the entire interjurisdictional emergency management system became actively involved in the response and recovery phases of the disaster process.

The degree of devastation in the affected areas was such that no single individual, organization, or jurisdiction could cope with it alone. The full complement of policies, plans, and resources available through the interjurisdictional emergency management system directed by FEMA was in effect. In short, the best efforts of current administrative policies and practices were placed in operation in response to this disaster.

The tornado disaster provided a sobering but timely opportunity to observe the activation of the interorganizational emergency management system and to assess its capacity for problem-solving. In the two weeks following the disaster, three groups were interviewed: ninety-seven citizens who experienced the disaster; 139 local government officials, ninety-two of whom were actively involved in the response process, from seven of the ten affected counties in western Pennsylvania; and ten federal officials who were responsible for administering federal programs of disaster assistance in the thirteen counties struck by tornadoes in Federal Region III.[28]

Specifically, our research was directed towards assessing the capacities of organizations involved in the disaster to increase interorganizational problem-solving as measured by the degree to which the four principal components were reported to be in operation.

- □ *open flow of information*: To what extent did decisionmakers at each level of problem-solving have adequate information to support appropriate and timely action to meet their responsibilities in the disaster management process?
- □ *interpersonal communication and trust*: To what extent did communications flow between as well as within groups and organizations involved in disaster response and recovery activities? To

Table 1. Time of Local Officials' Warning of
Approaching Tornado: "When did you first learn that
a tornado was in your vicinity?"

Warning time	N	Relative frequency (in percent)
4–6 hours	1	1.1
3–4 hours	3	3.3
2–3 hours	1	1.1
1–2 hours	16	17.8
30–59 minutes	6	6.7
15–29 minutes	8	8.9
5–14 minutes	15	16.7
Less than 5 minutes	30	33.3
No warning	1	1.1
Afterward	9	10.0
Total	90	100.0

Valid cases = 90
Missing cases = 2
Missing data excluded; percentages calculated on N.

what extent did these communication patterns generate or reflect
trust among the participants?

☐ *articulation of professional goals and norms*: To what extent were
citizens and officials aware of the risk to their lives and property?
To what extent were professional plans and procedures for emergency response developed and implemented?

☐ *systematic feedback mechanisms*: To what extent were those
involved in the disaster response and recovery process given the
opportunity to reflect on the process and to make suggestions for
future change?

In three of the four areas, study findings stand in sharp contrast to
the desired goals of interorganizational problem-solving. In reference
to the flow of information, study findings document serious discrepancies in the amount and sources of information available to citizens,
local officials, and federal officials, limiting their respective capacities
for action in the emergency management system. In the formal allocation of responsibilities in the Integrated Emergency Management System (IEMS) proposed by FEMA, local officials have the legal responsibil-

Table 2. Sources of Local Officials' Tornado
Warnings: "How did you learn that a tornado
was in your vicinity?"

Response	N	Relative frequency (in percent)
Neighbor/friend/ relative	4	4.6
C.B. radio	4	4.6
Radio news	4	4.6
Television broadcast	9	10.2
Communication from public service worker	13	14.8
Siren/bell	1	1.1
County emergency dispatch system	38	43.1
National Weather Service teletype	3	3.4
Other	12	13.6
Total	88	100.0

Valid cases = 88
Missing cases = 4
Missing data excluded; percentages calculated on N.

ity for first response in a disaster. Tables 1–4 show the pattern of response reported by ninety-two local officials in the tornado disaster.

As shown in table 1, the majority of local officials reported some warning of the approaching tornadoes. Of the officials responding to the question, 23.2 percent (twenty-one out of ninety) learned of the tornado more than an hour before it occurred; 35.2 percent had between five and fifty-nine minutes warning, but 32.3 percent had less than five minutes warning. Table 2 shows that 61.3 percent of the local officials learned of the approaching tornado through official communication channels—the County Emergency Dispatch System, National Weather

Table 3. Actions Taken by Local Officials
as the Tornado Approached: What did you do when you realized
the tornado was actually coming toward you?"

Action	N	Relative frequency (in percent)
Tried to warn community	45	38.1
Tried to contact other public service personnel	7	5.9
Tried to contact family members	20	16.9
Tried to warn friends and neighbors	8	6.8
Sought shelter immediately	7	5.9
Other	23	19.6
Believed there was no danger	8	6.8
Total	118	100.0

N (actions) = 118
Missing data excluded; percentages calculated on N (actions).

Service teletype, or communication from another public service official, while 24 percent learned of the danger through unofficial means —radio, television, family, friends, or neighbors. Once they received the information the large majority of local officials took action as reported in table 3. Of the 118 actions reported, fifty-two (or 44 percent) were directed toward trying to warn the community or to alert other public service personnel. Table 4 cites the methods used to warn citizens of the approaching tornado, reporting that 44 percent (twenty-six of fifty-nine) included preestablished community warning or public emergency broadcast systems.

These data show that the emergency management system—with some slippage—was functioning at the local level of government during the disaster. The majority of local officials received warning of the tornadoes and acted upon that information to warn the citizens of their communities with the means available to them.

In startling contrast, however, was the reception of that information by the citizens. Table 5 reports that the large majority of the citizens, 71.3 percent (sixty-two out of eighty-seven responding to the question) received less than five minutes warning before the tornado struck. Only 5.7 percent (five citizens) learned of the approaching tornadoes an hour or more before they occurred. Further, as shown in table 6, only one citizen out of ninety-two responding to the question (1 percent) learned of the tornadoes through an official emergency warning system. Almost half of the citizens (49.1 percent) learned of the danger through self-perception or informal means—they heard it or saw it, or learned of the tornadoes through family, neighbors, or friends. Another 29.2 percent learned of the tornadoes through unofficial means, radio, television or C.B. radio.

These data document a serious breakdown in the flow of information between local officials and the citizens, limiting the problem-solving capacity of both groups as they sought to respond to the staggering demands of the tornado disaster. The discrepancy in warning time between citizens and local officials is summarized in table 7. A difference of means test calculated on the findings reported for the two

Table 4. Methods Used by Local Officials
to Warn Their Community: "What means, if any,
did you use to alert citizens of the community to
the approaching tornado?"

Method	N	Relative frequency (in percent)
Community warning system	13	22.0
Public Emergency Broadcast System	13	22.0
Vehicle with loudspeaker	7	11.9
Telephone ring-down	9	15.3
House-to-house canvass	3	5.1
Other	14	23.7
Total	59	100.0

N (method) = 59
Missing data excluded; percentages calculated on N (methods).

Table 5. Time of Citizens' Warning of
Approaching Tornado: "When did you first learn that a tornado
was in your vicinity?"

Warning time	N	Relative frequency (in percent)
3–4 hours	1	1.1
2–3 hours	2	2.3
1–2 hours	2	2.3
30–59 minutes	2	2.3
15–29 minutes	8	9.3
5–14 minutes	9	10.3
Less than 5 minutes	62	71.3
Afterward	1	1.1
Total	87	100.0

N = 97
Valid cases = 87
Missing cases = 10
Missing data excluded; percentages calculated on N.

groups resulted in a T value of 2.90 with a significance level of <.004, or a probability of less than 4 in 1,000 that the differences reported between the two groups could have occurred by chance.

At the federal level, the same discontinuity of information flow adversely affected the problem-solving capacity of federal officials in the intergovernmental administration of disaster relief. Table 8 presents a weighted index of what information federal officials would have found most useful in assessing the impact of the tornadoes, as well as how much information was available to them on each characteristic. As the data show, they rated the information available to them as at best middling (3.1 on a five-point scale) to no information at all (1 on a five-point scale).

Especially significant is the comparison of available to desired information regarding emergency plans for local government. Under federal guidelines for the integrated emergency management system, each community is expected to develop its own emergency plan and relay it to the next level of government, the county. The county in turn develops an emergency plan for its jurisdictional responsibilities, incorporating plans and information from the set of communities within its boundaries into its data base. The counties relay this information on to the state, which in sequence passes it on to the federal administration in emergency management. According to the official plan, federal officials should have full access to vital characteristics regarding communities involved in any disaster. Again, these data reveal that the present flow of information does not adequately support the problem-solving process between jurisdictional levels in the emergency management process.

In the second area—that of interpersonal communication—the data show that despite the interorganizational and interjurisdictional demands of the emergency management process, intragroup communication was high while intergroup communication was low. Each group communicated more frequently and more easily with those in its small, informal network than with those at different jurisdictional levels. The greatest number of communications were to family, friends, and neighbors while only 11.1 percent of communications were to local officials.

When asked to evaluate how well local, state, and federal agencies worked together to gather, analyze, or share needed information, 21.9 percent of local officials responded "not at all effective" or "not so effective," while 25.5 percent responded "very" or "quite" effective. More significant, nearly one-third (32.6 percent) did not respond to

Table 6. Sources of Citizens' Tornado Warnings:
"How did you learn that a tornado
was in your vicinity?"

Response	N	Relative frequency (in percent)
Heard it	4	4.4
Saw it	25	27.2
Family	3	3.3
Neighbor, friend	13	14.2
C.B. radio	1	1.0
Radio	9	9.8
TV	17	18.4
Emergency warning	1	1.0
Other	19	20.7
Total	92	100.0

Valid cases = 92
Missing cases = 5
Missing data excluded; percentages calculated on N.

Table 7. Citizens' and Local Officials' Warning of
Approaching Tornados

Scale of warning time before tornado		Citizens		Local officials	
		N	Percent	N	Percent
10	4–6 hours	0	0	1	1.1
9	3–4 hours	1	1.2	3	3.3
8	2–3 hours	2	2.3	1	1.1
7	1–2 hours	2	2.3	16	17.8
6	30–59 minutes	2	2.3	6	6.7
5	15–29 minutes	8	9.2	8	8.9
4	5–14 minutes	9	10.3	15	16.7
3	Less than 5 minutes	62	71.3	30	33.3
2	No warning	1	1.2	1	1.1
1	Afterward	0	0	9	10.0
	Total	87	100.1	90	100.0

For citizens: valid cases = 87; missing = 10; mean = 3.609; S.D. = 1.315. For officials: valid cases = 90; missing = 2; mean = 4.378; S.D. = 2.134. Difference of means = .769; standard error = .265; T-value = 2.90; DF = 149; P<.004. Missing data excluded; statistics calculated on valid cases. Percentages are rounded to one decimal point.

this question, demonstrating a reluctance to make a judgment about the effectiveness of interagency performance on this critical task. Thus, more than half (54.5 percent) of the local officials responded negatively or did not respond at all to this question on interjurisdictional cooperation. Recognizing a lack of trust between jurisdictional levels, federal officials reported the need for continual interchange of information among participating public agencies to improve the emergency management process. (At the Disaster Field Office in Meadville, Pennsylvania, the federal coordinating officer scheduled daily staff meetings to coordinate information within and between federal and state agencies, two of which were observed by the senior author.)

On a related issue, local officials did not have available to them during the response process advanced communications technology which would have facilitated both intragroup and intergroup communication. Of 110 facilities represented by respondents in the survey, only 3 (2.7 percent) had access to interactive telephone and computer systems. Slightly more than half of the facilities (51.8 percent) used the county dispatch system, while more than one-third (35.5 percent) used a community dispatch system. Ten percent of the cities used telephone switchboards, which were vulnerable to disruption in an emergency.

Further, officials relied heavily on local police and fire dispatch systems to communicate both incoming requests for assistance (45.7 percent, or 42 of the 92 local officials participating in the survey reported using local dispatch systems for this purpose) and outgoing messages across service agencies (41.6 percent, or 38 of the 92 respondents). These local dispatch systems are vulnerable to overload in a disaster due to limited channel capacity, but in most small jurisdictions, they

Table 8. Weighted Index of Community-related Information Desired by Federal Officials in the Administration of Disaster Relief

Rank	Information characteristic	Index of desired information	Index of available information
1	Residential concentrations	4.3	3.1
2	Population concentrations	4.2	3.5
3	Emergency plans for local governments	3.3	2.7
3	Utilities	3.3	3.3
4	Transportation access	3.0	2.9
5	Industrial plants and construction	2.8	1.5
6	Medical facilities	2.7	1.8
7	Infrastructure: roads, bridges, tunnels	2.1	1.8
8	Public broadcast facilities	1.9	2.5

N = 9

Scale: 5 = most helpful; 1 = least helpful. Index of desired information: Original ratings of nine federal officials for each of these characteristics (5 = most helpful to 1 = least helpful) were multiplied by their respective weights and divided by N to arrive at the value shown. Index of available information: Original rating of ten federal officials for each of these characteristics (5 = complete information available; 1 = no information available) were multiplied by their respective weights and the totals divided by N to arrive at the value shown.

represent the best means of communication available. Clearly, local officials need improved communications facilities for effective problem-solving.

In reference to the third area, the articulation of professional norms and goals (criteria used to screen and evaluate information to facilitate problem solving) 48.1 percent of the citizens interviewed reported that they "never got information" from public officials or agencies about what to do in a tornado. Fewer citizens, but still over one-third (34.8 percent) reported they received no information from public officials regarding other kinds of emergencies. More vivid were the responses from citizens who voluntarily stated they had "never seen a tornado before" and "didn't know what to do." In contrast, 65 percent of the citizens stated that warning systems would have helped them most to protect themselves, their families, and their property from the tornado. The majority of citizens acknowledged that the introduction of professional means of identifying the level of risk in emergencies would help them to take protective measures. Without public education to assist citizens in interpreting the symptoms of a tornado and in taking appropriate safety measures, emergency warnings or public announcements by local officials have little effect.

When asked for their professional judgment regarding the effectiveness of the emergency plans in their communities, only 12 percent of the local officials who participated in disaster response activities reported "very effective." Nearly twice that proportion, 22.8 percent of the officials, reported the plans in their communities to be "not so effective," "not at all effective," or reported "no plan in community." These data demonstrate that local officials were operating to meet the demands of the disaster in their communities without the degree of professional planning that would have facilitated their emergency response process.

Federal officials, as well, reported the need for better management of information among the organizations participating in the emergency response and recovery process. Individual comments stated the desirability of more professional training and interaction between the jurisdictional levels in the emergency management system.

On the final requirement for an effective interorganizational problem-solving process—reflection and redesign—all three groups surveyed evidenced thoughtful review of the process. Of the citizen respondents, 91 percent had suggestions for change, focusing primarily on better means of warning and information flow, professional planning, and education. Among local officials nearly 47 percent offered suggestions for change, emphasizing the need for improved communication, organization, coordination, and cooperation. Federal officials stressed the importance of managing the information for their decision process, recommending the utilization of appropriate computer technology to assist in coping with both the great volume and rapid rate of change in information involved in disaster management.

These findings document the importance of reflection and redesign for the problem-solving process. More significant, they demonstrate that the participants in this tornado disaster are aware of this need and are already engaging in reflection on how to improve the problem-solving process for future emergencies. This is a critical stage for the thoughtful review of performance at each level of the interorganizational emergency management process and a necessary first step in its redesign for more effective performance as a system.

Toward Increasing Problem-solving
Capacity between Organizations

The data from the surveys of citizens, local officials, and federal officials involved in the tornado disaster in western Pennsylvania underscore the importance of the four components addressed in this chapter as essential to interorganizational problem-solving. In this case it is clear that the information requirements for interorganizational problem-solving in a disaster of this magnitude and scope overwhelmed existing patterns of information flow, professional planning, and interpersonal communication. Citizens, local officials, and federal officials found serious discrepancies between the amount and kinds of information available to them and the amount and kinds of information that would have helped them to meet the demands of the disaster more quickly, appropriately, and efficiently. Interorganizational problem-solving requires a distinctive mode of information gathering, processing, and dissemination that will extend human problem-solving capacities in complex, uncertain settings.

The most interesting finding of the study, however, is that significant proportions of each group surveyed are aware of this discrepancy between available and desired information. This awareness, highest immediately following a disaster, can serve as a vital element in initiating change at each level in the intergovernmental emergency management process. Advances in telecommunications and computer technology provide the technical capability for interorganizational decision support. Designing and implementing their appropriate use becomes central to the effective development of interorganizational problem-solving in an integrated emergency management system. Increasing the technical capacity to manage information would facilitate and extend the substantial degree of interorganizational learning demonstrated by citizens and public officials involved in the emergency response and recovery activities following the western Pennsylvania tornado disaster.

The Impact of Stress on Emergency Service Personnel: Policy Issues in Emergency Response
⚡ Jeffrey T. Mitchell

The Problem

Few policy issues related to disaster management have been so effectively ignored as that of stress and its effects upon emergency responders. Until very recently disaster managers and workers alike have functioned under what amounts to a "nonpolicy." That is, they have, through lack of knowledge of the stress problem, continued to work at the scenes of disasters, hoping that psychological stress would not have an impact on them. They have falsely believed that their training, experience, or luck would prevent them from encountering the negative aftereffects of overwhelmingly stressful events.

The absence of an adequate stress policy for emergency workers and their managers led tornado relief workers in western Pennsylvania in 1985 to work thirty-six hours without adequate rest, food, and relief, reducing their effectiveness in the relief effort and creating, for some, recurring problems in public service performance.

The same nonpolicy on stress was evident in the recent El Salvador earthquake (October 10, 1986) relief efforts. Insufficient numbers of rescue workers produced a situation that required excessively long hours of rescue work at the scene of collapsed buildings. Some rescuers accepted thirty-six- to forty-eight-hour tours of duty in the intense effort to get trapped victims out alive in the immediate postdisaster period. Without a preplanned stress management policy, workers were subjected to erratic and poorly timed rest breaks and long hours without food. Even though a disaster psychologist was at the scene as an advisor, the immediate demands of the disaster preempted operations managers from considering or initiating a stress management policy for rescue personnel. As a result, rescue workers experienced severe fatigue, some physical illness, and an overall less efficient use of their potential capacity in the rescue effort. Emotional aftereffects also tended to be more tenacious than they might have been in the presence of an appropriate preplanned stress management policy.[1]

In contrast, when stress effects on emergency personnel are considered prior to the incident, the impact can be significantly reduced. In a marked departure from the usual nonpolicy on stress, the Los Angeles Fire Department quickly implemented at least the rudiments of a stress management policy during operations at the Cerritos plane crash. The fire department had previously reviewed other situations and found stress to be a significant factor in the deterioration of performance of rescue personnel. Command officers arranged to have mental health professionals brought to the scene for immediate counseling and stress education when necessary. In addition, prior service crews were rotated through the disaster site on a regularly scheduled basis and their exposure to distressing actions was reduced. Crews were given opportunity to ventilate their feelings and reactions before being returned to their normal duty stations, and psychological debriefings were held for all department personnel who worked at the scene. Those debriefings were held by mental health professional staff ten days after the incident. As a result, fewer service personnel reported stress-related problems, which are common after such events.

The situations cited above clearly indicate that stress policies for disaster workers are most effective when established before a disaster. Otherwise they are unlikely to be implemented during the disaster.

Disaster managers have realized only very recently that disaster workers are subject to the same psychological syndrome frequently encountered by combat troops—called post-traumatic stress disorder. This disorder is described in the third edition of the *Diagnostic and Statistical Manual* (1980) of the American Psychiatric Association as an anxiety reaction experienced by almost everyone who is exposed to an overwhelmingly frightening or horrifying event. Those who experience such horrible events as war, disasters, physical and emotional violence, extreme threat, or major loss frequently display physical, cognitive, emotional, and behavioral symptoms that may last for weeks and months after the terrible event. Some individuals, especially those who lack a supportive environment capable of counteracting the aftershocks of an emotionally powerful event, may experience symptoms of post-traumatic stress disorder for many years after the event. Some experiences are so catastrophic to some individuals that they are unable to recover completely during their entire lives.

The common signs and symptoms of post-traumatic stress disorder that have been noted in those with the condition, including disaster workers, are intrusive memories of the event, disturbing dreams, an intensified startle response, a loss of interest in significant activities, feelings of depression and estrangement, sleep disturbance, intense guilt feelings, memory impairment, and avoidance of certain activities that remind them of the traumatic event.

In an as yet unpublished study, this author has found that more than 86 percent of disaster workers experience some symptoms of post-traumatic stress disorder within twenty-four hours after their experiences at the scenes of major emergencies. Roughly 40 percent display symptoms three weeks after the event and about 20 percent will still be experiencing symptoms six months to a year after the event. Approximately 10 percent may be profoundly distressed by the event. That is, they are unable to continue in that line of work, they experience a personality change, their marriages and family life are disturbed, or they become physically ill.

For a constellation of reasons most managers and workers involved in disaster operations have resisted virtually all attempts to expand the knowledge base associated with disaster stress. Almost no attempt has been made, in the majority of American communities, to develop a set of disaster stress policies for emergency workers.

Resistance to the Acknowledgment of Stress

Among the many reasons that appear to be the foundation of the resistance to the development of both a knowledge base and policies for managing stress in disaster operations, the following are the most noteworthy:

The Macho Image. Many emergency personnel, at all levels of operations and management, believe that they are tough and must maintain a stance devoid of all emotional reaction in the face of catastrophic situations. The macho image is, in reality, an exaggerated extension of the very legitimate need to maintain the hyperalert status necessary to perform the demanding work of emergency intervention in a variety of dangerous and difficult situations.

Fear. A number of emergency personnel believe that they will be blocked from promotions if it were to become known that they had experienced psychological reactions to a disastrous event. They also fear that the public and, more important, their coworkers might lose respect for them if they admit that they are vulnerable to those events.

Denial. Emergency workers are usually quick to suppress their emotions and keep up a calm facade in the face of turmoil. They do not admit that the disaster is having any effect upon them. Perhaps, as Duston[2] points out, when denial is present in those under severe stress it indicates terror on the part of those who continue to use the defense in the face of obvious facts.[3]

Public Resistance. The public has long believed that emergency workers are specially trained to cope with their work and are therefore invulnerable to personal disruptions. The public functions under a false belief that emergency workers will not be able to rescue them and assist them in their emergency if those rescuers are vulnerable to the stress associated with witnessing human misery.

Economics. Training courses to assist emergency personnel in preventing or mitigating stress reactions after disaster work may be costly. Likewise, acknowledging that disaster stress exists and that it is extremely harmful to the health, job function, and personal lives of emergency personnel necessitates the development of policies to deal with the problem which might also put a demand on dwindling resources.

Costs of Stress to Individual
Emergency Workers and to Public Services

The many reasons that explain why stress policies have not yet been developed are not sufficient to warrant a continuation of the neglect of this important issue. In spite of the resistance to expanding the knowledge base associated with disaster stress in emergency personnel, some researchers during the last decade have been accumulating data which indicate that a large percentage of emergency workers are experiencing powerful physical and psychological "aftershocks" to their work in disasters. Emergency responders have displayed a wide range of physical, cognitive, and emotional symptoms during and after work at a disaster.[4] Nightmares, insomnia, depression, mental confusion, marital discord, job dysfunction, irritability, excessive fatigue, anxiety, gastrointestinal disturbance, migraines, and amnesia have persisted for months and sometimes years after emergency operations at an event had ended.[5] A recent study of 360 emergency personnel indicates that 313, or 86.9 percent, encountered noticeable psychological and physical symptoms as a result of their work at one or more major emergency events.[6]

Various emergency services across the nation have reported increased attrition rates among their personnel in the twenty-four months following a disaster. Losses of personnel have been estimated between 1 percent and 50 percent depending upon the circumstances of a disaster. Studies are now being organized to confirm these preliminary reports. If the reports are true, the losses to emergency systems are evident and often staggering. For example, according to emergency medical administrators, it usually costs a community between $6,000 and $12,000 to train a single paramedic. If several paramedics from the same community are required to leave their positions as a direct result of post-traumatic stress disorder suffered after being exposed to a disaster, the community may be hard pressed to find the funds to train replacements properly. Only now, in the light of a new awareness of the effects of stressful events on emergency personnel, are efforts being made to collect better data regarding the economic and management losses to public service agencies.

The Immediate Impact of Disaster Stress

Direct work with people in and of itself is emotionally stressful.[7] The added responsibility for the well-being and/or lives of others has been implicated as a source of serious stress in health care workers[8] and in police officers.[9] Excessive contact with people in need of help produces feelings of anger, embarrassment, anxiety, frustration, fear, and despair.[10]

Emotional consequences of severe stress are not the only effects encountered by emergency workers. Serious disease entities may arise in many people exposed to severe and/or recurrent stress. Mulvihill points out that the wear and tear caused by stress on the body produces structural changes such as the deformities of arthritis, stress ulcers, and hormonal imbalances.[11] Frankenhauser suggests that increases of catecholamines as a result of stress cause functional disturbances in body organs and systems that may eventually lead to disease.[12] Levine has associated high levels of the stress-triggered body hormones with psychosis, convulsions, and electrical brain wave activity disruption.[13] Holsti found that individuals subjected to high stress experienced distortions in time perspective and had increased error rates.[14] Individuals under stress also initiated less activity than usual and became more rigid in their thinking. Problem-solving behaviors decreased substantially. Keena found that emergency medical technicians experienced a 50 percent injury rate when they were working to free trapped auto accident victims but only a 22 percent injury rate while working at scenes where only property and no victims were involved.[15]

The range of symptoms of stress, both in quality and quantity, is impressive. Byl and Sykes report fatigue, dizziness, and anxiety in stressed workers.[16] Sedgwick found the following common symptoms exhibited in persons experiencing stress: withdrawal, somatic complaints, decreased ability to think clearly, an increase in distractability, self-consciousness, and reduced ability to master tasks.[17] Rigidity and inflexibility were reported by Lazarus,[18] while Titchener and Kapp found disorganization, sluggishness, poor emotional control, grief, despair, sleep disturbance, nightmares, obsessions, depression, anger, visual flashbacks, and feelings of helplessness and inadequacy in individuals faced with overwhelming stress such as in a disaster.[19] Mitchell has noted the appearance of similar symptoms in emergency personnel.[20] Lippert and Ferrara reported that police officers who take a human life in the performance of their duties experience strong feelings of guilt, anger, immobilization, and denial.[21]

Some emergency workers who were able to demonstrate proficiency in previous stressful situations may decompensate upon continued exposure to severe stress. They become gradually less functional and may develop crippling phobic avoidance behaviors. This very phenomenon was noted during the Second World War in England. Veteran fire brigades and rescue workers became increasingly more dysfunctional in the presence of repeated bombing raids. They reacted to the same types of dangers with decreasing activity levels, helplessness, aimless wandering, apathy, or mute, motionless behavior.[22] The mental stresses associated with disasters have been known to contribute to self-destructive behavior on the part of rescuers.[23]

Long-term Effects of Stress on Emergency Workers

Emergency personnel will often suppress emotional reactions experienced during the emergency because of the fear of being incapacitated by those emotions. The feelings may be transformed later into nightmares, flashbacks, and other expressions such as humor, excessive physical activity, or some maladaptive techniques such as emotional outbursts.[24] Frederick states that these symptoms and many others "can occur long after the crash site has been cleared and the physical injuries have been treated."[25]

Freeman noted that police officers who worked at the scene of an aircraft disaster were requesting counseling and other psychological support for a year afterward.[26] The use of psychological counseling services rose from five (11.9 percent) of forty-two police officers before the disaster to eleven of the forty-two (30.9 percent) in the year following the disaster. Some officers and other emergency workers had to be retired after working at an aircraft crash site.[27]

Eight weeks after the crash of Air Florida 90 in Washington, D.C., emergency service personnel (fire, emergency medical, police, and their administrators and supervisors) were still experiencing the following symptoms: anxiety, fear, feelings of guilt, depression, grief, doubts about themselves and their capabilities, anger, irritability, sleep disturbance, nightmares, nausea, withdrawal from contact with others, lowered sexual and eating appetites, visual flashbacks, a strong need to talk about the incident over and over again and to read printed material about and view still and motion photography of the incident, concern for the well-being of coworkers, excessive denial of any symptoms, a total withdrawal from any discussions or photographs of the incident, a need to fix blame, a desire to talk with the survivors they had aided, a strong need for reassurance that they had done their best, a very strong feeling of being unappreciated by superiors, and resentment for not having received appropriate credit in the media for their work during the disaster.[28]

Psychological Defenses Employed by Emergency Workers

Withdrawal is among the most common of the dynamics utilized by people under stress.[29] Emergency personnel as well are prone to use this less effective coping behavior in their efforts to manage their stress.[30] Withdrawal is usually accompanied by a decreased sensitivity to others and a focus on oneself.[31]

Often withdrawal from patients increases feelings of guilt and shame for emergency workers, especially those in the field of medicine.[32] They may then attempt to shift their attitudes about patients from positive to negative. For example, a passive patient is thought of as an object such as a rock or a vegetable.[33] If patients can be thought of in this way, it is easier to withdraw from them without feeling guilty. When it is not possible to think of people in the negative, emergency workers are likely to turn some of their frustration inward on themselves and the end result is a serious depression.[34]

Emergency personnel often attempt to suppress unpleasant memories. They may refuse to discuss their daily activities with their spouses and loved ones. They claim that this is to protect their loved ones from the horrors they have experienced. But it also serves very well as a buffer which prevents them from reliving those horrors.[35]

Many emergency workers frequently experience a problem in winding down after they have been exposed to the almost daily horrors of death, destruction, and coping with the needs of hurting human beings. The knowledge that a lowered alert status can lead to small mistakes which can have catastrophic consequences causes them to choose to remain in a chronic state of being hyperalert even when off duty. This hyperalert condition may be related to the psychological theory that cues about danger may also imply cues about one's security.[36] Most inactive emergency personnel do not know how to truly relax and use their off-duty time to their benefit.[37]

Mitigating the Impact of Disaster Stress

C. J. Frederick, the former director of the National Institute of Mental Health's Disaster Assistance Program, states that the severe disturbance in the physical and emotional equilibrium of emergency workers can be countered. He suggests that "appropriate mental health services available in moments of crisis and disaster could . . . reduce the long-term psychological and somatic impact of the event."[38]

The Critical Incident Stress Debriefing

Mitchell has developed a psychological debriefing process for emergency personnel.[39] The group process, called the Critical Incident Stress Debriefing (CISD), is led by a trained mental health professional and is designed to allow emergency workers to ventilate their feelings after a major situation. A CISD generally begins with an introduction in which the ground rules of the process are spelled out and the participants are encouraged to keep everything discussed confidential. Next, participants are asked to re-create the situation by providing as many pertinent details about the event as possible. They are then asked to describe their first thoughts related to the situation and then their reactions to it. They discuss what bothered them most and the signs and symptoms they experienced during and after the crisis event. The CISD then becomes an educational forum in which the participants hear how normal their reactions are in light of what others have experienced in similar events. Time is alloted for questions and for planning further steps to mitigate the impact of the event on the lives of the personnel.

The CISD process assists the majority of emergency personnel in understanding their reactions and it reassures them that what they are experiencing is normal and common to most of those who were involved in the incident. The CISD also allows for group support and an opportunity to find those who may be in need of short- or long-term therapy.

The CISD process is a mixture of exploring reactions, emotions, symptoms, myths, beliefs, and thoughts of emergency workers after an unsettling experience. Opportunity is also given in the typical debriefing to provide didactic material on the usual stress reactions that can be found in emergency workers.[40]

The CISD process has been employed in over 150 major events, including twenty-five events that are classified as disasters, such as the Barneveld, Wisconsin, tornado in June 1984. Reports from over a thousand emergency workers involved in debriefings have been very encouraging. They generally report that they have been able to express themselves to each other and to a concerned and well-trained clinician. They express relief that they were not alone in their reactions to a powerful event. The reassurance provided in the debriefing encourages them to express rather than suppress their emotions.[41] Long-term destructive aftereffects of a traumatic incident are less likely under such circumstances. The establishment of a network of concerned coworkers is often the main feature of a CISD which discourages isolation and emotional suppression. Further studies to assess the effectiveness of the CISD process are now under way.

Special teams of well-trained mental health professionals should be developed in the larger population centers of the nation, and these teams should work in concert with emergency personnel who share in the responsibility of assuring adequate mental health services in the form of psychological debriefings and short- and long-term therapy. Where teams are not available, mutual aid agreements between jurisdictions or a team organized and supported by a federal agency may be an alternative. These debriefing teams, which might be called "Emergency Services Support Units" or "Critical Incident Stress Debriefing Teams," would consist of fire, police, emergency medical, and psychosocial personnel. The teams could respond to the scene, should that be necessary, and provide on-site emergency mental health consultation to the commanders of field units as well as crisis intervention and emotional support to emergency workers and disaster victims. On-site consultation occurs far less frequently, however, than the other services of such a team.

In the majority of cases the Emergency Services Support Unit is brought into action in the days or weeks following any critical incident that has sufficient emotional power to cause overwhelming emotional reactions in emergency personnel. Group debriefings or individual short-term therapy can be provided, ideally, twenty-four to seventy-two hours after the impact of a critical incident or at any time thereafter when it appears most appropriate. The most effective teams are those that have been formed before the disaster, since it takes several months to develop the membership of a team, train the personnel, and advise the emergency workers that such a service is available to them. Start-up costs are usually the greatest. About a dozen teams have been developed across the nation at the time of the writing of this essay. Costs have ranged from between $3,000 and $8,000 to create an operational team. Many teams rely on volunteer mental health personnel or on already existing personnel in employee assistance programs or community crisis intervention programs. Each team needs a clinical director who is a mental health professional plus several mental health professionals who are team leaders or facilitators. Teams must also have peer counselors or facilitators who are carefully selected from among the public safety personnel. A team coordinator is a must. This person sets up the times and places for a debriefing and alerts the team. Some teams have a designated administrator in a lead agency. That is, a hospital, a fire department, or a police department may support the team and may have an administrator who assures that they have stationery, telephones, and transportation.

An Emergency Services Support Unit also serves several other roles, including follow-up at thirty-, sixty-, or ninety-day intervals and also at the first anniversary of a major traumatic incident. The provision of education regarding stress and crisis can also be a function of the Emergency Services Support Unit. Much of the material provided in educational programs may have a preventive value for emergency personnel and may mitigate the effects of critical incidents on them.

Team members need to be carefully selected. Work on an Emergency Services Support Unit or a Critical Incident Stress Debriefing Team is strenuous and many emergency personnel and clinicians are unsuited for such work. Emergency personnel who are chosen should have the respect of their fellow workers and should be known to be mature, stable, sensitive individuals who are able to maintain an extremely high degree of confidentiality. Many emergency service team members can be trained to provide crisis intervention for their fellow workers until a debriefing session can be organized by a mental health professional. In some cases a certain team member from the emergency services area may become so proficient as to serve as a cotherapist with the clinician.

Clinicians who serve on the team must be dynamic in their approach. The traditional Freudian or Rogerian styles usually do not work well for emergency personnel. What is necessary is a therapist with a directive style who is also very supportive in his or her approach. The therapist should be well versed in crisis intervention theory, should be experienced with the crisis intervention approach to therapy, and should have an understanding of stress, particularly post-traumatic stress disorder. Clinicians should also be experienced in group process and should have a thorough knowledge of human communication processes. Those who serve on the team should be cross-trained in emergency operations and disaster psychology. They should be willing to ride along occasionally with emergency workers in order to gain an understanding of the type of work these people do as well as their personalities.

Other Policies and Strategies for Mitigating Disaster Stress

One of the clearest policies that needs to be established is that of extensive pre-incident training. Every community should set aside the resources and the time necessary to prepare their emergency personnel for the exhausting task of disaster intervention. This training should not be limited to the technical aspects of emergency operations but should also include elements of stress management and the recognition of the warning signals of stress. Disaster workers need to understand the importance of teamwork and individual and organizational cooperation during interventions in the field. It is very important to emergency workers that they have well-developed communication skills.

Unclear, imprecise, lengthy, and ineffective communications may have catastrophic results during a disaster. Personnel should be well versed in the principles of crisis intervention for use with victims in a state of emotional turmoil and in need of immediate assistance. Pre-incident training should also emphasize problem-solving and decision-making skills. Personnel need to be taught to understand general principles and apply those principles to the specific events in which they are involved. Often well-developed cognitive processes are far more useful in disasters than the technical strategies.

Personnel arriving at a disaster site need as much information as possible to begin their work. The surprise element in disasters needs to be reduced since fear, mental confusion, increased anxiety, and a loss of self-confidence frequently result from sudden exposure to the unexpected. Pre-incident briefings should be a standard policy for new arrivals at a disaster site.

Communities would be wise to establish policies related to the resting and changing of assignments of emergency workers. Since the average person has a great deal of difficulty working under intense stress for more than one hour without making mistakes and becoming more vulnerable to personal injury, it is recommended that a fifteen-minute break be programmed in for every hour of intense activity. No worker should work under conditions of intense stress for more than two hours without a break. In addition, disaster workers should not be kept at a scene for longer than twelve hours. All disaster workers should be required to be physically away from the scene for a minimum of six to eight hours after spending twelve hours at the scene.

A common stress-management strategy is to alleviate frustration, anxiety, and fatigue by changing the tasks at hand. A carefully timed and executed change in activity often helps emergency personnel to avoid being overcome by too much of one type of activity for too long a period of time. It is appropriate to change a worker's type of activity after a rest period as long as that person's work is not so specialized as to cause disruption to the overall operation.

The biochemical reactions of the body to a stressful event may produce caustic chemicals with a high potential for deteriorating body tissue. These caustic chemicals are best eliminated or reduced by strenuous physical activity after the stressful event has been managed. Emergency managers would do well to establish policies that require a physical exercise period of at least one hour for all emergency personnel who have worked at a disaster. The timing of the physical exercise is crucial and should be accomplished within twenty-four hours of the disaster work. The earlier the exercise is initiated, the better will be the results. However, the physical condition of the workers and their ability to participate safely in a post-incident physical exercise program needs to be taken into consideration. No one exercise program will be suitable for all of the disaster workers.

Disaster workers need adequate food, shelter, privacy, and rest.

They may also need psychological, religious, and medical support. It is up to the management of an organization to assure that its workers are provided with these necessities. Individuals performing the disaster work may become too stressed to make clear decisions to their best interests and management personnel may need to intervene and structure their workers' involvement in the disaster event.

Organizations need to establish clear policies regarding the development of useful research data files. Data collection and the careful application of analytic strategies and evaluation procedures may do much in the years to come to enhance the currently limited knowledge base regarding the psychological impact of disasters on emergency workers. Honest and scientific evaluation of current procedures will enhance the development of management policies for the benefit of emergency personnel everywhere.

Conclusion

Events such as the San Diego air disaster, the collapse of the Hyatt Regency Hotel in Kansas City, and the devastating tornados in western Pennsylvania, Ohio, and Canada need not be meaningless and empty losses. They have dramatically opened our eyes to the devastating stresses that invade the lives of emergency personnel. Perhaps before it becomes too late we can realize that it is not necessary for emergency personnel to tolerate the heartbreak and pressures of their work without alleviation and support. The development of Critical Incident Stress Debriefing Teams as well as the disaster stress policies recommended in this essay may provide sufficient support to emergency personnel to counter the aftershocks of their work. Policies and strategies to attack the stress problem may alleviate disruption in their lives and serious threats to their mental and physical health.

Summary of the Components of Mental Health Services for Emergency Service Personnel

1. Personnel screening (choosing the best)
   a. Psychological testing

    b. Careful interviewing

2. Human elements training (preferably before the emergency)
   a. Crisis intervention skills
   b. Stress management strategies
   c. Human communications training
   d. Conflict resolution skills
   e. Disaster psychology
   f. Problem-solving and decisionmaking skills
   g. Other as necessary

3. Preplanned mental health services
   a. Critical incident stress debriefing teams
   b. Employee assistance programs
   c. Spouse support programs
   d. Family life programs
   e. Counseling programs
   f. Other as necessary

4. Incorporation of mental health personnel in disaster drills as well as disaster planning committees

5. Established written policies for mental health services in disasters
   a. Briefings to prepare new arrivals at a scene. The emphasis needs to be on reducing the surprise elements of a disaster incident.
   b. Staff rest policies (fifteen minutes rest for every hour of *intensive* activity)
   c. Policies related to assignment of duties or rotation to different duties at the scene
   d. Policies related to length of service at a specific disaster scene (no longer than twelve hours at the scene)
   e. Checking vital signs (BP, pulse, respiration) of all personnel every two hours to screen out potentially serious stress reactions
   f. Emergency counseling at the scene
   g. Mandatory physical exercise postincident (within twenty-four hours)
   h. Critical incident stress debriefings
   i. Policies related to food, shelter, and privacy for emergency workers

6. Periodic stress and mental health evaluations of emergency personnel when not involved in emergency operations

7. In-service training programs

8. Periodic evaluations of current stress reduction strategies

9. Research into new human elements programs
10. Development of written policies to guide emergency personnel in their interactions with the press and with dignitaries such as government officials at a scene
    a. Have press report to and speak with a designated public information officer (PIO)
    b. Request that no dignitary visits take place until all elements related to the impact, inventory, rescue, and initial recovery phases of a disaster are completed (preventing a diversion of resources from life-saving and rescue operations to dignitary protection, transportation, and communications)
    c. Have any dignitaries who choose to violate the above guidelines report to and be assigned a specific representative of the organization while at the scene

Recovery and Reconstruction

Recovery Following Disaster: Policy Issues and Dimensions
⚡ Josephine M. LaPlante

The Problem: Recovering from Disaster

When disaster strikes, communities and their residents can be thrown quite literally into another world. Normal, day-to-day social and economic functioning are disrupted and may cease altogether in the most severe events. As the furor of the clash between human settlement and nature's forces or man's carelessness recedes, what occurs? How does a community, struck those harsh blows, begin to put the pieces back together?

Immediately following the initial impact, all attention focuses on responding to the emergency and keeping losses to a minimum. Valiant search-and-rescue efforts are launched to locate and bring survivors to safety; emergency shelter, clothing, and food are dispensed. Altruistic behavior has been found to dominate the immediate postimpact period in most settings. Human ability to care and to translate that caring into an overwhelming helping response has been documented repeatedly. During this period of time, the pieces of the community's life are located and assembled, and the task of recovery begins.

Figure 1. Stages of Recovery Following Disaster

Phases of activity

	Phase one	Phase two
Characteristic activities		
Community level	Normal activities suspended or changed Search and rescue of victims Emergency shelters set up Emergency feeding/clothing Clearance of debris begins	Normal activities resumed Cessation of search Shelters closed Debris cleared

Recovery period begins – – – – – – – –

Periods	Emergency	
		Restoration

| Individual and household level | Social/family structure disrupted
Search and rescue of victims
Temporary housing sought
Food/clothing sought | Family/social ties may be restored
Mourning
Rebuilding or return to homes
Possible relocation
Health effects may become known |

Coping/recovery may begin – – – – – – –

Periods	Emergency	
		Restoration

Sources: Adapted from Sandra Sutphen, "Disaster in Lake Elsinore" (paper presented at the Western Political Science Association Annual Conference, San Diego, California, 1982); and J. Haas et al., eds., *Reconstructions Following Disasters* (Cambridge, Mass.: MIT Press, 1977).

Phase three   Phase four

Community rebuilds   Disaster memorialized

Jobs restored   Large-scale construction
Commerce resumes   Mitigation

- ►

Replacement/reconstruction

                            Long-term reconstruction

Return to work
Social activities resumed ─────────────────►
Health effects
Mental health effects   ─────────────────►

- - - Healing - ►

Long-term recovery

The Recovery Process

Recovery is a process of healing for communities and their residents. While recovery is often conceptualized as a phase of activity distinct from response, beginning after the emergency has receded, early coping behavior in fact initiates the recovery process while the community and its citizens are continuing response efforts. As steps to restore the vital functions and activities of the community begin to be undertaken, those pieces of the puzzle which once formed functioning systems are put and occasionally forced back into place. Thus the recovery process grows out of the response to disaster.

The processes of recovery, as well as efforts aimed at assisting that process, continue through the days and weeks after the disaster event. For both households and communities struck by the disaster, the period of recovery may need to extend well beyond the weeks and months that follow the immediate impacts of the disaster event. Figure 1 delineates a chronological model of the overlapping stages of the recovery process. Figure 1 is based upon a representation of the disaster recovery process developed by Haas,[1] which divided the overall community recovery process into a four-phase cycle. The Haas model is expanded here by the explicit consideration of the household recovery process as distinct from, yet related to, the community pattern.

Haas defined the four phases of recovery by studying communities' patterns of activities and coping behavior following a disaster event. The first period, the emergency phase, is typically a period of high consensus in the community, with much altruistic behavior aimed at preventing or reducing human suffering. Next, activities that will return the community to normal functioning are undertaken and initiate the second period, called the restoration phase. When a semblance of normal functioning is achieved, activities aimed at permanence begin the reconstruction phase: families return to homes, work, or school, and community rebuilding gets under way. Family and individual needs may come into conflict with community goals at this stage of recovery. The Haas model then presents a final stage which reflects activity at essentially the community level, called the commemorative, betterment, and development reconstruction phase. During this time of second-stage community reconstruction, plans and actions decided upon during the earlier reconstruction are implemented.

Each new phase of recovery evolves from previous activities. The length of each phase of the recovery cycle varies among communities and among households. The emergency phase is generally the briefest of the recovery periods, with each stage which follows becoming much longer in relation to previous stages. The second stage of reconstruction may stretch over many years in communities where substantial community development is initiated by the disaster event and the availability of financing.[2] Similarly, particularly hard-hit households and individuals may face long and arduous paths to total recovery, without a break between reconstruction phases.

Research on Recovery

Some communities, as well as individuals and families, show remarkable resilience in the face of adversity. Yet others never seem to return completely to what once existed. What determines who succeeds and who does not? The process of recovering after a disaster is complicated and not yet fully understood. Prior to the late 1970s research on disasters had largely focused on response. Since that time researchers have begun to delve into the recovery process, typically from one of two general perspectives: household recovery versus aggregate, community-level patterns.

Research Evidence: Community-level Recovery

The research findings on natural disasters indicate that a number of factors may influence the speed and quality of a community's recovery. Some are specific to the disaster, including particularly the size of the event and the scope of damage. Others are related to antecedent conditions, including economic resources for financing recovery. Results of various research studies have tended to contradict each other, primarily on findings related to community economic recovery patterns.

In the 1970s several groups of researchers sought to build upon past research while correcting methodological problems that had made comparison among events difficult. Haas and his coresearchers[3] published the results of their four-case longitudinal study in 1977, which demonstrated that predisaster trends, including economic and population change, are exacerbated by disaster. A positive association between increases in external disaster aid and speed of rebuilding was evident.

Wright et al.[4] conducted a nationwide study that utilized detailed census data on demographic, housing, and economic conditions within metropolitan areas and counties as the basis for regression analysis. The researchers first estimated each area's 1970 position using the 1960 data, then tested differences found to determine whether changes seen could be attributed to the disaster events. No discernible effects on changes in housing stocks or population at the county level were found, nor were consistent effects found to survive more than a very short period of time following the event. Wright noted a methodological problem, that "the comparison of average damages to average resources makes it implausible . . . that disasters would have residual and observable effects."[5]

Despite the less than clear findings that emerged from the Wright study, an important contribution was the development of a measure of disaster severity that is specific to the location of the event, which they called an impact ratio: Resources Lost/Available Resources. Total resources lost are expressed as a proportion of available resources, which allows an estimation of the net seriousness of the disaster within the community's own unique context. Wright notes that "the same physical event, when experienced by a small community, may have much more serious implications than when experienced by an SMSA."[6] In referring to an SMSA, Wright is using the initials for "Standard Metropolitan Statistical Area," a term in wide use among public administrators. Although findings from Wright et al. are generally considered to be contradictory to Haas's conclusions, the impact ratio concept actually supports some of Haas's contentions. Haas argues that reconstruction of heavily damaged communities cannot occur successfully without large influxes of outside aid, which assumes the proportional relationship between resources and severity advanced in the impact ratio model.

In 1979 Friesema et al.[7] presented findings from their longitudinal study of four communities which further fueled the recovery debate. Friesema defined two complementary components of loss estimates, the human side and the economic side, but noted the difficulty inherent in measuring losses. Their findings focused on economic recovery, and showed that all of the communities studied showed rapid progress toward recovery, regardless of the initial severity of the event. However, even the least aided community in the Friesema study received large amounts of outside assistance.

These and other studies of community level recovery have dealt largely with economic recovery. While the results have not been consistent, they do underscore the multidimensionality of the economic recovery process. True economic impacts are difficult to gauge. Immediately after the event, the determination of losses must be made to establish eligibility for state assistance and a presidential disaster declaration. Since the decision on whether a federal declaration is warranted determines what assistance the local communities and their residents are eligible for, time is of the essence. Nevertheless, the full economic impact of the event may not be known for some time. The "multiplier effect," the spending of income which generates production and subsequently new income, is often cited as the source of economic recovery when aid flows into a community. However, the multiplier can work in reverse: particularly when aid is not forthcoming, decisions not to rebuild or not to resume production can have longer-term spiraling effects.

Community versus Governmental Impacts

Most of the research on economics of disasters has focused on community-wide economic, rather than governmental fiscal and economic impacts. The research findings relating to communities have generally indicated that while some short-term impacts of disasters on the economies of communities affected have been positive, the short-term benefits are quickly dissipated, resulting in insignificant or uneven long-term effects.[8] Whether these findings extend to the fiscal viability of local governments requires further research.

It is the local governments who typically must finance early response and recovery as well as some portion of later recovery and reconstruction, depending on whether the community struck by disaster receives a presidential declaration, thereby enabling the local government to obtain matching aid for rebuilding. Friesema et al. did consider what are actually governmental impacts when it was hypothesized that disasters would hurt the property tax base and necessitate an increase in long-term expenditure levels. They were unable to find evidence at the level studied, the overall economy of the affected area.

In fact, the inability to find substantial governmental impacts may be a result of the approach utilized. The types of impacts hypothesized would have affected individual governments differently, depending upon the extent of damage, predisaster fiscal condition, and after-impact financial assistance flows. Many of the studies of disaster impacts are plagued by two classic problems: imprecise measures and use of an improper unit of analysis. Some of the obvious problems have been acknowledged by researchers on disaster impacts, but others have not. The continued use of aggregated figures and the averages which result from their manipulation may be threatening the validity of findings. The aggregation of effects over a wide area would tend to mask individual differences that result from disasters. In addition, public finance research has long been troubled by noncomparability of data across jurisdictions of different states, and even within the same state, when functions performed can differ markedly.

Chang, in a recent work exploring the impacts of Hurricane Frederic on the revenues of the city government of Mobile, Alabama, is unable to state conclusively whether his results in Mobile support a hypothesis of long-term increases in burden on taxpayers in the disaster area.[9] Thus the question of whether local governments whose communities are struck by disasters must impose increased cost burdens on their citizens is unresolved.

There is some evidence that long-term fiscal effects may differ for declared disasters versus localized, undeclared events where external aid is not forthcoming. Recent research on flooding in Pennsylvania is indicating that cases of recurrent events in disaster-prone areas, such as riverine and flash flooding, may be particularly threatening to a local government's long-term fiscal viability.[10] The impacts of disaster-related expenses on community debt burdens are cumulative over recurrences of disaster events, whether large or small. Communities forced to support the repeated repair and rebuilding of roads, bridges, and other physical infrastructures following "small" events may find that the impact on debt burdens is much more serious over time than one isolated event would indicate.

Research Evidence: Individual and
Household-level Recovery

There is little doubt that in any situation, the aggregate picture may be significantly different than the condition of the individual components. Thus studying recovery at only the aggregate, community level may mask important consequences of the disaster, and incorrectly estimate both the length of time required for full recovery and the actual extent of recovery at a given point in time. Wright's impact ratio approach, while devised to measure economic loss, can be extended to conceptualize and provide a framework for measuring loss at the household level. The net seriousness of the event for the household would be equal to the ratio of resources lost to total household assets and resources available to them. This approach is supported by research reported by Bolin, who has found that families with greater resources recover more quickly, while elderly and the poor face a more difficult period.[11] Any use of the impact ratio as a measure of magnitude of losses for households would require the inclusion of important intangible resources and personal characteristics including age, sex, and family and social support networks, in addition to any financial assets.

Personal and social impacts are particularly difficult to assess, for they typically defy quantification. Measures used as proxies for intangible losses, such as dead as a percentage of the population, percentage of the population forced to relocate, and percentage hospitalized fail to capture the full effect of those occurrences on the victims. Yet avoiding the inclusion of difficult variables can lead to estimates that significantly understate the real impact of a disaster event.

Melick has summarized the research on families and natural hazards.[12] In general, she found that there is enough evidence to support a number of conclusions. Long-term health and mental health consequences have resulted from disasters, particularly when there have been large numbers of deaths. While this is more difficult to assess, Melick notes that research evidence indicates that sleeplessness, nightmares in children, stress-induced illnesses, and chronic health problems endure long after the event. In addition, kin and friendship ties may lead to spillover effects, where nonvictims become victims of disaster. Long-term stress-related symptoms and mental health problems have been identified among disaster relief workers. Disasters thereby create another category of victim rarely considered in policy design. Melick underscores the need for research on high-risk populations, most notably women under sixty-five having low income and educational levels. Finally, Melick states that studies are showing that a majority of victims of disaster are reluctant to avail themselves of mental health services.

Evidence from Love Canal[13] and Three Mile Island[14] indicates that recovery following technological events may be an even more complex and presumably risky process than recovery after natural disasters. Research on health and mental health impacts of enduring events such as Love Canal indicate that physical illness, generational health-related problems, and stress-induced illness which may be both physical and mental health-related are more common than after natural disasters. Forced relocation following environmental damage may also take its toll, since research on relocation during the urban renewal era revealed long-term consequences.[15] Age is related to the ability to adapt, with both the elderly and the young less able to cope on their own. Support, whether from parents or other sources, through the process has had positive impacts on long-term adjustments. Sex is also related to coping behavior, with women being more susceptible to long-term problems.

Family recovery has been studied, but primarily within the natural disaster context. Bolin and Bolton have noted that families recover from disasters by establishing linkages with outside agencies, including the government and social services system.[16] Extended kin groups and extrafamilial linkages are used to assist with coping. Based upon his research on housing following disaster events, Bolin states that economic and housing recovery are prerequisites to successful emotional recovery.[17] Bolin notes that while there are programs to address family needs, the emphasis on returning the family to the status quo ante obscures long-term problems. Victims' mental health and the social-psychological dimensions of housing placement are not adequately considered. In addition, the equitable allocation of disaster assistance is not included in the current policy framework which looks more at recovery of the place, that is, the community.

Local Governments and Emergency Management

The research on recovery indicates that local government's response to disaster can play an important role in shaping the path of recovery at both the community and household levels. Yet local governments may be the forgotten partners in disaster recovery. While local government responsibilities for developing and functioning mitigation policy, as well as the central functions they play in disaster response, have been the theme of both research and training efforts, the important direct and indirect roles these local governments assume and have thrust upon them in disaster recovery are easily overlooked. Local government agencies are at the forefront before and during a disaster event, and more often than realized, after the event as well.

Rubin and Barbee have been conducting research on local government recovery decisionmaking processes in a number of communities following natural disasters since 1979.[18] They note that local officials are involved not only in complex intergovernmental processes but also in key public policy choices that can shape the future of the community.[19] Strategic choices are made by local decisionmakers during the response and early recovery periods which will shape both immediate and long-range recovery. Key determinants of their effectiveness which Rubin and Barbee have identified include an ability to act, reason to act, and knowledge of what to do.[20] These findings highlight the importance of training for local government officials on how to go about assessing both community and citizen needs following a disaster.

Integrating Community and Household Perspectives

Turning to figure 2, we may now reconsider the chronological framework from the distinct perspectives of overall community-level recovery and the process of recovery for individuals and families. In both cases the recovery processes are characterized by activities that grow out of the activities of the previous period and then wind down, often overlapping the next period as well. Emergency phase activities, during which attention focuses on saving lives and meeting basic human needs, are generally similar whether the activity is considered at a

Figure 2. Recovery as an Interdependent Process

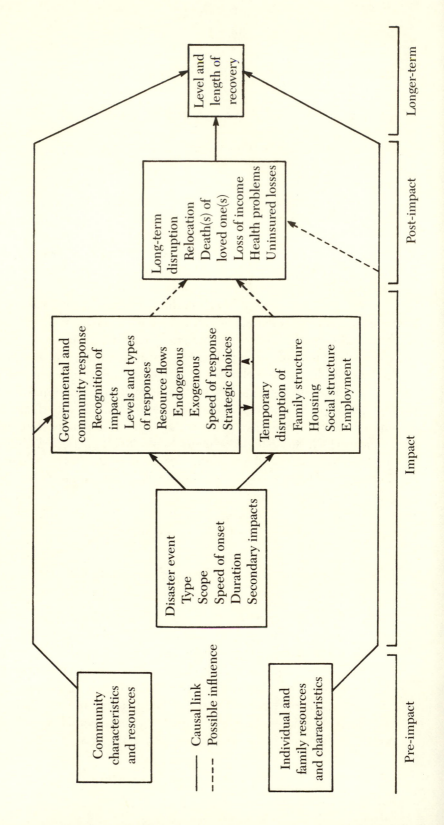

microlevel or aggregated to the broader community level. While individual households will be differently affected by the disaster, attention typically focuses on salvaging what is left and preventing more losses. The "total community" impacts versus household level impacts become more apparent during the restoration phase. For some households the return to normalcy, the initiation of healing, and the process of recovery will progress smoothly. For others, who must first bury and mourn their dead, rebuild their homes, or face permanent relocation, the healing will be more elusive.

Figure 3 extends work done by Haas and his colleagues with the introduction of the elements of choice and gatekeeping.[21] Choices occur at a number of points in the recovery process, whether knowingly or unknowingly by the families and individuals affected. Families and individuals make choices about what aid they seek. At times choices are made for them by governmental and community agencies that establish eligibility and access to services through their gatekeeping choices. Figure 3 indicates at each point in the process of moving toward recovery possible patterns of interrelationships among community and personal characteristics, actions taken, and both short-term and longer-range outcomes that can be expected to occur based upon the literature on disaster recovery. Figures 2 and 3 are in part causal models, with many lines indicating selective impacts dependent upon given characteristics and decisions of individuals as well as governmental agencies.

Gatekeeping in disaster relief actually occurs at two key points. The first level of gatekeeping occurs when total losses are calculated, then used to determine whether a whole range of disaster assistance is made available to a community.[22] The second stage of gatekeeping occurs at the point of assistance or other postdisaster helping. Neither all communities nor all disaster victims within one community share equally in available recovery assistance.

Formulating Policy for Disaster Recovery

Before the question of what constitutes effective recovery policy can be adequately addressed, researchers and policymakers must direct their attention to a number of points.

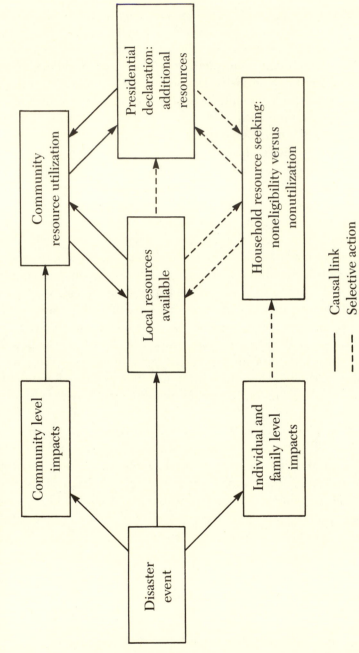

Figure 3. Aggregate versus Individual Level
Resource Availability and Utilization

People and Places Face Disaster

The literature base on the urban impacts of federal policies provides us with an important analogy. Policymaking on urban renewal and the federal highway system was frequently done in a vacuum. The priorities of the agency involved were considered without any particular regard either to interrelationships with other federal programs and possible negative impacts, or to the people in the communities who would be affected by the policy. Edel, writing on the question of "people" versus "places" in urban policymaking noted that policies that are designed spatially but with the objective of helping people may meet with three problems. First, they are subject to ecological fallacy: eligibility criteria may be incorrectly specified. For example, not all poor people live in poor places, nor are all people in poor places poor. Second, benefits may be diverted from people to the owners of land. Third, confusing economic and social relationships may cause confusion. Edel suggests that effects of programs on people need to be distinguished from effects on places.[23]

The complex processes that make up local social and economic systems cannot be considered in isolation. As figures 2 and 3 suggest, important interdependencies among those systems and the intergovernmental system require explicit consideration of both intended effects and any possible negative impacts of policies on people, places, and governmental units. Policies should be evaluated prior to implementation to determine whether the likelihood that intended recipients will benefit is high. The history of federal social programs through the 1960s illustrated the types of problems that occur when the necessary links between inputs, activities, outputs, and outcomes were not logically in place even at the program design stage.

Important differences between the community as a whole and its households which may determine in large part the overall pattern of recovery are evident in the early period following a disaster. Yet the perception of the disaster from the outside may be that the impact was "severe" or "not too severe," while within the community the impact may range from minimal to extreme. One family may be left untouched, while the family next door sees their home destroyed and a loved one killed. The random nature with which disasters select their victims is well known; the devastation that can confront those few singled out by a seemingly minor event is less recognized, and consequently the impacts on these households have gone largely unstudied.

Previous research on disaster severity has implicitly addressed the issue of people versus places. Wright has noted the problem of the parts suffering because the focus is on the whole. Family disasters, or catastrophic occurrences occurring at the family level that may not affect enough households in an area to be deemed a disaster, may have insidious impacts simply because they are unrecognized. They may be deemed inconsequential because they are not additive. A question that has not yet been researched is whether the impact of the lack of recognition actually exacerbates the effects of the personal disaster. In Centralia this ambiguity clearly escalated community conflict.[24]

Federal policy has been directed from above and as such is based on an aggregate picture, in terms of both needs and severity. What is rational and effective policy at the macrolevel may be the reverse at the community or individual level. Response which can effectively meet the needs of people *and* places following disaster will foster recovery of people and places. However, designing policy with such a goal will require an explicit consideration of the intended beneficiaries of the policy. In addition, knowledge of the likely impacts of the policy, both negative and positive, is a necessary prerequisite to the design of effective policy.

Classes of Hazard Events

Research on man-made, technological accidents, whether a chemical spill or a Three Mile Island, and on enduring technological events, such as Love Canal and Centralia, has begun to indicate the need for an examination of generally accepted definitions and impressions of what constitutes a disaster. Most disaster research has focused on episodic and natural events. The literature base that has evolved thus far on other kinds of events often assumes transferability of the bulk of accrued knowledge, while nonetheless unearthing differences. Table 4 presents an overview of the categories of hazard events. Various characteristics associated with disaster events are shown for each of the three broad categories of events. The differences are particularly marked between episodic events, whether natural or technological in terms of the agent, and the chronic events. Perry and Mushkatel cite differences between natural and episodic, technical accidents.[25] The enduring or chronic events, however, are strikingly different on a number of counts from the natural disaster and even from the "average" man-made accidents.[26] While it may not be inappropriate to conceive these

Table 4. Distinguishing Categories of Hazard Events

Usual characteristics associated with event	Type of event/Disaster agent		
	Natural disaster	Technological failure/ accident	Chronic technological event
Scope of impact	varies	varies	varies
Usual speed of onset	sudden	sudden	prolonged
Speed of problem recognition	rapid	rapid	prolonged
Duration of primary impact	short	varies	prolonged
Existence of secondary impacts	yes	yes	yes
Governmental mechanisms for timely response/ recovery	yes	varies	often not
Known technology for recovery	yes	varies	often not

Source: This table elaborates on the typology presented in R. Perry and A. Mush-katel, *Disaster Preparedness: Warning, Response, and Community Relocation* (Westport, Conn.: Greenwood Press, 1984).

classes of events as comprising a continuum, a better understanding of systematic differences is needed if disaster policy is to meet victim needs appropriately following various events.

The chronic, technological event is not always viewed as comprising a disaster, at least by policymakers. The existence of these cases comes to the public's eye slowly, and the real impact may be nearly impossible to assess. Cases of chronic technological hazard events such as hazardous waste at Love Canal or Centralia, Pennsylvania's, mine fire do not currently fall under FEMA's authority. Instead, the agency with jurisdiction over the agent takes charge, where the agent is known. For example, in the case of Centralia, the Bureau of Mines was involved in major studies on the mine fire. Timely response, as well as governmental actions during chronic events, and also hazardous accidents where blame may fall on them, are not in accord with our notions of responses to disaster, which have been based on research on natural disasters. How different these kinds of occurrences are and what the differences mean to policy formulation will require further research. In addition, the concepts of disaster severity and the impact ratio will require refinement to deal with cases where the full scale of the effects may be unknown. At Love Canal it was difficult for residents to obtain acknowledgment that health-related disorders were related to the chemical dump.[27] Centralians, subjected to stress over a twenty-three-year period, have had their health status studied by the state of Pennsylvania, with no conclusive evidence found.[28] Questions concerning the effects of Three Mile Island still linger in many minds. Long-term health impacts, particularly those that skip a generation, and mental health effects are extremely difficult to include in a severity assessment. Yet their inclusion is obviously critical when the determination of whether a disaster has occurred, and what its magnitude is, needs to be made.

Conclusion

A number of points stand out as requiring attention. First, the need to consider local government's fiscal ability is underscored by research. Despite some findings to the contrary, disasters may have important long-term economic and fiscal impacts on selected communities as well as families and individuals. The formulation of effective federal disaster assistance policy depends upon an explicit consideration of fiscal capacity.

Recent changes in the federal financing of recovery will place a new burden on local governments. The new legislation requires that state and local governments assume 25 percent of the cost of recovery in declared disasters. The actual distribution of the costs among the states and local governments is yet to be seen, but the outcome for local fiscal health, regardless of the proportion of the new state-local financing partnership each state decides to assume, is clear nonetheless. Increased local cost burdens will be associated with hazard events. The need to rethink the benefits and costs of mitigation projects under this restructured financing arrangement are evident. The question of who pays may change the benefits and costs of mitigation from the perspectives of the local governments. Costs of restoring the physical condition of a community, as well as long-term fiscal impacts of the event itself and recovery costs, must be factored into the calculation of the benefits of mitigation. In some cases, the balance towards mitigating against future events may change.

Finally, it is important to recognize that despite the oft-noted lack of use of research findings in policymaking, much policy is shaped by research findings. Much of the critical research on recovery cautions readers that the results may not extend to the individual level. While the comments allude to the specificity of the results to the particular level studied, there is no consideration of what implications different findings for other levels of analysis would have for the formulation of disaster assistance policies. Policymakers do use the results of research on disaster in their policy deliberations. Caveats, however, are easily overlooked or their significance not fully gleaned. Policymakers do not try to judge the quality of research. Questions of "appropriate" measures and the "correct" unit of analysis are the domain of professional peers. Reviewers of research findings recognize that compromises are often forced upon their colleagues by time and a lack of resources. They are willing accordingly to accept some imperfection, so long as the proper caveats are included. In the disaster policy area it may well be that compromises that have shaped policy in the past are now ratifying the policy directions of an administration which favors less federal involvement in all areas.

Recovery is a link in a chain of events, which can be helped by carefully planned policy at each stage. At different points throughout the emergency management cycle, critical decisions are made, whether by design or by default, that have important consequences for the future of communities and the citizens who populate them. Interactions between citizens and government officials can foster or hinder the course of recovery for communities and individuals. Response as well as disaster relief assistance, effectively targeted and equitably distributed, can increase the likelihood of recovery for the victims of disaster. Predisaster planning, including the assignment of responsibility and coordination of efforts, has been shown to be an important mitigating force against a disaster's potential impact on both the physical and human settlement that comprises a community. Policy design and disaster management are important intervening variables in the healing and recovery process. Policymakers have the responsibility to see that the composition of their policies in fact enhances, not diminishes, the opportunity for recovery.

Disaster Recovery and Reconstruction ⚡ Peter J. May

The Political Dilemmas: A Disaster Policy

Disasters bring visions of terrifying destruction. Mount St. Helens blows its top, lava pours down, ashes go skyward to fall like snow on cities, and a small river named the Toutle turns into a raging torrent of force. In such a disaster people and institutions are mobilized, ranging from local police and state troopers to the president of the United States who, upon the request of a governor, can declare a catastrophe a major disaster. That declaration starts the flow of federal funds and an intense period of combined federal, state, local, and private effort to put lives and property back together. In the jargon of disaster specialists, these highly visible activities are labeled disaster "recovery and reconstruction."

As discussed in earlier chapters in this book, there is more to disaster policy than recovery and reconstruction. Before, and even after, a disaster is the chance to prevent or to ameliorate losses through disaster mitigation and preparedness. These are the tasks to work on during a routine· day while waiting for the next disaster that again galvanizes efforts to recover from catastrophe. However mundane the actual tasks may be, mitigation and preparedness are central to an effective disaster policy and to lessening the work required in recovering from catastrophe. Disaster after disaster has shown institutions poorly prepared to handle the crisis and demonstrating unwise behavior after a disaster, including repeated reconstruction in hazard-prone areas.

Despite the good intentions of federal policymakers and others to encourage disaster mitigation and preparedness, the centerpiece of federal disaster policy is recovery and reconstruction provisions. This essay addresses the evolution of federal disaster policy with a particular focus on the reasons why efforts to clean up after disasters dominate policymaking activity in the disaster arena. Herein is the stage of the political environments in which disaster policymaking takes place. We shall see that it is useful to distinguish two different political worlds, from which emerge vastly different policies. As discussed in the last section of this chapter, the differences in these political worlds present federal policymakers with major political and implementation dilemmas in efforts to reshape disaster policy toward greater emphasis upon mitigation and preparedness.

The Political Worlds of Disaster Policy

Federal disaster policymaking takes place in two different political worlds. One world is that of "normal" politics where disaster policies have low political salience and, as a result, are relegated to the backwaters of legislative committees and agency activity. The second world is the "active" one of disaster policymaking that occurs in the aftermath of major catastrophes such as Hurricane Agnes, the Teton Dam failure, or a San Fernando earthquake. In this second world, disaster policy has high political salience featuring intensive media attention and politicians' desires to help disaster-struck communities. The two political worlds can be distinguished in a variety of ways. Table 1 summarizes the differences, and the discussion that follows outlines, with respect to the salience of disaster relief issues, the roles of Congress and federal agencies in policymaking and intergovernmental relationships.

One issue is the scale of disaster that distinguishes the two worlds. Catastrophic events of the order of magnitude of an Alaska earthquake, Hurricane Camille, San Fernando earthquake, Hurricane Agnes, or Mount St. Helens volcanic eruption trigger the more politically active

Table 1. Two Political Worlds of Disaster Relief Policymaking

Distinguishing features	Aftermath of catastrophes	Between catastrophes
Salience of relief issues	High	Low
Legislative roles and influence	Special legislation in the aftermath of catastrophic disasters	Generalized legislation shaped by congressional "disaster specialists"
Federal Disaster Agency roles and influence	Define content of disaster policy and thus shape policy	Policy influence limited to promulgating administrative regulations
Intergovernmental relationships	Central aspect of relief effort; episodic in nature	Not central
Resultant policies	Responsive to disaster at hand; skewed toward catastrophic events	Less affected by latest catastrophic disaster; generalized policies

(and visible) world. For the most part, hundreds of smaller events that occur each year belong to the other world. However, the threshold between the two is difficult to define. With this caveat in mind, let us consider the differences in disaster relief policymaking between the two worlds.

Salience of Relief Issues

Perhaps the sharpest distinguishing feature is the salience of disaster relief issues in each of the worlds. Between catastrophic disasters the threat of disasters—and presumably even more so the specifics of federal assistance policies—are not highly salient in policymakers' minds at any level of government. In the aftermath of catastrophic disasters, however, such issues are actually salient considerations for those policymakers representing disaster-struck areas as well as, to a surprising extent, salient issues for policymakers from other areas susceptible to natural disasters.

The results of a recent survey of officials who are expected to have a role in disaster policymaking at the state and local level (for example, governors, mayors, political party leaders, legislative leaders, real estate and banking officials) indicate the relatively low seriousness attached to natural hazards between major disasters.[1] For both groups of officials in hazard-prone areas the mean ratings of the perceived seriousness of floods, fires, hurricanes, tornadoes, and earthquakes ranked lower than the perceived seriousness of such things as inflation, welfare costs, traffic congestion, water and air pollution, and pornography. (The situation often is very different after disasters. These data were gathered during a period in which there were relatively few disasters nationally. One might note that considerable difficulties exist in measuring salience both with respect to measurement device and timing.) Indeed, among the eighteen problems that were specifically asked about, flooding ranked twelfth (making that concern less serious than concerns about pornographic literature), fires ranked thirteenth, hurricanes and tornadoes ranked fifteenth and sixteenth respectively (after race relations), and earthquakes ranked last (after too much economic growth).

This of course does not mean that the threat of disasters is of little concern in all states or localities. For some states—Colorado, Louisiana, and Pennsylvania—and for some localities—for example, Corpus Christi, Los Angeles, and Tulsa—which had more experience with disasters, the perceived seriousness of disasters ranked much higher. Nonetheless, the more general findings concerning the salience of natural hazards at times other than the aftermath of major disasters can be described as an "apathetic politics" characterized by ambivalent or contradictory policy positions among elites, and by neither strong advocacy nor opposition to disaster policy change.[2]

Legislative Activity

In the aftermath of catastrophic disasters the need for some form of relief assistance is obvious, but what constitutes an appropriate level of federal assistance is less apparent. The political visibility of the relief

Table 2. Disaster Relief Legislation

Year	Key relief provisions	Comments

Legislation Enacted during the Aftermath of Catastrophes

Year	Key relief provisions	Comments
1803–1947	128 separate acts providing relief in the aftermath of individual catastrophe	No standby authority existed for federal provision of relief
1950 (PL 81-875)	Disaster Relief Act of 1950: Authorized funding for repair of local public facilities upon presidential approval	Enacted after flooding in North Dakota and Missouri Provided standby authority
1951 (PL 82-107)	Authorized federal provision of emergency housing	Response to Kansas-Missouri flood of 1951
1953 (PL 83-134)	Permitted donation of federal surplus property to individuals	Response to 1953 Worcester, Massachusetts tornado
1962 (PL 87-502)	Added grants for repair of state facilities; added Guam, American Samoa, and Pacific Territories	Response to state and territorial needs
1964 (PL 88-451)	Special loan and grant provisions	Disaster-specific relief, Alaska Earthquake
1965 (PL 89-41)	Similar loan provisions to the Alaska earthquake	Disaster-specific relief, Pacific Northwest floods
1965 (PL 89-339)	Authorized cancellation of up to $1,800 on loan repayments	Disaster-specific relief, Hurricane Betsy
1966 (PL 89-769)	Disaster Relief Act of 1966: Rural communities made eligible Funding for damage to higher education facilities	Amendments to the 1950 act extending disaster-specific provisions from above acts.

Table 2. (continued)

Year	Key relief provisions	Comments
	Funding for repair of public facilities under construction	Indiana tornado in 1965 solidified the act's support
1968 (PL 90-448)	Added "riots or civil disorders" as categories for disaster loans	Response to urban riots
1969 (PL 91-79)	Disaster Relief Act of 1969: Funding for debris removal from private property Distribution of food coupons Unemployment compensation for disaster victims SBA, FHA, VA loan revisions Private timber purchase allowed	New general relief act which was limited to 15 months duration Followed California mudslide and Hurricane Camille
1970 (PL 91-606)	Disaster Assistance Act of 1970: Most provisions of the 1969 act, plus the following Grants to individuals for temporary housing/relocation Funding for legal services Community payments for tax loss Revision of SBA loan provisions	 Outgrowth of the 1969 act and Hurricane Camille response
1971 (PL 92-209)	Funding for repair, replacement, or reconstruction of nonprofit medical facilities	Amendment to 1970 act, arising from the 1971 San Fernando earthquake

Table 2. (continued)

Year	Key relief provisions	Comments
1972 (PL 92-385)	Hurricane Agnes relief program, special loans, and grants	Disaster-specific relief
1974 (PL 93-288)	Disaster Relief Amendments of 1974: Distinguished "major disaster" from "emergencies"	Outgrowth of extensive hearings about disaster relief
	Authorized funding for mental health counseling, recovery planning councils, community loans, state disaster planning, park and recreation repairs	Severe tornados in the Southwest were an impetus for final action
1977 (PL 95-89)	Lowered interest rates for disaster loans	Response to a severe drought

Legislation Enacted between Catastrophes

Year	Key relief provisions	Comments
1953 (PL 83-163)	Small Business Act of 1953: Authorized SBA to make loans "as the administration may determine to be necessary for floods or other catastrophes"	Outgrowth of the Disaster Loan Corporation and the Reconstruction Finance Corporation loan programs
1956 (PL 84-1016)	Federal Flood Insurance Act of 1956: Housing and Home Finance Administrator to establish flood insurance, loan contracts, and reinsurance programs	An "experimental program" advocated by Eisenhower Funding rejected by House in 1957, killing the program
1965	Extended Northwest	Making permanent

Table 2. (continued)

Year	Key relief provisions	Comments
(PL 89-59)	floods repayment provisions	earlier special relief provisions
1968 (PL 90-448)	National Flood Insurance Act of 1968: Provided for private insurers' selling of federally subsidized flood insurance	Outgrowth of 1956 failed program and a study called for after Hurricane Betsy, issued in 1966
1973 (PL 93-234)	Flood Disaster Protection Act of 1973: Expanded flood damage coverage and provided sanctions for communities in flood zones failing to participate	Provisions enacted to induce more participation. Agnes and Rapid City showed lack of insurance coverage
1975 (PL 94-68)	Revised formula for interest rates on loans, attached to governmental cost of borrowing	Retrenchment of liberal loan policies enacted after Hurricane Agnes
1976 (PL 94-305)	Authorized SBA loans for farmers	Seeking uniformity in loan programs
1977 (PL 95-128)	1977 Housing and Community Develop-ment Act: Relaxed flood insurance sanctions	Response to concern over federal intervention in local land use decisions
1977 (PL 95-124)	Earthquake Hazards Reduction Act of 1977: Multiagency research and planning effort	Provided greater federal "leadership" in earth-quake preparedness
1980 (PL 96-302)	Reauthorization of SBA loan program until 1984: SBA loans harder for farmers to obtain	Response to large increase in amount of farm loans under SBA program

Source: Executive Office of the President, Office of Emergency Management, *Disaster Preparedness* (Washington, D.C.: Government Printing Office, January 1972): 167–73.

effort and pressures to provide extraordinary levels of assistance are typically such that special disaster-specific relief legislation is introduced into Congress, thereby shifting disaster relief policy from the periphery to center stage. Between catastrophic events, disaster relief policymaking is left to a few disaster specialists within Congress. At such times the specifics of disaster relief policy are a central concern only of those specialists, the relevant federal agencies, and a limited number of interest groups representing state and local emergency services personnel.

The differences in legislative activity over time between the two political worlds of disaster relief policymaking are summarized in table 2. Without belaboring the substantive details, suffice it to note that until recently there has been considerable expansion of disaster relief grant and loan provisions and opportunties.[3] In more recent years, federally subsidized flood insurance has been made available and greater attention has been paid at the federal level to earthquake preparedness. These latter programs in particular represent shifts in congressional attitudes concerning the need for a federal role in helping states and localities avert disaster losses. More important for the present discussion, however, are the differences among the two groups of legislation dealing with disaster relief. Differences are evident in the amount of legislative activity, the content of the legislation, the related legislative debate, and the level of congressional support for enacting legislation.

Of the twenty-five key disaster relief-related laws enacted since 1950, some two-thirds were enacted in the aftermath of major catastrophes. Prior to 1950, except for some standby loan authorities, the only way the federal government got involved in providing relief was through legislation enacted after a disaster that provided particular kinds of federal assistance for that disaster. That changed in 1950 with the enactment of the Disaster Relief Act giving the president authority to obligate federal funds for the repair of public facilities in the aftermath of disasters that were deemed to be beyond state and local capabilities to address. Although his standby authority alleviated the need for congressional action in the aftermath of catastrophes, major catastrophes continued to occasion legislative activity. In some instances—for example, the Alaska earthquake, the Pacific Northwest floods, and Hurricane Betsy—the legislation was specific to the disaster at hand. In other cases—for example, the Palm Sunday tornado of 1965 in

Indiana and Hurricane Camille— the catastrophe served as a catalyst for forcing action on disaster relief bills that were being debated at the time.

Several reasons can be offered for catastrophes occasioning legislative activity. First, the perceived need for action is greater in that the gaps in existing relief provisions are more apparent. For example, the 1971 San Fernando earthquake resulted in damage to several nonprofit hospitals which at the time were not eligible for federal disaster grants. Second, and relatedly, given the visibility of catastrophes it is easier to get relief issues on legislative agendas.[4] For example, legislative activity in 1974 was stalled because of differences between an administration bill and another bill developed by Senator Burdick, the specialist at the time on disaster relief issues. Severe tornados in the Southwest provided an opportunity for breaking the legislative logjam and rushing enactment of the Burdick bill.

Legislators from disaster-struck areas have strong incentives to push for expanded legislation because they undoubtedly believe (with reason) that seeking additional assistance is a valuable constituent service which will be rewarded with favorable votes in the next election. Mount St. Helens is a noteworthy example in that the Washington state delegation, which happened to be led by the chairman of the Senate Appropriations Committee, was able to orchestrate quick congressional passage of a supplemental appropriation that was necessary at the time for funding federal disaster relief activity.

The content of disaster legislation also differs according to the political world in which it was enacted. Legislation enacted in the aftermath of catastrophes tends to reflect the disaster at hand, even if it is not meant to be specific to that disaster. Thus the 1971 amendments enacted in the aftermath of the San Fernando earthquake made permanent federal assistance for nonprofit hospitals. Sometimes expanded legislation is originally enacted on a disaster-specific basis, but later made permanent. This was the case for the 1969 and 1970 acts. The 1969 act originally was introduced to address some mud slides in California, was expanded into more general but temporary legislation after Hurricane Camille, and was made permanent as the 1970 act a year later.

The content of legislation enacted between catastrophes is much different. Here the efforts are aimed at uniformity of relief provisions across various legislative authorities, organizing the federal relief machinery, averting future disaster losses, and experimenting with new forms of assistance. In some instances legislation enacted between catastrophes is an effort to cope with problems encountered with legislation hatched in the political world of the aftermath of catastrophes. For example, the provisions of the 1973 flood insurance legislation were among other things, a response to the lack of flood insurance coverage for victims of Hurricane Agnes and the Rapid City flood, a problem compounded by generous relief provisions enacted after those disasters. Similarly, increases in interest rates for disaster loans enacted in 1975 were a response to the cost of the more generous legislation enacted after Hurricane Agnes. Thus cycles of legislative activity are evident in which major catastrophes become occasions for expanding federal relief benefits, and the time between catastrophes becomes an occasion for rethinking (and sometimes retrenching) federal responsibilities.

Efforts to expand federal assistance in the aftermath of catastrophes have gained political support within Congress through logrolling. In order to secure votes of representatives from disaster-prone areas, those requesting assistance have shown a willingness to support future relief assistance bills. For example, in debating relief assistance for Hurricane Betsy, Senator Long told Senator Proxmire, "As I told the senator privately, if his State should ever be visited with a similar disaster, he could count on my vote to help for his people."[5] In order to secure the votes of those whose districts had recently experienced disasters, retroactive features have been incorporated into the pending legislation. The provisions of the Hurricane Agnes legislation, for example, were applied to more than one hundred earlier disasters.[6]

Reflecting the distributional nature of relief assistance and related logrolling within Congress, bills enacted in the aftermath of catastrophes have passed with ease. (This, of course, does not mean that all bills introduced in the aftermath of catastrophes have been enacted.) All but four of the acts listed in table 1 were enacted with voice votes. For the remaining acts with roll call votes, the maximum numbers of House and Senate members voting against a bill are twenty-five and seven respectively. Not surprisingly, the bills enacted between catastrophes have been enacted with narrower margins. Here the issues — regulation of land use, retrenchment of relief benefits, reorganizations of federal agencies — have been more controversial and the debate more polarized.

Federal Disaster Agency Roles

The federal agency role in shaping disaster relief policy also differs in the two political worlds. In the aftermath of catastrophes, federal relief agencies have discretion, within certain limits, in negotiating the specifics of relief provision. These negotiations have been occasions for introducing fairly substantial policy changes. More generally, the cumulative actions of federal agencies in responding to various disasters define the content of federal disaster relief policy. Between catastrophes, the emphasis of federal relief agencies is on promulgating administrative regulations often designed to overcome problems encountered in the most recent catastrophe.

The Mount St. Helens relief experience exemplifies the way in which agency-level decisions made in the aftermath of particular catastrophes can shape overall relief policy. One of the concerns of FEMA —the federal agency which administers the Disaster Relief Act— is to make sure that federal assistance supplements state and local relief efforts rather than supplants them. This is in keeping with the congressional intent of the 1950 and subsequent relief acts. Prior to Mount St. Helens the state commitment had been a negotiated one, written into a federal-state agreement that specified the conditions under which federal assistance was being granted. Typically states agreed to either a fixed obligation of funds, a commitment to undertake certain relief activities, or a commitment to bear a fixed share of relief costs.

In the case of Mount St. Helens and subsequent disasters a new policy was established by federal officials. As a part of the agreement, federal officials specified that the state would pay 25 percent of relief costs for public facilities. This was a higher amount than states had typically borne in the past and far greater than what the states involved expected to pay. Despite many efforts by state officials and some congressmen to get the federal agency to revise this policy, the agency remained steadfast, citing the desire to make federal assistance "truly supplemental" and presidential concurrence with the cost-sharing provision.

General Accounting Office reviews of disaster relief activities have been a major impetus for disaster agency policymaking between catastrophes. Since 1978 there have been eight major reviews of disaster relief operations, not counting other reviews of the flood insurance program, FEMA management procedures, and reviews of civil defense programs.[7] The reviews address such things as cash flow problems experienced by disaster-struck communities waiting for federal funds, duplication of benefits brought about by some victims receiving payment for disaster losses from multiple agencies, controversies over the federal regulations governing request for disaster assistance, and the time period for which federal assistance is available. For many of the issues addressed in the reviews, the federal agency response has been to adopt new administrative regulations.

Intergovernmental Relations

Because the details of federal assistance for any particular disaster are negotiated by state and federal officials, the tenor of relief efforts is influenced by intergovernmental relationships. Such relationships tend to be episodic in nature, shaped more by the experience in providing relief for the disaster at hand than by previous contacts.

Many of the disaster relief experiences and related intergovernmental relationships have been quite positive, while others have been conflict-ridden. Because the federal disaster relief partnership rests heavily upon state-level cooperation in negotiating relief provisions and rendering assistance, the implementation of relief programs is delayed and the burdens of disasters are prolonged when conflicts erupt.

The variation in federal and state relations in the aftermath of catastrophes can be explained by several factors. In part such variation is a consequence of the discretion that federal and state officials have to tailor relief programs to the disaster at hand. In part the variation is the result of congressional passage of special relief legislation and of the intervention of members of Congress who represent disaster-struck areas at the scene of a disaster in helping to work out constituents' difficulties in receiving assistance. In part the variation is the result of differences in strategies adopted by state and local officals in attempting to secure or expand the amount of federal assistance.

Implications for Disaster Policy

As the result of triggering the highly salient political world, major catastrophes have had two influences on federal disaster policy—best characterized together as a "ratchet-like" effect. First, the policy at any point in time is likely to be defined in terms of the most recent catastrophic event. This in turn skews disaster policy more generally toward extreme events. Second, the recurrence of catastrophes has become occasion for further expanding the scope of and opportunities for federal funding for recovery and reconstruction. This in turn has resulted in increased federal outlays for federal disaster programs. The expansion of federal outlays has led to the search for ways to limit federal disaster relief expenditures in particular and disaster losses more generally.

The Political Dilemma

Herein lies the political dilemma of disaster policymaking. On the one hand, the politically most popular policy—expanding federal disaster assistance for recovery and reconstruction—is both costly and does little to control longer-run growth of disaster losses. On the other hand, the policies that are believed to be most effective in these latter respects—preparedness and mitigation—are politically less salient and therefore unlikely to receive much attention during the "active" stages of federal disaster policymaking.

The history of federal disaster policymaking, as briefly reviewed in this chapter, demonstrates the political appeal of recovery and reconstruction and the more divisive politics associated with the mitigation aspects of disaster policy. Expanded federal disaster loan and grant provisions for recovery and reconstruction have been enacted many times in the past thirty years, each with substantial support within Congress. In contrast, it took many years from the time that the concept of nonstructural mitigation was first introduced within Congress until it became part of any disaster legislation. Even now, mitigation provisions are relatively limited.

The Implementation Dilemma

Placing more emphasis upon hazard mitigation and preparedness also creates an implementation dilemma. On the one hand, federal officials have a strong stake in promoting hazard mitigation and preparedness— in order to lessen federal costs for disaster recovery—but little direct control over the effectiveness of such efforts. For federal disaster policy to have an impact in lessening disaster losses, the programs that the federal govenment establishes must alter the behavior not only by persons in federal agencies but also by personnel in subnational governments and ultimately by individual citizens. On the other hand, subnational governments and individuals owning property in hazardous areas control the effectiveness of mitigation and preparedness policies, but for the most part actions consistent with such policies are low on their list of priorities.

In principle, the recent efforts to control the growth of federal disaster relief outlays and to control the longer-run growth of disaster losses make eminent sense. By increasing preparedness capacities, governmental entities are better situated to issue warnings or respond in a fashion that helps minimize disaster losses. Through land use revisions and other hazardous development modifications, disaster losses can be averted.

The difficulty is that citizens and governmental officials often do not feel an urgency to undertake such actions. Evidence for the low priority that individuals and officials assign to disaster preparedness and mitigation has been provided in earlier chapters in this book. More generally, one of the central themes of the literature about human response to catastrophes is the marked indifference in the attitudes of those who live in hazardous areas or are otherwise exposed to hazards. People who reside in hazardous areas tend not to worry about the "coming" earthquake, flood, hurricane, or nuclear power plant accident until it happens. Believing they have little control over such events, they tend to be fatalistic about the occurrence of catastrophes.

Conclusions

There is no easy resolution of these dilemmas, for disaster policy needs to strike a balance between efforts to recover from disasters and efforts to avert losses. In striking that balance, policymakers need to consider the factors that facilitate or constrain policy change as reflected by the differing political worlds of disaster policy.

One of the challenges for policymakers who desire to reduce the growth of disaster losses is to stimulate more effort in the "normal" world of disaster policymaking. This would reduce the political pressure for responding to problems posed by the most recent catastrophe and avoid formulating disaster policy on the basis of extreme events. Such a shift in policymaking requires a clear and consistent advocate—among policymakers—for increasing hazard mitigation and preparedness efforts. It also requires lessening the incentives for individuals to simply wait until disasters occur, then rebuild.

Policy Issues in International Context

Decisionmaking under Disaster Conditions ⚡ Yehezkel Dror

Multiple Perspectives

Decisionmaking under disaster conditions (DDC) is a complex and multifarious process. Even though a large literature deals with the subject and related processes, such as command in war,[1] external relations, and security crisis management,[2] no good theoretic basis is available for analyzing and explaining actual DDC behavior or for significantly improving it. In the absence of relevant theory, learning from experience is inhibited. Therefore, this essay aims toward constructing a suitable theoretic frame for observing, studying, and improving DDC.

In this essay parts of a comprehensive model of policymaking[3] are applied to DDC. DDC is examined with the help of multiple perspectives[4] that are applied both behaviorally to explain actual DDC behavior and prescriptively to identify improvement needs and to design improvement proposals.

Without exhausting the range of useful perspectives, this essay selects the following seven for exploring DDC: (1) facing adversity; (2) producing images; (3) compressed time; (4) tragic choice; (5) fuzzy gambling; (6) strain and stress; and (7) group processes, individuals, and organizational settings.

Even though they are incomplete and in part overlapping, these multiple perspectives permit exploration of often neglected facets of DDC. This inquiry is but a step towards a general theory of DDC, which in turn should be anchored in a comprehensive approach to crisis decisionmaking and to decisionmaking as a whole.

Crisis decisionmaking in general and DDC in particular should also be looked at as a mode of social problem-handling processes as a whole and governmental policymaking especially. When a more narrow view of DDC is adopted, it must still be considered within broader policymaking processes, in particular those directed at preventing disasters and at hardening society against disasters. For instance, installation of emergency relief systems in the chemical industry can prevent Bhopal-like calamities. Enforcement of earthquake-resistant building codes or obligatory insurance against disaster damages illustrate disaster consequence-mitigating policies.

Therefore DDC should, at the very least, be considered within a broader view of disaster-management by society and government as a main component of societal disaster-coping systems. This point of theoretic importance also has very practical implications. Allocation of resources for disaster prevention should be considered together with allocation of resources for DDC and allocation of resources for disaster damage mitigation. These alternatives are competing uses of limited social resources that can be allocated to disaster coping in the inclusive sense of that term.

This essay addresses the narrower subject of DDC, but its broader context should be kept in mind. It proceeds by examining the seven above-mentioned perspectives, with special attention to their implications for understanding actual DDC behavior and improvement needs. Then, on the basis of the behavioral analysis, as summarized in a theoretic intermezzo, some recommendations for improvements are proposed.[5]

Behavioral Exploration

DDC behavior is examined and analyzed with the help of seven theoretic perspectives. The concept of DDC covers a range of different disasters, although excluding foreign affairs, security crises and related situations (such as terrorism incidents and criminal activities), and economic

crises. Nuclear plant disasters, earthquakes, famine, and sudden out-
break of a serious epidemic are quite different in nature, with variations between cases and their societal and political settings. Though
therefore necessarily generalized, the following exploration aims at
exposing some important behavioral features of DDC shared in nearly
all cases, despite much variation. This behavioral exploration also presents some main improvement needs, with a "debugging" strategy that
aims at reducing major error propensities.

Facing Adversity

A main feature of DDC is the facing of some extreme adversity. This
determines the main goal of DDC, namely to reduce the costs of the
adversity, both direct and indirect. Long-range societal and sociopsy-
chological impacts, such as traumatization, are often ignored, but important to consider.[6]

The acute adversity facing DDC explains much of actual DDC behavior, such as tendencies toward maze-decisionmaking—that is, erratic
behavior responding in ad hoc fashion to parts of the calamities as they
slowly reveal themselves, up to decision-spasms. Adversity also produces some of the main features of DDC discussed as separate perspectives, such as strain and stress.

The adversity features of DDC raise an interesting issue. Can or
should one utilize the adversity in order to achieve various disaster-
unrelated goals impossible to realize under ordinary conditions? Underlying this query is the desire to make various changes in reality, such
as clearing slum areas, for example. Under ordinary conditions such
changes may be infeasible, because of the strength of pro-status-quo
variables and the costs of slum clearance. But disasters loosen up
reality and may permit quite a number of interventions, which may
not really be necessary for handling the particular disaster but can be
done under its umbrella. The utilization of disaster for desired changes,
with nature providing the "destruction" part of what Joseph A.
Schumpeter called "constructive-destruction,"[7] constitutes a challenge
for DDC. The issue is ignored in relevant literature as well as practice.
This point is all the more important because of its prescriptive
implications.

Interesting as well as important is the impact of disaster shocks on
main national policies, in the sense of learning from the extreme
adversity. In principle, such learning can be correct, or can constitute

"underlearning" or "overlearning." Various policies adopted in Japan as a result of earthquake disasters illustrate correct learning, while the Dutch Delta Project can, in part, be considered as a case of "overlearning" from a counterprobabilistic disaster.[8] Stricter restrictions on nuclear power plants following some accidents illustrate debatable learning, regarded as underlearning or overlearning depending on ideological and political stance.

Longer-range policy results from disaster go beyond the concept of DDC, because they involve policymaking as a result of the disaster but not under disaster conditions. Often longer-range policy results of disasters are more important than DDC effects in the narrow sense, leading directly into politics, public opinion, and broader aspects of culture. Cultural attitudes toward risk often condition and are conditioned by political and policy results of various disasters, with significant differences between countries.[9] Though largely outside the scope of this essay, such impacts of disasters and their containment are very important, including the economic impacts of changes in risk perceptions and attitudes to risks following dramatic but low-probability incidents. As such longer-range consequences are also influenced by DDC, it is up to DDC to take them into account and direct activities to them. This leads directly to the image-producing effects and functions of DDC.

Producing Images

The political, policy, and social learning processes caused by disasters and their handling add an important and difficult dimension to DDC, namely image production. This dimension includes communication, public relations, and mass media handling. The public impacts of disaster and DDC are influenced more by images diffused through the mass media than by the exact facts, with unavoidable and sometimes very large differences between those two. While disasters are not produced in order to affect the mass media, as is the case in many terrorism incidents, the presentation of the disaster by the mass media can have very important immediate effects. The media may either provide timely warning or create mass panic. The images of disaster and DDC lingering in the minds of various publics influence the longer-range political, policy, and cultural consequences of disaster and DDC.

Image production is therefore an important aspect of DDC. Its ethical, political, and technical problems are formidable, starting with the principle of freedom of the media and ranging to hesitation about including public relations experts on DDC staffs. Indeed, the very idea of devoting scarce attention and other decisionmaking resources to image-influencing activities during the pressures of a disaster may seem an anathema to DDC. Yet in terms of mitigating and influencing disaster results as the main task of DDC, image production must be taken into account. It is an important perspective for looking at DDC.

Compressed Time

A main feature of DDC, shared with all of crisis management and indeed an element of its definition, is intense time pressure. Events occur very fast and require immediate response that also engenders longer-range implications. DDC does not deal necessarily with a single event but sometimes with a continuous process. That is, DDC may respond to single, repeated, or continuous calamity events/processes, which in turn may or may not be influenced in their continuous dynamics by the DDC.

The distinction between single-event calamities, continuous calamities, and series of calamities, or pandemics, is very important for DDC. To take an historic example, the plague in medieval Europe was a pandemic.[10] Terrorism at present illustrates a pandemic, with periodic outbreaks and surges constituting acute calamities, as do earthquakes in some areas and famine in parts of Africa. Implications for DDC are many, including the possibility of establishing dedicated DDC that specializes in particular calamities and operates on a continuous basis, as compared with broad-spectrum DDC that must be geared to face diverse and often unpredictable calamities.

Some implications of time compression for actual DDC behavior are included in the concept of strain and stress. But others are quite understudied. In particular, implications for fatigue and for continuous vigilance require attention. It is the consequences of the compressed time dimension of DDC that pose important challenges to DDC improvement. Ways to upgrade decisionmaking quality within strict time constraints are needed, with the costs of delay increasing often exponentially. What are needed are decisionmaking shortcuts and time-saving decisionmaking aids and procedures, as well as arrangments to reduce the psychological effects of time pressures that erode decision quality.

Tragic Choice

Morally demanding, psychologically depressing, and politically nearly impossible are the tragic choices[11] often imposed on DDC. Harsh choices have to be made in terms of allocation of very limited resources to pressing needs, only some of which can be met. This choice is made all the more difficult by "lottery values," as discussed below, and by the often striking life and death features of DDC. Intense pressures put on DDC by various agents, including often well-intended local and international groups, further aggravate tragic choice situations.

Two additional aspects of tragic choice in DDC are essential for understanding actual DDC behavior. These aspects are often hidden. First, the form in which the questions for decision are formulated during DDC largely shapes the priorities that are actually allocated to different goals and values.[12] A second special aspect of tragic choice in DDC is the allocation of attention.

As Herbert Simon points out,[13] attention is the scarcest of all of decisionmaking resources. Allocation of attention within the pressing and demanding circumstances of DDC, with many events clamoring for decisions, is a very difficult process. Very dramatic events tend to receive more attention than they deserve in terms of objective significance, and accidental sequences of information inputs shape the allocation of attention. Prescriptively, attention allocation tools that apply deliberately explicit criteria are needed. However handled, attention allocation in the face of demand overloads is a tragic choice, adding to strain and stress and other facets of DDC.

Fuzzy Gambling

A dominant and often overwhelming feature of DDC is uncertainty. This characteristic is illustrated in multiple ways. For instance:

1 The calamity itself is unpredicted, at least in location and scope and often in its basic features.
2 The unfolding dynamics of the calamity is shrouded in fog, with many actual events being unknown to DDC till much later.
3 Often cardinal future scenarios of the calamity dynamics cannot be predicted.
4 Second, third, and further levels of calamity effects are often indeterminate. For instance, involved populations may either panic or organize very effective self-help measures, with quite different

implications for DDC. Such levels of calamity effects often are unpredictable and cannot be unknown without long time lags.

5 Many results of DDC actions cannot be predicted, with a high probability of unanticipated and frequently undesired consequences, including the possibility of counter intended "ironies of calamity."

Because of these and other uncertainties built into calamities, all DDC involves "fuzzy gambling," in the sense that decisions must be made in the face of uncertainty, with much of the uncertainty being extreme and not reducible to probabilities. DDC involves gambling, that is, decisionmaking in the face of uncertainty. It is fuzzy because the rules of the gamble are unknown, largely unknowable, often indeterminate, and erratic. Catastrophe models and chaos mathematics apply more appropriately to calamity processes than do smooth curves and regular patterns.[14]

"Lottery value" choice is unavoidable in nearly all DDC. "Lottery values" involve choice between different levels of risk, including irreducible uncertainty. These are basically value choices—but very imposing ones which are usually not explicated and further increase the burden of tragic choice. In DDC hard choices between different bundles of risks and uncertainties are unavoidable; therefore, improvement of lottery value judgment is another important facet in upgrading DDC.

The view of DDC as fuzzy gambling has far-reaching implications. Many of the inadequacies of DDC can be explained in terms of inherent weaknesses of human decisionmaking in the face of uncertainty.[15] Further, many of the professional ideas for improving decisionmaking in the face of uncertainty do not apply to the fuzzy aspects of DDC. Most so-called decision analysis[16] is not applicable because it relies upon subjective probabilities, which in DDC are more of a delusion than a reasonable basis for action. More recent ideas on risk management often are not applicable either, leaving an intellectual and theoretical vacuum hindering upgrading of cardinal fuzzy gambling aspects of DDC.[17]

Strain and Stress

Applying the psychology of decisonmaking under strain and stress is a promising way to increase understanding of DDC behavior and to explore possibilities for improvement.[18] Additional applications of decision psychology to DDC are needed. For instance, the shattering effects of calamities on cognitive maps and on reference theories may explain some DDC characteristics.

Well known but usually not frankly discussed are the effects of strain and stress on human biological and bioneurological performance, which often result in decay of DDC quality. This decay leads to an esoteric but very important field of recommendations involving ergometric considerations, work and rest discipline, and controlled and monitored use of psychotropic chemicals to upgrade decision performance of key personnel.

Strain and stress cast grave doubts on gaming simulations of DDC and other crisis behavior. The absence of real-life strain and stress makes many crisis exercises (especially with students) quite dissimilar from actual DDC. Crisis management theory, based on doubtful gaming,[19] needs reevaluation, as well as simulated DDC operations, exercises, and experiments under realistic strain and stress conditions.

Group Processes, Individuals, and Organizational Settings

The group processes aspects of DDC are relatively well covered in the literature, even if in somewhat different contexts.[20] But some relevant DDC features have escaped adequate scrutiny. These include, among others:

1 The location of final decision authority in single superiors or small collegial bodies. The interaction between group processes in DDC and the command element poses important issues, all the more so because of the needs of decision shortcuts due to time pressure.

2 Actual devolution of decision authority on individuals, often of low rank, because time pressures prevent group processes and hierarchical controls from working.

3 The interaction between the professional staffs of DDC and political decisionmakers.

Because of such specific features, standard images of group processes need much adjustment in the study and improvement of DDC.

DDC takes place within organizational contexts. Therefore findings on organizational behavior in conditions of ambiguity apply to DDC.[21] Still, most literature in organizational behavior does not explain DDC behavior. For example, the commitment and personal involvement revealed in much DDC behavior does not fit many "cold" and "calculated" modes of organizational bureaucratic politics and reward-maximization theories dominating organization theory. Whatever the applicability of organization theory, DDC takes place in organizations. Therefore improving the overall organizational setting of DDC is a central approach to increasing its effectiveness.[22]

Theoretic Intermezzo

The above perspectives lead to an important conclusion. Many of the inherent features of DDC have a congenital limit or, in economic terms, a constrained maximum production function. DDC at its hypothetical best is still a haphazard process, with many built-in weaknesses and error propensities.

Even at its hypothetical best, DDC will be error-prone because of inherent difficulties and limitations. This conclusion is important for the evaluation of DDC and for application of various political and legal forms of accountability to it. Recognition of the probability of error in even very good DDC leads to the need to install error-absorbing and error-balancing processes, mainly as a post-DDC activity.

Another set of implications from pluralistic views of DDC deals with improvement possibilities. In principle, improvement of any process can be approached in two main ways, with various mixes between them. The first and easier way is debugging, that is, to observe and study the process in action, to identify its obvious weaknesses, and to intervene so as to rectify these weaknesses. The second, more difficult but more penetrating way is to design preferable models of the process, to identify gaps between that model and reality, and to intervene in order to make the actual process more closely approximate the preferable model.

The first approach is more practical. It can help to avoid some more glaring weaknesses of the examined process, but it has strict limitations. In particular, debugging, too, depends on models of the process as it should be for identification of errors, but the underlying models are mental, tacit, and not subjected to explicit evaluation and justification. Therefore, identification of obvious weaknesses may be misleading and at best limited to manifest phenomena rather than to

in-depth propensities for error. This weakness is all the more pronounced when complex processes are considered for improvement.

A good example illustrating the limits of debugging and the need for
more advanced models as bases for improvement is supplied by the
Cuba missile crisis. That case demonstrates the advantage of positive
redundancy, in the sense of multiple parallel teams considering independently the more difficult issues posed by the crisis. While the idea
of "multiplexing" as a mean structural device for reducing the probability of error has been justified theoretically by Von Neumann in
1950,[23] it contradicts naive common sense, which regards all duplication as wasteful. Therefore the idea of positive redundancy in the
thinking processes of DDC will often be missed by intuitive debugging,
requiring explicit preferable models instead.

The complexities of DDC require theoretical analysis and design of
preferable models to serve as bases for significant improvement. Debugging by experienced practitioners can help to get rid of glaring weaknesses, but it can also produce incorrect and counterproductive
"improvements" and it is likely to miss many needs and possibilities for
real improvement. In respect to DDC, good theory constitutes an essential basis for good practice.

Recommendations for Action

A variety of recommendations for improving DDC can be derived from
the multiple perspectives presented above and their underlying models. The following eight recommendations for action illustrate such
recommendations and also serve to illustrate different approaches to
the improvement of DDC.

Application of these recommendations to concrete situations requires
specification in terms of particular needs and possibilities. A qualita-
tive cost-benefit estimate is necessary to decide what resources to
allocate to which DDC improvement recommendations. Choices between
different recommendations are best made in terms of a selective radi-
calism improvement strategy that selects a limited number of DDC elements for radical redesign. This strategy is often preferable to incremental improvements spread over many domains of DDC or to overall
DDC nova-design, that is, the substitution of an entirely new DDC
design for the previous strategy. When the expected negative value of

calamities is very high and the current DDC is very weak, it may be necessary to engage in overall redesign and even nova-design of the DDC, considering the perspectives and prescriptions in an integrated way. In any case, a number of elements of DDC must be improved in coordinated ways because of internal interdependencies, such as the relationship between introduction of innovative processes and upgrading of DDC staff.

The recommendations presented below are conjectural,[24] with some having a stronger base in available data and some being more daring. An experimental attitude to the upgrading of DDC is needed, with recommendations to be tested and further developed continuously.

The proposed recommendations deal with eight main dimensions of DDC: (1) authority and functions; (2) facilities; (3) internal structure and organization; (4) decision processes and procedures; (5) staffing; (6) integrative simulated operations exercises; (7) DDC research, development, and pilot-testing; (8) policymaking for DDC.

Authority and Functions

Clear establishment of the legal authority of DDC is critical in disaster conditions. Particularly when multiple jurisdictions are involved, clear authority to make decisions and activate multiple agencies is vital. The alternative of relying on willing cooperation of multiple jurisdictions is unlikely to operate spontaneously during DDC without earlier agreement and simulation exercises.

The question of DDC authority is central not only to the orchestration of multiple public agencies during disaster operations, but also to involvement of citizens groups and various private bodies, such as mass media, in DDC. In many countries special legal emergency regimes provide DDC with all necessary powers, subject to later account. But in the United States emergency powers are granted only in a state of war. Instead, agreements are required to specify lines of authority and mutual assistance prior to the emergency. Such agreements need evaluation and revision following DDC experiences, to meet future needs better. Allocation of legal authority is an integral part of DDC preparation and simulation and requires appropriate legal advice.[25]

It is necessary to define the function of DDC in relation to other activities and units dealing with disaster possibilities and consequences. Activities to reduce the probability of disasters and handling of long-term consequences of disasters are outside the scope of DDC. Their relations should be clarified so as to permit DDC to concentrate on its main functions, namely coping with the disaster itself in real time.

Facilities

Without suitable facilities, the quality of DDC is seriously impaired. Emergency operating center facilities need careful preparation, including, for instance, reliable communication networks. DDC facilities need to be designed to meet human needs, reducing strain, fatigue, and other DDC-damaging effects. Rest and relaxation areas and control of noise and smoke illustrate minimal requirements.

DDC does not require facilities reserved for its exclusive use, which may be unnecessarily costly. Various public facilities can be adjusted to serve as DDC operations centers with relatively small investments. But lack of adequate facilities will impair DDC unnecessarily. In addition, adequate preparation of resources needed for operations and capacity to mobilize these resources are integral to adequate preparations for disasters. Plans to make available such resources need to be exercised within DDC-simulated operations exercises.

Internal Structure and Organization

A number of structural and organizational principles can augment DDC, creating an adaptive, rapidly learning, and crisis-accommodating agency. Some of these principles include:

- [ ] Built-in positive redundancy and multiplexing, with parallel teams considering critical decisions so as to compress time.
- [ ] Clear-cut decisionmakers, preferably individuals rather than collective bodies, with defined division of authority, to accelerate decisions and establish accountability.
- [ ] Internal division of labor, combined with full elasticity, so that staff and functions can be shifted around and staff resources can be reallocated according to urgency and nature of disaster.
- [ ] Special units in charge of select processes, including intelligence and implementation monitoring. Without a special unit in charge of intelligence, constant data collection, and revision of situational estimates, as needed for high-quality DDC, these activities will be neglected in favor of urgent action and distorted by various biases. Intelligence collection and presentation requires profes-

sionalism, for instance, in the assessment and presentation of uncertainty. Similarly, without a defined unit monitoring implementation, the actual impact of DDC on field operations will often diminish, without responsible DDC officials being adequately aware of operational constraints and inadequacies.

☐ Distinct units are also needed to manage issues that do not seem pressing and that, therefore, tend to be displaced from attention. Management of longer-range psychological effects of disasters, for example, needs to be integrated into DDC rather than left for later. Unless assigned to a specific unit, such an issue is usually neglected. Related to the already discussed need for a special unit is inquiry into the image-producing effects of DDC.

☐ Brain trusts, drawing upon outside volunteer experts, should be formed to consider special issues. Such brain trusts are not integrated into the main stream of DDC. They are thus protected from some of the crisis pressures and are able to consider critical issues thoroughly but rapidly.

A hierarchal structure is most effective for DDC. Collegial, consensual, and coordinational arrangements do not permit rapid and clear-cut decisionmaking with due accountability, essential for DDC. Therefore a hierarchical structure with a defined top DDC decisionmaker and clear-cut though elastic line-staff relationships is recommended.

Often DDC units will be composed of representatives of different organizations that are not subordinate to DDC officials, such as police, national guard, health services, etc. Still, for all but very minor disasters, a disaster coordinating director who can temporarily give orders to all units involved in disaster operations is essential for adequate disaster management. Often a political superior will be the top decisionmaker, such as governor of a state. In such cases, the DDC director should operate in the name of the top political decisionmaker, with a direct "hot line" or other close communication means with the latter. In case of multijurisdictional disaster management, suitable prearrangements are needed to assure necessary hierarchical authority, as stated above.

A DDC management unit, directly subordinated to the DDC director and in charge of the operations of DDC itself, is central to the DDC organizational structure. Within the DDC management unit, experts in DDC processes and procedures are needed to review the quality of decisionmaking and to adjust processes and procedures as needed.

This role may be filled by a chief DDC scientist. This person or unit would observe DDC in operation and intervene to correct wrong processes. Such an expert would also keep a detailed action diary and would be in charge of postdisaster learning processes to improve DDC in the future.

Special consideration needs to be given to DDC as a man-machine operation, as many DDC processes can be aided by suitable data banks and computer programs. The timesaving aspects of man-machine systems make them especially attractive for DDC, where time is one of the scarcest resources. Micro- and minicomputers may well meet many DDC needs, making large hardware installations with all their complexities and sensitivities often unnecessary. Microcomputer networks, with each main DDC unit and function having its own computer and with automated interflow of information, may best meet DDC requirements below a scale justifying heavier hardware. To assure smooth operation and necessary elasticity, all staff need to be fully competent in using the man-machine system and in operating all main stations. The man-machine system needs built-in redundancy and backup facilities to operate fully under various disaster conditions, including the disruption of power lines.

Decision Processes and Procedures

Decision processes and procedures are at the core of DDC and therefore need careful consideration and preparation. Many of the detailed processes and procedures depend on the specific types of disaster to be managed by discrete DDC units. On a more general level, needed processes and procedures include the following:

  □ Preprogrammed, carefully exercised and updated procedures for activating DDC, including rapid mobilization of staff and preparation of equipment and facilities for operations.
  □ Continual estimation and current portrayal of the disaster situation. This information is best displayed using interactive computer graphics and information systems that are simultaneously available to the principal decisionmaking and analysis stations in DDC.
  □ Appropriate models for decision analysis are essential to assure decision quality under extreme time pressures. Some of the simpler decisions, such as in the domain of logistics, can in part be

automated on the basis of suitable operations research models. Most decisions will be heuristic in nature, but still can be assisted by suitable policy analysis models, using in part computerized decision support systems. These systems are urgently needed, but are not available at present.

□ Special attention must be given to conditions of uncertainty, to avoid its repression or displacement. All policy analysis models and programs used in DDC need to be sensitive to uncertainty in order to avoid inappropriate methods, such as arbitrary allocation of subjective probabilities. This need illustrates the necessity for research and development to develop knowledge and methods appropriate for meeting the real needs of DDC.

□ Creativity, in the sense of inventing good ideas for managing disaster predicaments, needs to be encouraged during DDC. The structural ideas of parallel staff work and of a separate brain trust are directed in part at this need, illustrating the fusion between functional and structural improvements of DDC.

□ Necessarily, standard operating procedures will play a major role in DDC, but they must not be permitted to repress improvisation. Despite all possible preparations, DDC is in many respects a process of improvisation. Accordingly, good DDC combines various preparatory processes, such as contingency planning, with increasing ability for improvisation. The standard operating procedures accordingly should recognize the crucial importance of improvisation and provide suitable frameworks for it, rather than repressing it.

These are only a few recommendations for improving DDC processes and procedures. Processes and procedures constitute the core of DDC, with structures, facilities, and staff designed in principle to improve the processes.

Staffing

Processes and procedures constitute the core of DDC, but the primary factor in determining DDC performance is the human beings engaged in DDC and its related activities. Therefore, developing the capacity of staff is the single most important approach to improving DDC, although raising the standards of staff needs to be planned and implemented in relation to processes, procedures, structures, etc., so as to improve the capacity of staff to engage in principal DDC activities. Changes in procedures, structures, facilities, authority, etc. without parallel development of staff are futile.

In dealing with DDC staffing a number of separate aspects need careful attention and improvement:

1 *Staff composition.* The staff must include experts in the various fields relevant to particular disasters, such as toxic materials, as well as in particular disaster-consequence managing professions, such as medicine and civil construction. In addition, DDC staff must include DDC process professionals, such as experts in policy analysis, decision psychology, and crisis management.

2 *Staff professionalization.* The staff as a whole needs professional training in DDC, in order to develop appropriate professionalism in action.[26] To do so, a variety of staff development modes have to be used, such as intensive simulated operations exercises and modular training with the help of intensive workshops.[27] Helpful in encouraging a sense of professionalism in DDC may be setting up a professional association in crisis management, with a DDC subsection, arranging conferences and other shared professional activities, strengthening informal networks of staffs.

3 *Crisis management experts.* Urgently needed for improving DDC are crisis management experts. Such experts are not being systematically trained at present. To prepare crisis management experts, innovative programs are needed at public policy schools or at a center to be set up on a national level, for instance by FEMA.

4 *Politicians and* DDC. The politicians who are in charge of DDC need some suitable training too. Participation at simulated operations exercises and specially designed workshops may be the most practical means for preparing politicians for their critical roles in DDC.

Integrative Simulated Operations Exercises

A principal mode to integrate various improvements of DDC, as well as to test the improvements and train DDC practitioners and professionals, is integrative simulated operations exercises in DDC. Unless a DDC center is exercised under realistic conditions periodically, it has no chance of performing well in case of disaster. The recommendation to exercise DDC staff and operations periodically is a major one that is supported by available experiences and theoretical analysis alike.

Exercising DDC is a complex endeavor with a professional basis of its own in both gaming and military staff exercises. Some of the nontechnical issues involved are illustrated by the following recommendations:

☐ Integrative operations exercises need to be done periodically. But simulating DDC under realistic conditions and in all dimensions is a resource-consuming activity. Therefore an annual full-scale exercise is reasonable for most DDC centers.

☐ Parts of DDC can and should be exercised more frequently, in preparation for the annual full-scale exercise.

☐ Realistic conditions should be simulated as far as possible; for example, starting at night and continuing the exercise for real-time periods, with all involved hardship and fatigue. Other realistic conditions that need to be fully reflected include much uncertainty, jurisdictional disputes, and mass media pressures.

☐ Diverse scenarios should be utilized and tied to contingency planning. But the fact that real disasters will probably be quite different from all considered contingencies should be emphasized.

☐ The persons who in fact will engage in DDC must, of course, be those participating in the exercises.

☐ Real-time monitoring is essential, with careful discussion of the exercise and written analysis of the experiences to facilitate organizational learning.

☐ The participation of politicians who will be in charge in real disasters is very desirable, but often difficult to achieve.[28] Surrogate arrangements include participation of principal advisors and assistants of the politicians in the exercise, together with full presentation of the findings from the exercises to the appropriate politicians.

Development of suitable methods and materials for realistic exercises is a principal task for DDC research and development.

DDC Research, Development, and Pilot-testing

The need for DDC research, development, and field-testing is demonstrated by the many unresolved problems and needed methods confronted throughout this essay. Wherever one turns knowledge needed for DDC improvement is missing.[29] Therefore intense research and development are essential.

As DDC is an applied activity, the criterion for evaluating relevant knowledge is its utility for improving DDC. Field-testing is essential before an improvement proposal can be regarded as valid enough to be widely adopted. Simulation exercises are useful, but experience with actual DDC under real disaster conditions is essential for final testing of research and development products. Building the necessary knowledge base requires a network for collecting experiences, a means of processing it for valid innovations, and a diffusion of experience-supported improvements.

Research and development and experimentation require planning, support, suitable organizational bases, and interdisciplinary professional teams. Integrating DDC research and development and testing into overall crisis management, with special attention to relevant work in national defense, is necessary. This requirement leads directly into policymaking.

Policymaking for DDC

DDC is simultaneously a dispersed activity of importance to many localities and a national necessity. Consequently, an integrated approach to policymaking is necessary. To realize the scope of needed policymaking, the already mentioned location of DDC within broader disaster-coping functions should be taken into account, such as policies to prevent disasters and policies for managing longer-range disaster consequences. FEMA is seeking to adopt such an integrated and broader approach. It is a very complex task that requires adequate political support, time, attention, and resources for successful implementation.

Embedment in Governance Retrofitting

An even broader perspective for looking at DDC is to view disaster response and crisis management in general as a form of policymaking under adversity and of societal problem-handling processes. The possibility of utilizing disasters for constructive destruction, as already considered, reinforces the need to look at DDC within policymaking as a whole. DDC development can be regarded as one of many modes for retrofitting governance to improve the capacity to govern. Such a perspective leads to further possibilities for improving crisis management and DDC in conjunction with other governance retrofitting endeavors.

In conclusion, the one last perspective is to look at DDC as a humane emergency activity directed at helping human beings in acute misery, comparable to traumatic medicine in moral imperative. It is this ethical, overriding dimension of DDC that differentiates it from most other forms of crisis management and makes it an especially appealing professional activity, vocation, and even calling. This perspective requires practitioners of DDC to make strenuous efforts to improve their ability to help persons in acute distress. This is the shared endeavor to which this essay is devoted and which serves as the ethical justification for the demands for DDC development put forth here.

Disaster Management in the Netherlands: Planning for Real Events
⚡ Uriel Rosenthal

Introduction

In several respects the Netherlands can be considered a disaster-prone country. It has

- a very dense population (about fourteen million people in an area half as large as the state of Indiana)
- the world's largest concentration of petrochemical industry in the metropolitan Rijnmond area
- two nuclear power plants, as well as others just a few miles across the border on Belgian and West German territory—all within close distance to urban regions
- a high density of private and public transport by road, railways, and waterways, with a road infrastructure in the coastal region resembling that of the largest metropolitan areas in the world
- very dense air traffic in the Amsterdam area
- the transportation of hazardous materials by road and water to and from the industrial areas of West Germany
- and, although the perennial battle against the sea seems to have been won at long last, natural circumstances that make possible the occurrence of violent storms and other natural disasters

In the postwar period the Netherlands has been struck by one large-scale disaster. In February 1953 a flood hit the southwestern part of the country, taking the lives of nearly two thousand people. Since then only a few events have met the usual criteria set by the international disaster literature. In January 1962, in a train collision near Harmelen, ninety people were killed. A November 1975 explosion in a chemical plant in Beek resulted in fourteen people killed. In May 1976 a train accident in the Rijnmond area killed twenty-four passengers. And in May 1977 a hotel fire in the center of Amsterdam resulted in the deaths of thirty-three people.

The shortness of this list of disasters might suggest that, apart from sheer luck, the Netherlands stands out as an example of advanced disaster-prevention policies and of a firm disaster-preventing culture. On a crossnational comparative level, there may be some reason to accept this perspective. But from the inside the picture is less reassuring. Emergency management, disaster management in particular, is left too much and too easily to technicians, legal specialists, and a handful of civil servants. The main policy problem with regard to disaster management in this country, then, is the gap between the technical, bureaucratic-legalistic official approach, on the one hand, and the political and sociospychological processes that will dominate any future disaster scene, on the other hand.

In this chapter I will focus on four aspects of disaster management in the Netherlands. First, attention will be paid to the discrepancies between the official conceptualization of disaster and the political and bureaupolitical reality that imposes itself in actual disaster contexts. A second topic involves the tensions between the official design for disaster management and some sociological and psychological facts that appear to be intimately linked with disaster events (and indeed to a larger extent than many seemingly natural steps resulting from the official rules and regulations). Third, I will discuss some questions regarding the organizational infrastructure of disaster management in the Netherlands. Here the major issue is the responsibilities of the public authorities and several community emergency organizations. Some rather drastic changes in the intraorganizational network are taking place. Disaster management seems to be one of the few instances of administrative reform actually carried out in recent years.

The fourth topic brings us to a fundamental paradox of emergency management. We are dealing with plans, organizations, and people oriented towards events which they are supposed to prevent from taking place in the first place, and which come as a surprise and in unexpected dimensions and forms. The persisting question is along which lines adequate preparations can be made and how disaster-relevant organizations can keep up their morale without succumbing to the syndrome of "winning the last war."

In my analysis I shall draw on Dutch disaster studies. An extensive study has been undertaken on the flood disaster of February 1953. Some smaller pieces of research have examined the Harmelen train accident of January 1962 and the explosion in the petrochemical plant near Beek.[1]

Case 1—The Flood Disaster of February 1953

In the night of Saturday, January 31, through early Sunday, February 1, 1953, the province of Zeeland in the southwestern part of the Netherlands was hit by a flood. The flood was caused by a combination of natural forces: a spring tide and a heavy storm. Nearly two thousand people were killed. The flood came at a very unfortunate moment —just before Sunday, in a region characterized by a strong belief in the sanctity of that day. In addition, many people had a vivid memory of the flood caused by the bombing of the dikes by the Royal Air Force on one of the Zeeland islands in 1944–45 and, by false analogy, underestimated the impact of the disaster. It should also not be forgotten that the catastrophe struck a region which was indeed in the process of building up its infrastructure after five years of German occupation.

Soon after the first rumors, facts, and figures reached the unaffected part of the Dutch population, the disaster took political and psychological shape as a national event, if not a national catastrophe. The initial rescue operations were coordinated by the military staff center in the governmental residence, The Hague. This was partly due to the very prompt response of the military authorities (in particular some naval officers) to the first calls for help on Saturday night. While communications between the municipal authorities in Zeeland and the provincial as well as the central government were breaking down, and one of the islands (Schouwen-Duiveland) became a "forgotten island" for nearly one and a half days, the military took the lead in containing the disaster to the stricken area. This policy, which gave priority to containment over a full-fledged mobilization of manpower and materials for local rescue operations, was affirmed by the key cabinet ministers on Sunday afternoon, February 1.

On Monday, February 2, the authorities in The Hague gradually became aware of the scope of the emergency situation in specific regions in the disaster area. In several places the absence of massive rescue efforts led to an antagonistic attitude on the part of the people towards Middleburg (the provincial capital) and The Hague. In the town of Zierikzee the local population eventually turned on the municipal authorities. Tensions came into the open when the municipal government decided to evacuate the larger part of the population. Neither a number of visits by members of the Royal House and by top-level government officials nor compulsory measures could prevent the evacuation from becoming a complete failure.

By the middle of the first week of February the authorities had a fairly adequate notion of the scope and impact of the disaster. Organized and professional relief, though seriously hindered by a shortage of equipment, got under way. A coordination commission led by the Home Secretary had to find its way amidst some twenty-five to thirty agencies. It also had to deal with the problem of civil-military relations in the disaster area. From the end of the week on, the disaster process became bureaucratized, except for the forgotten island of Schouwen-Duiveland and the town of Zierikzee. The central and provincial authorities adopted a restrictive policy regarding the "mass assault" or convergence of onlookers on the disaster area.[2] Much energy was invested in the precise application of emergency rules and regulations.

As to the recovery and restoration of the flooded areas, three elements should be mentioned. First, there was a strong nationwide feeling that this should never happen again. It resulted in the implementation of the so-called Delta plan: the closure of the estuaries in the Zuid-Holland and Zeeland area. Second, much attention was paid to material restoration and the issue of financial compensation. Different groups opposed different governmental proposals. Again, the report of the National Academy of Sciences Committee on Disaster Studies stated that "criticism was generally directed collectively against the government."[3] Third, a latent function of the flood disaster was to accelerate social and political change. Restoration indeed became identical with innovation. In some towns and villages the old social and political structure was "flooded" by the water. In other places predisaster cracks in the social system burst open. Here the disaster actually helped to settle the latent tension that had been building up in the preceding ten or fifteen years.

Case 2—The Harmelen Train Accident
of January 1962

At 9:19 AM, Monday, January 8, 1962, two passenger trains collided near Harmelen. One of the trains (coming from Utrecht) carried 900 passengers, the other 180. Ninety-three people, including both engineers, were killed. About thirty passengers were seriously injured. Material damage amounted to about ten million guilders (fifty million at current value). The accident was the biggest railway crash in Dutch history. Regarding the facts of the case, it has been established that the Utrecht train had left the station with a delay of six minutes and, consequently, should have waited for the other train to pass it at a switch near Harmelen. For reasons which still remain unclear, the engineer of the Utrecht train ignored both the yellow warning signal and the red signal. A last-second emergency braking procedure could not prevent the collision.

At 9:30 AM two Civil Defense physicians arrived at the scene of the disaster, after receiving some vague information from the municipal police. They were able to get Civil Defense personnel and material to the spot within thirty minutes. The Civil Defense personnel joined the many passengers and local residents who came to the rescue. Professional assistance units of the Dutch Railways (NS) came in at about 10:30 AM. Their boss—the president-director of the NS—had already taken charge of the rescue operations. Ambulances of the Municipal Health Service of Utrecht were also already present.

From 10:30 until about 11:00 AM the rescue operation was seriously hindered by several unexpected developments. First, a nonstop stream of volunteers rushed to the scene of the accident. Second, this mass convergence occurred at the very moment that various authorities were becoming informed about the calamity. Several emergency and emergency-relevant organizations had just become aware of the fact that something serious had happened that morning and started taking part in the operations. For instance, the provincial governor was informed only at 10:50 AM. Due to a cumulation of misunderstandings, state police officials and other potential informants had taken for granted that the highest authority in the province had been among the first to know of the dreadful event. The Utrecht Red Cross did not receive information beyond the level of rumors, and the Central Command in The Hague remained fully uninformed until 11:20 AM. The next day the Utrecht chief of the Red Cross blamed the Municipal Health Service and the provincial governor for their neglect of the Red Cross. A third obstacle was the overloading of the rather primitive communications network.

By 11:15 AM the Utrecht Municipal Health Service had managed to transport the injured passengers to nearby hospitals, where many coordination and intake problems were evident; some hospitals were unprepared for this kind of an emergency. The head of the Health Service was hindered in his efforts by the late and rather superfluous arrival on the disaster scene of a variety of authorities, assistance units, and equipment. Irrespective of their general relevance in disaster rescue operations, they simply had no task to perform and for that reason impeded rather than contributed to a prompt treatment of the most urgent problems. Irritations and frustrations on the part of some public authorities led to premature statements on responsibilities and faults. One day later a prestigious evening journal openly admitted that it had lost control over the incoming news and consequently had not been as careful as usual in presenting the news. Inexperience with this kind of situation led the prime minister to a very dubious judgment of popular sentiments about what was going on. It was against his advice that Queen Juliana came back from her ski vacation in Austria.

The official reports on the Harmelen crash all pointed to the need for automatic controls systems in the railway network. The Dutch government promised that by 1975 the entire railway network would be provided with automatic control. However, due to budgetary, technical, and administrative problems, this promise turned out to be illusory. In 1976 a train collision near Rotterdam (twenty-four people were killed) called attention to the dramatic fact that one of the busiest lines of the Dutch railways was still lacking automatic control. Indeed, in 1982 a similar story had to be told on the occasion of another severe collision on the same line. Lack of funds was the main obstacle to the introduction of such technologies.

Case 3—The DSM explosion of November 1975

On Friday, November 7, 1975, at 9:50 AM, a heavy explosion took place
at a naphthaline cracker on the grounds of the DSM chemical plant in
the southern town of Beek. After the explosion, which killed fourteen
people and inflicted serious injuries upon twenty workers, the cracker
and three petroleum tanks caught fire. Eight hours later, at 5:50 PM,
the fire spread to some other places in the tank park; for some time
there was a serious danger of a really unmanageable compounded
catastrophe. The last tank continued burning for several days.

The medical and fire brigade units of the DSM arrived immediately;
they exhibited great competence and courage. Within the hour, those
seriously wounded had been taken to hospitals. Regional health services arrived soon enough to be of some use as well. The fire brigades
of five municipalities were present from about 10:15 AM; they showed
less expertise than their DSM colleagues.

A lack of administrative, technical, and especially psychological
comprehension was apparent in the performance of quite a number of
public authorities. They were hindered to a significant extent by the
peculiar fact that personnel from no less than thirteen municipal governments, including mayors, aldermen, city councillors and civil servants, were involved in one way or the other, officially or voluntarily.
At the same time the Civil Defense apparatus did not take an active
part in managing the disaster until the evening. The president-director
of DSM later explained this delay by stating that the disaster had not
been a disaster in the legal sense and, consequently, he had not asked
for Civil Defense assistance. He did not understand that many people
saw this statement as additional evidence of a condescending attitude
on the part of DSM towards the regional community.

In the aftermath of the calamity it became clear that there had been
many warning signals, including Civil Defense reports on the dangerous location of the tank park. The mayors in the region affirmed the
need for a disaster plan that would prevent frictions and coordination
problems from escalating geometrically among the thirteen municipalities. Eventually the DSM disaster became an important facilitating
factor in the reduction of the number of municipal corporations from
thirteen to a manageable three.

The DSM disaster also had a triggering impact on disaster legislation
in The Hague. Government officials felt obligated to take more seri-

ously the possibility of industrial disasters. It was certainly due to the vivid memory of this disaster that from 1977 on, preparations for an interim bill on disaster planning were started. The bill was accepted in 1981.

The Conceptualization of Disaster:
Official versus Political Factors

Very recently, the Dutch Parliament passed a new Disaster Act. It defines disaster as an event that endangers the life and health of many people or causes severe harm to material interests, and that requires coordinated efforts on the part of agencies and organizations from various fields of expertise.[4] This conceptualization of disaster reflects the principles of disaster management in the Netherlands. A very general notion of the social and economic disruption of a community is combined with an explicit demand for governmental activity and for coordination between governmental agencies. This urge for coordination between agencies and organizations from various fields of expertise could be conceived of as a prescriptive statement. One might suggest that it is a necessary condition in order to achieve some degree of cooperation in a competitive setting. But nothing like this has been at the root of this orientation to disaster management. On the contrary, it looks more as if the recent Disaster Act has yielded to a typically legalistic approach. If the law says that public agencies and organizations should cooperate and coordinate their activities, there is nothing more to say—the more so because nobody would ever expect public officials to make things difficult for each other in the face of severe threats to the social system.

The Disaster Act includes several provisions with regard to disaster planning procedures. Municipal councils are supposed to draw up a disaster plan comprising a survey of the agencies which would take part in disaster activities. The mayor, who has the primary responsibility during disasters, is obliged to make a specific operational plan including a decisionmaking scenario for possible calamities on local territory. Although this would point to a decentralized approach to disaster prevention and disaster decisionmaking, the Disaster Act does not limit itself to arrangements for the local authorities. Due to the definite tendency to seek solutions through coordination and comprehensive planning, it rather breathes a spirit of centralization. As a self-evident supplement to the prescriptions for the local level, provincial plans are made obligatory. The Disaster Act indeed follows the trend towards closing the gap in the relations among the different levels of government in the Netherlands. When things get tough, as in disasters and other emergencies, local autonomy should give way to intervention by the provincial authorities. In turn, provincial administrators should follow the instructions from the central government.

Disaster legislation, and more specifically the legal conceptualization of disaster, appears to bet on two structural principles for disaster management: smooth cooperation between multiple agencies and organizations from various fields of expertise, and a reliance on assistance from beyond the immediate surroundings of the scene of the accident. The problematical side of this perspective is that it reinforces the naive conception that many authorities and public agencies hold about the reality of disaster management. Disaster management is presented as a depoliticized, technical process. The entire design is based on the idea that disasters will evoke feelings of solidarity and harmony among public officials and their agencies. It implies a denial of the bureaupolitics as well as of the high politics of disaster management. It ignores the fact that disasters, like all other kinds of crises, are political events in the purest sense.

The Bureaupolitics of Disaster Management

According to one of the dominant models of bureaucratic politics, bureaucratic agencies (both public and semipublic bodies) try to increase their power and attempt to promote their organization's prestige. Success in promoting an organization's prestige supposedly depends on its capacity to propagate and exhibit expertise and high morale, if possible under difficult circumstances.[5] It is not surprising, then, that disasters would be among the key events leading to bureaupolitical competition and conflict between emergency organizations. Such organizations not only fight for a common reason, but are well aware of the fact that disaster situations may be critical to the power and prestige they will hold in the postdisaster period. For some emergency organizations, such as the Red Cross, the Civil Defense, and the emergency units of the health services, disasters are rare occasions to display their social utility. But many other organizations, with socially relevant tasks to perform under normal circumstances (for instance, the police, medical institutions, and civil service bureaus) also have much to gain (or to lose) during disaster events.

As soon as the rescue phase moves to remedy and recovery, bureaupolitical tensions tend to come to the fore—sometimes even sooner. There is no activity which, by its specific substance, will never be the subject of competition and conflict. Helping the victims of a disaster often involves a bitter contest between the Red Cross, the Salvation Army, and an intriguing variety of welfare institutions. It has been aptly phrased the war of the Samaritans.[6]

During the flood disaster of February 1953, bureaupolitics flourished inside and outside the disaster area. At the outset the military, which was the first to arrive at various stricken places, was welcomed very warmly and was sometimes even asked to assume responsibilities well beyond their competence. But after a few days civil-military relations became increasingly strained. In the second week the central government decided to withdraw most military units from the disaster area. At that time the first signals had already been heard about competitive maneuvers of the Red Cross versus Civil Defense, state versus municipal police, clerical versus governmental welfare agencies. Later on, interservice rivalries between the navy on the one hand, and the air force and the army, on the other hand, come into the open.

The Harmelen train accident of January 1962 and the DSM explosion of November 1975 also gave rise to manifest confrontations between public or semipublic agencies. In January 1962 the open quarrels between representatives of the Red Cross and the health authorities were a conspicuous example of bureaupolitics. In November 1975 there were bitter accusations on the part of the Civil Defense authorities against the local authorities and the DSM directors for not having asked them to come to the scene of the accident.

Nothing relating to this kind of stress and tension will be found in official documents on disaster management in the Netherlands—let alone in disaster legislation. It is a long way from the official view and conceptualization of disasters to the disaster reality of bureaupolitical infighting and competition. Unfortunately, nothing more can be expected in a setting dominated until now by technicians and legal specialists. Technicians tend to take an apolitical stand towards social and political processes. Legal specialists in this somewhat neglected policy area stick to the illusion that if the Disaster Act prescribes coordination and cooperation, disaster reality will adapt itself to this instruction. When confronted with the many instances of competition and conflict, they stress the importance of unequivocal directives to coordinate. They simply ignore the fact that, on the contrary, this may result in an invitation to plan comprehensive schemes and design detailed scenarios that will not stand the test of disaster reality.

The High Politics of Disaster Management

The conceptualization of disaster in Dutch legislation is associated with the assumption that one cannot expect a local government, not to speak of a local community, to respond adequately to calamitous events. This does not mean that disaster legislation restricts itself to recording the rights and duties of the provincial and national authorities. As we have seen, the Disaster Act assigns primary responsibility for disaster management to the local authorities, while the role of the provincial and central authorities appears to focus upon giving assistance to the local emergency agencies.

However, this is only part of the picture. The basic thought behind Dutch disaster legislation actually involves the simple notion that a pure disaster requires assistance from outside the local domain. It is up to the provincial governor to intervene whenever he has the impression that a disaster is not manageable by the local authorities. And it is up to the secretary of the interior to take decisions in case of catastrophes involving more than one province. This may easily induce the provincial and central authorities to interfere with any disaster, irrespective of its impact and its consequences beyond the local area. External assistance seems to imply influence from higher levels of government.

Thus the Netherlands is no exception to the rule that disasters, like other crisis situations, are accompanied by the centralization and concentration of power and, if possible, by the central appropriation of successes in disaster management. During the flood disaster of February 1953, civil servants were sent from The Hague to the disaster area and received their instructions from the secretary of the interior; strategic decisions were taken by an ad hoc cabinet committee and the general staff in the government residence. The Harmelen train accident and the DSM disaster were wound up in such a short time that the central authorities did not get the chance really to intervene with the rescue and remedy operations. On the other hand, after both disasters, various cabinet members had a busy time in answering a variety of quite detailed questions from MPs.

There is a twofold irony in the tendency to couple the concept of disaster with the idea that such an event cannot be handled properly by local authorities and that a disaster becomes more disastrous as it attracts assistance from more remote places. First, as the reports on the Harmelen train collision and the DSM explosion show, external assistance may arrive at a moment when things are already more or less under control. The rather late arrival of Red Cross units or Civil Defense equipment may interfere with, rather than contribute to, disaster management. It should be added that for such organizations proximity to the disaster is no guarantee of timely involvement. It can happen that a local unit of a nationwide emergency organization (like the Civil Defense) is simply overlooked and awaits the instructions from the higher levels.

Second, intervention by the national authorities often is a burden rather than a relief to the people on the scene of the accident. These officials make psychological blunders caused by a lack of empathy and understanding. They consider it politically important to visit the disaster location, not realizing that they take precious time from the local authorities and operational leaders.[7] They forget that they are less important than several agencies under their supervision. They are very busy in talking strategy and in anticipating public and political indignation, but they do not take specific measures to alleviate the problems on the scene of the accident. Usually, then, the high politics of disaster management has a very negative influence on the morale and effectiveness of emergency organizations and volunteers.

The Dutch Context: The Neglect of Sociological and Psychological Facts

It is not very useful to compare the American and Dutch approaches to disaster management without taking into account the crucial differences in social and political culture. Consequently, one should be careful in transplanting the American perspective of self-help and communal action to the Dutch context.[8] Besides, one should be aware of the ideological overtone in the American perspective which makes it somewhat difficult to distinguish between the appreciation of such notions as the expansion of the citizenship role and the reality of governmental intervention.[9]

The Dutch context in which disaster management takes place can best be described as legalistic and government-oriented. All those playing a part in disaster planning and disaster management tend to focus primarily on what is going on in the legislative process. They spend most of their time in discussing the possibilities of making governmental rules and procedures more perfect. They attach extreme value to comprehensive planning. Returning to the legal definition of disaster, we can say that they pay exclusive attention to the second part of the concept which involves the need for interorganizational coordination and planning. They leave it to unworldly social scientists to suggest that a legalistic, government-oriented approach to disaster planning and disaster management may leave out of consideration a most important dimension of disaster reality. Disasters are seen as real disasters to the extent that they are officially declared to be so. Sociological and psychological processes are considered to be of secondary importance. If it is a long way from the official view and conceptualization of disaster to the reality of bureaupolitical fighting and competition, the way to the social and psychological elements of disaster reality is even longer. A grasp of this reality demands from technical and legal specialists some comprehension of regularities which, despite their predictability, do not find expression in the standard procedures and planning schemes.

Disasters: Collective Stress

Barton has defined disasters as situations characterized by collective stress.[10] This definition clearly takes a stand opposite to the legal concept of disaster mentioned above. It turns the ranking list of disaster topics upside down. Sociological and psychological issues become pivotal, at the expense of inner-oriented discussions within the official sphere on better and more detailed planning procedures and coordinating devices.

Collective stress may find expression in seemingly irrational aversion to smoothly organized and professional relief operations; the convergence towards the scene of the accident and the decisionmaking arena by volunteers; opposition to evacuation; and reproaches to government officials which at first glance seem to be without any reason. In the Netherlands, until now, such phenomena have not been given proper attention. If mentioned at all they are treated as deviations from a normal process and as further evidence of the irrational response of the common man to emergency circumstances. Indeed such reactions may in fact be interpreted as confirming the need for rigorous disaster planning and for procedures which leave nothing to chance.

Aversion to Organized and Professional Relief

During the flood disaster of February 1953, aversion to organized and professional relief assumed grave proportions. In the first and most critical stage, no such relief was available. At some places both authorities and members of emergency units became victims of the illusion of centrality.[11] In other locations they simply yielded to what has been called social regression: giving priority to rescuing their own families.[12] In addition, some of the most severely hit areas remained deprived of assistance from outside for a long one and a half days. There were strong feelings of having been betrayed; belief in the authorities and their organizations was shattered. The containment policy of the central government served only to reinforce this attitude. All this contributed to a more or less strong aversion to professional emergency groups, coming late, with misplaced airs of resolution.

At the train disaster of January 1962 and the DSM explosion of November 1975, somewhat different processes occurred. The train incident is a particularly interesting case. First aid actually was offered by passengers who had not been injured and by citizens living in the immediate proximity of the scene of the accident. Soon afterward professional help was provided on a fairly individual basis. Aversion to organized and professional relief grew with the rather late arrival of emergency units. Again, they came too late and were too eager to get their share of the praise.

With the DSM explosion, another pattern can be discerned. Here several emergency organizations with no role to play in the total impact area shifted their attention to the fringe zone.[13] Some failed to grasp the atmosphere of anger and anxiety in the region. The overt quarrels between a number of public and semipublic institutions did not help to restore confidence.

Disaster planners and rule-makers in the Netherlands hardly take seriously the aversion to professional relief. Of course, professional emergency organizations are well aware of this phenomenon; but they draw no conclusions from such observations. Little is done to reconsider the relation between unorganized and organized relief. Informal situation-bound leadership, for instance, is generally considered a threat to proper disaster organization. In fact, it has often been equated with civil disobedience. To take another example, the probability of social regression is ignored officially and consequently has not led to a discussion on the pros and cons of internal versus external relief organizations.

Convergence

The collective stress characteristic of disaster events also expresses itself in the general convergence towards the disaster area and the decisionmaking arena. Volunteers hurry to the scene of the accident; gapers fill the roads in the vicinity of the site; civic spirit is converted into good pieces of advice, which in no time overstrain the communication networks. In this respect there is no difference between American and Dutch disaster events, though the eagerness of Dutch citizens to take a closer look at the scene or convey their solutions to authorities is extraordinarily strong.

Yet it seems a bit of an exaggeration on the part of the authorities to call this sort of behavior "a disaster within the disaster," as the Dutch prime minister did during the first days of the flood disaster of 1953. This is, however, quite typical of the way in which convergence behavior is handled by Dutch authorities and disaster planners. Disaster policies are restrictive. The disaster area is to be closed off as soon as possible. People are to get back to normal activities. There is an excessive concern with ignoble motives of volunteers and, as a result, too much attention is given to rules preventing looting and illegal practices in disaster areas.

It is difficult for disaster specialists in the Netherlands to accept convergence as an inevitable part of the disaster process. They hesitate to use knowledge from past events and even from disaster exercises for a better design of the communications network. They would rather see the network overstrained than admit the kinds of facts they prefer to ignore. Only recently, a sense of reality seems to have gotten through to them. But they are still far from the open acceptance of such facts

—let alone from developing a strategy to make use of the advantages which social initiative and volunteer action may have.

Opposition to Evacuation

Starting from a definition of disaster as a situation of severe collective stress, one may safely assume that evacuations intervene quite drastically in people's lives. Psychologically, it is understandable that if evacuation involves moving people from a place not yet hit by a disaster, it may take much persuasive if not coercive power to accomplish this move. Except for situations where a massive and immediate evacuation is the only way to stave off impending danger, there is the additional complication that the evacuation authorities need to know about the social structure of the groups to be evacuated. Most important, the collective stress of a disaster event may unleash pent-up tensions between citizens and authorities. Evacuation decisions, then, are a perfect trigger in this regard, the more so because the implementation of such decisions is necessarily put into the hands of a tightly structured "crisis bureaucracy."

The Dutch experience with evacuations has not been very favorable. During the flood disaster of 1953, the opposition of the Zierikzee population assumed dramatic proportions. In some smaller disaster events—for instance, a break in a dike near Amsterdam in 1960 and a vapor cloud in the Rotterdam area in 1979—the authorities met with several unexpected difficulties. The special case of the creeping disaster of contaminated land in the town of Lekkerkerk, which led to a very stressful evacuation of a whole neighborhood in 1980, is worth special mention.

Nevertheless, consistent with the neglect of the social and psychological dimensions of disaster is the fact that disaster officials and planners tend to stick to extensive evacuation schemes and are relatively quick to decide that an evacuation is needed. Their hesitation to take action with regard to creeping disasters and their aloof attitude towards citizens who, despite reassuring official statements, indeed demand to be evacuated from polluted land, are special cases. In disaster events as well as during disaster exercises there is usually a strong urge to evacuate the population in the vicinity of the disaster site. The typical response to deficiencies in the evacuation process is to refine the procedures and scenarios; the main answer to popular opposition to evacuation has been, and continues to be, the strengthening and extension of the legal powers to enforce evacuation decisions. The authorities appear to take a distinctly top-down approach. What else could one expect from public authorities confronted with popular obstruction under emergency circumstances?

Reproaches to Government Officials

Throughout history, rulers and political elites have been made to pay the price for man-made as well as for natural disasters. In the Netherlands, with its rather government-oriented culture, government is often held responsible for whatever adversity may befall the population. During the first days of the flood disaster of 1953, one of the most widely asked questions pointed at the mistakes and failures of the Netherlands Waterways Authority; in the next period, rumors and information regarding the authorities went hand in hand with various stories about personal enrichment and corruption of officials. The train collision near Harmelen necessarily involved the public enterprise of the Dutch Railways and that fact alone invited political questions on safety standards and safety investments. In the public debate following the DSM explosion, attention was focused on the role of the public authorities regarding disaster prevention and disaster management. One study has shown that chemical explosions and vapor clouds caused by production accidents in private firms induced people in the Rijnmond area to call the police for help and to attack the public authorities for letting such things happen.[14]

From a collective stress perspective it is not surprising that disasters give rise to antigovernment sentiments and that government officials become the subject of reproach and complaints. Disasters, like any other emergency situation, are a most distinct manifestation of the vulnerability of social and communal organization. They show clearly that no arrangements, including those of governments, can prevent them from happening. The paradoxical conclusion must be that, to a certain degree, there is no reason for disaster planners to try for improvements to eliminate rumors and reproaches. Unfortunately, however, disaster planning in the Netherlands seems to aim at perfection and to strive for perfect disaster government. Apart from impressing on disaster managers and other public authorities the necessity of professional integrity, one cannot expect them to stand above the stressful dynamics of a disaster.

Disaster Management: A Suitable Case for Organizational Development

A widespread saying among disaster specialists in the Netherlands is "No disaster, please, until 1989." Since the 1970s disaster management in this country has been the subject of permanent discussion and much confusion. Recent legislation, first and foremost the new Disaster Act, may seem to create legal clarity concerning the responsibility structures in the public sphere, but nobody really knows what will be the implications of attendant changes in the interorganizational network. One can only hope that the abolition of the Civil Defense—the object of bad press and public criticism since its very beginning—and the emergence of the fire departments to a prominent place in disaster management will not be put to the test until 1989. By that year the fire departments in the Netherlands should be well prepared for their new task.

The Disaster Act of 1985

The Disaster Act of 1985 reflects the dominating views on disaster management in the Netherlands. First, it is based on the premise that complex disaster events require a coordinated intervention from the regional or national levels of government. In contrast to politics and government as usual, emergency management should not be hindered by such "luxurious" principles as local autonomy, grass roots democracy (including self-help), and self government. Thus the Disaster Act lends special powers to the provincial governor to overrule the municipal authorities in case of a disaster; the provincial government does not need to wait for a formal disaster declaration on the part of local authorities.

A similar story can be told of the powers and responsibilities assigned to the national authorities. The more complex the situation, the more central the attribution of powers and responsibilities. The Disaster Act testifies to the fact that emergencies may bring under public scrutiny the fundamental characteristics of the political and administrative system. Despite the ideology of decentralization, the practice of centralization prevails.

Second, the Disaster Act shows a nearly obsessive concern with planning on different levels of government. It mandates that all municipal corporations should have a disaster plan; such plans should be the basis for more detailed operational schemes. On the provincial level, plans should bear upon the coordination of intermunicipal assistance and cooperation. While at present there is an increasing antipathy to comprehensive planning in the Netherlands, the Disaster Act does not seem to be an example of effective and global planning. Again, the emergency context appears to be a good yardstick in assessing the relevance of moods, beliefs, and opinions in the political-administrative system. Despite the antiplanning mood, the practice of detailed and comprehensive planning still prevails.

From Fire Fighting to Disaster Management:
A Bad Bargain?

In November 1984 the under secretary of the interior received thunderous applause from the National Congress of Fire Chiefs when he told the fire chiefs that there would be no changes in the plans to give them the operational leadership during disasters. The passage of the Disaster Act was to bring an end to the protracted conflict between a variety of emergency organizations. From then on the fire chiefs would have to work hard to prepare their departments for a leading role in disaster planning and disaster management. They could reckon with a rather substantial share of the forty million dollars which the Dutch government had earmarked for the overall reorganization process. After all, the home secretary made a very advantageous bargain, substituting a multifunctional standing organization for the relatively expensive Civil Defense apparatus. They would receive about one hundred and fifty million guilders (fifty million dollars) to get ready for this task.

The great majority of the fire chiefs in the Netherlands have welcomed the Disaster Act as a victory over a number of (potential) competitors, including the Civil Defense and to a certain extent the police. They are quite confident that they have gotten a good deal. Against the criticism of a handful of policy and organizational analysts, they stress the fact that there is quite a difference between the operational leadership within and outside a disaster area and the legal responsibility for the decisions and actions that will explicitly remain with the mayor.

They have also taken good notice of the four-year period which is granted them in order to get accustomed to this complicated, but manageable task. And without stating the perception openly, they tend to admit that they have been rewarded generously for what is to be done in the coming years.

However, one may wonder if this perspective does not point up a gross underestimation of what disaster management, in the true sense of the word, is all about. There is a tremendous difference between fire fighting and disaster management. With the kinds of arguments they present, the fire chiefs actually show that they do not really understand the implications of operational leadership in a disaster context. First, it is very naive to believe that political authorities and public opinion would distinguish clearly between the operational leadership of a fire chief and the formal responsibility of the mayor. If things go wrong during a disaster, it would be a small step to hold the fire chief responsible while forgetting about the mayor's legal responsibility. This would be all the easier because one could expect a fire chief to take very seriously bureaucratic loyalty to his political superiors.[15]

Second, and closely related to this rather grim scenario, the promise of a four-year tryout will be forgotten at the very moment a large-scale disaster occurs. Nobody will accept excuses for a lack of familiarity with disaster management. The malproportion in most fire departments between a thin layer of professionals and a large group of voluntary rank and file—it will be said—has been well known all along. Problems resulting from the absorption of superfluous Civil Defense personnel will be waved away; fire chiefs, it will be said, should not keep complaining about a few minor flaws in an arrangement they themselves have so eagerly sought.

Have the Dutch fire departments, and their officers in particular, bought a bad bargain? Certainly they are better off than Civil Defense, which is a solid piece of evidence for the mortality of government organizations.[16] It is not clear whether the police and some other potential competitors for the operative leadership on the scene of future accidents should feel disappointed. On the other hand, such auxiliary institutions as the Red Cross, the Health Services, and specialized agencies of the armed forces combine an appropriate task with a more comfortable position in the second line.

One lesson can be drawn from this analysis. With their new task in the field of disaster management, Dutch fire chiefs should realize that their organization is moving towards a more central place in the

area of disaster policy. This calls for a reappraisal of the internal as well
as the external functions of the larger Dutch fire departments. As far as
the fire officers are concerned, they should take much more interest in
the interorganizational aspects of disaster management. The rank and
file volunteers should gradually get accustomed to the idea that disasters other than fires may occur. They will have to get used to a situation
where the fire chief talks politics and policy. These conditions make a
convincing case for organizational development. It would be no waste
of money to use a portion of the tryout budget for these purposes.

Planning and Reality?

A legalistic culture and a rather strong belief in comprehensive planning still are characteristic of the Dutch political and governmental
system. From this perspective the emphasis of Dutch disaster policies
on rules, regulations, and more or less specific planning schemes
simply fits in with the dominant policy styles in this country. But there
is no reason to submit to such observations. As the cynical saying goes,
the Netherlands suffers from a chronic shortage of disasters. This reinforces the tendency to bureaucratize disaster policies. Politicians need
the trigger of a real disaster to give serious attention to disaster prevention and disaster management. Rules, regulations, and detailed planning procedures are a perfect substitute for a public and political
debate on emergencies and unscheduled events. This approach allevi-
ates the pressure to undertake the basic steps of disaster analysis as
well as to engage in disaster politics.

As reassuring as it may seem to conceive of disaster planning as just
one among many categories of planning, there is no reason to submit to
such notions. Disaster planning confronts us with the antithesis of
common reality. Disasters come unexpectedly; they involve a disruption of normal patterns of life; they shatter patterns of expectations;
they define emergency situations; they require critical rather than
routine decisions. Disaster planning, then, lends substance to the
commonly stated need to predict the unpredictable.

In the Netherlands the predicament is "solved" by a tendency to
reason by analogy: the syndrome of "winning the last war." Disaster
policies become oriented to the past instead of the future; they are
based on supposedly known facts instead of creative imagination. Disas-

ter scenarios usually do not reach beyond extrapolations of the most recent calamity, thus imposing incremental solutions upon a typically nonincremental context.[17]

It should be added that disaster planners in the Netherlands tend to neglect the few facts that appear to recur in subsequent disasters. Gradually we are able to say something about a number of political, sociological, and psychological regularities in disasters. It would require a reorientation in this policy world to settle for a more balanced view on the decisionmaking qualities of governments and the people. After all, governments fall short of being smooth, synoptic machines finding rational solutions to sudden problems, while citizens do not simply fall prey to atrophic behavior and apathy. Simple disaster arithmetics of one-third inertia and one-third hyperactivity might make social dimensions of planning easier to integrate into the usual schemes; but they do not hold in reality.[18]

We do have reasons to look back, but not for easy analogies, simple extrapolations, and quasiscientific cliches. We should plan for reality, not for a pseudoreality made of rules and rigid structures. Disasters are real events, not occurrences on paper.

Science and the State in Latin America: Decisionmaking in Uncertainty ⚡ Bruno Podesta and Richard Stuart Olson

Problematic Science: Earthquake Prediction

Building codes, land use regulations, and preparedness planning are the standard tools to protect societies from natural disasters. In the case of earthquake threat, however, a new possibility has emerged over the last two decades: scientific earthquake prediction.

Published in 1975, a study by the National Research Council expressed the scientific optimism of the time about earthquake prediction:

> Within the past 5 years, many seismologists have become convinced that a new development is imminent, namely, the prediction of earthquakes. By prediction seismologists mean that the place, time, and magnitude of the quake are specified within fairly close limits, with the consequence that accelerated planning to save life and property is possible. Established methods for identifying high-risk areas depend largely on the past incidence of quakes and the mapping of fault structures. The new methods rely primarily on premonitory signs, such as changing physical properties of rocks under stress and surface tilting, that occur in advance of a quake. Predic-

tion capability does not lessen the importance of other approaches to earthquake mitigation, but it adds one potentially telling weapon to the arsenal.[1]

As plate tectonic theory and precursor identification proved more complicated than initially believed, however, the optimism was tempered, and a subsequent National Research Council panel was more cautious as well as more sensitive to the problematic of prediction:

> Geological technology will probably reach a point within the foreseeable future at which scientifically credible earthquake predictions can be made. Constructive use of this new prediction technology will depend to a considerable extent on the accuracy and reliability of our knowledge about how people and organizations will respond to these predictions and warnings. Inadequate attention to the social consequences of using a particular technology may have counterproductive results.[2]

Overlooked in many of the discussions of the coming ability to predict earthquakes was the fact that by the very nature of plate tectonic theory and the global distribution of earthquakes, earthquake prediction was quite likely to be international. Furthermore, because earthquake prediction research tends to be concentrated in developed countries, inevitable problems would arise when the prediction was for a less-developed country.

The purpose of this paper is to explicate a classically problematic earthquake prediction: the so-called Brady-Spence earthquake prediction for the Lima-Callao area of Peru. More specifically, our paper focuses on the decisionmaking and management difficulties, especially but not exclusively on the Peruvian side, of dealing with a "made in U.S." earthquake prediction. The situation developed over a five-year period and eventually became a highly public—and publicized—issue.

It is unfortunate that so many people, not simply scientists, believe that science, the pursuit of truth, takes place in a political vacuum. All events have context, and the context often determines specific effects and the course of subsequent events. Science is certainly no exception.

The Brady-Spence prediction can trace its roots back to a 1976 article published by Dr. Brian T. Brady, but the prediction itself did not become a public, that is, societal, issue until late in 1979 when the media picked up the story. Illustrating the importance of timing and context, the prediction began to have a profound impact on Peruvian society shortly thereafter. Understanding the phenomenon, however, requires that we understand the context.

State Structure, Regime Change, and Science in Peru

Peru, like many countries of Latin America, has fluctuated between military and civilian regimes since independence. This historical competition has cemented antagonistic ideologies and behaviors on both sides. Coincidentally, the two sectors of Peruvian society that played significant roles in the handling of the Brady-Spence case, the state apparatus and the scientific community, were caught in a regime change which began in 1979.

Presidential elections took place on May 18, 1980, bringing to an end twelve years of a dictatorial military regime. On July 28 of the same year a democratic system was once again attempted by Peruvian society with Fernando Belaunde Terry as President. Belaunde had been deposed in 1968 by the same military that was returning power to him.

The military governments of 1968–80 had significantly expanded the presence of the state in all areas of national life, with an emphasis on planning as the instrument to carry out policies of social change. The predominant vertical and hierarchical mentality, characteristic of military training, was translated to state organization, consequently affecting its operations.

To the vertical organization of state ministries, however, the military also superimposed a horizontal organization of systems (of planning or national defense, for example) with the goal of achieving coordination across state organizations. Nevertheless, with the change of regime in July 1980 and even some months prior to this, a series of trends that gave precedence to the role of the private sector (understood here as the private productive sector, primarily industrial, commercial, and financial) over the state became apparent. The planning system rapidly lost force within the public apparatus, and state institutions ceded ground before these new privatization trends. Thus the Brady-Spence earthquake prediction encountered a political "accident": the military was in retreat as the civilians, by means of a wide range of parties and political fronts, began to retake control of the nation.

Additionally, Peruvian institutions remained immersed in the paradox of extreme formalism on one hand and lax informality on the other. This paradox is characteristic of bureaucratic conduct in many Latin American countries and, to a certain degree, determines the functioning of institutions. An anecdote from real life clearly exemplifies the enormous space which has traditionally existed for personal decision-making in the administration of Latin American public institutions. A parliamentary member once responded to one of his colleagues when asked how he handled requests for favors, "My dear sir, the solution is very simple: For my friends, everything. For my enemies, the law and regulations."

The scientific community in Peru is very heterogeneous. Some disciplines have achieved a significant level of development and can count on adequate institutional support, research resources, and the accumulated work of several decades. Yet others show little activity and lack the necessary physical, institutional, and human resources to be viable. For this reason it is difficult to refer to the scientific community as a whole.

In Peru geophysics (of which seismology is a subfield) constitutes one of the few cases in which, through years of research, technical training, and institutional financing, the discipline has managed to achieve a position of prestige and national and international recognition. Although this is not without current problems, it is a trajectory begun many years ago.[3]

In Peru the earth sciences in general developed early because they were tied to the interest in mining. At the beginning of the century two specialized publications appeared that were to constitute an important step for the growth of the discipline: the *Boletin del Cuerpo de Ingenieros de Minas* and the *Boletin de la Sociedad de Geologia*. Several geographers, interested in describing and studying the geography of the country, also became involved in geology.

Nevertheless, the most important event occurred in 1922 when the Carnegie Institute of Washington installed the Huancayo Geophysics Station, where a systematic recording of seismological information was initiated despite the fact that seismology, as such, still did not exist. This observatory, aimed at satisfying the needs of North American specialists for scientific knowledge, gained international prestige for provision of quality data and for its special geographical location.

In 1947 the ownership and control of the Huancayo facilities were transferred to Peru, thus creating the Instituto Geofisico Peruano

(Peruvian Institute of Geophysics, IGP). A decade later the International Geophysical Year attracted the attention of many foreign institutions, and the IGP was lauded for the quality of its seismological work.

In the following years the IGP grew and consolidated itself to the point where, in the 1960s, it sent a group of its professionals to pursue doctoral studies abroad. Contrary to the brain-drain phenomenon, ten of the eleven who left the country under this program returned.

Seismology in Peru, as in advanced high altitude biology, achieved this significant level of development because of one pioneer figure who not only introduced up-to-date scientific knowledge but at the same time concerned himself with creating the necessary institutional framework, forming new technical teams, and achieving solid international ties. It was Peruvian scientist Alberto Giesecke who played this role in seismology. Thus, when the prediction of the North American physicist Brady was made public, the influence of Giesecke in diverse Peruvian institutions and his personal prestige enabled him to carry out a "linkage" function among the scientific community, the state, the press, and North American institutions.

At that time Giesecke was (1) a member of the board of directors of the Consejo Nacional de Ciencia y Tecnologia (National Council of Science and Technology, CONCYTEC); (2) director of the Centro Regional de Sismologia para America del Sur (Regional Seismology Center for South America, CERESIS); and (3) a member of the board of directors of IGP, in addition to being its operational head for many years.

Therefore, when the Brady-Spence prediction appeared in a period of marked political uncertainty, the IGP and Giesecke were the natural places to turn for the press, state and private institutions, high schools, and the public in general.

The Development of a Controversy

The 1970 Earthquake

In 1970 northern Peru was struck by a large earthquake which dislodged part of a mountain, causing it to slide down into a populated valley below. Seventy thousand people were killed. It was a national trauma for the people and government of Peru.

The response was slow and not well organized. Preparedness was obviously lacking. The political and institutional consequences of the disaster were felt immediately, and some were translated into policy initiatives. The most important was that the military, then in power, created the Civil Defense System. Alongside External and Internal Defense, Civil Defense formed part of National Defense. It was made responsible for dealing holistically with emergencies caused by natural disasters and was to interrelate with the public apparatus. Civil Defense remained primarily dependent on the armed forces for support, however. It is important to keep this fact in mind because the 1970 earthquake formed a powerful emotional backdrop against which the Brady-Spence case developed.

The 1976 Brady Article

In late 1976 Dr. Brian T. Brady, a research physicist for the U.S. Bureau of Mines (USBM) in Denver, published the last in a series of four articles on a theory of earthquakes in the European scientific journal, *Pure and Applied Geophysics*.[4] In this article Brady argued that he had observed a structure to rock failure that was as applicable to mines and earthquakes as to laboratory situations. His approach represented an unprecedented combination of geophysics, microphysics, and mathematics. He asserted that it was possible to derive precisely the time, place, and magnitude of an earthquake if past and present information about a location's seismicity were available. The model developed by Brady was fundamentally deterministic and contrary to the probabilistic approach commonly used in seismology.

In his article Brady indicated in a preliminary way that a major earthquake just off the coast of Lima could be expected. At this time his statements were only a forecast, not a prediction. Subsequently Brady explained to his Bureau of Mines superiors that he "purposely buried" the Peruvian forecast in the 1976 article so as to avoid "widespread publicity."[5] The name of Dr. William Spence, a geophysicist for the U.S. Geological Survey (USGS) in Golden, Colorado (near Denver), became identified with the prediction, because Spence had provided Brady with important data on a 1974 Peruvian earthquake sequence and worked with him on the plate tectonic context for the theory.

The Prepublic Stage

Late in 1976 Leonidas Ocola of the IGP was in the United States and
saw galley proofs of the Brady article. On arriving in Lima he
informed IGP scientist Daniel Huaco and Alberto Giesecke about the
article.[6] Enrique Silgado, in charge of researching Peru's seismic history, wrote to Brady on December 20, 1976, saying that Brady should
be aware of his research.[7] During that same month Alberto Giesecke,
as director of CERESIS, began to make arrangements for a group of
Latin American specialists to visit China to learn firsthand about that
country's experiences with earthquakes.

On January 11, 1977, Brady wrote a letter to Silgado thanking him
for the information provided. Silgado's research findings suggested to
Brady that his own conjectures (that is, the forecast) were correct.
Later in that same year, on August 25, Brady presented a report to
William Spence's immediate superior, Louis C. Pakiser of the USGS,
reiterating his position that a serious situation was developing near
Lima and upgrading his statements to a prediction.[8] This report was
read in the United States and Peru; Peruvian journalists also saw it but
nonetheless were forbidden by the military government to publish
anything about it.

Three months later, on November 18, 1977, in Golden, Colorado, a
meeting requested by Giesecke of H. William Menard, director of the
USGS, was convened. Spence of the USGS and Brady of the USBM (who
Giesecke met personally for the first time) both attended the meeting.
Here is was decided that Brady would not publish anything further
without prior coordination with the Peruvian government.

Soon after this meeting Brady began to receive unpublished seismic
information from the IGP, working with it for approximately one year.
It was also decided in the November meeting that another meeting
would be called after Brady and Spence had studied the new IGP data.
Starting early in 1977 the Ministry of Education (to which IGP
pertained) began to receive copies of the pertinent reports and
correspondence.[9]

The year 1978 was a period of relative calm, which is explained in
part by the fact that the IGP waited until Brady and Spence had
studied the information they had been sent. Nevertheless, in the highest government levels some actions continued to develop.

Giesecke has noted that on August 6, 1978, "the IGP presented a
complete, confidential report to the Peruvian government, through

the Ministry of Education, and requested additional funds for the acquisition of seismological stations and the hiring of personnel, as much in response to the Brady prediction as for, primarily, the need to accumulate basic information required to evaluate future seismic activity."[10] During the same month the minister of education, General José Guabloche, asked Alberto Giesecke for a written report on the prediction, for the president of the republic (General Francisco Morales Bermudez). Giesecke was also to inform the Ministry of Foreign Relations, the director of the National Institute of Planning, and the secretary of Civil Defense.

During January 1979 several important developments took place. Brady informed Giesecke that he remained certain of his prediction. Giesecke then wrote to USGS headquarters requesting a meeting of the seismologists of both the IGP and the USGS to evaluate the prediction. On February 1 the USGS responded to Alberto Giesecke, telling him that the meeting would take place on May 24, 1979. The aim of the meeting was to review and discuss matters related to earthquake threat in Peru. In the meeting, however, the USGS was not going to take a definite position on the Brady prediction.

Giesecke also met with the U.S. ambassador in Peru, Harry W. Shlaudeman, to discuss the possibility of establishing a working relationship between the USBM and the IGP and suggesting that Brady be permitted to dedicate part of his work schedule to continuing his work on the prediction.

On May 24, 1979, the meeting that Alberto Giesecke had requested in January was convened in Golden. According to Giesecke,

Eighteen people attended, including a representative of the Peruvian Embassy in Washington [and] four IGP specialists. . . . The IGP presented reports to the Ministries of Education, Foreign Relations, and the National Planning Institute, manifesting the low degree of credibility merited by the prediction, but reiterating the importance of intensifying seismic observation and research, and, in passing, completing the follow up of the parameters in the Brady theory. In the following months, permanent communication was maintained among the IGP, CERESIS, and Doctors Brady and Spence, providing these last two with the latest information concerning seismic activity in the central region of Peru.[11]

On August 19, 1979, a "research group" from CERESIS began a trip to the People's Republic of China with the aim of "trying to give their

best and share what they knew concerning the science of earthquakes."[12] Alberto Giesecke and Leonidas Ocola of Peru and eight
other Latin American specialists composed this group.

The last few months of the year saw the beginning in Peru of "Plan
Alfa Centauro," brought about to confront emergencies caused by natural disasters. Conceived by Civil Defense as a comprehensive plan, it
foresaw the completion of more than twelve specific hazard-related
studies in the metropolitan zone of Lima-Callao.

On November 7, 1979, Alberto Giesecke made the first formal presentation about the Brady-Spence prediction to Peruvian vice-ministers,
directors of state agencies, and the Red Cross. The objective of the
meeting, which took place in the offices of Civil Defense, was to assess
agency preparedness in the face of natural disasters and to agree on a
strong recommendation to substantially increase the funds of the IGP.[13]
The meeting was so large that leaks were inevitable. The first news of
the prediction appeared in the Peruvian media three days later.

The Public Stage

On January 4, 1980, U.S. Ambassador Shlaudeman personally prepared and sent to Washington a long cable (classified confidential)
entitled "The Politics of an Earthquake Prediction." At our request the
State Department provided us a copy with only a few minor excisions.
The cable is so coherent and captures the essence and the dilemmas of
the prediction (on both the U.S. and Peruvian sides) so well that it is
worth quoting at length:

> As the Department may be aware, Dr. Brian T. Brady of the U.S.
> Bureau of Mines has predicted that a cataclysmic earthquake will
> strike the south-central coast of Peru and the north coast of Chile on
> or about July 31, 1981. Dr. Brady's theory posits a mainshock of
> M9.8 (which, as I gather it, would be the biggest earthquake since
> scientists began to measure these phenomena), with an epicenter in
> the Pacific about 75 kilometers off Lima. . . .
>
> Dr. Brady first suggested this frightening possibility in 1976 in an
> article published in a scientific journal. He subsequently agreed
> with Dr. Alberto Giesecke, Chief of the Peruvian Geophysical Insti-
> tute, to publish no more on the specific prediction pending coordi-
> nation with the GOP. Peruvian geophysicists held a full-dress review
> of the prediction and the underlying theory with Dr. Brady and

other concerned USG scientists in May of last year at Golden, Colorado, but the GOP has yet to take any official public cognizance of the
matter. There have, however, been several references in the local
press to unspecified, "alarmist" earthquake predictions, and the Lima
rumor mill has been working overtime of late.

Word of Dr. Brady's prediction began to leak out when in November it became the subject of serious attention in the upper levels of
the GOP. It is not clear why such interest was aroused at that point,
but the timing may have been connected to consideration of the
budget allotment for Civil Defense activities in the coming year. In
any event, Dr. Giesecke was asked to make a presentation to the
Council of Ministers last month. The thrust of what he had to say
was that Dr. Brady's theory is far from proven but that it is sufficiently
serious in scientific terms to call for attempts at verification. Dr.
Giesecke proposed a supplementary budget for his institute. . . .

After some deliberation, the Council of Ministers decided not to
spend the money. Dr. Giesecke was told that the GOP would rely on
Civil Defense. He told me that he was disappointed but planned to
go back with a more modest proposal. He hopes for some kind of
go-ahead from the GOP so as to be able to request special assistance
from USG agencies. He continues to insist with what strikes me as
unassailable logic that the Peruvian military's concern for national
security would be more realistically engaged in his problem than in
the "threat" from Chile.

The word is also out that the GOP plans a special effort in Civil
Defense. [deletion, 1.5 lines] have asked me if I think those plans
have to do with earthquakes or something else, such as an attack on
Chile, or an effort to bring the population under firmer military
control in preparation for a "Third Phase" of the government of the
armed forces. [deletion, 6.5 lines] Dr. Giesecke in a memorandum
of October 2 to the Ministry of Education observed that :

"The prediction itself can cause damage comparable to the effects
of a large earthquake. The prediction has foreseeable social, economic and political consequences which can develop into a dangerous and chaotic situation—it is therefore urgent that policies be
adopted regarding the management of all the information concerning the prediction—the government has the responsibility to inform
the public truthfully and to educate the people."

The GOP so far apparently does not agree. The president side-
stepped a question about the prediction during his televised meet-

ing with the diplomatic corps on December 31 by responding that
there is always the danger of earthquakes in Peru, and the country
should prepare by emphasizing Civil Defense and employing better
construction in its buildings.

I am inclined to agree with Dr. Giesecke that it would probably be
best to get all this out into the open for responsible public discussion. I have encouraged him to pursue this aspect of the problem
with the GOP. But I can understand the reluctance in the latter
quarter. The rumors and fears of catastrophe or sinister plots may
fade—at least until September is closer on us—if the lid is kept on
and if, as I suspect will be the case, the Civil Defense effort proves
to be more talk than action.

In any event, the subject is one that will require our close attention and discreet handling in the months ahead. Because of Dr.
Brady's nationality and affiliation, the USG is very much involved.[14]

Then, according to Giesecke, on February 19,

the Director of the IGP (and of CERESIS) was invited by the Council
of Ministers and the President of the Republic to make a presentation explaining the (Brady problem) and to propose corresponding
actions. The results of this meeting were: (1) to place the administration of seismic prediction in charge of the Secretary of National
Defense within the concept of national security; (2) to accept that it
was advantageous for the national welfare to invest financial resources
in a long range program aimed at achieving a national capacity in the
field of seismic prediction; (3) to approve, in principle, an expansion
of the IGP budget to begin . . . a program of activities directed
towards seismic prediction.[15]

As a result of this meeting, IGP was authorized one million additional dollars to pursue the prediction. Shortly thereafter, General
Ramon Miranda Ampuero, executive secretary of National Defense,
sent a general communiqué to the armed forces making them aware of
a possible emergency and, at the same time, asking the directors of the
newspapers and television stations to decrease public tension. He also
requested Civil Defense to reduce the level of simulation exercises
and evacuations to decrease public anxiety. "We are not Chinese, disciplined and obedient," one of the ex-military officials interviewed said.
"One could not think in terms of evacuations. Nor did we have the
resources to do so. We had to do what we could. In February or March

of 1980, it was decided to minimize the importance of the case due, among other reasons, to the impossibility of managing the social consequences."

An especially important event occurred in October 1980. In San Juan, Argentina, a technical meeting organized by CERESIS took place in which Brady and Spence presented their prediction. From there they traveled to Chile and later to Peru, meeting with President Belaunde on October 29. News leaked out that the prediction was discussed in the presidential meeting. This served to increase anxiety and alarm among the population.

In the last two months of 1980 Alberto Giesecke, in the name of President Belaunde, made an official request to the United States government for an evaluation of the Brady-Spence prediction by the National Earthquake Prediction Evaluation Council (NEPEC, advisory board of the USGS).

1981, Tension Increases

Early in 1981 the Peruvian navy distributed an informative bulletin called "Tsunamis: Sistema de Alerta en el Pacifico Sur" to the inhabitants of La Punta and Chucuito (in Callao) during the night. This bulletin described a tsunami (violent displacement of water originating in the ocean after an earthquake, when the epicenter is located in the ocean) and the immediate measures to be taken for survival. Because of the characteristics of the peninsula, however, the local reader could easily deduce that his or her possibilities of dying from the effects of a tsunami were great (La Punta and Chucuito had only one street along which people could exit). Panic sales of apartments were reliably reported.

On January 26–27 the NEPEC met to hear Brady. At the end of the meeting NEPEC recommended that the Peruvian government not attach much importance to the prediction. This conclusion was endorsed by the USGS. The NEPEC report was made available to the press, and a video tape of the meeting was shown at the IGP offices in Lima. At the same time, however, no official statement was made in Peru about the situation, merely a reprinting of the translated NEPEC statement.

On April 2, 1981, Alberto Giesecke sent a letter to Roger Guerra-Garcia, president of CONCYTEC, suggesting that he request another evaluation of the prediction from CERESIS. The request was formalized, and on May 18, 1981, Ramon Cabre, S.J., president of the board of directors of CERESIS, sent a report to CONCYTEC. The document, which made no firm conclusion either for or against the prediction, was sent by CONCYTEC to President Belaunde.

Brady had specified June 28 as the exact date for the earthquake, but he changed it several times. A few weeks before the target date, William Spence withdrew support for the prediction, saying the necessary precursory seismicity had failed to occur. June 28, 1981, arrived and passed. No earthquake. On July 2 the U.S. embassy in Lima sent an unclassified cable to Washington entitled "The Earthquake that Wasn't." Again neatly reflecting both Peruvian and United States concerns, the key sections are as follows:

The visit of Dr. John Filson . . . of the U.S. Geological Survey, from June 25 through 29 proved most useful. His stay was highlighted by two press conferences devoted almost entirely to questions about the Brady prediction. Front-page treatment was given by the media to Dr. Filson's reiteration at those conferences of the U.S. National Earthquake Prediction Evaluation Council's rejection of the Brady prediction.

Peruvian authorities were also active in publicly rejecting the Brady prediction, and in terms more unequivocal than previously. The chief of the prestigious Peruvian Geophysical Institute spoke out against the scientific validity of the Brady theory and the Institute's scientific director of seismology denied that recent earthquakes in the southern mountains of Peru (Ayacucho) had anything to do with the Brady prediction.

The most prominent public statement against the Brady prediction was that of President Belaunde. The president claimed to the media that a trip he was making on the 28th to Pisco to dedicate the La Puntilla fish freezing and canning plant and other public works was being undertaken in defiance of Brady's prediction of the earthquake epicentered in the sea to the west of that town. The president's gesture came in neat counterpoint to the Air Force's quietly pulling their planes out of the low-lying sea front airbase at Pisco (at which the Belaunde party landed). The Air Force apparently had misread the prediction to include a 60 foot tsunami (tidal wave) at the time of the predicted first mainshock. The Air Force was not alone in its miscue. The country's first census in many years was postponed from the 28th in part to avoid the predicted earthquake.

The reaction to the passing of the predicted day has been one of relief and exhilaration, best typified by the June 29 *Expreso* headline: "Peru, Si! Brady, No!"[16]

Conclusion

The Brady-Spence affair offers several lessons about policy- and decisionmaking dilemmas in situations of high threat but high ambiguity. First, scientific technology in the First World is especially difficult for Third World countries to evaluate and manage. The situation becomes even more problematic when, as in this case, the Peruvians faced a U.S. scientific community deeply divided over the solidity of the underlying prediction theory and methodology.

Second, stakes tend to be markedly asymmetrical. For the U.S. scientific community and government, the Brady-Spence prediction was primarily a research issue and a bureaucratic problem. For the Peruvians, however, thousands of lives and the heart of their nation were at stake. This is not to say that U.S. scientists and officials were unconcerned about the life stakes in Peru, but distance insulated them from the immediacy of the problem.

Third, the Peruvian context into which the Brady-Spence prediction dropped was very complicated and profoundly affected the way in which the prediction and its repercussions were handled. One point not fully appreciated by most outsiders is that "Peru," like the "United States," is an abstraction and, in specific case analysis, not a very useful one. For example, it is a fact of life for academics and researchers in Peru that science and scientists in general enjoy little public or political respect. Therefore the Brady-Spence prediction landed in a medium that received it reluctantly, and not solely because of its negative content. Peruvian concern with "higher priority" development items was aggravated by a deep economic crisis that accentuated the scarcity of resources and shortened perspectives in all social sectors.

At the same time, vivid memories remained of the death and destruction caused by the 1970 earthquake, and Peru between 1976 and 1980 was governed by the same military leaders who had faced the 1970 disaster and were sensitive to situations that could alter internal security. Finally, Peru relied on a prestigious institution, the IGP, which in spite of being scientific—and thus marginal—had achieved significant press coverage and had made itself heard in the state hierarchies.

In other words, there was a relative receptiveness to the prediction and its possible consequences among those who governed the country between 1976 and 1980. During this period of military government, receptiveness translated into an effort to deal with the situation by means of a comprehensive strategy (Plan Alfa Centauro).

For its part, the IGP was responsible for all scientific aspects of the problem and, because of the presence of Alberto Giesecke, an actor with unique characteristics, a personal linkage component joined, in a permanent although changing form, the highest levels of the executive branch, national scientific institutions (IGP and CONCYTEC), regional agencies (CERESIS), and other foreign and international agencies.

But the executive branch, Civil Defense, and the IGP were incapable of evaluating the Brady-Spence prediction. Nor did they have, as can be proven throughout, control mechanisms to deal with such a process. This left them in a vulnerable and somewhat dependent position.

In spite of obvious government efforts to deal with the situation, what stands out is the relative lack of coordination, which then worsened as the military government ended in 1980. This observation also emphasizes the lacunae of "top-down" planning, which was incapable of starting participatory mobilization because attempts to involve the population had not succeeded.

The lack of coordination has very old origins. Although the military government created systems and sectors in an effort to make public administration both horizontal and integrated, this reform had its limits. The rapid growth of the state, bureaucratic behavior that tended to block all rationalization processes, and the control orientation of military hierarchies combine to explain the limited reach of bureaucratic reform. Then the change from a military to a civilian regime in early and middle 1980 made the efforts to coordinate the response to Brady-Spence even more problematic.

Finally, at first glance the dependence aspects of the Brady-Spence case appear overwhelming. The prediction itself, the NEPEC evaluation, and various aid requests all derived from or relied on the United States. But one should not be fooled by appearances. This was not a simple mechanical relationship of scientific dependency. Although seismology initially developed because of external mining interests, a national strategy of forming technical teams was soon begun, turning the IGP into a prominent institution. From then on the IGP role in the scientific community and the country increased in importance.

Peruvian scientific and technological institutions are aware that they are not an important concern of leaders and politicians. Similarly, they are aware that they have to use critical situations to advance their positions and make certain conquests, even if these are not durable. Institutions therefore try to attain budget increases, favorable legislation, the assignment of some locale, and/or the exoneration of austerity measures; seldom do they propose long-term objectives. Having a clear strategy in the face of the Brady-Spence prediction, however, the IGP represented a significant difference in approach.

The IGP positioned itself to take advantage of the scientific and political conjectures to raise the consciousness of the public, politicians, and directors of institutions in the face of the prediction. At the same time, the IGP attempted to achieve some material benefits for itself. In terms of the first goal the IGP was able to link various institutions to its own strategy and gained access to the highest levels of government and to foreign and international agencies. Consequently, it managed to strengthen itself as the only specialized, scientific institution capable of contributing to a better knowledge of the seismic situation of the country.

Furthermore, it was clear that external actors (the United States) did not present themselves as a monolithic block, but as appreciated by the more insightful national actors, were neither always interrelated nor coherent. This is especially valid and important in the case of the United States, where a broad gamut of institutions (USGS, USBM, USAID) with different policies and bureaucratic missions existed.[17] This "polycentric" aspect facilitated the design in Peru of a strategy which attempted to turn the situation into concrete advantages.

A Final Word: The Armero, Colombia, Disaster of 1985

On the night of November 13, 1985, a volcanic eruption on Nevado del Ruiz in central Colombia melted part of the permanent icecap, sending a large lahar down the mountain. As Colombia and the world soon learned with horror, the city of Armero was buried, with the approximate death toll set at 22,000. Other towns were also affected, adding another 5,000 people to those killed.

Within a few weeks several facts emerged that caused significant public consternation. First, the mountain had been rumbling (i.e., showing "precursors") for months and was under intense investigation by Colombian and U.S. scientists. Second, hazard maps had been prepared based on historical eruptions and current topography, and they indicated with frightening accuracy that Armero was in great danger; but the necessary warning and evacuation systems had not been put in place. Third, the population of Armero received contradictory messages (eruption detected, but "stay calm") a few hours before the lahar hit. Political scapegoating ensued, including a public call for the impeachment of the governor of Tolima, the department most affected by the disaster.

Another set of problems came several weeks later, when Colombian scientists and members of a U.S. Geological Survey team alerted the Colombian government and the U.S. embassy of a possible "second eruption," the effects of which would have reached other, densely populated downstream towns.

We return again to the fundamental decisionmaking dilemma of prediction situations, in this case for a volcano: what actions should government order when the scientific state of the art can only specify something between a possibility and probability? Of course, the costs of inaction are high, but *only* if the event occurs. On the other hand, ordering evacuation can be politically and economically costly if the event does *not* occur. These were the problems confronting the Colombian government in the weeks before and after the major eruption of November 13.

Frankly, decisionmakers in the Third World who must confront the problematic science of forecasts and predictions need a set of internationally agreed-upon guidelines to protect themselves. Ideally, the United Nations or a regional body should schedule a series of scientific meetings to hammer out a generic "what to do when" under a variety of likely scenarios. Without guidelines, decisionmakers will continue to find themselves very far out on a political limb when faced with major "predicted" disasters.

Integrating Emergency Management

Policy Analysis as the Study of Implements: Analytical Tools in Disaster Management ⚡ Richard F. Elmore

Science, Engineering, and Craft in
the Analysis of Disaster Management Policy

Policy analysis means different things to different people. For many academics it means the application of theory to problems of public policy. For these academics the theoretical tenets of economics, political science, and sociology—to name a few—are points of departure for hypotheses about the formation and impact of public policies. This kind of policy analysis is typically not done for specific clients, but rather for colleagues, appreciative critics, or connoisseurs. It views policymaking as a series of natural experiments, providing an opportunity to test hypotheses and develop general statements about cause and effect. The value of this kind of analysis is judged primarily by how well it meets disciplinary standards of inquiry and whether it extends theory. If it meets these criteria it is assumed to be useful. Whether policymakers actually use this analysis is a secondary matter. Its impact on public policy is rarely direct.

For shorthand purposes, I will call this kind of policy analysis "science."[1] It shows itself in a multitude of forms: geologists study the location and magnitude of potential seismic activity in certain soil and bedrock conditions; economists analyze the effects of the distribution of substantial amounts of international goods and supplies to affected populations following a disaster upon the local economies; biologists and physicians monitor the effects of exposure to radioactive elements upon living cells, and so forth. In all these cases, studies must be "good science" before they can be called "good policy analysis." The hallmarks of good science are grounding in theory and fidelity to established rules of evidence and inference. The academic disciplines are the custodians of theory and rules.

Operating in tandem with this science of policy analysis is another kind of analysis done for specific clients with specific interests in particular problems. Its impact on public policy is intended to be direct, although it often is not.[2] Its value is judged primarily by its responsiveness to the interests of the client and secondarily by whether it meets established canons of inquiry, although the fact that it meets certain canons of inquiry often enhances its value to the client. The feature that distinguishes this kind of analysis from what I have called science is the contractual relationship between the client and the analyst. Because of the incentives involved in this relationship, trade-offs between disciplinary canons and the interests of the client are common. Resources are limited, time is restricted, the scope of relevant questions is often narrower than that of discipline-based policy analysis.[3] The client is often less interested in having the best analysis, judged by disciplinary canons, than in having a timely analysis that answers a narrow range of policy questions in ways that can be defended in the political arena. These trade-offs between canons of inquiry and the interests of the client make some academics squeamish. Nonetheless, a semiprofession of policy analysts has emerged to meet the demand for this kind of analysis. Many academics move back and forth between discipline-based and contractual policy analysis without great difficulty, often using the same data for both purposes. The practice and professional ethics of contractual policy analysis are ill-defined, but many practitioners are clearly adept at doing analysis that is both good science and responsive to the client's interests.

To extend the analogy with science, we might call this contractual kind of policy analysis "engineering." The client, in effect, says "build me a bridge." The policy analyst either agrees to build the bridge within the specifications set by the client, or refuses. Once construction begins, the analyst follows accepted professional canons of design but also makes key trade-offs between those canons and the interests of the client. There is no necessary conflict between building good (safe) bridges and satisfying the needs of the client, but the contractual relationship requires trade-offs—or at least more explicit trade-offs than in discipline research. Any of the studies noted above as examples of science (seismic activity, international disaster assistance, or exposure to radiation) could also be done as engineering. The key difference would be the presence of a specific client—the United States Geological Survey, the Office of Foreign Disaster Assistance, the Nuclear Regulatory Commission—whose interests would define the scope of the analysis.

Having thus defined two types of policy analysis—science and engineering—we are left with a large residual category that I will call "craft."[4] Included in this category are activities such as (1) preparing a two-page memorandum on earthquake building code standards for a city councilmember; (2) writing a position paper for the secretary of state on the delivery of disaster assistance to underdeveloped countries; (3) drafting legislative language on criminal penalties for toxic waste spills for a governor to propose to a state legislature; and (4) structured reflection on policy problems, such as floodplain management, by decisionmakers themselves—legislators, elected or appointed executives, and career officials. It is commonplace in policy analysis textbooks either to disregard this kind of activity altogether or to refer to it as "art." For reasons I will elaborate momentarily, I think art is far too pretentious a term.

The craft of policy analysis is different from science and engineering in that it tends to be tightly bounded by particular problems, particular institutions, particular political preferences, and a particular period of time. Its value is judged primarily by whether it poses workable political solutions within these tight constraints. In the heat of battle, people who make policy and manage its implementation understandably want practical solutions to this or that problem. They are less interested in whether a solution generalizes to a broader class of problems, and usually not interested at all in whether a particular solution contributes to theory. Craft is more like engineering than science, but it is distinctively different from engineering in at least two respects. First, in the craft of policy analysis the client and the analyst are often one in the same person. Decisionmakers themselves do much of their own analysis, often without self-consciously thinking of themselves as analysts. In this sense, they are like Molière's character who spoke prose all his life without knowing it. With experience, though, these actors gain skill in the craft of analysis, and they convey this skill by example to their colleagues and subordinates. Like any craft, analysis can be taught by practice, example, and imitation, often better than it can be taught through formal explanation. Second, even when analyst and client are different people their relationship is less formal in craft than in engineering. Because of the immediacy of the problems that craft addresses, the particularistic nature of its solutions, and the pragmatic nature of its value, the products of craft are much less susceptible to evaluation than the products of engineering. Over the long term, an analyst or decisionmaker can develop a reputation for skill in the craft, based largely on his or her ability to influence the direction of events by bringing the right kind of analysis to bear at the right time. In the short term, though, it is difficult to say whether a particular exercise of craft is good or bad, because it is difficult to define the precise role of analysis in any given decision.

The term craft is particularly appropriate for describing the day-to-day, particularistic work of people actively engaged in policymaking and management.[5] Craft, in its common use, denotes the application of skill to making a tangible product with some practical use. Craftspeople are usually distinguished from artists, for example, by the fact that they apply their skill to the production of useful artifacts that also have aesthetic value. Likewise, in policy analysis, craft is defined by the tangible product—the memo, the deadlock-breaking option, the key piece of data, the influential paper—that moves a particular decision or a complex set of political relations from one stage to another. The tangible product and the immediacy of its application are the key determinants of good craft; if the product also happens to be good science or good engineering, so much the better. In addition, craft carries a connotation of guile, cunning, calculation, and subtle wit which, for better or worse, accurately captures the role that analytic skill plays in the game of policy and management. Practically speaking, analysis is done not because it is good to do, or even because it produces "better" decisions, by some external standard, but because it gives one party a potential advantage over another in a competitive situation. Hence, the term craft conveys the sense of analysis as an instrument of influence.

This distinction between science, engineering, and craft helps to frame some central problems of policy analysis. Doing science on policy questions, producing studies for clients, and marshaling information and options in support of immediate decisions are all part of the same enterprise. Because they involve different standards of value and very often different people in different roles, we often fail to see them as different sides of the same phenomenon. Worse yet, failing to see them as parts of the same enterprise can result in a destructive kind of intellectual imperialism. This imperialism takes a number of forms. One is a tendency to use the standards of one kind of analysis to discredit another. Scientists disdain engineers for their narrow focus and their client orientation, suggesting darkly that the data have been "cooked" to suit the needs of the client. Engineers disdain scientists for their unwillingness to dirty their hands by rubbing theory against reality. Craftspeople disdain scientists and engineers for being unwilling or unable to answer direct questions about what ought to be done about this particular problem right now. And so it goes.

Another form of imperialism is the professionalization of analysis. Periodically, some individuals and institutions (professional schools and associations, for example) attempt to define a class of people called "policy analysts," who because of experience, training, or a shared paradigm constitute a professional elite. The arguments for defining policy analysts as a special class are usually couched in appeals to society's well-being, which is the case with most attempts to professionalize important social activities. Marking off policy analysis as a profession, the argument goes, would allow analysts to develop professional standards, to apply those standards to the membership of the elite, and to distinguish charlatans from the real analysts. Not surprisingly, the major proponents of professionalization are what I have called above scientists and engineers. Also not surprisingly, the standards they recommend typically entail academic training, not mastery of the craft. One seldom hears arguments for the professionalization of analysis from craftspeople, perhaps because they have other sources of professional identity or because they view the label "policy analyst" as too restrictive a definition of what they actually do.

Professionalization of policy analysis, in attempting to make a profession out of a basic cognitive task, turns that task into a form of intellectual imperialism. Analysis, in the day-to-day conduct of public affairs, is not unlike breathing in the day-to-day conduct of life in general. It is not an optional activity that some people do and some people don't; it is a source of sustenance, an activity necessary to the competent performance of a job. Analysis provides the raw material from which decisions are made and actions are framed. Professionalizing analysis means, in effect, separating those who decide from those who analyze, relieving those who decide from the responsibility for thinking about how to decide, and creating a self-interested elite with analysis as its distinctive advantage.

At the level of craft, distinctions between analyzing, deciding, and acting are blurred and often irrelevant. When pressure mounts for a change in policy or management, the premium is on available information, feasible options, and packages of benefits that bind divergent interests together. Decisionmakers select information and options based on their availability, their political potency, and their instrumental value in building coalitions. The analytic skill required to do these things is formidable and complex, but it is only one component of effective action in a political environment, and a component not easily distinguished from others of equal importance—negotiating, motivating, persuading, and the like. Formal analysis, in the sense of science or engineering, is a highly differentiated activity. What we gain in methodological rigor, theoretical coherence, and precision from formal analysis we often lose in lack of timeliness, feasibility, and persuasiveness.

Three main lessons emerge from this discussion of the science, engineering, and craft of analysis. First, all three types of analysis are part of the same enterprise, though they operate in different incentive structures and are judged by different standards. Second, and more important, no clear hierarchy exists among types of analysis. There is no external standard on which to base a judgment that science is "better" analysis than engineering, which in turn is "better" than craft. Judgments about which kind of analysis is better are based solely on the internal standards of proponents of one kind of analysis or another. Third, attempts to professionalize analysis are based on a misunderstanding of the central and undifferentiated role that analysis plays in the craft of deciding and managing.

Growth of the Study of Implements

Policy analysis, then, is composed of three very different kinds of activity, pulled in divergent directions by their internal values and incentives, converging only coincidentally and occasionally on actual decisions. This state of affairs results from a preoccupation with internal standards and incentives, and a failure to look at what holds the science, engineering, and craft of policy analysis together in a single enterprise.

Definitions of the field of policy analysis have focused to date on analytic method, because they are framed by scientists, or the occasional scientist-engineer—people who are typically more comfortable with method than with craft. A robust analytic paradigm has emerged over time from this literature. In essence, the paradigm breaks analysis into discrete, related steps: define the problem, deduce criteria from the nature of the problem and the preferences of decisionmakers, frame distinguishable alternative courses of action, evaluate these options using the criteria specified earlier, and present the relative strengths and weaknesses of competing options.[6] This paradigm has a number of advantages. It is simple. It is clear. But it also allows for virtually infinite elaboration and embellishment. Its simplicity means that it can be taught to students at widely different levels of sophistication—the naive and inexperienced student learns how to think clearly, the more quantitatively sophisticated but inexperienced student learns to put analytic techniques in a broader frame of reference, the experienced but quantitatively unsophisticated student learns to pull common sense around a more explicit framework, and so forth.

This paradigm has at least two major disadvantages, however. First, it equates analysis with analytic method. It says, in effect, "When you are thinking this way, you are being analytical, but when you are thinking in other ways, you are not." Master the method and you learn how to be analytical. This equation of analysis with method is the special conceit of scientists and engineers, who, after all, judge their own work largely in terms of consistency with methodological prescriptions. At the level of craft, getting the method right is only part of what it means to be analytical. For craftspeople, being analytical also means understanding how options fit within existing political interests, administrative structures, and resource constraints; it means having a strategic sense of which short-term gains will lead to long-run results consistent with one's objectives; it means seeing the relationship between the content of an option and a strategy for enacting it; and it means shaping the language of options and arguments to draw supportive coalitions around them.

Second, insofar as the conventional paradigm of policy analysis does take account of the concerns of craft, it does so by grafting them onto the paradigm as marginal embellishments rather than treating them as separate and distinct analytic problems requiring special skills. Are political and administrative feasibility important? Fine. Let's add them as criteria and develop techniques for assessing them at a level of rigor consistent with other measures of effect. Are short-term and long-term objectives different? Fine. Let's break the analysis into stages, applying the paradigm first to short-term objectives and then to longer-term concerns. Is the language of analysis important in determining its political effect? Fine. Let people with political sensitivity fine-tune the language of analysis within the existing paradigm to reflect the common language of politics. In other words, scientists and engineers tend to deal with the problems of craft by folding them into the conventional paradigm, rather than studying the practice of craft for clues about the limits of the paradigm.

For some time now, three separate currents of thought have begun to converge on a different way of thinking about policy analysis. One of these currents is the study of policy implementation. The distinctive contribution of this line of analysis has been to call attention to the fact that policies are shaped as much, if not more, by the institutions that implement them as by the policymakers who frame them. In the words of Eugene Bardach, paraphrasing Clausewitz, "Implementation is the continuation of policymaking by other means." The second current of thought is an older one, dating back to Theodore Lowi's well-worn typology of distributive, redistributive, and regulatory policies. The central message, picked up and developed by J. Q. Wilson, among others, is that different types of policies involve distinctively different packages of incentives which in turn result in distinctively different patterns of political support. Erwin Hargrove first made the connection between these two currents of thought, arguing that one could predict patterns of implementation by specifying the bases of political support and opposition for different types of policies.[7]

The third current of thought is more recent, and potentially more important, than the other two. In an unpublished paper Eugene Bardach conceptualizes policymaking around three standard technologies or "implements," that he calls inducement, enforcement, and benefaction. Each type of implement, he argues, leads to a characteristic set of implementation problems; combinations of implements lead to more complex but still predictable problems. Different implements require different types and levels of resources, defined by Bardach as money, political support, administrative competence, and leadership. Later, Lester Salamon, in a paper addressing the growing role of "third party government," argued that implementation analysis had become "stuck in a rut" by focusing on programs and policies as the unit of analysis. This focus concealed important changes in the institutions and mechanisms that governments were using to implement policy. A more fruitful tack, he argued, was to focus on the "generic tools" of government intervention, rather than policies or programs, and to determine how those tools come to be used, and how combinations of them vary in their effects. Each type of tool, he argues, has its own "political economy" that can be understood systematically. Among the tools Salamon singled out for special attention were grants-in-aid, loan guarantees, direct loans, and conditional payment schemes. Of particular interest to Salamon were the trade-offs faced by policy-makers in the choice between "direct" methods of intervention (administered directly by government agencies) and "indirect" methods (use of financial incentives and regulations to induce third-party agencies to provide government services).[8] Salamon has since developed a major line of research around these themes.[9]

Also included in this third line of thought is Peter May's work on crafting policy alternatives. May argues that, at the level of craft, constructing policy alternatives consists essentially of finding the basic elements that policymakers and managers can influence, establishing the feasible range of manipulation of those elements, and then constructing packages of elements that respond to the problem policymakers are trying to solve. May's approach is particularly useful when it is applied with attention to the institutional and political context of a particular problem. It yields practical solutions and it eliminates much of the pompous rhetoric of analysis that often accompanies the conventional paradigm. It focuses on the questions, "What levers can we pull, in what combination, with what effect on the problem we're trying to solve?" In this sense, May's conception of policy analysis meshes well with the work of Bardach and Salamon and with the demands of craft for particular solutions to particular problems in particular institutional settings.[10]

These three converging lines of thought have considerably influenced conceptions of policy implementation. The problem of implementing policy appears to be more one of how to alter the particular mix of elements or implements in a policy, through policymaking or management decisions in response to unforeseen events, than one of what happens to a particular policy as it travels from a legislature through an administrative agency to some ultimate unsuspecting target. The focus of implementation analysis has shifted from assessing whether policies have been "successfully implemented" (whatever that means) to how to manage the implementation process for desired results, using changes in policy, organization, and political coalitions. Using implements as the unit of analysis, rather than policies or programs, has, I would argue, materially increased both the analytic power and the practical utility of this work.

These lines of thought represent a shift away from viewing policy analysis as the application of a standard analytic paradigm toward viewing policy analysis as the study of implements. This shift could have important consequences for the relationship between science, engineering, and craft in policy analysis.

First, implements are a unit of analysis that all practitioners of policy analysis can understand and use. For scientists and engineers, they are "independent variables." For craftspeople, they are specific changes in this or that policy. There may be disagreements about how to define a particular variable or implement, but the language of controllable and noncontrollable elements and the idea that these elements have a feasible range of control is one that has power across all types of policy analysis.

Second, we already have considerable knowledge about the theory and behavior of people and organizations in response to some standard policy implements. Economists, for example, have studied the problems of enforcement and compliance in regulatory policy and the response of governments to restricted and unrestricted grants. Political scientists have made considerable headway in defining the conditions under which diffuse and targeted benefits and costs can be expected to generate organized political activity in response to government action. These developments are happy coincidences, since academics did not start out to study these subjects with the idea that they would improve the science and craft of policy analysis. Nonetheless, these developments are available to policy analysts.

Third, development of a common focus on implements potentially allays the problem of intellectual imperialism among practitioners of policy analysis because it shifts away from method and toward problem-solving. At the level of science, people can do tightly designed, theoretically sound studies of particular implements, using prescribed methods and extending theory. At the level of engineering, people can do responsive analyses focused on a limited number and range of implements. At the level of craft, people can maintain their focus on feasible actions in tightly constrained settings. The study of implements focuses attention on what to do, rather than on whether the methods used in deciding what to do can pass disciplinary muster.

The Case of Three Mile Island

If policy analysis can usefully be considered the study of implements, the more difficult problem is what this shift in perspective means for the practice of analysis, as science, engineering, and craft.[11] The case of Three Mile Island can be used to illustrate the implications of this point of view for analysis of policy disaster.

The basic facts of the Three Mile Island accident are by now widely known. Two workers, performing routine maintenance while the Three Mile Island Unit 2 (TMI-2) was in full operation, accidentally choked off the main feedwater system supplying coolant to the reactor. This event triggered the plant's automatic emergency system, shutting down the reactor and activating emergency feedwater pumps. The emergency pumps failed to work, however, because workers had closed pump valves in an earlier maintenance procedure and failed to reopen them. The lack of coolant in the reactor vessel resulted in a precipitous increase in temperature and pressure, triggering a relief valve, which then stuck open. Reactor operators, aware that temperature and pressure were climbing, but unaware that the relief valve was stuck, read control room instruments as indicating that there was too much rather than too little coolant in the reactor. They reduced the flow of coolant to the reactor vessel, causing the remaining water to turn to steam, creating bubbles in the cooling system, blanketing fuel rods, and causing control room instruments to malfunction. Discovering that the two key valves to the emergency feedwater pumps were closed, two minutes after the initial shutdown, reactor operators opened the valves. But they were still unaware of the open relief valve. After becoming disturbed at the amount of water leaving the reactor, they shut down all reactor cooling pumps. Fuel rods in the reactor began to disintegrate, releasing radioactive gases, which were then vented.[12]

The lessons from the Three Mile Island accident can be reduced to six main points. First, safety problems initially grow out of mundane events. These events do not ordinarily cause accidents. In fact, the log books that utilities are required to keep on reactor operation for the

Nuclear Regulatory Commission (NRC) are full of thousands of such events. These events are an integral feature of the technology of nuclear power generation.

Second, the TMI-2 accident grew not out of a single event but out of a cascade of mundane events, none of which was serious enough by itself to cause a major accident. Engineers have considerable skill in designing redundant systems and in modeling their reliability. These skills were required to be applied to the design of all nuclear power plants, including TMI-2. Redundant design was not sufficient to prevent the accident that occurred at TMI-2.

Third, the transition from a collection of mundane events to a near-disaster occurs in a very short time, while the diagnosis and treatment of the problem takes a relatively long time. Of the three most critical events at TMI-2—the initial failure of the emergency feedwater system, the failure of the relief valve, and the operators' throttling back of the emergency injection system—the first two occurred in thirteen seconds, and the third occurred within four and one-half minutes. After that, it took operators over two hours to discover and close the stuck relief valve, and nearly sixteen hours to stabilize the disintegrating reactor core.

Fourth, the occurrence of mundane events can be traced to broader failures of design, management, and regulation. Among the major failures discovered by post-TMI-2 investigators were (1) poor selection and training of plant operators; (2) rigid and inflexible distinctions in the organization of nuclear plants into "hand" work (low-level technicians) and "mind" work (engineers and managers); (3) inadequate conduct and supervision of plant maintenance; (4) poor human factors engineering in the design of control systems; (5) failure of utilities to compile, and the NRC to use, information on previous near-accidents; and (6) overreliance on self-regulation by utilities and weak inspection and enforcement by the NRC.

Fifth, some of these defects in design, management, and regulation can be traced to defects in policy. Among the policy defects uncovered by post-TMI investigations were (1) failure by NRC to specify clear regulatory objectives and enforcement goals for the safe operation of nuclear plants; (2) regulatory designation of several critical subsystems, such as cooling systems, as "nonnuclear," thereby removing them from the purview of safety regulation; (3) failure to look seriously at the organization of nuclear plants, rather than their technology, as a potential source of safety hazards; (4) unclear division of responsibility between NRC commissioners and staff on safety matters; and (5) federal statutory limits on utilities' liabilities for damages occurring as a result of accidents.

Sixth, some of the defects in design, management, and regulation can be traced to the economic structure of the industry. The production of electrical energy with nuclear technology entails (1) high fixed costs and low variable costs relative to other forms of technology; (2) relatively high opportunity costs of shutdowns for plant maintenance, measured by the price of alternative energy that must be purchased to replace the energy lost through shutdowns; (3) a regulated rate structure that allows utilities to pass capital costs with relative ease to consumers, and, in the case of investor-owned utilities, to minimize risks for investors; and (4) as noted above, strict statutory limits on liability for accident damages. Taken together, these economic factors result in the construction of large plants, the use of those plants to meet "base load" requirements (the stable, fixed demand of an electrical generating system), the scheduling of shutdowns for refueling purposes only, and the performance of much routine maintenance with plants in full operation.

The major conclusion that emerges from this inventory is the extraordinary complexity and interdependence of factors bearing on the accident at TMI-2 and nuclear plant safety in general. The tendency of scientists and engineers, faced with this level of complexity, is to find some simplifying theoretical construct that will allow a neat, parsimonious solution. At the level of craft, though, all such solutions are partial; the relationships among the pieces—technological, economic, political, and organizational—have to cohere in some way to get a practical solution. In addition, the standard analytic model tells how to frame options once we know what the relevant pieces are, but doesn't tell us how to find the relevant pieces or how to relate them to the central questions of what is controllable over what range.

This diagnosis leads to an analysis of the implements surrounding the problem of nuclear plant safety. Some of these implements are standard fixtures of regulatory policy: plant design standards, safety performance standards, higher entry qualifications for plant personnel, better training, a greater degree of on-site inspection by the NRC representatives, higher penalties for noncompliance and for failure to report incidents, awards and protection for whistle-blowers. Other implements can be designed around the economic incentives of the industry: raising the liability of utilities for damages or providing compensation for down-time due to inspection and maintenance. These implements are the province of federal policymakers. Still other implements might focus on streamlining the organizational structure of utilities and plants: reducing the distinctions between low-level and high-level operating technicians, shortening lines of control and communication between utility executives and plant managers, and introducing positive incentives for early identification of maintenance and operation problems. These are implements that might be used by utilities, as a form of self-regulation, if the regulatory and economic incentives were correctly designed.

This kind of analysis, then, entails mapping various discrete "solutions" onto pieces of the problem, less in the manner of formal hypothesis-testing and more in the manner of searching for promising patterns in the solution to a complex puzzle. One can imagine such an analysis producing packages of implements that combine changes in regulatory policy, economic incentives, and organization in various ways to produce a range of options. Furthermore, we can see the role that science and engineering play in this process of mapping implements onto problems. Economic theory can tell us at what point the expected value of liability or regulatory penalties becomes high enough to create an incentive for utilities to manage plants safely. Human factors studies can tell us what training measures and entry qualifications are consistent with certain expectations about human performance in critical situations. Operations analysts can tell us the design and costs of maintenance systems that are consistent with certain expectations about reducing the frequency of critical events. This is science in the service of policy, but with a key difference from the usual practice of policy analysis as science. Instead of using a policy problem as a natural experiment for testing hypotheses, the focus on implements forces the mobilization of inquiry around key dimensions of the solution.

Having said this, we are still left with the question of why we would expect these new solutions to work any better than the old ones. Mobilizing theory around problems does not necessarily lead to better policies. After all, the system that permitted the accident at TMI-2 had the benefit of some very sophisticated science and engineering. The answer lies not just in mobilizing theory around problems—the specialty of science and engineering—but also in adapting theory to the special problems of the technology, the economics, the organization, and the politics of the industry where the problem resides—the specialty of craft. The solutions, if there are any, lie at the intersection of science, engineering, and craft, not inside the domain of one or the other—hence the importance of a language of analysis, the language of implements, that emphasizes this intersection.

Ethical Issues in
Emergency Management Policy
⚡ Ernest Partridge

Ethics and Policy

We begin with an affirmation that there are "ethical issues in emergency management policy." This may seem a strange and pointless recitation of the obvious. Public officials, crisis managers, public safety personnel, and others directly involved with hazards and disasters need not be reminded that in the performance of their respective roles and duties they will be faced with compelling, crucial, and forced ethical choices involving the protection and even the saving of lives and properties. They face these choices in all phases of emergency —*mitigation, preparedness, response*, and *recovery*—that is, before, during, and after disasters. These choices, regarding how they will act in the anticipation and in the event of an emergency, are unavoidably laden with values.

Yet many theorists (notably some economists and political scientists) have attempted to "simplify" and even eliminate ethical issues from policy analysis by reducing values to some arrangement of facts or empirical concepts, such as cost-benefit ratios, or preferences, or cultural norms. Such so-called positive criteria of value have the apparent advantage of precision and determinateness. However, since these criteria are also irrelevant to the solution of ethical questions, these advantages count for little in policy deliberations.

While such theoretical attempts to establish "value-free policy science" have recently given way to the criticisms of moral philosophers, many administrators and legislators have failed to recognize this development in applied ethics.[1] Thus when disaster management policy is debated before congressional committees economists, political scientists, geographers, engineers, and others are conspicuous in the roster of expert witnesses—and appropriately so. For the most part, however, moral philosophers are conspicuous only by their absence.

The decline and subsequent return of ethical analysis and debate in public policymaking constitutes a fascinating chapter in the recent history of ideas. However, a review of that controversy is neither necessary nor desirable at this time. A simple analysis of the concept of policy should suffice to prove that policymaking is fundamentally a value-laden activity.

After encountering numerous descriptions, conceptions, definitions, and theories of policymaking, I have concluded that at the very least policy can be defined as a general decision, arrived at deliberately and stated explicitly, which is intended to bind and direct future activities and investments (in funds, time, and energy) of the decisionmaker(s). Implicit in the term decision is a choice among distinguishable options. Furthermore, these are choices among graded options, that is, some of these options will be judged preferable to others and (presumably) the option chosen will be judged optimal. These options are graded (at least in part) according to how each is judged to affect the welfare, rights, and responsibilities of persons, and how effectively these options are judged to accomplish these and other presupposed value objectives. At the close of his deliberations the policymaker says, in effect, "Having evaluated the available options, I propose that we should do the following." In sum, by policymaking we mean, at the very least, a deliberative choice among graded options, each of which will variably affect the welfare and rights of human beings. That definition effectively entails that this activity is value-laden.

If we grant that policymaking is inherently a value-laden activity, need this concession trouble the disaster management specialist? After all, aren't the ethical premises in emergency management policy rather simple, straightforward, and uncontroversial? Isn't there, in effect, only one ethical imperative facing that specialist: "Minimize the losses of life and property"? Who could dispute that premise?

A moment's reflection will show that even that premise is anything but simple, straightforward, and uncontroversial. To begin with, it is not simple but compound—lives and property. Still worse, disaster policy and disaster management decisions often involve conflicts of lives versus property. In addition, decisions regarding the protection of lives and property are weighed according to a variety of separate scales of evaluation, such as costs and benefits (dollars), risks (probabilities), time (hours to years). Each scale of evaluation proliferates moral controversy. More fundamentally, a decision to evaluate policy in terms of the aggregate net value of the consequences of that policy draws attention away from the rights of, and justice to, individuals and toward the "bottom line" maximization of some impersonal good such as utility. Most moral philosophers will acknowledge that the utility versus justice question is one of the most perplexing and persistent issues with which they must deal. (These difficult ethical issues, all too briefly and abstractly presented here, will shortly be illustrated by an extended example—an emergency scenario.)

As such questions proliferate—lives versus property, assessment of risks, long- versus short-term consequences, justice versus utility, etc. —we find that they display the qualities of what are called "tragic choices." First, they are, in William James's words, momentous, they present live options, and they are forced (that is, to do nothing is to make a significant choice). Furthermore, these choices are among exclusive "goods" (we can't have them all), and (more seriously) among unavoidable "bads" (necessary evils). Emergency management policy gives us a stark and compelling reminder that the Sunday school view of morality as a contest between good and evil is radically restrictive and short-sighted. In the face of impending and actual catastrophes, good intentions and moral stamina, however important, will not suffice to give us the best decisions. Relevant information and moral intelligence are also required.

How are these ethical questions of disaster policy to be settled? In behalf of whose interests and preferences? Whose perspective upon these policy issues is to have precedent? Here we touch a theoretical "nerve" of the philosophical analysis of public policy. The problem of the point of view of hazards policy pervades this entire volume, thus saturating these discussions and this issue with ethical significance.

Each point of view implies a different policy. This rule can be readily appreciated as it applies to the following problem, one of acute concern to disaster management professionals. Ordinary citizens living in hazardous areas generally do not, before the occurrence of natural disasters, act in their own best interests. In such circumstances it appears that well-known psychological mechanisms of *denial* interfere with and defeat proposals to invest appropriate amounts of time, funds, and concern before the event.[2] Thus we find that public preference and opinion are usually at odds with public interest. Because of this discrepancy between the public's preference and interest, hazards professionals seeking to serve the public interest must often strain at the limits of democratic legitimacy and act in a manner that might be described as paternalistic. What point of view justifies this behavior? Perhaps the point of view of the hypothetical disaster victim. From this perspective, the hazards policymaker and policy implementor acts, before a disaster, as the citizen suffering from the disaster would have him act. But wouldn't such a point of view be overly cautious and conservative? After all, the vast majority of our days are disaster-free. Perhaps the optimum point of view would be that of a hypothetical individual who possesses general knowledge regarding risks, costs, benefits, and his basic needs and desires as a human being, but who is denied knowledge of the particular times and circumstances of his life. The point of view of such a hypothetical observer would thus encompass the perspectives of both the anguished disaster victim and the complacent citizen in predisaster conditions.[3]

The question of point of view is one of the most fundamental issues of moral philosophy. It is also implicit (and often explicit) in all policy theory and policy practice, for it is a ground of legitimacy for such theory and practice. As the point of view changes, so does the policy. A point of view fundamentally affects one's assessment of the values of life and property, as life and property are variously encountered and evaluated in a myriad of differing contexts and circumstances.

This is but a partial indication of a myriad of morally controversial problems that are generated by an analysis of the seemingly simple, obvious, and noncontroversial premise that the moral objective of emergency management policy is to minimize losses of life and property. The linkage between ethical issues and emergency management policy might be further illustrated by a hypothetical situation that may well be faced in the near future.

The Pasadena Paradigm

Imagine that an ad hoc emergency meeting of select members of the seismology faculty and staff has assembled at the California Institute of Technology in Pasadena. Also in attendance are seismologists from other campuses, from the United States Geological Survey (USGS) office in Menlo Park, and from appropriate California state and local offices. The meeting is a response to some ominous data that have just arrived from field studies along the San Andreas fault, some fifty kilometers to the north. These studies report alarming changes in data that were heretofore quite stable over the years and decades. They now report releases of radon gas in deep wells and mines, (and/or) changes in water tables, (and/or) quiescence in an asperity zone surrounded by microquakes, (and/or) crustal deformation along the fault, (and/or) a drop and then a rise in P-wave velocities. (The parenthetical "and/or" indicates the author's desire to remain neutral regarding various theories of earthquake prediction, none of which need be assumed or preferred in this scenario.)

We assume that at the time of this hypothetical meeting, earthquake prediction theory will have advanced to the point that a consensus can be reached regarding the implications of these findings. That consensus is that the next great earthquake in southern California is about to take place, and that it will, in effect, be a repetition of the Fort Tejon earthquake of January 9, 1857.[4] The prediction contains the following basic components:

Magnitude: 8.3
Epicenter: Tejon Pass
Time: Four weeks in the future, ± one week[5]
Probability: 60 percent

We have imagined, to this point, an exercise in applied science. Surely everyone in that conference room in Pasadena, though fully aware that such an event was "due," nonetheless devoutly wishes that the evidence indicated otherwise. But as good scientists, they all acknowledge that their preferences are irrelevant to the seismological data before them; the San Andreas fault will not alter its alignment by a millimeter to accommodate these preferences. In that sense these facts are totally detached from the values of those who recorded them, and by those to be affected by them. However, once these scientific assessments, analyses, and projections have been made, values enter the situation and with them, disaster management specialists. Two days later key members of the first meeting reconvene, with invited experts in the theory and practice of emergency management. The first question of ethical import is obvious and compelling: "What are we to do with this information and this prediction?" That question generates a large list of additional ethical questions, the most immediate of which is, "Shall we disclose our findings, or shall we withhold them?" (Here the problem of lives versus property, noted above, arises again.) The following decision grid of four cells results from the intersection of two pairs of possibilities: one physical (the occurrence or the non-occurrence of the earthquake), and the other moral (to disclose or not to disclose the prediction):

	Earthquake	No earthquake
Disclosure		
No disclosure		

(To simplify this analysis, I am ignoring such "gray issues" as degrees of magnitude, variable location of the epicenter, vagueness and ambiguity of the disclosure, etc.)

Certainty would eliminate the live ethical issues. If the seismologists were certain that a repeat of the Fort Tejon earthquake were to occur at a specified date, their clear obligation would be to disclose this information (the NW cell). If they were virtually certain that it would not occur, then of course they have nothing to disclose (the SE cell).

The problems arise with regard to the SW and NE cells—undesirable outcomes that might result from a forced decision under conditions of uncertainty. If a prediction and disclosure are made and no earthquake takes place, there will likely be a high cost in property value loss and economic dislocation. Furthermore, the credibility of the seismologists might be severely compromised (the "cry wolf" problem). However, if disclosure is withheld and the earthquake occurs a great many individuals will be killed and injured who might otherwise be spared. The seismologist is faced with a tragic choice: a choice between two "bads" (loss of life versus economic loss) and, conversely, two "goods" (preservation of life versus preservation of property values). Once again, our simple value assumption of lives versus property breaks down into complexity and controversy. Nor is that the only moral issue before the scientists, and shortly thereafter, before many more individuals and groups—public, corporate, and private.

The scientists and disaster managers in Pasadena hesitate. Might it be possible to improve probability assessment and the accuracy of the other variables in the prediction? It is possible, but it will take time—as much as a week. Perhaps the probability factor may be reduced below 30 percent (<30 percent or >70 percent). If, after review, the magnitude is revised to <7, emergency services will be able to cope much more appropriately and effectively. But valuable time will be lost; indeed, the event may occur while the review is under way. Another tragic choice: How much time versus how much confidence? How are these factors to be weighed, prior to balancing?

The decision is made to disclose the prediction, with appropriate caution and discretion. That moral choice settled, still more appear. How do we determine which mode of caution and discretion is appropriate. Who is to be notified? Surely the governor, the mayor of Los Angeles, and FEMA. Who else? The Los Angeles *Times*? CBS News and Dan Rather? The *National Enquirer*? The highest journalistic bidder? Where do we draw the line? What rationale directs the drawing of that line? What are they to be told? Just the "facts"? Public officials, journalists, and ordinary citizens are impatient with scholarly qualifications and unable to cope with scientific details and technicalities. Thus it will not do to bind up the pile of unedited technical data and toss it "over the transom" into the mayor's office. Abridgement, assessment, and summarization of the data must be done. What rules are to guide this preparation of the data?

Once disclosure is made, the seismologists become vulnerable to public ridicule and lawsuits, should their prediction prove to be false. (Conversely, had they chosen otherwise, they might still have been subject to lawsuits, were it to be discovered after an earthquake that they had deliberately withheld a prediction of that event—yet another "catch-22" dilemma.) A prediction, carefully qualified with precise scientific concepts and terminology, may be sensationalized by the press. Thus what they are willing and obligated to disclose must be a function not only of the integrity of their professional colleagues (in the review process) and of their codes of professional conduct (stated or otherwise), but also of the anticipated and actual conduct of public officials, the media, the legal profession, and indeed the general public. Thus the decision of the assembled seismologists and crisis managers cannot be derived entirely from abstract rules and in isolation from considerations of the conditions of the society upon which that decision will soon have an impact. Rather, because they have both a right and a responsibility to assess and anticipate the moral quality of the responses of affected professions and the public, their decision must take into account the interactions among the operative norms, the moral ecology, of the community. (We will return to this consideration in the next section.)

As we have seen, the tragic choices facing the conferees at Cal-Tech are inescapably moral choices. The conferees can also be said to be morally responsible for their decisions—again, a condition from which they cannot escape. Their predicament is due to a convergence, at that time, place, and circumstance, of the four essential conditions of responsibility—namely, that whatever they decide:

- They will *know*, or be capable of anticipating (before the event), the consequences of their decision (not totally, of course, but enough for their decision to be morally significant).
- They will be *capable* of making that decision and acting upon it.
- They will have a *free choice*. (They could have chosen otherwise.)
- Their decision will be acknowledged to have consequences of *value significance*, affecting the lives, welfare, and rights of other persons.

Should they choose to disclose the prediction, the burden of responsibility will be extended to others whose circumstances encompass these four conditions—the governor, various mayors, lawyers, the media, etc. A generation earlier this burden of responsibility would not have fallen upon a similar collection of specialists, professionals, and administrators, for the knowledge and capability conditions would have been virtually absent. Lacking any of the four criteria, there is no responsibility. Thus the hypothetical conference in Pasadena displays, in microcosm, the macrocosm of our scientific/technological civilization, wherein the exponential growth in knowledge and power bestows upon policymakers, legislators, administrators, and managers, a parallel expansion of moral responsibility.

Therefore it will not do for the decisionmakers in Pasadena to plead that they are not philosophers and therefore have no moral theories or moral responsibilities. They cannot escape their public responsibility. Whatever they choose to do (and this includes doing nothing), their decision will necessarily (a) reflect their knowledge of consequences,

(b) be a choice among options, (c) variably affect the future, and (d) have consequences of value significance (affecting the lives, welfare, property, and rights of persons). Furthermore, their decision will reflect upon their worth as persons (that is, their moral virtue). Finally, that decision will exemplify a moral theory, at least implicitly.[6] The moral component of their decision will not be determined simply by going over the scientific data once again, or sending researchers back to the field for still more facts.

This scenario illustrates moral issues that apply more to the preparedness and response phases of emergency management, and less to the mitigation and recovery phases. Other scenarios would direct our attention to still more ethical issues applying to other phases of emergency management. However, from even this simplified example, some significant moral aspects of emergency policymaking and policy implementation have become apparent.

Professional Ethics: Its Functions and Objectives

The professionals assembled in the hypothetical conference room at Cal-Tech will, if conscientious, be guided by codes of professional conduct, either formally enacted and articulated or implicitly sensed. Thus, as we explore ethical issues in emergency management policy, it would be appropriate to examine the function of professional codes of ethics.

Professional codes of ethics are commonly perceived to be like decalogues—lists of dos and don'ts (primarily don'ts) describing the bounds of acceptable and realms of forbidden conduct on the part of the professional. Thus committees that write professional codes are perceived as moral legislators, and others that enforce these codes are seen as moral police. To be sure, the decalogue function is an important element of a professional code of ethics, but it is not the only function and perhaps not even the most important. In addition to the claims of the profession against the practitioner, there are matters of reciprocating claims and expectations of the practitioner regarding his colleagues, of the profession and practitioners against other professions, against public officials and institutions, against the code of law, and against the public at large. Thus a comprehensive code of ethics includes not only a statement of duties and responsibilities (moral claims *against* the agents), but also a statement of rights and expectations (claims *by* and *in behalf of* the agent). In this second sense, a professional may claim from his colleagues candor, honesty, loyalty, and expectations of support. (For example, a conscientious seismologist prepared to announce an earthquake prediction will honor his peers' prohibition against seeking notoriety and self-promotion through sensationalism. In exchange for this restraint he might claim, against his colleagues, a right to have his prediction receive peer review and evaluation and, if the results are favorable, he has a claim to peer support as he discreetly discloses his prediction.)

In the code of conduct, the explication of the practitioner's rights, duties, responsibilities, and expectations results in an enhancement of personal, professional, and public advantage, through the professional's improved knowledge of the likely consequences of his conduct. Accordingly, the objectives of codes of professional conduct are not simply moral, they are also pragmatic (practical). They serve not only as moral policemen but also as facilitators of effective and appropriate action—as, one might say, "rules of the professional road." Thus, for example, a public communications expert in the office of the mayor of Los Angeles would, upon receiving the prediction from the Pasadena group, need to know the most expeditious means of releasing this information to appropriate officials and then, through the media, to the general public. That official's decision would surely be facilitated by an informed expectation of the degree of civic responsibility and moral restraint exhibited by the media, members of the legal and medical professions, and still other professionals. Codes of professional conduct might clarify and ensure that expectation. But apart from these moral considerations, codes of conduct may explicate agreed-upon procedures of doing intra- and extramural business—procedures that need not claim intrinsic moral significance by themselves.

There may be little moral difference among a set of available professional procedures until a collective choice is made. Once decided, however, the practitioner is obliged to follow these "rules," so that others may deal with him in an effective and efficient manner. Professional codes thus serve to define roles and interactions—within and beyond the profession. Thus they might better be called "codes of conduct *and procedure*."

Codes of conduct should express claims against other professions and should include statements of conditions and contingencies that will govern professional dealings with the members of other professions, contingent upon how those other professionals reciprocally behave. Thus, to return to our example, a seismologist's moral responsibility with regard to his prediction cannot be determined in isolation from the conditions of the world beyond his professional practice. Rather, as Garrett Hardin has put it, "the morality of [that] act is a function of the state of the system"[7]—namely, the system of society and the interaction of its component institutions and professions. For example, if the media can be expected to respond with the flamboyance of the *National Enquirer*, a different response is called for. Personal and professional ethics must therefore be a function of the "moral ecology" of society—the dynamic interaction of the norms, behavior, institutions, and professions of the social environment.

Let us return to the conference room in Pasadena. These seismologists, engineers, and crisis managers, having agreed that there is a high probability of a catastrophic earthquake in about a month, find themselves amid cross-currents of moral obligations—to themselves, to their profession, and to the general public. First, they have a duty to warn the public, presumably through appropriate government agencies and perhaps the media (who will learn of it anyway). On the other hand they, their institutions, and their families have a right to be protected from professional and financial ruin. How secure are their personal and professional lives once they give a candid warning? How does this security affect their burdens of professional responsibility?

As they attempt to answer these questions, the professionals must assess, predict, and come to terms with the moral ecology of their society—with the responsibilities, respectively, of governmental officials, media, and the legal profession. In the best of worlds (alas, not our world) one would find beyond one's profession, operative preferences (a) in government, for public safety over political advantage; (b) in the media, for accuracy over sensationalism; and (c) in law, of protected expression over litigation—all of which would protect and thus morally require candid disclosure on the part of the seismologist and the crisis manager. The professionals do not, however, have comparable responsibility if interacting institutions and professionals lie in ambush.

Codes of professional conduct can thus serve a vital social function, not merely as decalogues of "thou shalt not" imperatives, but rather as compacts between the profession and society, defining and regulating professional behavior and setting expectations and common understanding, both within and beyond the profession. As "agreements in principle" and statements of expectation, professional codes serve to reduce the "anguish of indecision" and hazards of unpredictability. Moreover, if they enjoy a consensus of the profession, they provide informal peer sanction. Like other "rules of the road," these codes are best drawn up in times of quiet and unhurried reflection, with wise and informed anticipation before the fact. Yet, as general rules they cannot anticipate all applications in the brutal, particular, anxious reality of an actual disaster. Thus initiative and improvisation—what Comfort calls "creative insight within rational bounds"[8]—must be an essential objective of the education and the practice of the professional disaster managers.

Given that one of the primary objectives of emergency management is effective, appropriate, and coordinated response to disasters, and given that codes of professional conduct and procedures may enhance the mutual expectations of how the active and interested parties and professionals will in fact respond before, during, and after an emergency, it follows that it is a primary and urgent duty of each profession involved in disaster policy and management to prepare and articulate a well-ordered, well-considered, and comprehensive code of conduct.[9] This obligation falls under the rule that "forewarned is forearmed." The preparation of these codes, integrated with the codes of ethics of other involved professions, may thus be regarded as one of the primary aspects of the preparation phase of emergency management policy.

A Postscript and an Invitation

How well has the foregoing analysis solved the dilemma of the hypothetical seismologists and emergency managers in the Pasadena paradigm? Have we instructed them as to whether or not they should disclose their findings, and, if so, to whom and in what manner? It would appear that we have offered them little guidance. But these appearances are deceiving. We have (hypothetically) cautioned them about widespread errors in ethical and policy decisionmaking. We have acquainted them with important relevant concepts and methods of ethical and policy decisionmaking. But we have offered no direct answers regarding the disposition of their prediction, for to do so would be an impertinence.

While many may be disappointed with this result, that disappointment betrays a misconception of the philosopher's role. Applied philosophers who are invited to confer with scholars and professionals of various fields of applied science, engineering, and the "help professions" routinely encounter such questions as these:

□ From a lawyer: "When is my obligation to my client overridden by my obligation to society?"
□ From an architect-engineer working in a seismically active region: "What can a philosopher tell me about balancing my obligations to my client with my obligation to the eventual tenants of this building?"
□ And from the disaster policymaker: "If public opinion and preference do not support disaster mitigation efforts that are in the public interest, how would a philosopher direct me to treat this dilemma?"

A responsible philosopher has remarkably little to say about any of these questions that is directly, explicitly normative and definitive. He does not because he lacks the factual competence to speak on these issues. Why then should the philosopher be consulted on these matters? Because the legislator, the lawyer, the architect, and the policymaker may lack a background in conceptual analysis and moral assessment to arrive at an informed and critically astute answer. Quite probably, however, through his practical professional experience, the practitioner has acquired excellent moral intuitions, which might be improved and integrated through critical reflection and clarification.[10] Working in concert, with due respect for each other's professional knowledge and skills, the professional practitioner and the philosopher may examine these issues with a combined skill and insight that far exceeds the sum of their separate competences.

Accordingly, to questions such as the above the philosopher might first say, "Please inform me of the facts, concepts, and theories that might bear upon this case" and "share with me your sense of the morally correct answer, and your justification for this belief." After reflecting upon these answers to these queries, he then might say, "Let me suggest some possible answers to these ethical questions, and let us together assess their adequacy. Also let me acquaint you with some fundamental concepts which we in our profession have found to be valuable in facing such issues as these. Finally, let me further suggest some methods of moral decisionmaking that have proven fruitful, and let me warn you of others which have not."

The philosopher's role in policymaking, then, is not to arrive upon the scene of policy debate with packaged answers, but to arrive with skills that will assist a common, open, and urgent inquiry.[11]

Synthesis in Disaster Management: Linking Reason with Action in Learning Systems
⚡ Louise K. Comfort

The Problem: Developing Professional Judgment to Cope with Conditions of Uncertainty

As the preceding essays have shown, the conditions characterizing the policymaking process in disaster management include uncertainty, organizational interaction, complexity, and escalating demands for professional performance.[1] Under stable conditions, professional training for decisionmaking involves progressive experience with increasingly complex problems in actual settings. Yet decisionmaking in disaster requires the exercise of professional judgment that operating personnel rarely have the opportunity to develop in actual settings. With relatively few professional guidelines, responsible emergency personnel confront demands for decisions in actual disasters based upon disparate, conflicting, incomplete sources of information under critical pressures of time. What form of reasoning contributes to the development of professional judgment in conditions of disaster? Is there a logic of decisionmaking under evolving disaster conditions that can be captured and articulated in a set of professional skills to assist emergency personnel in meeting the massive demands of an actual disaster? This inquiry returns to the problem of linking reason to action in learning systems.

Earlier essays in this volume have documented the inadequacy of rational methods of planning, information search, and analysis to meet the needs of decisionmakers under disaster conditions.[2] Even the most carefully devised emergency plan is unlikely to anticipate all of the requirements for action in any given disaster. Repeatedly, decisionmakers have acknowledged the shortcomings of their prepared plans, if they have them, in actual emergencies.[3] More serious is the charge that rational planning, well-intentioned but ill-conceived, may actually inhibit the problem-solving process in the dynamic, uncertain conditions of disaster.[4]

The existing model of decisionmaking in disaster management assumes a logic of certainty. Emergency managers seek to establish control over the uncertain conditions of disaster through jurisdictional plans, standard operating procedures, and lines of command. The assumptions underlying the command and control mode during the period of actual response to a disaster are not challenged in this essay. To do so would weaken the degree of control that is essential in an actual emergency situation. But this essay acknowledges that experienced decisionmakers also develop a capacity for professional judgment that demonstrates a significant amount of creativity.[5] In practice, they form judgments based upon incomplete, often conflicting information, guided by a set of professional standards and a disciplined body of knowledge. They become experts in the field, weaving together from prior experience, present knowledge, and new information a capacity to assess emergency situations more accurately and to make decisions more appropriately than those new to the field. This experienced form of reasoning fits no previously specified model of decisionmaking; yet it consistently results in decisions that are more appropriate to the evolving demands of the disaster than those conforming only to formal emergency plans. The reasoning patterns of experienced decisionmakers appear to combine skills of rational analysis with creativity and public interest concerns, allowing them to integrate disparate elements of information from the emergency environment back to reformulate the problem in more productive ways.

The Logic of Uncertainty

Reasoning processes used by decisionmakers operating under uncertain conditions have engendered significant study and reflection among scholars and practicing professionals.[6] Recognizing that it is desirable to enhance creativity in professional decisionmaking in the complex conditions of disaster, the paradox is that the only technology for doing so is rational analysis. Immediately decisionmakers encounter the limits of rational models designed for operation in stable conditions.[7]

Two significant trends of thought have developed in response to this dilemma. One trend, perhaps the most widely known and most frequently considered in the field of organizational theory, seeks to transform ill-structured problems into well-structured ones that human minds, with limited cognitive capacity, can understand and for which they can devise appropriate alternatives for action. This approach toward problem-solving is presented cogently by Herbert A. Simon is his essay, "The Structure of Ill-Structured Problems."[8] Simon argues that it is possible to cope with ill-structured or vaguely defined problems by conceptually transforming one large problem into a set of smaller, well-structured problems that can more easily be bounded by rational thought. Three basic assumptions underlie Simon's conception of this reasoning process, which can be illustrated in reference to emergency management.

First, by defining the goal or "desired outcome" in emergency management activities as the protection of life and property of the citizenry, emergency service personnel may use that goal as a selective guide to appropriate action in a complex, uncertain emergency environment. That is, they do not need to consider all possible problems that may afflict the citizenry, only those most relevant to the goal. The goal, interpreted in specific terms by the professional emergency service personnel, becomes a device to limit the number and scope of problems considered for emergency action.

Second, by decomposing the large problem identified within the scope of emergency action into smaller segments, emergency service personnel may then design appropriate action for smaller, more comprehensible problems, mobilizing the resources and knowledge available to them in clear, focused, readily observable measures. For example, major responsibilities for disaster operations in city jurisdictions are frequently allocated among police, fire, and public works departments. The results of actions taken in a given segment, e.g., the fire service, may then serve as the basis for formulating the next step in the sequence of rational acts directed toward achieving the stated goal in that segment.

Third, by evaluating the actions taken in the separate segments of the defined problem area against the overall goal of protection of life and property, emergency service personnel can assess the effectiveness of their collective actions. Through feedback they may identify their errors and correct their mistakes, thereby improving their performance in the process.

Simon's conception of problem-solving recognizes human ability to learn from carefully sequenced actions. The logic of this approach, however, is classically rational, using schemes of classification to decompose large, complex, ill-defined problems into smaller, more immediate, and more specific tasks that human minds can more easily comprehend and accept for action. The weakness of this approach, however, is that its effectiveness depends upon the appropriateness of the initial categories into which the different segments of the problem are sorted. There is no guarantee that the decisionmakers, using this approach, will discover whether vital categories have been omitted, or others have been inappropriately defined, in their problem-solving processes. The mechanism of feedback operates to encourage this discovery, but the logic of this process is one of discovering discrepancies between the observed phenomena and the existing categories. It is expressed in classical logic by the Barbara syllogism:

Men die.
Socrates is a man.
Socrates will die.[9]

The Barbara syllogism represents a logic of subject classification and does not necessarily compel a reexamination of the functions expressed by the differing subjects. It is reasoning that establishes structural relationships, and errors in performance are discovered only within the identified structures. For example, the logic of mutual assistance agreements among local jurisdictions in western Pennsylvania assumed that a communications capacity between participating communities would be in operation in all disasters. When this structural relationship was not met in the 1985 tornado disaster, the reasoning process failed. The basic organizational structure, once established, was not questioned. Performance, deriving from inappropriate organizational structure, proved inadequate in meeting the needs of the tornado-stricken town of Atlantic.

A second form of reasoning has a time-honored record in decision-making processes in uncertain, dynamic environments. Discussed by Gregory Bateson in describing evolutionary processes, this form of reasoning is illustrated by the "grass" syllogism:

> Grass dies.
> Men die.
> Men are grass. [10]

It is a logic of predicates, in which the common element of classification is the function which the two subjects, dissimilar in outward appearance, share. To identify the commonality of function between the two subjects requires the researcher to reformulate the question under study in a totally new way. The benefit of this type of reasoning in highly uncertain and dynamic conditions is that it is grounded in process and regards performance or "what works" as the basis for decision. Organizational structure, emerging from the experience of action in the emergency environment, is subject to review and adaptation in order to achieve fit performances.

For example, in the Mexican earthquake disaster the devastating collapse of nearly a thousand buildings, trapping thousands of people in tons of rubble, defied any preconceived plan for rescue operations. Neighbors and students helped to free survivors by passing chunks of debris hand to hand. Sophisticated seismic detection equipment identified sounds of life. Search dogs sniffed out live survivors buried under heavy concrete walls. Heavy earth-moving equipment lifted concrete barriers to uncover possible survivors. All elements, dissimilar subjects, shared the function of contributing to the rescue operations. Military helicopters with powerful lifting mechanisms for moving heavy debris were rejected because the noise of their engines and propellers interfered with other rescue activities. [11]

The different elements of the rescue operation are sorted not by subject but by function; not by nationality but by performance. Those that functioned effectively in the Mexican disaster are likely to be retained in the set of professional rescue techniques to be used in the next catastrophic urban earthquake disaster. Those that proved ineffective in performance are likely to be dropped. In the highly uncertain environment of disaster management, this kind of evolutionary development of practical performance allows the reconceptualization of organizational and interorganizational functions in more effective ways.

Synthesis in Practicing Emergency Management

Skills of synthesis are vital in interpreting the emergency environment for professional action. Men, technology, and information combine interactively in the dynamic, uncertain environment of disaster. The logic of predicates allows the development of a learning organizational system in emergency management, which can then be refined in smaller segments by the logic of subject classification.

In a learning system, the roles and responsibilities of public managers with emergency responsibilities shift significantly from those outlined in a traditional organizational model of command and control. Professional emergency managers become coordinators of activities undertaken by multiple organizations and individuals to protect lives and property in their respective communities. Through strategies of change, they invite the respective participants in public and private organizations to review their collective performance in light of current conditions of risk and to modify their actions accordingly. Through strategies of continuity, they reinforce proven structures of organizational performance and maintain their operation effectively. Through strategies of integration, public managers weigh differing interests, needs, and resources, balancing risk against responsibility in an evolving interpretation of public interest under conditions of disaster. The paradox of disaster management is overcome, albeit temporarily, by learning systems. It is a recurring task, one in which the dilemmas of policy and management are redrawn in the unique conditions of each disaster. Designing the appropriate fit between policy and practice remains the continuing task of disaster management. It is most effectively accomplished within learning systems.

Notes

Designing Policy for Action

1 Charles Perrow, *Normal Accident: Living With High-Risk Technologies* (New York: Basic Books, 1984).

2 Arnold Meltsner and Christopher Bellavita discuss the connecting links between policy and organization in their thoughtful book, *The Policy Organization* (Beverly Hills, Calif.: Sage, 1984). I prefer the term "organizational network" to policy organization as it conveys the interactive, flexible character of these links.

3 See Louise K. Comfort, "Integrating Organizational Action in Emergency Management: Strategies for Change," *Public Administration Review* 45, special issue (January 1985): 155–64.

4 See, for example Louis O. Giuffrida, *Emergency Management: The National Perspective* (Emmitsburg, Md.: National Emergency Training Center, monograph series, vol. 1, 1983), and David McLoughlin, "A Framework for Integrated Emergency Management," *Public Administration Review* 45, special issue (January 1985): 165–72.

5 See Louise K. Comfort, "Action Research: A Model for Organizational Learning," *Journal of Policy Analysis and Management* 5 (1985): 100–18.

6 James G. March and Herbert A. Simon, *Organizations* (New York: Wiley Press, 1958). See also the accounts of organizational efforts to cope with complexity in the essays by Comfort and Cahill, Kartez, and Kelley and LaPlante in this volume.

7 Chris Argyris, *Reasoning, Learning and Action* (San Francisco: Jossey Bass, 1982.)

8 John Holland, *Adaptation in Natural and Artificial Systems* (Ann Arbor: University of Michigan Press, 1975).

9 Herbert A. Simon, *The Sciences of the Artificial* (Cambridge: MIT Press, 1969, 1981).

10 See the concept of social entropy discussed by Eugene Bardach in his book, *The Implementation Game* (Cambridge: MIT Press, 1977).

11 Louis O. Giuffrida, director of the Federal Emergency Management Agency, states: "Protection of its citizens and their property is a legal and moral responsibility of the American government, as it is of any government." Giuffrida, *Emergency Management*, p. 2.

12 Interviews, Mercer County Fire Personnel, Mercer County Fire Chiefs' Association, monthly meeting, Jackson Center, Pennsylvania, June 24, 1985.

13 Lawrence B. Mohr, *Explaining Organizational Behavior* (San Francisco: Jossey Bass, 1982).

14 See James G. March and Johan P. Olsen, "The New Institutionalism: Organizational Factors in Political Life," *American Political Science Review* 78 (September 1984).

15 See Louise K. Comfort and Anthony G. Cahill, "Increasing Problem-solving Capacity Between Organizations: The Role of Information in the May 31, 1985, Tornado Disaster in Western Pennsylvania," in this volume.

16 See table 5 in Comfort and Cahill, in this volume.

17 Herbert A. Simon, *Models of Discovery* (Englewood Cliffs, N.J.: Prentice-Hall, 1977), chap. 5.3, "The Structure of Ill-Structured Problems," reprinted from *Artificial Intelligence* 4 (1973): 181-201.

18 See Louise K. Comfort, "International Disaster Assistance in the Mexico City Earthquake," *New World* 1, no. 2 (Fall 1986): 12–43.

19 Ernest R. Alexander, "Design in the Decision-Making Process," *Policy Sciences* 14 (1982): 285.

20 Louise K. Comfort, "Information Search Processes in Emergency Management," in Sallie Marston, ed., *Terminal Disasters: Computer Applications in Emergency Management* (Boulder: Institute of Behavioral Science, University of Colorado, monograph no. 39, May 1986).

21 Simon, *The Sciences of the Artificial*, p. 190.

22 See the discussion in Comfort, "Integrating Organizational Action."

23 Comfort and Cahill, "Increasing Problem-solving Capacity."

24 See especially the work by Chris Argyris and Donald Schön, published together and separately from 1970 to 1986. They develop the theory together in *Theory and Practice: Increasing Professional Effectiveness* (San Francisco: Jossey-Bass, 1974), and refine it separately in subsequent works.

25 Michael D. Cohen, "Conflict and Complexity: Goal Diversity and Organizational Search Effectiveness," *American Political Science Review* 78 (June 1984): 435–51.

26 Ibid.

27 Allen Newell and Herbert A. Simon, *Human Problem Solving* (Englewood Cliffs, N.J.: Prentice-Hall, 1972); Cohen, "Conflict and Complexity"; John J. Kirlin, "A Political Perspective," in Trudi C. Miller, ed., *Public Sector*

Performance (Baltimore: Johns Hopkins University Press, 1984).

28 Comfort, "Action Research."

29 Lotfi Zadeh, "Fuzzy Sets as a Basis for a Theory of Possibility," in *Fuzzy Sets and Systems* (Amsterdam: North-Holland, 1978); Lotfi Zadeh, *Fuzzy Sets and Their Applications to Cognitive and Decision Processes* (New York: Academic Press, 1975).

30 March and Olsen, "The New Institutionalism," 741.

31 Harold L. Wilensky, *Organizational Intelligence* (New York: Basic Books, 1967); Martha Feldman and James G. March, "Information in Organizations as Signal and Symbol," *Administrative Science Quarterly* 26 (1981): 171–86.

32 See the concept of "deutero learning" presented by Argyris in *Reasoning, Learning and Action.*

33 See the discussion by Meltsner and Bellavita, *The Policy Organization,* in chap. 5, "Members: Part-Time Participation in a Full-Time Organization."

34 Simon, *Sciences of the Artificial;* Robert Axelrod, *The Evolution of Cooperation* (New York: Basic Books, 1984).

Structuring Problems for Policy Action

1 Paul Watzlawick, John Weakland, and Richard Fisch, *Change: Principles of Problem Formation and Problem Resolution* (New York: W. W. Norton, 1974), pp. 81–82.

2 Charles Perrow, *Normal Accidents: Living with High-Risk Technologies* (New York: Basic Books, 1984), p. 83; and G. L. Wilson and P. Zarakas, "Anatomy of a Blackout," *IEEE Spectrum* (February 1978): 38–46.

3 William N. Dunn, *Public Policy Analysis: An Introduction* (Englewood Cliffs, N.J.: Prentice-Hall, 1981), p. 97.

4 David Dery, *Problem Definition in Policy Analysis* (Lawrence: University Press of Kansas, 1984), p. 4.

5 Charles E. Lindblom and David K. Cohen, *Usable Knowledge: Social Science and Social Problem Solving* (New Haven: Yale University Press, 1979), p. 50.

6 Russell L. Ackoff, *Redesigning the Future: A Systems Approach to Societal Problems* (New York: John Wiley, 1974), p. 21.

7 Dunn, *Public Policy Analysis,* p. 98.

8 Ackoff, *Redesigning the Future,* p. 8.

9 Howard Raiffa, *Decision Analysis* (Reading, Mass.: Addison-Wesley, 1968), p. 264.

10 Ian I. Mitroff and Frederick Betz, "Dialectical Decision Theory: A Meta-Theory of Decision Making," *Management Science* 19 (1972): 11–24.

11 See Dery, *Problem Definition,* p. 57.

12 Ibid., p. 58.

13 Chris Argyris, *Reason, Learning and Action* (San Francisco: Jossey-Bass, 1982).

14 Edward Wenk, Jr., *Margins for Survival* (Oxford: Pergamon Press, 1979), pp. 72–102.

15 Ian I. Mitroff and James R. Emshoff, "On Strategic Assumption-Making: A Dialectical Approach to Policy and Planning," *Academy of Management Review* 4 (1979): 1–12.

16 Ian I. Mitroff and Richard O. Mason, *Creating a Dialectical Social Science* (Boston: D. Reidel, 1981), pp. 73–86.

17 Ibid.

18 David McLoughlin, "A Framework for Integrated Emergency Management," *Public Administration Review* 45, special issue (January 1985): 166.

19 Thomas L. Saaty, *The Analytic Hierarchy Process* (New York: McGraw-Hill, 1980).

20 Kenneth R. Hammond, et al., "Social Judgment Theory," in Martin F. Kaplan and Steven Schwartz, eds., *Human Judgment and Decision Process* (New York: Academic Press, 1975), pp. 271–312; Stephen Toulmin, *The Uses of Argument* (Cambridge: Cambridge University Press, 1958).

21 Ralph G. Lewis, "Management Issues in Emergency Response," in this volume.

22 Kim S. Cameron, "Effectiveness as Paradox: Consensus and Conflict in Conceptions of Organizational Effectiveness," *Management Science* 32 (May 1986): 539–53.

23 Ibid., pp. 545–46.

24 Ibid., p. 549.

25 Ibid., pp. 545–46.

Current Policy Issues in Mitigation

1 Thomas Pavlak discusses these stages in the preceding chapter. Also see National Governors' Association, *1978 Emergency Preparedness Project Final Report* (Washington, D.C.: U.S. Government Printing Office).

2 See Christoph Hohenemser, Roger Kasperson, and Robert W. Kates, "Causal Structure: A Framework for Policy Formulation," in Hohenemser and Kasperson, eds., *Risk in the Technological Society*, AAAS Selected Symposium no. 5 (Boulder, Colo.: Westview Press, 1982), pp. 109–139.

3 See Charles Perrow, *Normal Accidents: Living with High-Risk Technologies* (New York: Basic Books, 1984), for an insightful discussion of relationships among scientific advancements, disasters, and social responsibility.

4 Flooding, for example, was one of the costliest types of disasters in 1984 and was the crisis cited most often by governors in their requests for presidential aid. See Anders Wijkman and Lloyd Timberlake, *Natural Disasters: Acts of God or Acts of Man?* (Washington, D.C.: Earthscan, 1984) for a discussion of the worldwide flood problem.

5 See Ian Burton, "Cultural and Personality Variables in the Perception of Natural Hazards," in J. F. Wohlwill and D. H. Carson, eds., *Environment and the Social Sciences Perspectives and Applications* (Washington, D.C.: American Psychological Association, 1972), pp. 184–95; and Raymond J. Burby and

Beverly A. Cigler, "Effectiveness of State Assistance Programs for Flood Hazard Mitigation," in R. Charbeneau, ed., *Regional and State Water Resources Planning and Management* (Bethesda, Md.: American Water Resources Association, 1984), pp. 179–88.

6 See *Public Administration Review* 45, special issue (January 1985) for articles on the governmental framework for dealing with hazards, especially articles by Roger E. Kasperson and K. David Pijawka, 7–18; Bruce B. Clary, 20–28; and Rae Zimmerman, 29–39. Also see David Sink, "An Interorganizational Perspective on Local Emergency Management," *Policy Studies Review* 4 (May 1985): 698–708.

7 A controversial discussion of the interactions between technology and environment is found in Mary Douglas and Aaron Wildavsky, *Risk and Culture* (Berkeley: University of California Press, 1982).

8 Roger E. Kasperson and K. David Pijawka, "Societal Response to Hazards and Major Hazard Events: Comparing Natural and Technological Hazards," *Public Administration Review* 45, special issue (January 1985): 7–18.

9 Perrow, in *Normal Accidents*, discusses this point.

10 See Advisory Board on the Built Environment, National Research Council, *Multiple Hazard Mitigation: Report of a Workshop on Mitigation Strategies for Communities Prone to Multiple Natural Hazards* (Washington, D.C.: National Academy Press, 1983); and David McLoughlin, "A Framework for Integrated Emergency Management," *Public Administration Review* 45, special issue (January 1985): 165–72.

11 Representative works on beliefs about the seriousness of risk and subjective probability of experiencing risk include Paul Slovic, Howard Kunreuther, and Gilbert White, "Decision Processes, Rationality, and Adjustment to Natural Hazards," in Gilbert White, ed., *Natural Hazards: Local, National, Global* (New York: Oxford University Press, 1974), pp. 187-204; Ian Burton, Robert Kates, and Gilbert White, *The Environment as Hazard* (New York: Oxford University Press, 1978; and Gilbert White, *Natural Hazards: Local, National, Global* (New York: Oxford University Press, 1974).

12 Dennis S. Mileti, "Human Adjustment to the Risk of Environmental Extremes," *Sociology and Social Research* (April 1980): 327–347, reviews this literature.

13 Examples of the research literature are Thomas E. Drabek, Alvin H. Mushkatel, and Thomas S. Kilijanek, *Earthquake Mitigation Policy: The Experience of Two States* (Boulder, Colo.: Institute of Behavioral Science, University of Colorado, 1983); and Ronald W. Perry and Alvin H. Mushkatel, *Disaster Management: Warning, Response, and Community Relocation* (Westport, Conn.: Quorum Books, 1984).

14 James D. Wright, Peter H. Rossi, Sonia R. Wright, and Eleanor Weber-Burdin, *After the Clean-Up: Long-Range Effects of Natural Disasters* (Beverly Hills, Calif.: Sage Publications, 1979).

15 See Burton, Kates, and White, *The Environment as Hazard*; Janice Hutton and Dennis Mileti, *Analysis of Adoption and Implementation of Community Land Use Regulations for Floodplains* (San Francisco: Woodward-Clyde, 1979), as examples of the literature.

16 On intellectual limitations relating to risk see Amos Tversky and Daniel

Kahneman, "Judgment Under Uncertainty: Heuristics and Biases," *Science* 185 (September 27, 1974): 207–32; and Daniel Kahneman, Paul Slovic, and Amos Tversky, eds., *Judgment Under Uncertainty: Heuristics and Biases* (New York: Cambridge University Press, 1982). Also useful is Paul Slovic, B. Fischhoff, and S. Lichtenstein, "Facts and Fears: Understanding Perceived Risk," in R. Schwing and W. Alberts, eds., *Societal Risk Assessment: How Safe is Safe Enough?* (New York: Plenum, 1980), pp. 181–216.

17 On flood hazard insurance see Howard Kunreuther, R. Ginsberg, L. Miller, P. Sagi, P. Slovic, B. Borkan, and N. Katz, *Disaster Insurance Protection: Public Policy Lessons* (New York: John Wiley, 1978).

18 Overconfidence and risk assessment is treated in Slovic, Fischhoff, and Lichtenstein, "Facts and Fears," pp. 181–216.

19 Yair Aharoni, *The No-Risk Society* (Chatham, N.J.: Chatham House, 1982), offers an analysis of how we have shifted risks from ourselves as individuals to our society collectively, along with an examination of consequences.

20 There are a number of legal cases involving the National Flood Insurance Program (NFIP). See, for example, *Texas Landowners Rights Association* v. *Harris*, 453 F. Supp. 1025 (D.C.C. 1978); and *Town of Falmouth, Mass. Board of Selectman* v. *Hunter*, 427 F. Supp. 26 (D. Mass. 1976).

21 A discussion of persuasion, incentives, and penalties, along with a review of mandates and informational strategies, is presented in Kasperson and Pijawka, "Societal Response," 7–18.

22 For example, see Jon A. Kusler, "Liability as a Dilemma for Local Managers," *Public Administration Review* 45, special issue (January 1985): 118–22.

23 See Ibid., for a review of liability issues.

24 For costs and cost estimates on selected hazards, as well as financing strategies see William J. Petak and Arthur A. Atkisson, *Natural Hazard Risk Assessment and Public Policy* (New York: Springer-Verlag, 1982); and Allen K. Settle, "Financing Disaster Mitigation, Preparedness, Response, and Recovery," *Public Administration Review* 45, special issue (January 1985): 101–6.

25 For a discussion and data regarding the state role in land use planning and management see Raymond J. Burby, Steven P. French, Beverly A. Cigler, Edward J. Kaiser, David J. Moreau, and Bruce Stiftel, *Flood Plain Land-Use Management: A National Assessment* (Boulder, Colo.: Westview Press, 1985).

26 See Beth W. Honadle, *Capacity-Building (Management Improvement) for Local Governments: An Annotated Bibliography*, RDRR-28 (Washington, D.C.: U.S. Department of Agriculture, Economic Statistics Service, March 1981), p. 1; and Honadle, "A Capacity-Building Framework: A Search for Concept and Purpose," *Public Administration Review* 41 (September/October 1981): 575–80.

27 On the importance of design and information development, see the essay by Louise Comfort in this volume.

28 Raymond J. Burby and Daniel A. Okun, "Land Use Planning and Health," *Annual Review of Public Health* 4 (1983): 47–67.

29 Early examples of this literature include Roland N. McKean, *Efficiency in Government Through System Analysis* (New York: John Wiley, 1958); and Robert H. Haveman, *The Economic Performance of Public Investments* (Baltimore: Johns Hopkins University Press, 1972).

30 Burby and Okun, "Land Use Planning and Health," present an excellent discussion of the weaknesses of both structural and nonstructural mitigation approaches, including much of what is presented here.

31 A review of mitigation strategies by two planners is David R. Godschalk and David J. Brower, "Mitigation Strategies and Integrated Emergency Management, *Public Administration Review* 45, special issue (January 1985): 64–71.

32 Raymond J. Burby and Steven P. French, "Coping with Floods: The Land Use Management Paradox," *Journal of the American Planning Association* 47 (July 1981): 289–300. Also see Burby et al., *Flood Plain Land-Use Management*; Drabek, Mushkatel, and Kilijanek, *Earthquake Mitigation Policy*.

33 A summary of the early economic literature on this topic is found in Jerome W. Milliman, "An Agenda for Economic Research on Flood Hazard Mitigation," in Stanley A. Changnon, Jr., William C. Ackermann, Gilbert F. White, and J. Loreena Ivens, eds. *A Plan for Research on Floods and Their Mitigation in the United States* (Champaign, Ill.: Illinois State Water Survey Division, 1983).

34 See Kahneman, Slovic, and Tversky, eds., *Judgment Under Uncertainty*, for an examination of the ways that people's intuitive inferences, predictions, probability assessments, and diagnoses do not conform to the laws of probability theory and statistics, making hard data on costs for either damages or mitigation difficult to use in the policy process.

35 See Dennis S. Mileti, "Human Adjustment to the Risk of Environmental Extremes," *Sociology and Social Research* 64 (April 1980): 327–42.

36 See P. F. Ricci, L. A. Sagan, and C. G. Whipple, eds., *Technological Risk Assessment* (Boston: Martinus Nijhoff, 1984); K. S. Shrader-Frechette, *Risk Analysis and Scientific Method: Methodological and Ethical Problems With Evaluating Societal Hazards* (Boston: D. Reidel, 1985); and Ray A. Waller and Vincent T. Covello, eds., *Low-Probability High-Consequence Risk Analysis: Issues, Methods, and Case Studies* (New York: Plenum, 1984).

Natural Hazard Mitigation and Development

1 The Flood Control Act of 1936 was the first attempt by the United States government to prevent natural hazards through large-scale projects like dams. The National Flood Insurance Act of 1968 emphasizes a regulatory approach as discussed later in this article.

2 This is discussed in Donald J. Zeigler, James H. Johnson, Jr., and Stanley D. Brunn, *Technological Hazards* (Washington, D.C.: Association of American Geographers, 1983), pp. 8–11.

3 William J. Petak, "Emergency Management: A Challenge for Public Administration," *Public Administration Review* 45 (January 1985): 4. See also William J. Petak and Arthur A. Atkisson, *Natural Hazard Risk Assessment and Public Policy* (New York: Springer-Verlag, 1982).

4 Petak, "Emergency Management."

5 Anders Wijkman and Lloyd Timberlake, *Natural Disasters: Acts of God or Acts*

of Man? (Washington, D.C.: Earthscan, 1984), pp. 18–32.

6 See Randall W. Scott, ed., *Management and Control of Growth*, vols. 1, 2, and 3 (Washington, D.C.: The Urban Land Institute, 1975); ICMA Management Information Service, "Public-Private Sector Cooperation: Concepts and Ambiguities," *National Civic Review* 69 (July 1980): 365–70, 394.

7 See Charles E. Lindblom, *Politics and Markets* (New York: Basic Books, 1977).

8 Sam Bass Warner, *The Urban Wilderness* (New York: Harper and Row, 1972), chap. 2.

9 A useful discussion of this relationship can be found in Paul E. Peterson, *City Limits* (Chicago: University of Chicago Press, 1981).

10 See Robert Dahl, *Who Governs?* (New Haven: Yale University Press, 1961); Barbara Ferman, *Governing the Ungovernable City* (Philadelphia: Temple University Press, 1985); Paul Kleppner, *Chicago Divided* (DeKalb: Northern Illinois University Press, 1985); Nelson W. Polsby, *Community Power and Political Theory* (New Haven: Yale University Press, 2d ed., 1980); Todd Swanstrom, *The Crisis of Growth Politics: Cleveland, Kucinich and the Challenge of Urban Populism* (Philadelphia: Temple University Press, 1985).

11 See especially Bruce Brugmann and Greggar Sletteland, eds., *The Ultimate Highrise: San Francisco's Mad Rush Toward the Sky* (San Francisco: San Francisco Bay Guardian, 1971).

12 See Scott, *Management and Control of Growth*, pp. 5, 6.

13 See Peter H. Rossi, James D. Wright, and Eleanor Weber-Burdin, *Natural Hazards and Public Choice* (New York: Academic Press, 1982).

14 This geological vulnerability has promoted responsible public and private parties to establish the Southern California Earthquake Preparedness Project (SCEPP), which is funded jointly by the State of California and the Federal Emergency Management Agency. The main purpose of SCEPP is to stimulate preparedness for earthquake-related events in the most heavily populated areas of southern California.

15 John Whittown, *Disasters: The Anatomy of Environmental Hazards* (London: Allen Lane Penguin Books, 1980), chap. 11.

16 Wijkman and Timberlake, *Natural Disasters*, p. 11.

17 Petak and Atkisson, *Natural Hazard Risk Assessment*, p. 44.

18 Raymond J. Burby and Steven P. French, "Coping with Floods: The Land Use Management Paradox," *Journal of the American Planning Association* 47 (July 1981): 289–98.

19 U. S. Department of the Interior, *Report of the Barrier Islands Work Group*, 1978. See also Robert Dolan, Bruce Hayden, and Harry Lius, "Barrier Islands," *American Scientist* 68 (January–February 1980): 16–25.

20 Bruce B. Clary, "The Evolution and Structure of Natural Hazard Policies," *Public Administration Review* 45 (January 1985): 22.

21 Ibid.

22 Ibid., 23. See also Peter J. May and Walter Williams, *Disaster Policy Implementation: Managing Programs Under Shared Governance* (New York: Plenum, 1986).

23 Senior Executive Policy Center, Federal Emergency Management Agency, *Conference Report—Legal Issues in Emergency Management*, August 1 to 3, 1984,

Emmitsburg, Md., pp. 4–9.
24 Wijkman and Timberlake, *Natural Disasters*, p. 137.
25 Petak and Atkisson, *Natural Hazard Risk Assessment*, p. 6.

Design and Implementation of Disaster Mitigation Policy

1 William J. Petak, *"Development of Earthquake Hazard Reduction Policies in the Cities of Long Beach and Santa Ana,"* presented at the University of Redlands, 1982.
2 This chapter is based on Lidia L. Selkregg (principal investigator), Richard L. Ender, John Choon K. Kim, Stephan F. Johnson, Susan Gorski, and Jane Preuss, *Earthquake Hazard Mitigation: Planning and Policy Implementation —The Alaska Case*. All of the materials incorporated in this work were developed with the financial support of the National Science Foundation Grant CEE8112632, 1984. However, any opinions, findings, conclusions, or recommendations expressed are those of the authors and do not necessarily reflect the views of the foundation.
3 Eugene Bardach, *The Implementation Game* (Cambridge, Mass.: MIT Press, 1977); Jeffrey Pressman and Aaron Wildavsky, *Implementation* (Berkeley: University of California Press, 1973).
4 George C. Edwards, III, *Implementing Public Policy* (Washington, D.C.: Congressional Quarterly Press, 1980).
5 Petak, "Development of Earthquake Hazard Reduction Policies."
6 George C. Edwards, *Implementing Public Policy*.
7 W. Henry Lambright, "Earthquake Prediction and the Governmental Process," paper presented at Hazards Research Policy Development and Implementation Incentives Focus on Urban Earthquake, workshop at University of Redlands, Calif., June 24–26, 1982.
8 Allan B. Jacobs, *The Seismic Safety Plan for San Francisco: Its Preparation and Adoption*, in proceedings of the P.R.C.–U.S.A. Joint Workshop in Earthquake Disaster Mitigation through Architecture, Urban Planning and Engineering, Beijing, China, 1982.
9 Graham T. Allison, *The Essence of Decision: Explaining the Cuban Missile Crisis*, (Boston: Little, Brown, 1971); Herbert A. Simon, *Administrative Behavior*, 2d edition (New York: Macmillan, 1957); James G. March and Herbert A. Simon, *Organizations* (New York: Wiley, 1958).
10 William J. Petak and Arthur Atkisson, "Intergovernmental Problems in Policy Implementation: A Case Study of Seismic Standards of California Building Codes," unpublished manuscript, April 1981; Alan J. Wyner, "Urban Land Use Planning for Seismic Safety in California," in *Third International Earthquake Microzonation Conference Proceedings*, vol. 2 of 3, June 28–July 1, 1982; Peter J. May, "Federal-State Relations and Disaster Relief Formulation," paper presented at the Western Political Science Association's Annual Meeting, San Diego, Calif., 1982; W. Henry Lambright, "Earthquake Prediction and the

Governmental Process," paper prepared for Hazards Research Policy Development and Implementation Incentives Focus on Urban Earthquakes, workshop at University of Redlands, Calif., June 24–26, 1982; Arthur G. Svenson and John G. Corbett, "Earthquakes, Hurricanes, and the Mitigation of Risk at the Local Level: Comparing Policy Response in California and Florida," paper presented at the annual meeting of the Western Political Science Association, Denver, Colorado, 1981; Richard Stuart Olson and Douglas D. Nilson, Jr., "Public Policy Analysis and Hazards Research: Natural Complements," *Social Science Journal* 19 (January 1982); Working Group on Earthquake Hazards Reduction, Office of Science and Technology Policy, Executive Office of the President, *Earthquake Hazard Reductions: Issues for an Implementation Plan*, 1978; Stanley Scott, *Policies for Seismic Safety: Elements for a State Governmental Program* (San Diego: Institute of Governmental Studies, University of California, 1979); Sandra Sutphen, "Disaster in Lake Elsinore: Can Forty Agencies Help This Little Town?" paper presented at the Western Political Science Association Annual Conference, San Diego, Calif., 1982.

11 Wyner, "Urban Land Use Planning for Seismic Safety."

12 Olson and Nilson, "Public Policy Analysis and Hazards Research."

13 Robert D. Miller and Ernest Dobrovolny, *Surficial Geology of Anchorage and Vicinity, Alaska*, U.S. Geological Survey Bulletin 1093 (Washington, D.C.: Government Printing Office, 1959).

14 Anchorage *Daily Times*, April 27, 1964.

15 Wyner, "Urban Land Use Planning for Seismic Safety."

16 Scott, *Policies for Seismic Safety.*

17 Martin Jaffee, *Earthquake Research in Urban and Regional Planning: A Research Agenda*, summary of the Conference on Earthquake Research in Urban and Regional Planning, April 16–17, 1983, Seattle, Wash.

18 U.S. Federal Emergency Management Agency, *An Assessment of the Consequences and Preparation for a Catastrophic California Earthquake: Findings and Actions Taken* (Washington, D.C., 1980).

19 James D. Wright et al., *The Indifferent Politics of Natural Hazards* (Amherst, Mass.: SADRI, 1980); Thomas E. Drabek, Alvin H. Mushkatel, and Thomas S. Kilijanek, *Earthquake Mitigation Policy: The Experience of Two States* (Boulder, Colo.: Institute of Behavioral Sciences, University of Colorado, 1983).

20 Claire B. Rubin, *Long Term Recovery from Natural Disasters: A Comparative Analysis of Six Local Experiences* (Washington, D.C.: Academy for State and Local Government, 1982).

21 Ibid.

22 Svenson and Corbett, "Earthquakes, Hurricanes, and the Mitigation of Risk"; Petak, "Development of Earthquake Hazard Reduction Policies."

23 Wyner, "Urban Land Use Planning for Seismic Safety."

24 Theodore Lowi, *The End of Liberalism* (New York: Norton, 1969).

25 Ralph H. Turner et al., *Community Response to Earthquake Threat in Southern California: Individual Awareness and Attitudes* (Los Angeles: Institute for Social Science Research, University of California, 1978); Richard L. Ender, *Matanuska-Susitna Borough Comprehensive Plan Survey*, vol. 1, *Sample Survey Results*, prepared for the Matanuska-Susitna borough, December 1984.

26 Joanne Nigg, "Putting the Public Back into Concern About Public Policy," newsletter of the Earthquake Engineering Research Institute, July 1980.

27 Arthur Atkisson and William J. Petak, "The Politics of Community Seismic Safety," unpublished manuscript, 1981.

28 Peter Bachrach and Morton S. Baratz, *Power and Poverty: Theory and Practice* (New York: Oxford University Press, 1970).

29 Atkisson and Petak, "Politics of Community Seismic Safety"; Wright et al., *Indifferent Politics of Natural Hazards.*

30 Personal interview with Ernest Dobrovolny, retired, U.S. Geological Survey, Denver, Colo., 1982.

31 Turner et al., *Community Response to Earthquake Threat in Southern California;* Arnold J. Meltsner, "Public Support for Seismic Safety: Where Is It in California?" *Mass Emergencies* 3 (1978); Wright et al., *Indifferent Politics of Natural Hazards.*

32 James L. Gibson et al., *Organizations: Behavior, Structure, Processes,* 5th ed. (Homewood, Ill.: Business Publications, 1985).

33 George Mader et al., "Microzonation and Land Use Planning," *Proceedings for the Joint U.S.—P.R.C. Microzonation Workshop,* United States National Science Foundation and the Peoples Republic of China State Seismological Bureau, Harbin, China, September 11–16, 1981.

34 Louise K. Comfort, "Designing Policy for Action: The Emergency Management System," in this volume.

Agenda-setting in Nonstructural Hazard Mitigation Policy

A major portion of this chapter is based upon research supported by the National Science Foundation under Grant #CEE-840525. Opinions, findings, conclusions or recommendations are those of the author and do not necessarily reflect the views of the National Science Foundation.

1 On community reaction to earthquakes, see Thomas A. Drabek, Alvin H. Mushkatel, and Thomas S. Kilijanek, *Earthquake Mitigation Policy: The Experience of Two States* (Boulder: Colo. Institute of Behavioral Science, University of Colorado, 1983); W. Henry Lambright, "Policy Innovation in Earthquake Preparedness: A Longitudinal Study of Three States," paper presented at the 1982 Annual Meeting of the American Political Science Association, Denver, Colo.; and Arthur A. Atkisson and William J. Petak, *Seismic Safety Policies and Practices in U.S. Metropolitan Areas: A Three City Case Study* (Redondo Beach, Calif.: J. H. Wiggins, 1981). On a broader scale, see Claire B. Rubin, Martin D. Saperstein, and Daniel G. Barbee, *Community Recovery from a Major Natural Disaster* (Boulder: Institute of Behavioral Science, University of Colorado, 1985).

2 John W. Kingdon, *Agendas, Alternatives, and Public Policies* (Boston: Little, Brown, 1984).

3 Yehezkel Dror, *Policymaking Under Adversity* (New Brunswick, N.J.: Transac-

tion Books, 1986). p. 153; and Nelson W. Polsby, *Political Innovation in America: The Politics of Policy Initiation* (New Haven: Yale University Press, 1984), p. 3.

4 An excellent case study highlighting this point is Barbara J. Nelson, "Setting the Public Agenda: The Case of Child Abuse," in Judith V. May and Aaron Wildavsky, eds., *The Policy Cycle* (Beverly Hills, Calif.: Sage, 1978), pp. 17–41.

5 See the discussion of risk selection in relation to culture in Mary Douglas and Aaron Wildavsky, *Risk and Culture* (Berkeley: University of California Press, 1983).

6 Roger W. Cobb and Charles D. Elder, *Participation in American Politics: The Dynamics of Agenda Building* (Baltimore: Johns Hopkins University Press, 1983).

7 John J. Kirlin, "A Political Perspective," in Trudi C. Miller, *Public Sector Performance* (Baltimore: Johns Hopkins University Press, 1984), pp. 161–192.

8 Michael D. Cohen, James G. March, and Johan P. Olsen, "A Garbage Can Model of Organizational Choice," *Administrative Science Quarterly* 17 (March 1972): 1–25. See also Daniel Kahneman, Paul Slovic, and Amos Tversky, eds., *Judgment Under Uncertainty: Heuristics and Biases* (Cambridge: Cambridge University Press, 1982).

9 Evelyn Brodkin, review of John W. Kingdon, *Agendas, Alternatives, and Public Policy* in *Political Science Quarterly* 100 (Spring 1985): 165–166.

10 Roger Cobb, Jennie-Keith Ross, and Marc Howard Ross, "Agenda Building as a Comparative Political Process," *American Political Science Review* 70 (March 1976): 126–38.

11 Michael W. Kirst, Gail Meister, and Stephen R. Rowley, "Policy Issue Networks: Their Influence on State Policymaking," *Policy Studies Journal* 13 (December 1984): 247–63.

12 Kingdon, *Agendas, Alternatives, and Public Policies.*

13 Ibid., p. 20.

14 See Arnold Meltsner's characterization of the "policy entrepreneur" in his book, *Policy Analysts in the Bureaucracy* (Berkeley: University of California Press, 1976).

15 Peter H. Rossi, James D. Wright, and Eleanor Weber-Burdin, *Natural Hazards and Public Choice* (New York: Academic Press, 1982).

16 This chapter presents part of a comprehensive analysis of the attitudes and attributes of key local and state influentials concerning natural hazard mitigation and public policies. This analysis is currently being written.

17 The objective risk measures used in table 1 were taken from William J. Petak and Arthur A. Atkisson, *Natural Hazard Risk Assessment and Public Policy* (New York: Springer-Verlag, 1982), the same source that Rossi and his colleagues used to determine hurricane risk in their study.

18 For a discussion of floodplain regulations in the United States, see H. Crane Miller, "Context and Impacts of Floodplain Regulations in the United States," in Earl J. Baker, *Hurricanes and Coastal Storms* (Gainesville: University of Florida, Report No. 33, 1980), pp. 73–77.

19 David R. Godschalk and Kathryn Cousins, introduction to "Coastal Management: Planning on the Edge," *Journal of the American Planning Association* 51 (Summer 1985): 263.

20 *Conn. Gen. Stat. Ann.* 25-69 et seq.

21 This quotation was taken from a response to a questionnaire reported in Patricia A. Bloomgren, *Strengthening State Floodplain Management* (Boulder: Institute of Behavioral Science, University of Colorado, 1982), p. 64.

22 *Conn. Gen. Stat. Ann.* 25-68b et seq.

23 *Fla. Stat. Ann.* 161.011 et seq.

24 *Fla. Stat. Ann.* 161.52 et seq.

25 *La. Rev. Stat.* 38.301 et seq.

26 *La. Rev. Stat.* 38.84.

27 *N. J. Stat. Ann.* 58:16A-1 et seq.

28 *N. J. Stat. Ann.* 58:16A-50 et seq.

29 *N. J. Stat. Ann.* 52:14E-1 et seq.

30 *N. J. Stat. Ann.* 13:9A-1 et seq.

31 *N. J. Stat. Ann.* 13:19-1 et seq.

32 *N. Y. Envir. Conserv. Law* 25-0101 et seq.

33 *N. Y. Envir. Conserv. Law* 24-0101 et seq.

34 *N. Y. Envir. Conserv. Law* 36-0101 et seq.

35 *N. Y. Envir. Conserv. Law* 16-0101 et seq.

36 *N. C. Gen. Stat.* 143-215.51 et seq.

37 *N. C. Gen. Stat.* 113A-100 et seq.

38 For a discussion of the Coastal Zone Management Act, see William Matuszeski, "Managing the Federal Coastal Program: The Planning Years," *Journal of the American Planning Association* 51 (Summer 1985): 266–74; and for an analysis of its implementation in North Carolina, see David W. Owens, "Coastal Management in North Carolina: Building a Regional Consensus," *Journal of the American Planning Association* 51 (Summer 1985): 322–29.

39 *Pa. Stat. Ann.* tit. 32, 651 et seq.

40 *Pa. Stat. Ann.* tit. 32, 681–91.

41 *Pa. Stat. Ann.* tit. 32, 679.101 et seq.

42 *Pa. Stat. Ann.* tit. 32, 680.1 et seq.

43 *S. C. Code of Laws* 48-39-10 et seq.

44 *Va. Code* 10-151 et seq.

45 *Va. Code* 62.1-13.1 et seq.

46 *Va. Code* 62.1-44.108 et seq.

47 *Va. Code* 3.1-22.13 et seq.

48 See the discussion of policy communication in Arnold J. Meltsner and Christopher Bellavita, *The Policy Organization* (Beverly Hills, Calif.: Sage, 1983).

49 Rossi et al., *Natural Hazards and Public Choice*, pp. 39–67.

50 John Hartigan, "Model Blocks in Dentition of West Coast Mammals," *Systematic Zoology* 25 (1976): 149–60.

51 Rossi et al., *Natural Hazards and Public Choice*, pp. 52–55.

52 The dynamic aspects of coalition formation at the agenda-setting stage among organizational entities cannot be addressed in this essay since no longitudinal nor sociometric data were collected from key figures in the ten states. For a detailed discussion on that topic at the state level see Kirst, Meister, and Rowley, "Policy Issue Networks."

53 Kirlin, *A Political Perspective.*

54 Both Lambright, "Policy Innovation," and Elliott Mittler, "An Analysis of State
   Government Orientation Toward Earthquake Mitigation: Comparing Six States,"
   to be published in the *Proceedings* of the Third U.S. National Conference on
   Earthquake Engineering, 1986, report empirical evidence generally in agreement with these conclusions.

Current Policy and Implementation Issues
in Disaster Preparedness

Special thanks are due to the following persons who provided assistance in the
writing of this essay: Mr. David Morton, Natural Hazards Research and Applications Information Center, University of Colorado at Boulder; Dr. Rodger Kelley,
Fullerton Community Hospital and Quintessential Mass Casualty Consultant Services, San Clemente, California; and Mr. George Koortbojian, Hospital Council of
Northern California, San Bruno, California.

 1 The complexity of systems and the interdependence of their parts increases the
   likelihood of accidents and mitigates against their anticipation. See, for example, Charles Perrow, "Normal Accident at Three Mile Island," *Society* 18
   (July–August 1981): 17–26, reprinted in Frank Fischer and Carmen Sirianni,
   Critical Studies in Organization and Bureaucracy (Philadelphia: Temple University Press, 1984), pp. 287–305.
 2 See Ronald W. Perry and Alvin W. Mushkatel, *Disaster Response and Preparedness Among Minority Citizens* (Athens: University of Georgia Press, 1985);
   Perry and Mushkatel, *Disaster Management: Warning, Response and Community Relocation* (Westport, Conn.: Greenwood Press, 1984).
 3 National Governors' Association, "Comprehensive Emergency Management
   Bulletin," no. 1 (Washington, D.C.: NGA Office of State Services, April 1982),
   cited in Alvin W. Mushkatel and Louis F. Weschler, "Emergency Management
   and the Intergovernmental System," *Public Administration Review*, special issue
   (January 1985): 50.
 4 David McLoughlin, "A Framework for Integrated Emergency Management,"
   Public Administration Review 45, special issue (January 1985): 168.
 5 Daniel A. Mazmanian and Paul A. Sabatier, *Implementation and Public Policy*
   (Glenview, Ill.: Scott, Foresman, 1983), pp. 21–22. The method of study implementation by identifying problems and tracing their causes is called "backward
   mapping." See Richard F. Elmore, "Backward Mapping: Implementation
   Research and Policy Decision," in Walter Williams et al., eds., *Studying
   Implementation* (Chatham, N.J.: Chatham Publishers, 1982), pp. 18–35.
 6 This conclusion was manifest in the discussions of disaster preparedness in the
   *Proceedings of Conference XX: A Workshop on the 1886 Charleston, South
   Carolina, Earthquake and Its Implications for Today,* May 23-26, 1983, Charles-
   ton, South Carolina (Reston, Va.: U.S. Department of the Interior, Geological
   Survey, 1983, Open File Report, 83–843); the *Proceedings of Conference XV: A
   Workshop on "Preparing for and Responding to a Damaging Earthquake in the
   Eastern United States,"* September 16–18, 1981, Knoxville, Tennessee (Reston,

Va.: U.S. Department of the Interior, Geological Survey, 1982, Open File Report 82-220); and *Primer on Improving the State of Earthquake Hazards Mitigation and Preparedness* (Reston, Va: U.S. Department of the Interior, Geological Survey, 1984, Open File Report 84-772).

7 U.S. General Accounting Office, *States Can Be Better Prepared to Respond to Disasters* (Washington, D.C.: GAO, CED–80–60, March 31, 1980) and subsequent reports on specific programs. See the references to GAO reports in the following citations.

8 The notation that state and local officials lack the expertise and resources to provide adequate disaster preparedness and seek the guidance and support from the federal govenment is a recurring theme in the GAO reports relative to disaster preparedness and mitigation and in the conference proceedings cited earlier.

9 See, for example, Ian Campbell, "The Influence of Geologic Hazards on Legislation in California," *California Geology* (October 1977).

10 John W. Kingdon, *Agendas, Alternatives, and Public Policies* (Boston: Little, Brown, 1984), pp. 173–181.

11 Ibid.

12 The impact of the federalist system on emergency management is discussed more broadly in Mushkatel and Weschler, "Emergency Management and the Intergovernmental System"; Claire B. Rubin and Daniel G. Barbee, "Disaster Recovery and Hazard Mitigation: Bridging the Intergovernmental Gap"; and Peter J. May, "FEMA's Role in Emergency Management: Examining Recent Experience" (all in *Public Administration Review* [January 1985]).

13 See William L. Waugh, "Disaster Mitigation and Intergovernmental Relations: The Case of the Hyatt Skywalk Disaster," in Michael Charles and John Kim, eds., *Crisis Management: A Casebook* (forthcoming, 1988). For the view that state governments may not be willing to provide fiscal resources for local programs, see William L. Waugh, "Counties, States, and the Questions of Trust and Capacity in a Realigned Federal System," *Publius* (forthcoming); and Waugh, "Counties, States and the New Federalism: The Issue of Trust in Intergovernmental Relations," presented at the Southern Political Science Association Meeting, Nashville, Tenn., November 6–9, 1985.

14 This argument is fundamental to the debate over the relationship among federal, state and local governments. The models of perceptions and degrees of trust can be found in Deil Wright, *Understanding Intergovernmental Relations*, 2d ed. (Monterey, Calif.: Brooks-Cole, 1982).

15 This observation is based on interviews with persons involved with emergency management and was a recurring theme in the comments of several managers.

16 GAO, *States Can Be Better Prepared to Respond to Disasters* (1980); GAO, *The Federal Emergency Management Agency's Plan for Revitalizing U.S. Civil Defense: A Review of Three Major Plan Components* (Washington, D.C.: GAO, GAO/NSIAD-84-11, April 16, 1984).

17 May, "FEMA's Role in Emergency Management," pp. 40–48. May also comments on the "dual use" focus that was highlighted in President Carter's message on the reorganization that created FEMA.

18 Ibid.

19 FEMA's response to the GAO conclusion that the agency had not provided needed leadership for disaster programs was that the agency perceived its own role as "supplemental" rather than instrumental and that the "lead agency" role was not defined in the various legislative provisions.

20 GAO, *Review of the Emergency Management Agency's Role in Assisting State and Local Governments to Develop Hurricane Preparedness Planning* (Washington, D.C.: GAO, GAO/RCED-83-182, July 7, 1983).

21 GAO, *Stronger Direction Needed for the National Earthquake Program* (Washington, D.C.: GAO, GAO/RCED-83-103, July 26, 1983).

22 GAO, *Three Mile Island: The Most Studied Nuclear Accident in History* (Washington, D.C.: GAO, EMD-80-109, September 9, 1980). Also see GAO, *Further Actions Needed to Improve Emergency Preparedness Around Nuclear Power-plants* (Washington, D.C.: GAO, GAO/RCED-84-43, August 1, 1984).

23 GAO, *Implementation: The Missing Link in Planning Reorganizations* (Washington, D.C.: GAO, GGD-81-57, March 20, 1981).

Research-based Disaster Planning

This is an account of work supported by National Science Foundation Grant ECE 82-17550. Opinions are those of the authors.

1 California Seismic Safety Commission, *Transcript of the July 14, 1983 Hearings on the Coalinga Earthquake*, Report #SSC 83-10 (Sacramento, Calif.: The Commission, 1983).

2 J. Kartez, *Emergency Planning Implications of Local Governments' Adaptive Responses to Mt. St. Helens*, Working Paper 46 (Boulder: Institute of Behavioral Science, University of Colorado, 1982).

3 James B. Taylor, Louis A. Zurcher, and William H. Key, *Tornado: A Community Responds to Disaster* (Seattle: University of Washington Press, 1971).

4 Thomas E. Drabek, H. Tamminga, and Thomas S. Kilijanek, *Managing Multiorganizational Emergency Responses* (Boulder: Institute of Behavioral Science, University of Colorado, 1981).

5 Ibid., p. 243.

6 G. Hoetmer, "Emergency Management," *Baseline Data Reports*, vol. 15, no. 4 (Washington, D.C.: Urban Data Service, International City Management Association, 1983).

7 G. Hoetmer, "Interorganizational Relationships in Emergency Management: Fundamental to an Effective Disaster Response," paper prepared for NASPAA/FEMA Public Administration Faculty Workshop on Emergency Management, May 20–June 2, 1984, p. 1.

8 Allen H. Barton, *Communities in Disaster: A Sociological Analysis of Collective Stress Situations* (Garden City, N.Y.: Doubleday, 1970).

9 Committee on Disasters and the Mass Media, *Disasters and the Mass Media* (Washington, D.C.: National Research Council, 1980).

10 Ronald Perry, "Incentives for Evacuation in Natural Disasters," *Journal of the American Planning Association* 45 (1979): 440–47.

11 Russell R. Dynes, Enrico L. Quarantelli, and Gary A. Kreps, *A Perspective on*

Disaster Planning (Columbus: Disaster Research Center, Ohio State University, 1972).

12 J. Kartez, "Crisis Response Planning: Toward a Contingent Analysis," *Journal of the American Planning Association* 50 (1984): 9–21.

13 G. Fox, "Emergency Management," *Public Management* (January–February 1981); R. Kemp, "The City Manager's Role in Emergency Management," *Public Management* (March 1984): 9–12.

14 J. Kartez and W. Kelley, *Emergency Planning and the Adaptive Local Response to the Mt. St. Helens Eruptions* (Pullman: Environmental Research Center, Washington State University, 1980).

15 Fox, "Emergency Management."

16 Drabek et al., *Managing Multiorganizational Emergency Responses.*

17 M. Meyer and P. Belobaba, "Contingency Planning for Response to Urban Transportation System Disruptions," *Journal of the American Planning Association* 48 (1982): 545–65.

18 *Public Official Attitudes Towards Disaster Preparedness in California* (Sacramento, Calif.: California Seismic Safety Commission, 1979).

19 For an example see K. Hawley and M. Nichols, "A Contextual Approach to Modeling the Decision to Participate in a 'Political' Issue," *Administrative Science Quarterly* 27 (1982): 105–19.

20 Drabek et al., *Managing Multiorganizational Emergency Responses.*

21 Perry, "Incentives for Evacuation"; M. Lindell and Ronald Perry, "Evacuation Criteria for Emergency Response Plans in Radiological Transportation," *Journal of Hazardous Materials* 3 (1980): 335–48.

22 U.S. Mayors' Conference, *Emergency Management: A Mayor's Manual* (Washington, D.C.: U.S. Mayors' Conference, 1980).

23 Kemp, "City Manager's Role."

24 M. Whittaker, *Emergency Preparedness Project: Final Report* (Washington, D.C.: National Governor's Association, 1979).

25 The purpose of this exercise was not to evoke crude measures of the desirability and feasibility of each idea, but to use the occasion to draw out managers' views in their own words. Recognizing that many have never thought about these issues, some mechanism was needed to form the basis for discussing the pros and cons of each suggested practice. Participants were asked why they rated a strategy as particularly high or low in feasibility of adoption, for example, "Why do you think there is small chance of adopting a Media Center?" Although Perry, Lindell, and Greene (1981) have asked *citizens* if they support strategies such as a warning hotline, and Sood (1983) has canvassed selected officials about the feasibility of intergovernmental information centers, to our knowledge there has been no systematic comparison of managerial attitudes toward a range of research-based planning practices.

26 P. Anderson, "Decisionmaking by Objection and the Cuban Missile Crisis," *Administrative Science Quarterly* 28 (1983): 201–22.

27 R. Steers and L. Porter, *Motivation and Work Behavior,* 2d ed. (New York: McGraw-Hill, 1979).

28 S. Kiesler and L. Sproull, "Managerial Response to Changing Environments: Perspectives on Problem-sensing from Social Cognition," *Administrative Sci-*

ence Quarterly 27 (1982): 564–70; Amos Tversky and Daniel Kahneman, "Availability: A Heuristic for Judging Frequency and Probability," *Cognitive Psychology* (1973): 207–32.

29 Herbert A. Simon, *Administrative Behavior*, 2d ed. (New York: Free Press, 1957).

30 Robert Wolensky and Edward Miller, "The Everyday Versus the Disaster Role of Local Officials: Citizen and Official Definitions," *Urban Affairs Quarterly* 16 (1981): 483–504.

31 T. Caplow, H. Bahr, and B. Chadwick, *Analysis of the Readiness of the Local Communities for Integrated Emergency Management Planning*, contract no. EMW-83-C-1127 (Washington, D.C.: FEMA 1984).

32 Thomas E. Drabek, "Managing the Emergency Response," *Public Administrative Review* 45 (1985): 85–92.

33 Enrico L. Quarantelli, *Organizational Behavior in Disasters and Implications for Disaster Planning* (Emmitsburg, Md.: FEMA, National Emergency Training Center, 1984).

Federal Preparedness for Hazardous and Toxic Waste Disaster

1 U.S. EPA, *Superfund: What It Is, How It Works* (Washington, D.C.: Office of Solid Waste and Emergency Response, WH-562-A, December 1982), p. 1.

2 Stuart Diamond, "The Disaster in Bhopal: Lessons for the Future," *New York Times* (February 3, 1985), p. 1.

3 For accepted definitions of each of these phases of emergency management, see William J. Petak, "Emergency Management: A Challenge for Public Administration," *Public Administration Review* 45, special issue (January 1985): 3–6.

4 William L. Waugh, "Current Policy and Implementation Issues in Disaster Preparedness" (Atlanta: Institute of Public Administration, Georgia State University, 1985).

5 Michael Brown, *The Poisoning of America by Toxic Chemicals* (New York: Washington Square Press, 1981), p. 1. A dangerous substance has effects that are biologically magnified when it achieves successively higher concentrations in the tissues of living organisms as it moves up the food chain. Since human beings are at the top of the food chain, the effects of the substance may therefore pose the greatest threat to humans.

6 Paul R. Portney, "Toxic Substance Policy and the Protection of Human Health," in Paul R. Portney et al., eds., *Current Issues in U.S. Environmental Policy* (Baltimore: Johns Hopkins University Press, 1978), p. 107.

7 See Mary Douglas and Aaron Wildavsky, *Risk and Culture* (Berkeley: University of California Press, 1982).

8 Douglas and Wildavsky, *Risk and Culture*, p. 17.

9 Rae Zimmerman, "The Relationship of Emergency Management to Governmental Policies on Man-Made Technological Disasters," *Public Administration*

Review 45, special issue (January 1985): 29–39.

10 U.S. EPA, *EPA's Emergency Response Program* (Washington, D.C.: Office of Emergency and Remedial Response, November, 1982), p. 2.

11 Roger E. Kasperson and K. David Pijawka, "Societal Response to Hazards and Major Hazard Events: Comparing Natural and Technological Hazards," *Public Administration Review* 45, special issue (January 1985): 7–18.

12 Carl Pope, Samuel S. Epstein, and Lester O. Brown, *Hazardous Waste in America* (San Francisco: Sierra Club Books, 1982), p. 237.

13 U.S. Comptroller General, *Hazardous Waste Sites Pose Investigation, Evaluation, Scientific, and Legal Problems* (Washington, D.C.: U.S. General Accounting Office, April 24, 1981, CED-81-57), p. iv.

14 U.S. EPA, *Emergency Response Program*, p. 2.

15 Ibid., p. 4.

16 Ibid., p. 5.

17 Ibid.

18 Ibid.

19 Ibid., p. 8.

20 Ibid., p. 15.

21 Ibid., pp. 12–13.

22 U.S. FEMA, "Hazardous Materials Program Launched by FEMA," FEMA *Newsletter* (November–December 1984), pp. 2–3.

Management Issues in Emergency Response

1 Ilya Prigogine and I. Stengers, *Order of Chaos* (New York: Bantam Books, 1984).

2 Russell R. Dynes, Enrico L. Quarantelli, and Gary A. Kreps, *A Perspective on Disaster Planning* (Columbus: Disaster Research Center, Ohio State University Report, series 2, 1972), pp. 9–12.

3 Ibid., pp. 15–38.

4 Ibid.

5 Ronald W. Perry, M. K. Lindell, and M. R. Greene, *Evacuation Planning in Emergency Management* (Lexington, Mass.: Lexington Books, 1981).

6 Thomas E. Drabek, Harriet L. Tamminga, Thomas S. Kilinanek, and Christopher R. Adams, *Managing Multiorganizational Emergency Responses* (Boulder: Institute of Behavioral Sciences, University of Colorado, 1981).

7 N. C. Gross, J. Giacquinta, and M. Bernstein, *Implementing Organizational Innovations* (New York: Basic Books); Jeffrey Pressman and Aaron Wildavsky, *Implementation* (Berkeley: University of California Press, 1973); E. C. Hargrove, *The Missing Link: The Study of Implementation in Social Policy* (Washington, D.C.: The Urban Institute, 1975); P. Berman et al., *Federal Programs Supporting Educational Change*, vols. 1–5 (Santa Monica: Rand Corporation, 1974); W. Williams and R. E. Elmore, eds., *Social Program Implementation* (New York: Academic Press, 1976); W. Williams, *The Implementation Perspective*

(Berkeley: University of California Press, 1980); W. Williams et al., *Studying Implementation: Methodological and Administrative Issues* (Chatham, N.J.: Chatham House, 1982); Eugene Bardach, *The Implementation Game: What Happens after a Bill Becomes a Law* (Cambridge, Mass.: MIT Press, 1977); R. G. Lewis and J. R. Greene, "Implementation Evaluation: A Future Direction in Project Evaluation," *Journal of Criminal Justice* 6: 91–103; D. A. Mazmanian and Paul Sabatier, *Implementation and Public Policy* (Glenview, Ill.: Scott, Foresman, 1983).

8 G. J. Hoetmer, "Emergency Management," *Baseline Data Reports* 15, no. 4 (Washington, D.C.: International City Management Association, 1983).

9 Herbert A. Simon, *The New Science: A Management Decision* (Englewood Cliffs, N.J.: Prentice-Hall, 1971).

10 J. McKenney and P. Keen, "How Managers' Minds Work," *Harvard Business Review* (May–June 1979): 74–90.

11 Ibid.

12 H. Mintzberg, "Planning on the Left Side and Managing on the Right Side," *Harvard Business Review* (July–August 1976): 49–58.

13 F. E. Emery and E. C. Trist, "The Causal Texture of Organizational Environments," *Human Relations* 18 (1965): 20–26.

14 Tom Burns and G. M. Stalker, *The Management of Innovation* (London: Tavistock, 1961).

15 Carolyn Smart and Ian S. Vertinsky, "Designs for Crisis Decision Units," *Administrative Science Quarterly* 22 (December 1977): 640–57; R. F. Littlejohn, *Crisis Management: A Team Approach* (New York: American Management Association, 1983).

16 M. Crozier, *The Bureaucratic Phenomenon* (Chicago: Chicago University Press, 1963).

17 W. Ouchi, "The Relationship between Organizational Structure and Organizational Control," *Administrative Science Quarterly* (March 1977); G. Steiner, ed., *The Creative Organization* (Chicago: University of Chicago Press, 1979); N. R. F. Maier, *Problem Solving and Creativity in Individuals and Groups* (Belmont, Calif.: Brooks-Cole, 1970); L. Cummings et al., "Creative Behavior as a Function of Task Environment," *Academy of Management Journal* 18 (1975).

18 Littlejohn, *Crisis Management*, pp. 26–29.

19 Mintzberg, "Planning on the Left Side"; W. H. Agor, "Training Public Managers to Develop and Use Their Intuition for Decision Making," *Professional Development Handbook* (1983): 1–6.

20 Dynes, Quarantelli, and Kreps, *Perspective on Disaster Planning*.

Increasing Problem-solving Capacity between Organizations

1 Louise K. Comfort, "Action Research: A Model for Organizational Learning," *Journal of Policy Analysis and Management* 5, no. 1 (1985): 100–118.

2 Claire Rubin, *Community Recovery from a Major Disaster* (Boulder, Colo.: Institute of Behavioral Sciences, 1985); Comfort, "Action Research."

3 Louis O. Giuffrida, *Emergency Management: The National Perspective* (Emmitsburg, Md.: National Emergency Training Center, Monograph Series, vol. 1, 1983).

4 Thomas E. Drabek, Harriet L. Tamminga, Thomas S. Kilijanek, Christopher R. Adams, *Managing Multiorganizational Emergency Responses* (Boulder, Colo.: Institute of Behavioral Sciences, 1981).

5 A thorough overview of such networks may be found in Everett Rogers and D. Lawrence Kincaid, *Communication Networks: Towards A New Paradigm for Research* (New York: Free Press, 1981). See especially chap. 3, pp. 79–142.

6 Drabek et al., *Managing Multiorganizational Emergency Responses.*

7 Herbert A. Simon, *The Sciences of the Artificial* (Cambridge: MIT Press, 1969, 1981); Chris Argyris, *Reason, Learning and Action* (San Francisco: Jossey-Bass Publishers, 1982).

8 Herbert A. Simon, *Models of Discovery* (Boston: D. Riedel, 1977), p. 151.

9 Rudi Klauss and Bernard M. Bass, *Interpersonal Communication in Organizations* (New York: Academic Press, 1982).

10 Ibid.

11 Richard R. Nelson and Douglas Yates, eds., *Innovation and Implementation in Public Organizations* (Lexington, Mass.: Lexington Books, 1978).

12 Claudia Bird Schoonhoven, "Problems in Contingency Theory: Testing Assumptions Hidden Within the Language of Contingency Theory," *Administrative Science Quarterly* 26, no. 3 (September 1981): 349–377.

13 Ferdinand Tönnies, *Community and Society*, trans. and ed. Charles P. Loomis (1887; reprint, East Lansing: Michigan State University Press, 1957).

14 Ibid.

15 T. C. Dandridge, Ian Mitroff, and W. F. Joyce, "Organizational Symbolism: A Topic to Expand Organizational Analysis," *Academy of Management Review* 5 (1980): 77–82.

16 S. W. Woolgar, "The Identification and Definition of Scientific Collectivities," in Gerard Lemaine et al., eds., *Perspectives on the Emergence of Scientific Disciplines* (Chicago: Aldine Press, 1976), p. 34.

17 Comfort, "Action Research."

18 Joseph L. C. Cheng and William McKinley, "Toward an Integration of Organization Research and Practice: A Contingency Study of Bureaucratic Control and Performance in Scientific Settings," *Administrative Science Quarterly* 28, no. 1 (March 1983): 85–100.

19 Argyris, *Reason, Learning and Action.*

20 Simon, *Models of Discovery*, p. 146.

21 Jack Knott and Aaron Wildavsky, "If Dissemination is the Solution, What is the Problem?" *Knowledge: Creative, Diffusion, Utilization* 1, no. 4 (1979): 537–78.

22 Simon, *Sciences of the Artificial.*

23 Michael D. Cohen, J. G. March, and J. Olsen, "The Garbage Can Model of Organizational Choice," *Administrative Science Quarterly* 17 (March 1972): 1–25.

24 Michael D. Cohen, "The Power of Parallel Thinking," *Journalist Economic*

Behavior and Organization 2 (1981): 285–306; Michael D. Cohen, "Conflict and Complexity: Goal Diversity and Organizational Effectiveness," *American Political Science Review* 78, no. 2 (June 1984): 435–51.

25 Simon, *Sciences of the Artificial.*

26 *Pittsburgh Post Gazette*, June 2, 1985; Statement by John L. Patten, Director, Pennsylvania Emergency Management Agency, November 11, 1985.

27 *Pittsburgh Post Gazette*, June 4, 1985.

28 The study was supported by a research grant from the Natural Hazards Research and Applications Information Center, University of Colorado, Boulder, Colorado. The survey was conducted with the assistance of members of the policy seminar on Emergency Management, Graduate School of Public and International Affairs, University of Pittsburgh, Spring 1985. The authors gratefully acknowledge the financial support of the Natural Hazards Center and the dedication, effort and skill of the students in the conduct of this study.

The Impact of Stress on Emergency Personnel

1 Jeffrey F. Mitchell, professional observation as staff member of U.S. Dog team, sent to San Salvador by the U.S. Office of Foreign Disaster Assistance, October 11–16, 1986.

2 H. Duston, "The Consequence of Stress," *Clinical Roundtables* (Bloomfield, N.J.: Rocks Laboratories, Health Learning Systems, 1979).

3 D. O'Brien, "Mental Anguish, an Occupational Hazard," *Emergency* 12 (1979): 61; N. K. Graham, "Done in, Fed Up, Burned Out: Too Much Attrition in EMS," *Journal of Emergency Medical Services* 6 (1981): 24.

4 A. S. Kliman, "The Corning Flood Project: Psychological First Aid Following a Natural Disaster," *Emergency and Disaster Management: A Mental Health Sourcebook* (Bowie, Md.: Charles Press, 1975); H. G. Freudenberger and G. Richelson, *Burnout, the High Cost of High Achievement* (Garden City, N.Y.: Anchor, Doubleday, 1980); J. T. Mitchell, "Recovery from Rescue," *Response, the Magazine of Emergency Management* (Fall 1982): 7–10.

5 R. C. Illinitch and M. P. Titus, "Caretakers as Victims: The Big Thompson Flood," *Smith College Studies in Social Work* 48 (1976): 67; B. D. Colen, "Aircrash Rescue Workers Also Victims, Psychiatrist Says," *Washington Post*, July 9, 1979; J. Duffy, "The Role of CMHCs in Airport Disasters," *Technical Assistance Center Report* 2 (1979): 1; K. Freeman, "CMHC Responses to the Chicago and San Diego Airplane Disasters," *Technical Assistance Center Report* 2: 3; *Time* Magazine Staff, "Crash Trauma, Nightmares Plague Rescuers," *Time*, January 8, 1979, p. 61; N. K. Graham, "How to Avoid a Short Career," pt. 2, *A Journal of Emergency Medical Services* 6 (1981): 25; Mitchell, "Recovery from Rescue."

6 J. T. Mitchell, "Healing the Helper," in Bonnie Green, ed., *Role Conflict and Support for Emergency Workers* (Washington, D.C.: American Psychological Association, FEMA, and the National Institute for Mental Health), in press.

7 C. Maslach, "The Client Role in Staff Burn-Out," *Journal of Social Issues* 46 (1980).

8 S. R. Stanley and J. P. Saxon, "Occupational Stress: Implications for Vocational Rehabilitation Counseling," *Journal of Rehabilitation* 46 (1980).

9 C. Maslach and S. Jackson, "Burned Out Cops and Their Families," *Psychology Today* (May 1979): 59.

10 Maslach, "Client Role in Staff Burn-Out"; R. Kahn, "Job Burnout Prevention and Their Remedies," *Public Welfare* 36 (1978): 61; Maslach and Jackson, "Burned Out Cops"; C. Charniss, *Burnout, Job Stress in the Human Services* (Beverly Hills, Calif.: Sage, 1980); J. D. Adams, *Understanding and Managing Stress: A Book of Readings* (San Diego, Calif.: University Associates, 1980).

11 M. L. Mulvihill, *Human Diseases: A Systematic Approach* (Bowie, Md.: Robert J. Brady, 1980).

12 M. Frankenhauser, "Psychoneuroendocrine Approaches to the Study of Stressful Person Environmental Transactions," *Selye's Guide to Stress Research* (New York: Van Nostrand Reinhold, 1980).

13 S. Levine, "Stress and Behavior," *Scientific American* (January 1971): 26–31.

14 Ole R. Holsti, "Crisis, Stress and Decision-Making," *International Social Science Journal* 23 (1971): 53–67.

15 B. Keena, "What We've Learned About Firefighter Safety and Health," *Emergency Management* (Spring 1981): 33.

16 N. Byl and B. Sykes, "Work and Health Problems: An Approach to Management for the Professional and the Community," *Community Health* 9 (1978): 149–58.

17 R. Sedgwick, "Pyschological Response to Stress," *Journal of Psychiatric Nursing and Mental Health Services* (September–October 1975).

18 R. S. Lazarus, *Patterns of Adjustment and Human Effectiveness* (New York: McGraw-Hill, 1969).

19 T. L. Titchener and F. I. Kapp, "Family and Character Change at Buffalo Creek," *American Journal of Psychiatry* 133 (1976): 295–99.

20 Mitchell, "Recovery from Rescue"; J. T. Mitchell, "Emergency Medical Stress, APCO Bulletin," *Journal of Association of Public Safety Communication Officers* (February 1983).

21 W. Lippert and E. R. Ferrara, "The Cost of 'Coming Out on Top': Emotional Responses to Surviving the Deadly Battle," *FBI Law Enforcement Bulletin* (December 1981): 6–10.

22 A. J. Glass, "Psychological Aspects of Disaster," *Journal of the American Medical Association* 171 (1959): 222–25.

23 Calvin J. Frederick, ed., *Aircraft Accidents: Emergency Mental Health Problems* (Washington, D.C.: National Institute of Mental Health, U.S. Department of Health and Human Services, 1981).

24 O'Brien, "Mental Anguish"; A. Forstenzer, "Stress, the Psychological Scarring of Air Crash Rescue Personnel," *Firehouse* (July 1980): 50–52, 62.

25 Frederick, ed., *Aircraft Accidents*, p. 17.

26 Freeman, "CMHC Responses."

27 R. E. Cohen and F. L. Ahearn, *Handbook for Mental Health Care of Disaster Victims* (Baltimore: Johns Hopkins University Press, 1980).

28 Mitchell, "Recovery from Rescue."

29 J. Edelwich and A. Brodsky, *Burn-out, Stages of Disillusionment in the Helping Professions* (New York: Human Sciences Press, 1980).

30 Mitchell, "Emergency Medical Stress."

31 Sedgwick, "Psychological Response to Stress."

32 S. H. Appelbaum, *Stress Management for Health Care Professionals* (Rockville, Md.: Aspen Systems, 1981).

33 Maslach, "Client Role in Staff Burn-Out."

34 P. D. S. Patrick, "Burnout: Job Hazard for Health Workers," *Hospitals* (November 16, 1979): 87–90.

35 Maslach and Jackson, "Burned Out Cops."

36 S. M. Miller, "When is a Little Information a Dangerous Thing? Coping With Stressful Events by Monitoring Versus Blunting," *Coping and Health* (New York: Plenum, 1979).

37 D. H. Johnston, "Crisis Intervention," *Critical Care Update* 6 (1979): 5–20; Graham, "Done In, Fed Up, Burned Out."

38 Frederick, *Aircraft Accidents*, p. 6.

39 Mitchell, "Emergency Medical Stress."

40 Ibid.; and Mitchell, "Recovery from Rescue."

41 J. Judge, Deputy Chief, Baltimore County Fire Department, personal communication, December 1984.

Recovery Following Disaster

1 J. Haas, R. Kates, and M. Bowden, eds., *Reconstructions Following Disasters* (Cambridge, Mass.: MIT Press, 1977).

2 Ibid.

3 Ibid.

4 J. Wright, P. H. Rossi, S. R. Wright and E. Weber-Burdin, *After the Clean-up: Long Range Effects of Natural Disasters* (Beverly Hills, Calif.: Sage, 1979).

5 Ibid., p. 198.

6 Ibid., p. 205.

7 H. Friesema, J. Caporaso, G. Goldstein, R. Lineberry, and R. McCleary, *Aftermath: Communities After Natural Disaster* (Beverly Hills, Calif.: Sage, 1979).

8 Wright et al., *After the Clean-up*.

9 S. Chang, "Disaster and Fiscal Policy: Hurricane Impact on Municipal Revenue," *Urban Affairs Quarterly* 18 (June 1983): 511–523.

10 J. LaPlante, "1986 Fiscal Impacts of Recurrent Flooding," in Alan Williams, ed., *Proceedings: 1986 State Floodplain Management Conference*.

11 R. Bolin, discussions at Natural Hazards Workshop, Boulder, Colo., 1985.

12 R. Bolin and P. Bolton, discussions at Natural Hazards Workshop, 1985.

13 A. Levine, *Love Canal: Science, Politics and People* (Lexington, Mass.: D. C. Heath, 1982).

14 C. McKenna, "Three Mile Island," in M. Charles and J. C. Kim, eds., *Crisis*

Management: A Casebook (Springfield, Ill.: Charles C. Thomas, 1986).

15 T. Heller, "The Effects of Involuntary Relocation," *American Journal of Community Psychology* 10 (1982): 471–92.

16 Bolin and Bolton, discussions at Natural Hazards Workshop.

17 R. Bolin, "Disasters and Long-Term Recovery Policy: A Focus on Housing and Families," *Policy Studies Review* 4 (May 1985): 709–15.

18 C. Rubin and D. Barbee, "Disaster Recovery and Hazard Mitigation: Bridging the Intergovernmental Gap," *Public Administration Review* 45 (January 1985): 57–63.

19 Ibid.

20 Ibid.

21 Haas et al., *Reconstructions Following Disasters.*

22 Friesema et al., *Aftermath*, p. 145.

23 M. Edel, "People Versus Places in Urban Impact Analysis," in N. Glickman, ed., *The Urban Impacts of Federal Policy* (Baltimore: Johns Hopkins University Press, 1980), pp. 175–91.

24 J. LaPlante and J. S. Kroll-Smith, "Centralia: The Nightmare Which Would Not End," in M. Charles and J. C. Kim, eds., *Crisis Management: A Casebook* (Springfield, Ill.: Charles C. Thomas, 1986).

25 R. Perry and A. Mushkatel, *Disaster Preparedness: Warning, Response, and Community Relocation* (Westport, Conn.: Greenwood Press, 1984).

26 LaPlante and Kroll-Smith, "Centralia."

27 Levine, *Love Canal.*

28 LaPlante and Kroll-Smith, "Centralia."

Disaster Recovery and Reconstruction

This chapter draws upon the introductory chapters of two books by the author: Peter J. May, *Recovering From Catastrophes: Federal Disaster Relief Policy and Politics* (Westport, Conn.: Greenwood Press, 1985), and Peter J. May and Walter Williams, *Disaster Policy Implementation: Managing Programs Under Shared Governance* (New York: Plenum, 1986).

1 The survey results are reported in Peter H. Rossi, James D. Wright, and Eleanor Weber-Burdin, *Natural Hazards and Public Choice, The State and Local Politics of Hazard Mitigation* (New York: Academic Press, 1982), with chap. 3, pp. 39–67, being particularly relevant to this discussion.

2 The characterization of "apathetic politics" is taken from the title of the Rossi et al. original report to the National Science Foundation as cited and discussed in "The State and Local Politics of Natural Disasters," in James D. Wright and Peter H. Rossi, eds., *Social Science and Natural Hazards* (Cambridge, Mass.: Abt Books, 1981), pp. 44–88.

3 Not included in table 2 are loan programs for farmers as well as other, more minor relief programs. For a compilation of various disaster relief related legislative authorities see National Governors' Association, *Federal Emergency*

Authorities Abstracts (Washington, D.C.: U.S. Government Printing Office, May 1979).

4 The more general phenomena of crises triggering legislative action is discussed in Jack L. Walker, "Setting the Agenda in the U.S. Senate: A Theory of Problem Selection," *British Journal of Political Science* 7 (October 1977): 423–45.

5 Remarks by Senator Long in *Congressional Record, Senate 111*, 89th Cong., 1st sess., October 21, 1965, p. 27948.

6 The debate over how retroactive to make the legislation is contained in *Congressional Record, Senate 118*, 92nd Cong., 2nd sess., August 4, 1972, p. 26837.

7 See the following General Accounting Office Publications: *The Johnstown Area Flood of 1977: A Case Study for the Future* (CED-78-114, May 5, 1978); *Federal Snow Removal Reimbursement Policy: Improvements Being Made in Flood Fighting Capabilities in the Jackson, Mississippi, Area* (CED 80-36, December 18, 1979); *States Can Be Better Prepared to Respond to Disasters* (CED 80-60, March 31, 1980); *Poor Controls Over Federal Aid in Massachusetts After the 1978 Blizzard Caused Questionable Benefit Payments* (CED 81-4, January 26, 1981); *Requests for Federal Disaster Assistance Need Better Evaluation* (CED-82-4, December 7, 1981); *Improved Administration of Federal Public Disaster Assistance Can Reduce Costs and Increase Effectiveness* (CED-82-98, July 23, 1982); and *Federal Involvement in the Mount St. Helens Disaster: Past Expenditures and Future Needs* (RCED-83-16, November 15, 1982).

Decisionmaking under Disaster Conditions

1 For example, see Martin van Creveld, *Command in War* (Cambridge, Mass.: Harvard University Press, 1985).

2 Illustrations of crisis management literature dealing with security situations include M. Crecher, ed., *Studies in Crisis Behavior* (New Brunswick, N.J.: Transaction Books, 1979); Paul Bracker, *The Command and Control of Nuclear Forces* (New Haven: Yale University Press, 1983); Desmond Ball, *Can Nuclear War Be Controlled?* (London: International Institute for Strategic Studies, Adelphi Paper 169, 1981); Gerald W. Hopple, Stephen J. Andriole, and Amos Freedy, eds., *National Security Crisis Forecasting and Management;* (Boulder, Colo.: Westview Press, 1983); Daniel Ford, *The Button: The Pentagon's Strategic Command and Control* (New York: Simon and Schuster, 1985); and J. L. Richardson, "Crisis Management: A Critical Appraisal," paper submitted to World Congress of the International Political Science Association, Paris, 1985. Business crisis literature is illustrated by C. F. Smart and W. T. Stanbury, eds., *Studies on Crisis Management* (Toronto: Butterworth, 1978).

DDC has important characteristics of its own in comparison to security crises, such as absence of an "enemy," in the psychopolitical sense; less sensitivity of many features of disaster dynamics to DDC; absence of deliberate disinformation; easier definition of desirable outcome; and a less pronounced difference between the professional and the political levels; for example, see Alexander L. George, "Crisis Management: The Interaction of Political and Military Considerations," *Survival* 27 (September/October 1984): 223–34. Still, there is scope for much mutual learning between DDC and other forms of crisis management and for progress toward a comprehensive theory of crisis management.

3 See Yehezkel Dror, *Policymaking Under Adversity* (New Brunswick, N.J.: Transaction Books, 1986).

4 Compare with Harold A. Linstone et al., *Multiple Perspectives for Decision Making: Bridging the Gap Between Analysis and Action* (New York: Elsevier, 1984).

5 This paper is based in part on reprocessing of literature dealing with crisis management in other contexts, as illustrated in note 2, and on the growing literature dealing with DDC, such as: Gilbert F. White, ed., *Natural Hazards: Local, National, Global* (New York: Oxford University Press, 1974); Roger L. Wettenhall, *Bush Disaster: An Australian Community in Crisis* (Sydney: Angus and Robertson, 1975); Frederick C. Cuny, *Disasters and Development* (Oxford: Oxford University Press, 1983); and, rather unique and requiring urgent translation into English, Uriel Rosenthal, *Rampen Rellen Gijzelingen: Crisisbesluitvorming in Nederland* (Amsterdam: De Bataafsche Leeuw, 1984). Another basis is the work of the author on policymaking and in policy sciences in general, as reflected in, among others, Dror, *Policymaking Under Adversity*, and Dror, *Public Policymaking Reexamined* (supplemented ed., New Brunswick, N.J.: Transaction Books, 1983).

Important in many respects is the author's personal experience in crisis management and crisis management improvement, for instance, during his term of office as senior policy analyst and planning advisor of the Israel Ministry of Defense.

6 Still relevant and rather unique is Pitirim A. Sorokin, *Man and Society in Calamity: The Effects of War, Revolution, Famine, Pestilence Upon Human Mind, Behavior, Social Organization and Cultural Life* (New York: Dutton, 1942). See also S. Breznits, ed., *Stress in Israel* (New York: Van Nostrand, Reinhold, 1983).

7 See Joseph A. Schumpeter, *Capitalism, Socialism and Democracy* (London: Allen, Unwin, 1952), chap. 7.

8 See Ashok K. Dutt and Stephen Heal, "The Delta Works: A Dutch Experience in Project Planning," in Ashok K. Dutt and Frank J. Costa, eds., *Public Planning in the Netherlands* (Oxford: Oxford University Press, 1985), ch. 12, esp. pp. 187ff.

9 Relevant are Yair Aharoni, *The No-Risk Society* (Chatham, N.J.: Chatham House, 1981); and Mary Douglas and Aaron Wildavsky, *Risk and Culture: An Essay on the Selection of Technological and Environmental Dangers* (Berkeley: University of California Press, 1982). Related are the impacts of disasters and their management on future risk analysis and risk perception by different groups. Some relevant ideas are dispersed throughout Vincent T. Covello et al., eds., *The Analysis of Actual Versus Perceived Risks* (New York: Plenum, 1983).

10 The longer-range consequences of the plague in Europe demonstrate changing perception of the consequences of calamities with the passing of time. Immediate

horrible impacts gave way to important longer-range blessings. See Robert S. Gottfied, *The Black Death* (New York: Free Press, 1983); and Philip Ziegler, *The Black Death: A Study of the Plague in Fourteenth-Century Europe* (New York: Day, 1969).

11 For the concept see Guido Calabresi and Philip Bobbitt, *Tragic Choice* (New York: Norton, 1979).

12 See David Dery, *Problem Definition in Policy Analysis* (Lawrence: University Press of Kansas, 1984).

13 See Herbert A. Simon, "Rational Decision Making in Business Organizations," *American Economic Review* 69 (1979): 493–513.

14 See Yehezkel Dror, "Policy-Gambling: A Preliminary Exploration," *Policy Studies Journal* 12 (September 1983): 9–13.

15 See Daniel Kahnemann, Paul Slovic, and Amos Tversky, eds., *Judgment Under Uncertainty: Heuristics and Biases* (Cambridge: Cambridge University Press, 1982); and Dietrich Doerner et al., eds., *Lohhausen: Vom Umgang mit Unbestimmtheit und Komplexitaet* (Bern: Hans Huber, 1983).

16 Best developed in Howard Raiffa, *Decision Analysis* (Reading, Mass.: Addison-Wesley, 1968).

17 The author hopes to take up these issues in a book on policy-gambling, in progress.

18 See Irving L. Janis and Leon Manning, *Decision Making: A Psychological Analysis of Conflict, Choice, and Commitment* (New York: Free Press, 1977); and Ole R. Holsti and Alexander L. George, "The Effects of Stress on the Performance of Foreign Policy-Makers," *Political Science Annual* 6 (1975): 255–319.

19 Compare with Garry D. Brewer and Martin Shubik, *The War Game: A Critique of Military Problem Solving* (Cambridge, Mass.: Harvard University Press, 1979).

20 For example, see Irving L. Janis, *Groupthink: Psychological Studies of Policy Decisions and Fiascoes*, rev. ed. (Boston: Houghton Mifflin, 1982).

21 For example, James G. March and Johan P. Olsen, *Ambiguity and Choice in Organizations* (Bergen, Norway: Universitetsforlaget, 1976).

22 Some stimulating ideas are presented in Kenyon B. De Greene, *The Adaptive Organization: Anticipation and Management of Crisis* (New York: Wiley, 1982).

23 See John Von Neumann, "Probabilistic Logics and the Synthesis of Reliable Organisms from Unreliable Components," in C. E. Shannon and J. McCarthy, eds., *Automation Studies* (Princeton: Princeton University Press, 1950), pp. 83ff. Implications for design of policymaking systems, applying in principle also to DDC, are considered in Dror, *Public Policymaking Reexamined*, esp. p. 211.

24 A Popperian approach to formulation, support, and refutation of conjectures fits well the needs of DDC study and improvement, in line with the necessity for an appropriate philosophy of knowledge and philosophy of action base. See Sten A. Joensson and Rolf A. Lundin, *Methodological Problems in the Study of Organizational Behavior in Crises* (Gothenburg, Sweden: University of Gothenburg, Department of Business Administration, FE-Rapport 34, n.d.).

25 I leave open the controversial issue whether available legal powers in the United States, including the so-called legal doctrine of necessity, are perhaps

inadequate for some DDC needs.

26 See Donald A. Schon, *The Reflective Practitioner: How Professionals Think in Action* (New York: Basic Books, 1983).

27 Some relevant workshop designs and experiences of the author are described in Yehezkel Dror, *Advanced Workshops in Policy Analysis for Senior Decision-Makers: Lessons from Experience*, paper prepared for European Institute of Public Administration Round Table on Policy Analysis and Training of Public Servants, Maastricht, July 22–24, 1985. (Copies of the workshop outlines are available from the author on request.)

28 My own main explanation for the lack of participation by politicians in crisis exercises is their understandable reluctance to put themselves into a situation where they are monitored, evaluated, and "judged." Only very few politicians willingly accept such a challenge in earnest.

29 Interestingly, the private sector does not realize the potential demand for DDC supports. Thus, as far as I could find out, no suitable computer software is available, the various decision analysis programs which are on the market being unable to handle DDC uncertainties.

Other possibilities are illustrated by the adjustment of modern battlefield representation, display, and control systems to DDC. This is not an easy task, requiring much simplification, reduction in size and in costs. Still, the adjustment of systems such as MSE (Mobile Subscriber Equipment) to DDC poses a major challenge before research and development, including in the private sector.

Disaster Management in the Netherlands

1 ISONEVO/Committee on Disaster Studies of the National Academy of Sciences, *Studies in the Dutch Flood Disaster 1953* (Amsterdam, 1953); *Train Collision Harmelen 1962* (The Hague, 1962); A. L. M. van Eijnatten, "Explosion in a Naphtha Cracking Unit," in ISONEVO/Committee on Disaster Studies of the National Academy of Sciences, *Loss Prevention* (September 1977).

2 A. H. Barton, *Communities in Disaster* (Garden City, N.Y.: Doubleday, 1962), pp. 123–201.

3 ISONEVO, vol. 4, p. 58.

4 Disaster Act, sec. 1.

5 See M. H. Halperin, *Bureaucratic Politics and Foreign Policy* (Washington, D.C., 1974); F. Rourke, *Bureaucracy, Politics and Public Policy* (Boston: Little, Brown, 1969).

6 This term was introduced in connection with the Lengede mining disaster in West Germany (October–November 1963).

7 See Verta Taylor, "Future Directions for Study," in Enrico L. Quarantelli, ed., *Disasters: Theory and Research* (London and Beverly Hills, Calif.: Sage, 1978), p. 261.

8 Compare Russell R. Dynes, *Organized Behavior in Disaster* (Columbus, Ohio:

Heath-Lexington, 1974), pp. 214–15.

9 Dynes, *Organized Behavior*, p. 96.

10 Barton, *Communities in Disaster*, p. 38.

11 M. Wolfenstein, *Disaster: A Psychological Essay* (Glencoe, Ill.: Free Press, 1957).

12 ISONEVO, vol. 4, pp. 21–26.

13 J. W. Powell, *An Introduction to the Natural History of Disaster* (College Park: University of Maryland Press, 1954), p. 3.

14 Peter Ester, ed., *Social Aspects of the Environment Issue* (Assen: Van Gorcum, 1975); in Dutch.

15 An attitude similar to that of police and military officers. See Uriel Rosenthal, "The Bureaupolitics of Policing: The Dutch Case," in *Police Science Abstracts* 12 (1984): i–xiv.

16 Herbert Kaufman, *Are Government Organizations Immortal?* (Washington, D.C.: Brookings, 1976).

17 Yehezkel Dror, "Muddling Through: Science of Inertia," *Public Administration Review* (1964): 153–63; R. E. Goodin, *Political Theory and Public Policy* (Chicago: University of Chicago Press, 1982), pp. 39–56.

18 See also Ronald W. Perry, *The Social Psychology of Civil Defense* (Lexington, Mass.: Lexington Books, 1982), pp. 101–7.

Science and the State in Latin America

Research for this chapter was supported by the National Science Foundation under Grant CEE-824245. The authors bear sole responsibility for all statements of fact and interpretation.

1 National Research Council Panel on the Public Policy Implications of Earthquake Prediction, *Earthquake Prediction and Public Policy* (Washington, D.C.: National Academy of Sciences, 1975), p. 24. See also Frank Press, "Earthquake Prediction," *Scientific American* 232 (May 1975): 14–23.

2 National Research Council Committee on Socioeconomic Effects of Earthquake Predictions, *A Program of Studies on the Socioeconomic Effects of Earthquake Predictions* (Washington, D.C.: National Academy of Sciences, 1978), p. 1.

3 Alberto Giesecke, "El desarrollo de la geofísica," Congreso Nacional de Historia (Lima), November 11–16, 1984; and Bruno Podesta, "Moviendo el piso: La grave crisis de Instituto Geofísico y el terremoto administrativo," *Caretas* (Lima) 847 (1985): 52–53.

4 The *Pure and Applied Geophysics* articles were as follows: Brian T. Brady, "Theory of Earthquakes I: A Scale Independent Theory of Rock Failure," 112 (1974): 701–25; "Theory of Earthquakes II: Inclusion Theory of Crustal Earthquakes," 113 (1975): 149–67; "Theory of Earthquakes III: Inclusion Collapse Theory of Deep Earthquakes," 114 (1976): 119–39; "Theory of Earthquakes IV: General Implications for Earthquake Prediction," 114 (1976): 1031–93.

5 Internal U.S. Bureau of Mines memo from Brian Brady (USBM-Denver) to Robert Marovelli (USBM-Washington, D.C.), June 5, 1978.

6 Alberto Giesecke, "Algunos aspectos de la reaccion ante la prediccion de un terremoto en el Peru," *Revista Geofisica* (Mexico) 13 (1980): 45.

7 The research referred to is Enrique Silgado F., *Historia de los sismos mas notables ocurridos en el Peru* (1513–1974) (Lima: Instituto de Geologia y Mineria, 1978).

8 Memo from Brian Brady (USBM-Denver) to L. C. Pakiser (USGS-Golden), August 25, 1977. It became a prediction by not merely specifying place (75 km offshore Lima) and magnitude (8.5 ± 0.1) but also time (5.9 years from November 14, 1974).

9 Alberto Giesecke, "Case Study of the Peru Prediction for 1980–1981," UNDRO-UNESCO Seminar on Earthquake Prediction Case Histories (Geneva), October 12–15, 1982, p. 10.

10 Giesecke, "Algunos aspectos," p. 46.

11 Ibid.

12 Leonidas Ocola, *Analisis de la prediccion sismica China* (Lima: IGP, 1980).

13 Giesecke, "Case Study of the Peru Prediction," p. 11.

14 "Lima 00090," January 4, 1980.

15 Giesecke, "Algunos aspectos," p. 47.

16 "Lima 6427," July 2, 1981.

17 A complete study of the entire Brady-Spence affair will be found in Richard Stuart Olson, Joanne M. Nigg, and Bruno Podesta, *The Politics of Earthquake Prediction* (Princeton, N.J.: Princeton University Press, forthcoming, 1988).

Policy Analysis as the Study of Implements

1 In the discussion that follows I have deliberately blurred the useful distinction, initially made by Walter Williams, between policy analysis and policy research, where the former is "synthesizing information" to support decisions, and the latter is "using scientific methodologies to describe phenomena . . . and the relationships between them." See Williams, *Social Policy Research and Analysis* (New York: Elsevier, 1971), pp. 12ff. I have done so not because I disagree with the distinction, but because I wish to emphasize the social division of labor involved in the production of policy analysis and research.

2 See Carol Weiss, "Research for Policy's Sake: The Enlightenment Function of Social Research," *Policy Analysis* 3: 531–45; and Richard Elmore, "Social Policymaking as Strategic Intervention," in Edward Seidman, ed., *Handbook of Social Intervention* (Beverly Hills, Calif.: Sage, 1983), pp. 212–36.

3 The best account of these trade-offs is still James Coleman, "Policy Research in the Social Sciences," General Learning Press, 1972.

4 I am indebted to Aaron Wildavsky's discussion of the craft of policy analysis in *Speaking Truth to Power: The Art and Craft of Policy Analysis* (Boston: Little, Brown, 1979), pp. 385–406.

5 The etymology of *craft* indicates that it derives from Middle English, Anglo-Saxon, and German words for "strength, power, and force." Only in modern English did it begin to acquire the meaning "skill." In contemporary dictionaries the first definition typically emphasizes skill, while the second or third emphasizes guile, cunning, and deception. All definitions include reference to manual arts or dexterity in the production of tangible objects.

6 E. S. Quade, *Analysis for Public Decisions* (New York: Elsevier, 1975); Edith Stokey and Richard Zeckhauser, *A Primer of Policy Analysis* (New York: Norton, 1979); Garry Brewer and Peter deLeon, *The Foundations of Policy Analysis* (Homewood, Ill.: Dorsey, 1983).

7 Eugene Bardach, *The Implementation Game* (Berkeley: University of California Press, 1977); Theodore Lowi, "American Business, Public Policy, Case Studies, and Political Theory," *World Politics* 16 (1964): 677–715; J. Q. Wilson, "The Politics of Regulation," in J. Q. Wilson, ed., *The Politics of Regulation* (New York: Basic Books, 1980); Erwin Hargrove, "The Search for Implementation Theory," in Richard Zeckhauser and Derek Leebaert, eds., *What Role for Government? Lessons from Policy Research* (Durham, N.C.: Duke University Press, 1983), pp. 280–94.

8 Eugene Bardach, "Implementation Studies and the Study of Implements," paper presented to the 1980 Annual Meeting of the American Political Science Association; Lester Salamon, "Rethinking Public Management: Third-Party Government and the Changing Forms of Government Action," *Public Policy* 29 (1981): 255–75.

9 The results of this research are available upon request from Lester Salamon and Michael Lund, Urban Institute, Washington, D.C.

10 Peter May, "Hints for Crafting Alternative Policies," *Policy Analysis* 7 (1981): 227–44.

11 This section summarizes a more extended analysis contained in Richard Elmore, "The Safe Operation of Nuclear Power Plants: Implementing Federal Policy in the Aftermath of Three Mile Island," *International Journal of Mass Emergencies and Disasters* 2 (1984).

12 This description is drawn from Daniel Ford, *Three Mile Island: Thirty Minutes to Meltdown* (New York: Penguin, 1981), pp. 16–22; and David Okrent and Dade Moeller, "Implications for Reactor Safety of the Accident at Three Mile Island, Unit 2," *Annual Review of Energy* 6 (1981): 44–51.

Ethical Issues in Emergency Management Policy

The author, a philosopher, is a research associate at the Cooperative Institute for Research in Environmental Sciences and the Institute of Behavioral Science at the University of Colorado. This paper has benefited from the comments and criticism of Louise Comfort, Karl Kisslinger, and Clement Shearer, who are not responsible for the shortcomings that remain. Research and writing was supported by an Interdisciplinary Incentive Award from the Program in Ethics and Values in Science and Technology (EVIST), cosponsored by the National Science Foundation and the National Endowment for the Humanities (Award no. RII-8210282). The views expressed herein are those of the author, and do not necessarily reflect the positions and policies of these sponsoring agencies.

1 Prominent among those who have criticized the attempt at value-free policy science are Lawrence Tribe, Mark Sagoff, Alastair MacIntyre, and K. S. Shrader-Frechette. See also numerous publications by the Hastings Center and the Center for Philosophy and Public Policy (University of Maryland), many of which can function well as avenues to the issues and the literature of the value-free policy controversy.

2 Risa Palm's important study reveals that in California neither home buyers nor appraisers nor lending institutions set prices that reflect seismic hazards. "In sum," she writes, "the housing market has accepted [seismic risk] zonation with a giant yawn." Risa Palm, "Geography and Consumer Protection: Housing Market Responses to Earthquake Hazards Disclosure," *Southeastern Geographer* 25 (May 1985): 67, 69, 71. The paper summarizes an extensive study by Palm, Marston, Kellner, Smitty, and Budetti, *Home Mortgage Lenders, Real Property Appraisors and Earthquake Hazards* (Boulder: University of Colorado, Institute of Behavioral Science, 1983).

3 Such a hypothetical point of view is proposed by John Rawls in his celebrated and esteemed work, *A Theory of Justice* (Cambridge, Mass.: Harvard University Press, 1971).

4 This is the "scenario earthquake" studied by the California Division of Mines and Geology, James F. Davis et al., "Earthquake Planning Scenario for a Magnitude 8.3 Earthquake on the San Andreas Fault in Southern California," Special Publication 60 (Sacramento: California Department of Conservation, Division of Mines and Geology, 1982).

5 At the present state of the science, short-term predictions (hours and days) and long-term hazard assessments (probabilities over several years) are more reliable than such an intermediate time prediction as imagined here. However, this scenario raises the more interesting ethical issues. (My thanks to Clement Shearer for pointing this out.)

6 By this I mean that these ethical decisions will not be arbitrary, random, and incoherent. Rather, they will follow a pattern displaying a moral theory, just as colloquial speech displays a grammatical structure unknown to the uneducated speaker (or, in the case of "deep structures," the professor of linguistics). For more about "implicit moral theory" see Ernest Partridge, "Are We Ready for an Ecological Morality?" *Environmental Ethics* 4 (Winter 1984): 175–90. That paper draws upon important work by John Rawls, Noam Chomsky, and Lawrence Kohlberg.

7 Garrett Hardin, "The Tragedy of the Commons," *Science* 162 (December 1968): 1245.

8 Louise K. Comfort, "Designing Policy for Action: The Emergency Management System," this volume.

9 Well-coordinated codes of conduct and procedure would thus help to bring about and sustain what John Rawls calls a "well-ordered society"; namely, a society in which the parties know not only that they will behave rationally and

justly but also that others will behave likewise, and that this knowledge and
expectation is mutual and reciprocated—that is, "they know that others know
that they know." Rawls, *A Theory of Justice*, pp. 4, 453ff.

10 For important recent work on "moral intuitions" and "the moral sense," see the
work of Lawrence Kohlberg and, once again, John Rawls, *A Theory of Justice*,
pp. 46ff. My ideas along these lines (following the ideas of Kohlberg and Rawls)
may be found in my "Are We Ready for an Ecological Morality?"

11 This role of the philosopher is not unlike what Comfort, in this volume, calls
"the function of design in emergency problem-solving," namely, "to structure
the elements of decision—information, timing, known constraints, interaction
among participants—in a process which is likely to yield the most appropriate
choice in the most timely fashion." To this list I would add "value clarification
and assessment" in terms of such philosophical criteria as consistency, coherence, and comprehensiveness.

Synthesis in Disaster Management

1 See the model of professional design presented in Louise K. Comfort, "Designing
Policy for Action: the Emergency Management System," this volume.

2 See, for example, Richard L. Ender and John Choon Kim, "The Design and
Implementation of Disaster Mitigation Policy"; Jack D. Kartez and William J.
Kelley, "Research-based Disaster Planning: Conditions for Implementation";
Louise K. Comfort and Anthony G. Cahill, "Increasing Problem-solving Capac-
ity between Organizations," all in this volume.

3 Kartez and Kelley, "Research-based Disaster Planning"; Comfort and Cahill,
"Increasing Problem-solving Capacity."

4 Carolyn Smart and Ian S. Vertinsky, "Designs for Crisis Decision Units," *Administrative Science Quarterly* 22 (December 1977): 640–57.

5 See, for example the discussion by Yehezkel Dror in "Decisionmaking Under
Disaster Conditions," this volume.

6 See, for example, James G. March and Johan P. Olsen, *Ambiguity and Choice
in Organizations* (Oslo: Universitetsforlaget, 1976; 2d ed., 1979); Lotfi Zadeh,
Fuzzy Sets and Their Application to Cognitive and Decision Processes (New
York: Academic Press, 1975); Herbert A. Simon, "The Structure of Ill-Structured
Problems," in *Models of Discovery* (Englewood Cliffs, N.J.: Prentice-Hall, 1977);
Yehezkel Dror, *Policymaking Under Adversity* (New Brunswick, N.J.: Transac-
tion Books, 1986); and Gregory Bateson, "Men are Grass: Metaphor and the
World of Mental Process," *The Lindisfarne Letter* (West Stockbridge, Mass.:
Lindisfarne Press, 1980).

7 Daniel Kahneman, Paul Slovic, and Amos Tversky, *Judgment Under Uncertainty:
Heuristics and Biases* (Cambridge: Cambridge University Press, 1982); Louise
K. Comfort, "The Limits of Rationality in Public Agencies and Programs,"
paper presented at the Annual Meeting of the American Society for Public
Administration, San Francisco, California, April 13–16, 1980.

8 Simon, "The Structure of Ill-Structured Problems."

9 This well-known syllogism is quoted by Bateson in "Men are Grass."

10 Ibid.

11 Louise K. Comfort, interviews conducted in Mexico City with international administrative personnel involved in disaster rescue and recovery operations following the September 19, 1985, earthquake. The interviews were conducted during the period September 27–October 12, 1985. The author gratefully acknowledges the Natural Hazards Information and Applications Center, University of Colorado; the University Center for Social and Urban Research, the University Center for International Studies, and the Graduate School of Public and International Affairs, all of the University of Pittsburgh; and the Heinz Foundation of Pittsburgh for financial support for her study of the decisionmaking processes in the Mexico earthquake.

Bibliography

Ackoff, Russell L. *Redesigning the Future: A Systems Approach to Societal Problems.* New York: John Wiley, 1974.

Adams, J. D. *Understanding and Managing Stress: A Book of Readings.* San Diego: University Associates, 1980.

Agor, W. H. "Training Public Managers to Develop and Use Their Intuition for Decision Making." *Professional Development Handbook* (1983): 1–6.

Aharoni, Yair. *The No-Risk Society.* Chatham, N.J.: Chatham House, 1981.

Alexander, Ernest R. "Design in the Decision-Making Process." *Policy Sciences* 14 (1982).

Allison, Graham T. *The Essence of Decision: Explaining the Cuban Missile Crisis.* Boston: Little, Brown, 1971.

Anderson, William. *Disaster and Organizational Change: A Study of the Long-term Consequences of the 1964 Alaska Earthquake.* Columbus: Disaster Research Center, Ohio State University, 1969.

Applebaum, S. H. *Stress Management for Health Care Professionals.* Rockville, Md.: Aspen Systems, 1981.

Argyris, Chris. *Reasoning, Learning and Action.* San Francisco: Jossey-Bass, 1982.

————, and Donald A. Schön. *Theory and Practice: Increasing Organizational Effectiveness.* San Francisco: Jossey-Bass, 1974.

Atkisson, Arthur, and William J. Petak. "The Politics of Community Seismic Safety," unpublished manuscript, 1981.

Axelrod, Robert. *The Evolution of Cooperation.* New York: Basic Books, 1984.

Bachrach, Peter, and Morton S. Baratz. *Power and Poverty: Theory and Practice.*

New York: Oxford University Press, 1970.

Ball, Desmond. *Can Nuclear War Be Controlled?* London: International Institute for Strategic Studies, Adelphi Paper 169 (1981).

Bardach, Eugene. *The Implementation Game.* Cambridge, Mass.: MIT Press, 1977.

———. "Implementation Studies and the Study of Implements." Paper presented to the annual meeting of the American Political Science Association, 1980.

Barton, Allen H. *Communities in Disaster: A Sociological Analysis of Collective Stress Situations.* Garden City, N.Y.: Doubleday, 1970.

———. "The Emergency Social System." In *Man and Society in Disaster,* edited by G. W. Baker and D. W. Chapman. New York: Basic Books, 1962.

Bateson, Gregory. "Men are Grass: Metaphor and the World of Mental Process." *The Lindisfarne Letter.* West Stockbridge, Mass.: Lindisfarne Press, 1980.

Berman, Paul. "The Study of Macro- and Microimplementation." *Public Policy* 26, no. 2 (1978): 6–184.

Berman, Paul, et al. *Federal Programs Supporting Educational Change,* vols. 1–5. Santa Monica, Calif.: Rand Corporation, 1974.

Bolin, R. "Disasters and Long-Term Recovery Policy: A Focus on Housing and Families." *Policy Studies Review* 4 (May 1985): 709–15.

Bracker, Paul. *The Command and Control of Nuclear Forces.* New Haven: Yale University Press, 1983.

Brady, Brian T. "Theory of Earthquakes I: A Scale Independent Theory of Rock Failure." *Pure and Applied Geophysics* 112 (1974): 720–25.

———. "Theory of Earthquakes II: Inclusion Theory of Crustal Earthquakes." *Pure and Applied Geophysics* 113 (1975): 149–67.

———. "Theory of Earthquakes III: Inclusion Collapse Theory of Deep Earthquakes." *Pure and Applied Geophysics* 114 (1976): 119–39.

———. "Theory of Earthquakes IV: General Implications for Earthquake Prediction." *Pure and Applied Geophysics* 114 (1976): 1031–93.

Brewer, Garry, and Peter De Leon. *The Foundations of Policy Analysis.* Homewood, Ill.: Dorsey, 1983.

———, and Martin Shubik. *The War Game: A Critique of Military Problems Solving.* Cambridge, Mass.: Harvard University Press, 1979.

Breznits, S., ed. *Stress in Israel.* New York: Reinhold, 1983.

Brockriede, Wayne, and Douglas Ehninger. "Toulmin on Argument: An Interpretation Application." *Quarterly Journal of Speech* 46 (1960): 44–53.

Brown, Michael. *The Poisoning of America by Toxic Chemicals.* New York: Washington Square Press, 1981.

Brugmann, Bruce, and Greggar Sletteland, eds. *The Ultimate Highrise: San Francisco's Mad Rush Toward the Sky.* San Francisco: *San Francisco Bay Guardian,* 1971.

Brunswik, Egon. "Representative Design and Probabilistic Theory in Functional Psychology." *Psychological Review* 62 (1955): 193–217.

Burby, Raymond J., and Beverly A. Cigler. "Effectiveness of State Assistance Programs for Flood Hazard Mitigation." In *Regional and State Water Resources Planning and Management,* edited by R. Charbeneau, pp. 179–188. Bethesda, Md.: American Water Resources Association, 1984.

Burby, Raymond J., and Steven P. French. "Coping with Floods: The Land Use Management Paradox." *Journal of the American Planning Association* 47 (July 1981): 289–300.

Burby, Raymond J., and Daniel A. Okun. "Land Use Planning and Health." *Annual Review of Public Health* 4 (1983): 47–67.

Burby, Raymond J., et al. *Flood Plain Land-Use Management: A National Assessment.* Boulder, Colo.: Westview Press, 1985.

Burns, Tom, and G. M. Stalker. *The Management of Innovation.* London: Tavistock, 1961.

Burton, Ian. "Cultural and Personality Variables in the Perception of Natural Hazards," *Environment and the Social Sciences Perspectives and Applications,* edited by J. F. Wohlwill and D. H. Carson, pp. 184–195. Washington, D.C.: American Psychological Association 1972.

Burton, Ian, Robert Kates, and Gilbert White. *The Environment as Hazard.* New York: Oxford University Press, 1978.

Byl, N., and B. Sykes. "Work and Health Problems: An Approach to Management for the Professional and the Community." *Community Health* 9, no. 3: 149–58.

Calabresi, Guido, and Philip Bobbitt. *Tragic Choice.* New York: Norton, 1979.

California Seismic Safety Commission. *Public Official Attitudes Towards Disaster Preparedness in California.* Sacramento, Calif.: 1979.

California Seismic Safety Commission. *Report #ssc83–10.* Sacramento, Calif.: 1983.

Cameron, Kim S. "Effectiveness as Paradox: Consensus and Conflict in Conceptions of Organizational Effectiveness." *Management Science* 32 (May 1986): 539–53.

Campbell, Ian. "The Influence of Geologic Hazards on Legislation in California." *California Geology* (October 1977).

Caplow, T., H. Bahr, and B. Chadwick. *Analysis of the Readiness of Local Communities for Integrated Emergency Management Planning,* contract no. EMW-83-C-1127. Washington, D.C.: FEMA, 1984.

Chandler, A. D. *Strategy and Structure.* Cambridge: The MIT Press, 1962.

Chang, S. "Disaster and Fiscal Policy: Hurricane Impact on Municipal Revenue." *Urban Affairs Quarterly* 18 (June 1983): 511–23.

Charniss, C. *Burnout, Job Stress in the Human Services.* Beverly Hills, Calif.: Sage, 1980.

Cheng, Joseph L. C., and William McKinley. "Toward an Integration of Organization Research and Practice: A Contingency Study of Bureaucratic Control and Performance in Scientific Settings." *Administrative Science Quarterly* 28, no. 1 (March 1983): 85–100.

Cigler, Beverly A., Edward J. Kaiser, David J. Moreau, and Bruce Stiftel. *Flood Plain Land-Use Management: A National Assessment.* Boulder, Colo.: Westview Press, 1985.

Clary, Bruce B. "The Evolution and Structure of Natural Hazard Policies." *Public Administration Review* 45, special issue (January 1985).

Cohen, Michael D. "The Power of Parallel Thinking." *Journal of Economic Behavior and Organization* 2 (1981): 285–306.

―――. "Conflict and Complexity: Goal Diversity and Organizational Effectiveness." *American Political Science Review* 78, no. 2 (June 1984): 435–51.

————, J. G. March, and J. Olsen. "The Garbage Can Model of Organizational Choice." *Administrative Science Quarterly* 17, no. 1 (March 1972): 1–25.

Cohen, R. E. and F. L. Ahearn. *Handbook for Mental Health Care of Disaster Victims.* Baltimore, Md.: Johns Hopkins University Press, 1980.

Coleman, James. "Policy Research in the Social Sciences." General Learning Press, 1972.

Colen, B. D. "Aircrash Rescue Workers also Victims, Psychiatrist says." *Washington Post,* July 9, 1979.

Comfort, Louise K. "The Limits of Rationality in Public Agencies and Programs." Paper presented at the annual meeting of the American Society for Public Administration, San Francisco, California, 1980.

————. "Fitting Systematic Research Methods to Actual Social Conditions: The Quasi-experimental Approach to Social Research." Paper presented at the annual meeting of the American Political Science Association, Chicago, Illinois, 1983.

————. "Information Search Processes in Emergency Management: Computer Simulation as a Means of Improving Organizational Decision-making Capacity." In *Emergency Planning,* edited by John M. Carroll. San Diego, Calif.: Simulation Councils, Simulation Series 15, no. 1, 1985. (This article was later published in Sallie Marston, ed., *Terminal Disasters: Computer Applications in Emergency Management* [Boulder: Institute of Behavioral Science, monograph no. 39, May 1986].)

————. "Integrating Organizational Action in Emergency Management: Strategies for Change." *Public Administration Review* 45, special issue (January 1985): 155–64.

————. "Action Research: A Model for Organizational Learning." *Journal of Policy Analysis and Management* 5, no. 1 (1985): 100–118.

————. "International Disaster Assistance in the Mexico City Earthquake." *New World* (Fall 1986): 12–43.

Committee on Disasters and the Mass Media. *Disaster and the Mass Media,* Washington, D.C.: National Research Council, 1980.

Cook, T. D., and Donald T. Campbell. *Quasi-Experimentation.* Skokie, Ill.: Rand McNally, 1979.

Covello, Vincent T., et al. *The Analysis of Actual Versus Perceived Risks.* New York: Plenum, 1983.

"Crash Trauma, Nightmares Plague Rescuers." *Time* 61 (January 8, 1979).

Crecher, M., ed. *Studies in Crisis Behavior.* New Brunswick, N.J.: Transaction Books, 1979.

Crozier, M. *The Bureaucratic Phenomenon.* Chicago: University of Chicago Press, 1963.

Cummings, L., et al. "Creative Behavior as a Function of Task Environment: Impact of Objective, Procedures and Controls." *Academy of Management Journal* 18: (1975).

Cuny, Frederick C. *Disasters and Development.* Oxford: Oxford University Press, 1983.

Dahl, Robert. *Who Governs?* New Haven: Yale University Press, 1961.

Daily Times. Anchorage, Alaska, April 27, 1964.

Dandridge, T. C., Ian Mitroff, and W. F. Joyce. "Organizational Symbolism: A

Topic to Expand Organizational Analysis." *Academy of Management Review* (1980).

Davis, James F., et al. "Earthquake Planning Scenario for a Magnitude 8.3 Earthquake on the San Andreas Fault in Southern California." Sacramento: California Department of Conservation, Division of Mines and Geology, 1982.

De Greene, Kenyon B. *The Adaptive Organization: Anticipation and Management of Crisis.* New York: Wiley, 1982.

Dery, David. *Problem Definition in Policy Analysis.* Lawrence: University Press of Kansas, 1984.

Diamond, Stuart. "The Disaster in Bhopal: Lessons for the Future." *The New York Times.* February 3, 1985, p. 1.

Doerner, Dietrich, et al., eds. *Lohhausen: Vom Umgang mit Unbestimmtheit und Komplexitaet.* Bern, Switzerland: Hans Huber, 1983.

Douglas, Mary, and Aaron Wildavsky. *Risk and Culture.* Berkeley: University of California Press, 1982.

Drabek, Thomas E. "Managing the Emergency Response." *Public Administration Review* 45, special issue (January 1985): 85–92.

Drabek, Thomas E., Alvin H. Mushkatel, and Thomas S. Kilijanek. *Earthquake Mitigation Policy: The Experience of Two States.* Boulder: Institute of Behavioral Science, University of Colorado, 1983.

Drabek, Thomas E., Harriet Tamminga, and Thomas J. Kilijanek. *Managing Multiorganizational Emergency Responses.* Boulder: Institute of Behavioral Science, University of Colorado, 1981.

Dror, Yehezkel. "Advanced Workshops in Policy Analysis for Senior Decision-Makers: Lessons from Experience." Paper prepared for European Institute of Public Administration Round Table on Policy Analysis and Training of Public Servants, Maastricht, the Netherlands, July 22–24, 1985.

———. "Muddling Through: Science of Inertia." *Public Administration Review* (1964): 153–63.

———. "Policy-Gambling: A Preliminary Exploration." *Policy Studies Journal* 1 (September 1983): 9–13.

———. *Policymaking Under Adversity.* New Brunswick, N.J.: Transaction Books, 1986.

———. *Public Policymaking Reexamined.* New Brunswick, N.J.: Transaction Books, 1983.

Dunn, William N. *Public Policy Analysis: An Introduction.* Englewood Cliffs, N.J.: Prentice-Hall, 1981.

Duston, H. "The Consequence of Stress." In *Clinical Roundtables.* Bloomfield, N.J.: Rocks Laboratories, Health Learning Systems, 1979.

Dutt, Ashok K., and Stephen Heal. "The Delta Works: A Dutch Experience in Project Planning." In *Public Planning in the Netherlands,* edited by Ashok K. Dutt and Frank J. Costa. Oxford, England: Oxford University Press, 1985.

Dynes, Russell R. *Organized Behavior in Disaster.* Columbus, Ohio: Heath-Lexington, 1974.

Dynes, Russell R., Enrico L. Quarantelli, and Gary A. Kreps. *A Perspective on Disaster Planning.* Columbus: Ohio State University Disaster Research Center, 1972.

Edel, M. "People Versus Places in Urban Impact Analysis." In *The Urban Impacts of Federal Policy*, edited by N. Glickman. Baltimore: Johns Hopkins University Press, 1980.

Edelwich, J. and A. Brodsky. *Burn-out: Stages of Disillusionment in the Helping Professions.* New York: Human Science Press, 1980.

Edwards, George C., III. *Implementing Public Policy.* Washington, D.C.: Congressional Quarterly Press, 1980.

Elmore, Richard F. "Backward Mapping: Implementation Research and Policy Decisions." In *Studying Implementation*, edited by Walter Williams et al., pp. 18–35, Chatham, N.J.: Chatham, 1982.

———. "The Safe Operation of Nuclear Power Plants: Implementing Federal Policy in the Aftermath of Three Mile Island." *International Journal of Mass Emergencies and Disasters* 2 (1984).

———. "Social Policymaking as Strategic Intervention." In *Handbook of Social Intervention*, edited by Edward Seidman. Beverly Hills, Calif.: Sage Publications, 1983.

Emery, F. E., and E. C. Trist. "The Causal Texture of Organizational Environments." *Human Relations* 18 (1965): 20–16.

Ender, Richard L. *Matanuska-Susitna Borough Comprehensive Plan Survey*, vol. 1, sample survey results, prepared for the Matanuska-Susitna Borough, December 1984.

Ester, Peter, ed. *Social Aspects of the Environment Issue.* Assen: Van Gorcum, 1975.

Feldman, Martha, and James G. March. "Information in Organizations as Signal and Symbol." *Administrative Science Quarterly* 26 (1981): 171–86.

Ferman, Barbara. *Governing the Ungovernable City.* Philadelphia: Temple University Press, 1985.

Fischer, Frank. *Politics, Values, and Public Policy: The Problem of Methodology.* Boulder, Colo.: Westview Press, 1980.

Fleishman, Joel L., Lance Liebman, Mark H. Moore, and Donald P. Warwick. "The Ethics of Adminstrative Discretion." In *Public Duties: The Moral Obligation of Government Officials.* Cambridge, Mass.: Harvard University Press, 1981.

Ford, Daniel. *Three Mile Island: Thirty Minutes to Meltdown.* New York: Penguin, 1981.

———. *The Button: The Pentagon's Strategic Command and Control.* New York: Simon and Schuster, 1985.

Form, William, and Sigmund Nosow. *Community in Disaster.* New York: Harper, 1958.

Forstenzer, A. "Stress, the Psychological Scarring of Air Crash Rescue Personnel." *Firehouse* (July 1980).

Frankenhauser, M. "Psychoneuroendocrine Approaches to the Study of Stressful Person Environmental Transactions." *Selye's Guide to Stress Research.* New York: Van Nostrand Reinhold, 1980.

Frederick, Calvin J. *Aircraft Accidents: Emergency Mental Health Problems.* Washington, D.C.: National Institute of Mental Health, U.S. Department of Health and Human Services, 1981.

Freeman, K. "CMHC Responses to the Chicago and San Diego Airplane Disasters." *Technical Assistance Center Report* 2, no. 1 (1979).

Freudenberger, H. G., and G. Richelson. *Burnout: The High Cost of High Achievement.* Garden City, N.Y.: Anchor, 1980.

Friesema, H., J. Caporaso, G. Goldstein, R. Lineberry, and R. McCleary. *Aftermath: Communities After Natural Disaster.* Beverly Hills, Calif.: Sage, 1979.

George, Alexander L. "Crisis Management: The Interaction of Political and Military Considerations." *Survival* 27, no. 5 (September/October 1984): 223–34.

Gibson, James L., et al. *Organizations: Behavior, Structure, Processes.* 5th ed. Homewood, Ill.: Business Publications, 1985.

Gieseke, Alberto. "Algunos Aspectos de la Reacción ante la predicción de un Terremoto en el Peru." *Revista Geofisica* (Mexico) 13 (1980): 45.

———. "Case Study of the Peru Prediction for 1980–1981." UNDRO-UNESCO Seminar on Earthquake Prediction Case Histories, Geneva, October 12–15, 1982.

———. "El desarrollo de la geofisica." Congreso Nacional de Historia, Lima, November 11–16, 1984.

Giuffrida, Louis O. *Emergency Management: The National Perspective.* Emmitsburg, Md.: National Emergency Training Center, Monograph Series I (1983).

Glass, A. J. "Psychological Aspects of Disaster." *Journal of the American Medical Association* 171, no. 2 (1959): 222–25.

Godschalk, David R., and David J. Brower. "Mitigation Strategies and Integrated Emergency Management." *Public Administration Review* 45, special issue (January 1985): 64–71.

Goodin, R. E. *Political Theory and Public Policy.* Chicago: University of Chicago Press, 1982.

Gottfried, Robert S. *The Black Death.* New York: Free Press, 1983.

Graham, N. K. "Done In, Fed Up, Burned Out: Too Much Attrition in EMS." *Journal of Emergency Medical Services* 6, no. 1.

Graham, N. K. "How to Avoid a Short Career." *A Journal of Emergency Medical Services* 6, no. 2.

Gross, N. C., J. Giacquinta, and M. Bernstein. *Implementing Organizational Innovations.* New York: Basic Books, 1971.

Haas, J., R. Kates, and M. Bowden, eds. *Reconstructions Following Disasters.* Cambridge, Mass.: MIT Press, 1977.

Halperin, M. H. *Bureaucratic Politics and Foreign Policy.* Washington, D.C.: 1974.

Hammond, Kenneth R., ed. *Judgment and Decision in Public Policy Formation.* Boulder, Colo.: Westview Press, 1978.

———, et al. "Social Judgment Theory." In *Human Judgment and Decision Processes,* edited by Martin F. Kapland and Steven Schwartz. New York: Academic Press, 1975.

Hardin, Garrett. "The Tragedy of the Commons." *Science* 162 (December, 1968): 1243–48.

Hargrove, Ervin C. "The Search for Implementation of Theory." In *What Role for Government? Lessons from Policy Research,* edited by Richard Zeckhauser and Derek Leebaert. Durham, N.C.: Duke University Press, 1983.

———. *The Missing Link: The Study of the Implementation of Social Policy.*

Washington, D.C.: The Urban Institute, 1975.

Haveman, Robert H. *The Economic Performance of Public Investments.* Baltimore: Johns Hopkins University Press, 1972.

Hawley, K., and M. L. Nichols. "A Contextual Approach to Modeling the Decision to Participate in a 'Political' Issue." *Administrative Science Quarterly* 27 (1982): 105–19.

Heller, T. "The Effects of Involuntary Relocation." *American Journal of Community Psychology* 10, no. 4 (1982): 471–91.

Henle, Mary. "The Snail Beneath the Shell." *Abraxas* 1 (1971).

Hoetmer, G. "Emergency Management." International City Management Assoc., *Baseline Data Reports* 15, no. 4 (1983).

Hoetmer, G. "Interorganizational Relationships in Emergency Management." Paper prepared for NASPAA/FEMA Public Administration Faculty Workshop on Emergency Management, May 20–June 2, 1984.

Hohenemser, Christoph, Roger Kasperson, and Robert W. Kates. "Causal Structure: A Framework for Policy Formulation." In *Risk in the Technological Society*, edited by Hohenemser and Kasperson. Boulder, Colo.: Westview Press, 1982.

Holland, John. *Adaptation in Natural and Artificial Systems.* Ann Arbor: University of Michigan Press, 1975.

Holsti, Ole R. "Crisis, Stress and Decision-Making." *International Social Science Journal* 23 (1971): 53–67.

———, and Alexander L. George. "The Effects of Stress on the Performance of Foreign Policy-Makers." *Political Science Annual* 6 (1975): 255–319.

Honadle, Beth W. "A Capacity-Building Framework: A Search for Concept and Purpose." *Public Administration Review* (September/October 1981): 575–580.

———. *Capacity-Building (Management Improvement) for Local Governments: An Annotated Bibliography*, RDRR-28. Washington, D.C.: U.S. Department of Agriculture, Economic Statistics Service, March 1981.

Hopple, Gerald W., Stephen J. Andriole, and Amos Freedy, eds. *National Security Crisis Forecasting and Management.* Boulder, Colo.: Westview Press, 1983.

Hutton, Janice, and Dennis Mileti. *Analysis of Adoption and Implementation of Community Land Use Regulations for Floodplains.* San Francisco, Calif.: Woodward-Clyde, 1979.

Illinitch, R. C., and M. P. Titus. "Caretakers as Victims: The Big Thompson Flood, 1976." *Smith College Studies in Social Work* 48, no. 1.

ISONEVO/Committee on Disaster Studies of the National Academy of Sciences. *Studies in the Dutch Flood Disaster 1953.* Amsterdam: ISONEVO, 1953.

ISONEVO/Committee on Disaster Studies of the National Academy of Sciences. *Train Collision Harmelen 1962.* The Hague: ISONEVO, 1962.

Jacobs, Allan B. *Seismic Safety Plan for San Francisco: Its Preparation and Adoption.* In *Proceedings* of the P.R.C.-U.S.A. Joint Workshops in Earthquake Disaster Mitigation through Architecture, Urban Planning and Engineering, Beijing, China, 1982.

Jaffee, Martin. *Earthquake Research in Urban and Regional Planning: A Research Agenda.* Summary of the Conference on Earthquake Research in Urban and Regional Planning, Seattle, Washington, April 16–17, 1983.

Janis, Irving L. *Groupthink: Psychological Studies of Policy Decisions and Fiascoes.*

Boston: Houghton Mifflin, 1982.

———, and Leon Mann. *Decision Making: A Psychological Analysis of Conflict, Choice, and Commitment*. New York: Free Press, 1977.

Joensson, Sten A., and Rolf A. Lundin. *Methodological Problems in the Study of Organizational Behavior in Crises*. Gothenburg, Sweden: University of Gothenburg, Department of Business Administration, FE-Rapport 34.

Johnston, D.H. "Crisis Intervention." *Critical Care Update* 6, no. 4: 5–60.

Kahn, R. "Job Burnout Prevention and Their Remedies." *Public Welfare* 36, no. 2.

Kahneman, Daniel, Paul Slovic, and Amos Tversky, eds. *Judgment Under Uncertainty: Heuristics and Biases*. New York: Cambridge University Press, 1982.

Kartez, J. *Emergency Planning Implications of Local Government Adaptive Response to Mt. St. Helens*. Working Paper 46. Boulder: Institute of Behavioral Science, University of Colorado, 1982.

———. "Crisis Response Planning: Toward a Contingent Analysis." *Journal of the American Planning Association* 50, no. 1 (1984): 9–21.

———, and W. Kelley. *Emergency Planning and the Adaptive Local Response to the Mt. St. Helens Eruptions*. Pullman: Washington State University, 1980.

Kasperson, Roger E., and K. David Pijawka, "Societal Response to Hazards and Major Hazard Events: Comparing Natural and Technological Hazards." *Public Administration Review*, special issue (January 1985): 7–18.

Kaufman, H. *Are Government Organizations Immortal?* Washington, D.C.: 1976.

Keena, B. "What We've Learned about Firefighter Safety and Health." *Emergency Management* (Spring 1981).

Kiesler, S., and L. Sproull. "Managerial Response to Changing Environment: Perspectives on Problem-sensing from Societal Cognition." *Administrative Science Quarterly* 27 (1982).

Kingdon, John W. *Agendas, Alternatives, and Public Policies*. Boston: Little, Brown, 1984.

Kirlin, John J. "A Political Perspective." *Public Sector Performance*, edited by Trudi C. Miller. Baltimore: Johns Hopkins University Press, 1984.

Klauss, Rudi, and Bernard M. Bass. *Interpersonal Communication in Organizations*. New York: Academic Press, 1982.

Kleppner, Paul. *Chicago Divided*. DeKalb: Northern Illinois University Press, 1985.

Kliman, A. S. "The Corning Flood Project: Psychological First Aid Following a Natural Disaster." In *Emergency and Disaster Management: A Mental Health Sourcebook*. Bowie, Md.: Charles Press, 1975.

Knott, Jack, and Aaron Wildavsky. "If Dissemination Is the Solution, What Is the Problem?" *Knowledge: Creative, Diffusion, Utilization* 1, no. 4 (1979): 537–78.

Kunreuther, Howard, R. Ginsberg, L. Miller, P. Sagi, P. Slovic, B. Borkan, and N. Katz. *Disaster Insurance Protection: Public Policy Lessons*. New York: John Wiley & Sons, 1978.

Kusler, John A. "Liability as a Dilemma for Local Managers." *Public Administration Review* 45, special issue (January 1985): 118–22.

Labadie, J. "Problems in Local Emergency Management." *Environmental Management* 8, no. 6 (1984): 489–94.

Lambright, W. Henry. "Earthquake Prediction and the Governmental Process: A Longitudinal Study of Three States." Paper presented for Hazards Research Policy Development, and Implementation Incentives Focus on Urban Earthquake, Workshop at University of Redlands, Calif., June 24–26, 1982.

LaPlante, J. "1986 Fiscal Impacts of Recurrent Flooding." In *Proceedings: 1986 State Floodplain Management Conference*, edited by Alan Williams.

———, and J. S. Kroll-Smith. "Centralia: The Nightmare Which Would Not End." In *Crisis Management: A Casebook*, edited by M. Charles and J. C. Kim. Springfield, Ill.: Charles C Thomas, 1986.

Lawrence, P. R., and J. W. Lorsch. "Differentiation and Integration in Complex Organizations." *Administrative Science Quarterly* 12 (1967): 11–47.

Lazarus, R. S. *Patterns of Adjustment and Human Effectiveness*. New York: McGraw-Hill, 1969.

Levine, A. *Love Canal: Science, Politics and People*. Lexington, Mass.: D.C. Heath, 1982.

Levine, S. "Stress and Behavior." *Scientific American* (January 1971): 26–31.

Lewis, Ralph G. and J. R. Greene. "Implementation Evaluation: A Future Direction in Project Evaluation." *Journal of Criminal Justice* 6: 91–103.

Lindblom, Charles E. *Politics and Markets*. New York: Basic Books, 1977.

Lindblom, Charles E., and David K. Cohen. *Usable Knowledge: Social Science and Social Problem Solving*. New Haven, Conn.: Yale University Press, 1979.

Lindell, M., and R. Perry. "Evaluation Criteria for Emergency Response Plans in Radiological Transportation." *Journal of Hazardous Materials* 3 (1980): 335–48.

Linstone, Harold A., et al. *Multiple Perspectives for Decision Making: Bridging the Gap Between Analysis and Action*. New York: Elsevier, 1984.

Lippert, W., and E. R. Ferrar. "The Cost of 'Coming Out on Top.' Emotional Responses to Surviving the Deadly Battle." *FBI Law Enforcement Bulletin* (December 1981): 6–10.

Littlejohn, R. F. *Crisis Management: A Team Approach*. New York: American Management Association, 1983.

Long, Senator Russell B. Remarks in the *U.S. Congressional Record, Senate 111* pt. 21, 89th Cong., 1st sess., October 21, 1965: 27948.

Lowi, Theodore. "American Business, Public Policy, Case Studies and Political Theory." *World Politics* 16 (1964): 677–715.

Lowi, Theodore. *End of Liberalism*. New York: Norton, 1969.

McKean, Roland N. *Efficiency in Government Through System Analysis*. New York: Wiley, 1958.

McKenna, C. "Three Mile Island." In *Crisis Management: A Casebook*, edited by M. Charles and J. C. Kim. Springfield, Ill.: Charles Thomas Publishers, 1986.

McKenney, J., and P. Keen. "How Managers' Minds Work." *Harvard Business Review* (May–June 1979): 74–90.

McLoughlin, David. "A Framework for Integrated Emergency Management." *Public Administration Review* 45, special issue (January 1985): 165–72.

Mader, George, et al. "Microzonation and Land Use Planning." *Proceedings for the Joint U.S.-P.R.C. Microzonation Workshop*. United States National Science Foundation and the Peoples Republic of China State Seismological Bureau, Harbin, China, September 11–16, 1981.

Maier, N. R. F. *Problem Solving and Creativity in Individuals and Groups*. Belmont, Calif.: Brooks-Cole, 1970.

March, James G., and Johan P. Olsen. *Ambiguity and Choice in Organizations*. Oslo: Universitetsforlaget, 1976.

———. "The New Institutionalism: Organizational Factors in Political Life." *The American Political Science Review* 78, no. 3 (September 1984).

March, James G., and Herbert A. Simon. *Organizations*. New York: Wiley Press, 1958.

Maslach, C. "The Client Role in Staff Burn-Out." *Journal of Social Issues* 34, no. 4 (1978).

———, and S. Jackson. "Burned Out Cops and Their Families." *Psychology Today* 59 (May 1979).

Mason, Richard, and Ian Mitroff. *Challenging Strategic Planning Assumptions: Theory, Cases and Techniques*. New York: Wiley, 1981.

May, Peter J. "Federal-State Relations and Disaster Relief Formulation." Paper presented at the Western Political Science Association, San Diego, California, 1982.

———. "Hints for Crafting Alternative Policies." *Policy Analysis* 7 (1981): 227–44.

———. *Recovering from Catastrophes: Federal Disaster Relief Policy and Politics*. Westport, Conn.: Greenwood Press, 1985.

———, and Walter Williams. *Disaster Policy Implementation: Managing Programs Under Shared Governance*. New York: Plenum, 1986.

Mazmanian, D. A., and P. A. Sabatier. *Implementation and Public Policy*. Glenview, Ill.: Scott, Foresman and Co., 1983.

Meltsner, Arnold, and Christopher Bellavita. *The Policy Organization*. Beverly Hills, Calif.: Sage, 1984.

Meyer, M., and P. Belobaba. "Contingency Planning for Response to Urban Transportation System Disruption." *Journal of the American Planning Association* 48 (1982): 545–65.

Mileti, Dennis S. "Human Adjustment to the Risk of Environmental Extremes." *Sociology and Social Research* 64, no. 3 (April 1980): 327–47.

Miller, Robert D., and Ernest Dobrovolny. *Surficial Geology of Anchorage and Vicinity Alaska*. U.S. Geological Survey Bulletin 1093. Washington, D.C.: Government Printing Office, 1959.

Miller, S. M. "When is a Little Information a Dangerous Thing? Coping with Stressful Events by Monitoring Versus Blunting." In *Coping and Health*. New York: Plenum, 1979.

Milliman, Jerome W. "An Agenda for Economic Research on Flood Hazard Mitigation." In *A Plan for Research on Floods and Their Mitigation in the United States*, edited by Stanley A. Changnon, Jr., William C. Ackermann, Gilbert F. White, and J. Loreena Ivens. Champaign, Ill.: Illinois State Water Survey Division, 1983.

Mintzberg, H. "Planning on the Left Side and Managing on the Right Side." *Harvard Business Review* (July–August 1976): 49–58.

Mitchell, J. T. "Emergency Medical Stress." *Journal of Association of Public Safety Communication Officers* APCO Bulletin (February 1983).

———. "Healing the Helper." *Role Conflict and Support for Emergency Workers*, edited by Bonnie Green. Washington, D.C.: American Psychological Association, Federal Emergency Management Agency and the National Institute for Mental Health, 1985.

————. "Recovery from Rescue." *Response, the Magazine of Emergency Management* (Fall 1982): 7–10.

Mitroff, Ian I., and James R. Emshoff. "On Strategic Assumption-Making: A Dialectical Approach to Policy and Planning." *Academy of Management Review* 4 (1979): 1–12.

Mitroff, Ian I., and Richard O. Mason. *Creating a Dialectical Social Science.* Boston, Mass.: D. Reidel Publishing Company, 1981.

Mitroff, Ian I., and Francisco Sagasti. "Epistemology as General Systems Theory: An Approach to the Design of Complex Decision-making Experiments." *Philosophy of the Social Sciences* 3 (1973): 117–34.

Mohr, Lawrence B. *Explaining Organizational Behavior.* San Francisco: Jossey-Bass Publishers, 1982.

Mulvihill, M. L. *Human Diseases: A Systemic Approach.* Bowie, Md.: Robert J. Brady, 1980.

Mushkatel, Alvin W., and Louis F. Wechsler. "Emergency Management and the Intergovernmental System." *Public Administration Review* (January 1985): 49–56.

National Governors' Association. *1978 Emergency Preparedness Project Final Report.* Washington, D.C.: Government Printing Office, 1978.

National Governors' Association. *Federal Emergency Authorities Abstracts.* Washington, D.C.: Government Printing Office, May 1979.

National Governors' Association. *Comprehensive Emergency Management Bulletin,* no. 1, Washington, D.C.: NGA Office of State Services, April 1982.

National Research Council, Advisory Board on the Built Environment. *Multiple Hazard Mitigation: Report of a Workshop in Mitigation Strategies for Communities Prone to Multiple Natural Hazards.* Washington, D.C.: National Academy Press, 1983.

National Research Council, Committee on Socioeconomic Effects of Earthquake Predictions. *A Program of Studies on the Socioeconomic Effects of Earthquake Predictions.* Washington, D.C.: National Academy of Sciences, 1978.

National Research Council, Panel on the Public Policy Implications of Earthquake Prediction. *Earthquake Prediction and Public Policy.* Washington, D.C.: National Academy of Sciences, 1975.

Nelson, Richard R., and Douglas Yates, eds. *Innovation and Implementation in Public Organizations.* Lexington, Mass.: Lexington Books, 1978.

Newell, Allen, and Herbert A. Simon. *Human Problem Solving.* Englewood Cliffs, N.J.: Prentice-Hall, Inc. 1972.

Nigg, Joanne. "Putting the Public Back into Concern about Public Policy." *Newsletter,* Earthquake Engineering Research Institute, July 1980.

O'Brien, D. "Mental Anguish, An Occupational Hazard." *Emergency* 12, no. 3.

Ocola, Leonidas. *Analisis de la Predicción Sismica China.* Lima: IGP, 1980.

Office of Science and Technology Policy, Working Group on Earthquake Hazards Reduction, Executive Office of the President. *Earthquake Hazard Reductions: Issues for an Implementation Plan,* 1978.

Okrent, David, and Dade Moeller. "Implications for Reactor Safety of the Accident at Three Mile Island, Unit 2." *Annual Review of Energy* 6 (1981): 44–51.

Olson, Richard Stuart, Joanne M. Nigg, and Bruno Podesta. *The Politics of Earth-quake Prediction.* Princeton, N.J.: Princeton University Press, forthcoming, 1988.

Olson, Richard Stuart, and Douglas D. Nilson, Jr. "Public Policy Analysis and Hazards Research: Natural Complements." *Social Science Journal* 19, 1 (January 1982).

Ouchi, W. "The Relationship Between Organizational Structure and Organizational Control." *Administrative Science Quarterly* (March 1977).

Palm, Risa. "Geography and Consumer Protection: Housing Market Responses to Earthquake Hazards Disclosure." *Southeastern Geographer* 25, no. 1 (May 1985).

————, et al. *Home Mortgage Lenders, Real Property Appraisors and Earthquake Hazards.* Boulder: University of Colorado, Institute of Behavioral Science, 1983.

Partridge, Ernest. "Are We Ready for an Ecological Morality?" *Environmental Ethics* 4 (Winter 1984): 175–90.

Patrick, P. D. S. "Burnout: Job Hazard for Health Workers." *Hospitals* (November 16, 1979): 87–90.

Perrow, Charles. *Complex Organizations: A Critical Essay.* Glenview, Ill.: Scott, Foresman, 1972.

————. "Normal Accident at Three Mile Island." *Society* 18 (July–August 1981): 17–26. Reprinted in *Critical Studies in Organization and Bureaucracy,* edited by Frank Fischer and Carmen Sirianni. Philadelphia: Temple University Press, 1974.

————. *Normal Accidents: Living with High-Risk Technologies.* New York: Basic Books, 1984.

Perry, Ronald W. "Evacuation Decision-Making in Natural Disasters." *Mass Emergencies* 4, no. 1 (1979): 25–38.

————. "Incentives for Evacuation in Natural Disasters." *Journal of the American Planning Association* 95 (October 1979): 440–447.

————. *The Social Psychology of Civil Defense.* Lexington, Mass.: Lexington Books, 1982.

————, M. K. Lindell, and M. R. Greene. *Evacuation Planning in Emergency Management.* Lexington, Mass.: Lexington Books, 1981.

Perry, Ronald W., and Alvin W. Mushkatel. *Disaster Management: Warning, Response and Community Relocation.* Westport, Conn.: Quorum Books, 1984.

————. *Disaster Response and Preparedness Among Minority Citizens.* Athens: University of Georgia Press, 1985.

Petak, William J. "Development of Earthquake Hazard Reduction Policies in the Cities of Long Beach and Santa Ana." Presented at the University of Redlands, 1982.

————, ed. "Emergency Management: A Challenge for Public Administration." *Public Administration Review* 45, special issue (January 1985).

Petak, William J., and Arthur Atkisson. "Intergovernmental Problems in Policy Implementation: A Case Study of Seismic Standards of California Building Codes." Unpublished manuscript, April 1981.

————. *Natural Hazard Risk Assessment and Public Policy*. New York: Springer-Verlag, Inc., 1982.

Peterson, Paul E. *City Limits*. Chicago: University of Chicago Press, 1981.

Podesta, Bruno. "Moviendo el piso: La grave crisis de Instituto Geofisico y el terremoto administrativo." *Caretas* (Lima) 847 (1985): 52–53.

Polsby, Nelson W. *Community Power and Political Theory*. 2d edition. New Haven: Yale University Press, 1980.

Pope, Carl, Samuel S. Epstein, and Lester O. Brown. *Hazardous Waste in America*. San Francisco, Calif.: Sierra Club Books, 1982.

Portney, Paul R. "Toxic Substance Policy and the Protection of Human Health." In *Current Issues in U.S. Environmental Policy*, edited by Paul R. Portney et al. Baltimore: Johns Hopkins University Press, 1978.

Powell, J. W. *An Introduction to the Natural History of Disaster*. College Park, Md.: University of Maryland, 1954.

Pressman, Jeffrey, and Aaron Wildavsky. *Implementation*. Berkeley: University of California Press, 1973.

Prigogine, Ilya, and I. Stengers. *Order Out of Chaos*. New York: Bantam, 1984.

Quade, E. S. *Analysis for Public Decisions*. New York: Elsevier, 1975.

Quarantelli, Enrico L. *Organizational Behavior in Disasters and Implications for Disaster Planning*. Emmitsburg, Md.: FEMA, National Emergency Training Center, 1984.

Raiffa, Howard. *Decision Analysis*. Reading, Mass.: Addison-Wesley, 1968.

Rawls, John. *A Theory of Justice*. Cambridge, Mass.: Harvard University Press, 1971.

Ricci, P. F., L. A. Sagan, and C. G. Whipple, eds. *Technological Risk Assessment*. Boston: Martinus Nijhoff, 1984.

Richardson, J. L. "Crisis Management: A Critical Appraisal." Paper submitted to World Congress of the International Political Science Association, Paris, 1985.

Rittell, H. W. J., and M. M. Webber. "Dilemmas in a General Theory of Planning." *Policy Sciences* 4 (1973): 155–69.

Rogers, Everett, and D. Lawrence Kincaid. *Communication Networks: Towards a New Paradigm for Research*. New York: Free Press, 1981.

Rogers, George O., and Jiri Nehnevajsa. *Behavior and Attitudes Under Crisis Conditions: Selected Issues and Findings*. Washington, D.C.: Government Printing Office, contract no. EMW-C-0736, February, 1984.

Rosenthal, Uriel. "The Bureaupolitics of Policing: The Dutch Case." *Police Science Abstracts* 12, no. 5 (1984): i–xiv.

————. *Rampen Rellen Gujzelingen: Crisisbesluitvorming in Nederland*. Amsterdam: De Bataafsche Leeuw, 1984.

Rossi, Peter H., et al. "The State and Local Politics of Natural Disasters." In *Social Science and Natural Hazards*, edited by James D. Wright and Peter H. Rossi, 44–88. Cambridge, Mass.: Abt Books, 1981.

Rossi, Peter H., James D. Wright, and Eleanor Weber-Burdin. *Natural Hazards and Public Choice: The State and Local Politics of Hazard Mitigation*. New York: Academic Press, 1982.

Rourke, F. *Bureaucracy, Politics and Public Policy*. Boston: Little, Brown, 1969.

Rubin, Claire B. *Long Term Recovery from Natural Disasters: A Comparative*

Analysis of Six Local Experiences. Washington, D.C.: Academy for State and Local Government, 1982.

————, et al. *Community Recovery from a Major Natural Disaster*. Boulder: Institute of Behavioral Science, University of Colorado, 1985.

Rubin, Claire B., and D. Barbee. "Disaster Recovery and Hazard Mitigation: Bridging the Intergovernmental Gap." *Public Administration Review* 45, special issue (January 1985): 57–63.

Saaty, Thomas L. *The Analytic Hierarchy Process*. New York: McGraw-Hill, 1980.

Salamon, Lester. "Rethinking Public Management: Third-Party Government and the Changing Forms of Government Action." *Public Policy* 29 (1981): 255–75.

Schön, Donald A. *The Reflective Practitioner: How Professionals Think in Action*. New York: Basic Books, 1983.

Schoonhoven, Claudia Bird. "Problems in Contingency Theory: Testing Assumptions Hidden Within the Language of Contingency Theory." *Administrative Science Quarterly* 26, no. 3 (September 1981): 349–77.

Schumpeter, Joseph A. *Capitalism, Socialism and Democracy*. London: Allen & Unwin, 1952.

Scott, Randall W., ed. *Management and Control of Growth*, vols. 1, 2, 3. Washington, D.C.: The Urban Land Institute.

Scott, Randall W. "Public-Private Sector Cooperation: Concepts and Ambiguities." *National Civic Review* 69 (July 1980): 365–70, 394.

Scott, Stanley. *Policies for Seismic Safety: Elements for a State Governmental Program*. San Diego: Institute of Governmental Studies, University of California, 1979.

Sedgwick, R. "Psychological Response to Stress." *Journal of Psychiatric Nursing and Mental Health Services* (September/October 1975).

Settle, Allen K. "Financing Disaster Mitigation, Preparedness, Response and Recovery." *Public Administration Review* 45, special issue (January 1985): 101–6.

Shrader-Frechette, K. S. *Risk Analysis and Scientific Method: Methodological and Ethical Problems with Evaluating Societal Hazards*. Boston: D. Reidel Publishing Co., 1985.

Siegel, S., and T. W. Kaemmerer. "Measuring the Perceived Support for Innovation in Organization." *Journal of Applied Psychology* 63 (1978): 553–62.

Simon, Herbert A. *Administrative Behavior*. 2d ed. New York: Macmillan, 1957.

Simon, Herbert A. *The New Science: A Management Decision*. Englewood Cliffs, N.J.: Prentice-Hall, 1971.

————. *Models of Discovery*. Boston: D. Riedel, 1977.

————. "Rational Decision Making in Business Organizations." *American Economic Review* 69, no. 4 (1979): 493–513.

————. *The Sciences of the Artificial*. Cambridge, Mass.: MIT Press, 1969, 1981.

Sink, David. "An Interorganizational Perspective on Local Emergency Management." *Policy Studies Review* 4 (May 1985): 698–708.

Slovic, Paul, Howard Kunreuther, and Gilbert White. "Decision Processes, Rationality and Adjustment to Natural Hazards." In *Natural Hazards: Local, National, Global*, edited by Gilbert White, pp. 187–204. New York: Oxford University Press, 1974.

Slovic, Paul, B. Fischhoff, and S. Lichtenstein. "Facts and Fears: Understanding

Perceived Risk." *Societal Risk Assessment: How Safe Is Safe Enough?*, edited by R. Schwing and W. Alberts, Jr., pp. 181–216. New York: Plenum, 1980.

Smart, C. F., and W. T. Stanbury, eds. *Studies on Crisis Management*. Toronto: Butterworth, 1978.

Smart, Carolyn, and Ian S. Vertinsky. "Designs for Crisis Decision Units." *Administrative Science Quarterly* 22, no. 4 (December 1977): 640–57.

Sorokin, Pitirim A. *Man and Society in Calamity: The Effects of War, Revolution, Famine, Pestilence Upon Human Mind, Behavior, Social Organization and Cultural Life*. New York: Dutton, 1942.

Stanley, S. R., and J. P. Saxon. "Occupational Stress: Implications for Vocational Rehabilitation Counseling." *Journal of Rehabilitation* 46, no. 2 (1980).

Steers, R. M., and L. W. Porter. *Motivation and Work Behavior*, 2d edition. New York: McGraw-Hill, 1979.

Steiner, G., ed. *The Creative Organization*. Chicago: University of Chicago Press, 1965.

Stokey, Edith, and Richard Zeckhauser. *A Primer of Policy Analysis*. New York: Norton, 1979.

Strauch, Ralph E. "A Critical Look at Quantitative Methodology." *Policy Analysis* 2 (1976): 121–44.

Sutphen, Sandra. "Disaster in Lake Elsinore: Can Forty Agencies Help This Little Town?" Paper presented at the Western Political Science Association Annual Conference, San Diego, California, 1982.

Svenson, Arthur G., and John G. Corbett. "Earthquakes, Hurricanes and the Mitigation of Risk at the Local Level: Comparing Response in California and Florida." Paper presented at the Annual Meeting of the Western Political Science Association. Denver, Colorado, 1981.

Swanstrom, Todd. *The Crisis of Growth Politics: Cleveland, Kucinich and the Challenge of Urban Populism*. Philadelphia: Temple University Press, 1985.

Taylor, James B., et al. *Tornado: A Community Responds to Disaster*. Seattle: University of Washington Press, 1970.

Taylor, Verta. "Future Directions for Study." In *Disasters: Theory and Research*, edited by Enrico L. Quarantelli. London and Beverly Hills, Calif.: Sage, 1978.

Texas Landowners Rights Association v. Harris, 453 F.Supp. 1025 (D.C.C. 1978).

Thompson, James D., and Robert W. Hawkes. "Disaster, Community Organizations, and Administrative Process." In G. W. Baker and D. W. Chapman, *Man and Society in Disaster*. New York: Basic Books, 1962.

Titchener, T. L., and F. I. Kapp. "Family and Character Change at Buffalo Creek." *American Journal of Psychiatry* 133, no. 3: 295–99.

Tönnies, Ferdinand. *Community and Society*. Translated from German and edited by Charles P. Loomis. Originally published in Germany in 1887. East Lansing: Michigan State University Press, 1957.

Toulmin, Stephen. *The Uses of Argument*. Cambridge: Cambridge University Press, 1958.

"Trouble in Silicon Valley." *Newsweek* (February 25, 1985): 92–94.

Turner, Ralph H., et al. *Community Response to Earthquake Threat in Southern California: Individual Awareness and Attitudes*. Los Angeles, Calif.: Institute for Social Science Research, University of California, 1978.

Tversky, Amos, and Daniel Kahneman. "Judgment Under Uncertainty: Heuristics and Biases." *Science* 185 (September 27, 1974): 1124–31.
———. "Availability: A Heuristic for Judging Frequency and Probability." *Cognitive Psychology* (1973): 207–32.
U.S. Comptroller General. *Hazardous Waste Sites Pose Investigation, Evaluation, Scientific, and Legal Problems.* CED-81-57. Washington, D.C.: General Accounting Office, April 24, 1981.
U.S. Congressional Record, 92nd Cong., 2d sess., 1972. Vol. 118, pt. 21.
U.S. Department of the Interior. *Primer on Improving the State of Earthquake Hazards Mitigation and Preparedness.* Open File Report 84-772. 1984.
U.S. Department of the Interior. *Proceedings of Conference XV: A Workshop on "Preparing for and Responding to a Damaging Earthquake in the Eastern United States."* Open File Report 82-220. 1981.
U.S. Department of the Interior. *Proceedings of Conference XX: A Workshop on the 1886 Charleston, South Carolina, Earthquake and Its Implications for Today.* Open File Report, 83-843. 1983.
U.S. Department of the Interior. *Report of the Barrier Islands Work Group,* 1978.
U.S. Environmental Protection Agency. *EPA's Emergency Response Program.* Washington, D.C.: Office of Emergency and Remedial Response, November 1982.
U.S. Environmental Protection Agency. *Superfund: What It Is, How It Works.* Washington, D.C.: Office of Solid Waste and Emergency Response, WH-562-A, December 1972.
U.S. Federal Emergency Management Agency (FEMA). *An Assessment of the Consequences and Preparations for a Catastrophic California Earthquake: Findings and Actions Taken.* Washington, D.C.: 1980.
U.S. Federal Emergency Management Agency. "Hazardous Materials Program Launched by FEMA." *FEMA Newsletter.* November/December 1984: 2–3.
U.S. Federal Emergency Management Agency, Senior Executive Policy Center. *Conference Report—Legal Issues in Emergency Management,* pp. 4–9. Emmitsburg, Md. August 1–3, 1984.
U.S. General Accounting Office. *The Federal Emergency Management Agency's Plan for Revitalizing U.S. Civil Defense: A Review of Three Major Plan Components.* NSIAD 84-11. Washington, D.C., 1984.
U.S. General Accounting Office. *Federal Involvement in the Mount St. Helens Disaster: Past Expenditures and Future Needs.* RCED-83-16. Washington, D.C., 1982.
U.S. General Accounting Office. *Federal Snow Removal Reimbursement Policy: Improvements Being Made in Flood Fighting Capabilities in the Jackson, Mississippi Area* (CED 80-36). Washington, D.C., 1979.
U.S. General Accounting Office. *Further Actions Needed to Improve Emergency Preparedness Around Nuclear Powerplants.* RCED-84-43. Washington, D.C., 1984.
U.S. General Accounting Office. *Implementation: The Missing Link in Planning Reorganizations.* GGD-81-57. Washington, D.C., 1981.
U.S. General Accounting Office. *Improved Administration of Federal Public Disaster Assistance Can Reduce Costs and Increase Effectiveness.* CED-82-98. Washington, D.C., 1982.

U.S. General Accounting Office. *The Johnstown Area Flood of 1977: A Case Study for the Future*. CED-78-114. Washington, D.C., 1978.

U.S. General Accounting Office. *Poor Controls Over Federal Aid in Massachusetts After the 1978 Blizzard Caused Questionable Benefit Payments*. CED-81-4. Washington, D.C., 1981.

U.S. General Accounting Office. *Requests for Federal Disaster Assistance Need Better Evaluation*. CED-82-4. Washington, D.C., 1981.

U.S. General Accounting Office. *Review of the Emergency Management Agency's Role in Assisting State and Local Governments to Develop Hurricane Preparedness Planning*. RCED-83-182. Washington, D.C., 1983.

U.S. General Accounting Office. *States Can Be Better Prepared to Respond to Disasters*. CED-80-60. Washington, D.C., 1980.

U.S. General Accounting Office. *Stronger Direction Needed for the National Earthquake Program*. RCED-83-103. Washington, D.C., 1983.

U.S. General Accounting Office. *Three Mile Island: The Most Studied Nuclear Accident in History*. EMD-80-109. Washington, D.C., 1980.

U.S. Mayors' Conference. *Emergency Management: A Mayor's Manual*. 1980.

van Creveld, Martin. *Command in War*. Cambridge, Mass.: Harvard University Press, 1985.

van Eijnatten, A. L. M. "Explosion in a Naphtha Cracking Unit." *Loss Prevention* (September 1977).

Von Neumann, John. "Probabilistic Logics and the Synthesis of Reliable Organisms from Unreliable Components." In *Automation Studies*, edited by C. E. Shannon and J. McCarthy. Princeton, N.J.: Princeton University Press, 1950.

Walker, Jack L. "Setting the Agenda in the U.S. Senate: A Theory of Problem Selection." *British Journal of Political Science* 7 (October 1977): 423–45.

Waller, Ray A., and Vincent T. Covello, eds. *Low-Probability High-Consequence Risk Analysis: Issues, Methods, and Case Studies*. New York: Plenum, 1984.

Warner, Sam Bass. *The Urban Wilderness*. New York: Harper and Row, 1972.

Watzlawick, Paul, John Weakland, and Richard Risch. *Change: Principles of Problem Formation and Problem Resolution*. New York: Norton, 1974.

Waugh, William L. "Counties, States, and the Questions of Trust and Capacity in a Realigned Federal System." *Publius* (forthcoming).

———. "Counties, States, and the New Federalism: The Issue of Trust in Intergovernmental Relations." Presented at the Southern Political Science Association Meeting. Nashville, Tenn., November 6–9, 1985.

———. "Current Policy and Implementation Issues in Disaster Preparedness." Atlanta: Institute of Public Administration, Georgia State University, 1985.

———. "Disaster Mitigation and Intergovernmental Relations: The Case of the Hyatt Skywalk Disaster." In *Crisis Management: A Casebook*, edited by Michael Charles and C. Kim. Springfield, Ill.: Charles Thomas, 1986.

Weiss, Carol. "Research for Policy's Sake: The Enlightenment Function of Social Research." *Policy Analysis* 3: 531–45.

Weller, J. *Organizational Innovation in Anticipation of Crisis*. Columbus: Disaster Research Center, Ohio State University, 1974.

Wenger, Dennis E., Charles E. Faupel, and Thomas F. James. *Disaster Beliefs and Emergency Planning*. Final Report to the National Science Foundation.

Newark: University of Delaware, 1980.

Wenk, Edward, Jr. *Margins for Survival*. Oxford, England: Pergamon Press, 1979.

Wettenhall, Roger L. *Bush Disaster: An Australian Community in Crisis*. Sydney, Australia: Angus and Robertson, 1975.

White, Gilbert. *Natural Hazards: Local, National, Global*. New York: Oxford University Press, 1974.

Whittaker, M. *Emergency Preparedness Project: Final Report*. Washington, D.C.: National Governors' Association, 1979.

Whittown, John. *Disasters: The Anatomy of Environmental Hazards*. London: Allen Lane Penguin Books, 1980.

Wijkman, Anders, and Lloyd Timberlake. *Natural Disasters: Acts of God or Acts of Man?* Washington, D.C.: Earthscan, 1984.

Wildavsky, Aaron. *Speaking Truth to Power: The Art and Craft of Policy Analysis*. Boston: Little, Brown, 1979.

Wilensky, Harold L. *Organizational Intelligence*. New York: Basic Books, 1967.

Williams, Walter. *The Implementation Perspective*. Berkeley: University of California Press, 1980.

————. *Social Policy Research and Analysis*. New York: Elsevier, 1971.

————, and R. E. Elmore, eds. *Social Program Implementation*. New York: Academic Press, 1976.

Williams, Walter, et al. *Studying Implementation: Methodological and Administrative Issues*. Chatham, N.J.: Chatham House, 1982.

Wilson, G. L., and P. Zarakas. "Anatomy of a Blackout." IEEE *Spectrum* (February 1978): 38–46.

Wilson, J. Q. "The Politics of Regulation." In *The Politics of Regulation*, edited by J. Q. Wilson. New York: Basic Books, 1980.

Wolensky, Robert, and Edward Miller. "The Everyday Versus the Disaster Role of Local Officials: Citizen and Official Definitions." *Urban Affairs Quarterly* 16 (June 1981): 483–504.

Wolfenstein, M. *Disaster: A Psychological Essay*. Glencoe, Ill.: Free Press, 1957.

Woodward, J. *Industrial Organization: Theory and Practice*. London: Oxford University Press, 1965.

Woolgar, S. W. "The Identification and Definition of Scientific Collectivities." In *Perspectives on the Emergence of Scientific Disciplines*, edited by Gerard Lemaine, R. MacLeod, M. Mulkay, and P. Weingart. Chicago: Aldine Press, 1974.

Wright, Deil. *Understanding Intergovernmental Relations*. 2d edition. Monterey, Calif.: Brooks-Cole, 1982.

Wright, James D., Peter H. Rossi, Sonia R. Wright, and Eleanor Weber-Burdin. *After the Clean-Up: Long-Range Effects of Natural Disasters*. Beverly Hills, Calif.: Sage, 1979.

Wright, James D., et al. *The Indifferent Politics of Natural Hazards*. Amherst, Mass.: SADRI, 1980.

Wyner, Alan J. "Urban Land Use Planning for Seismic Safety in California." In *Third International Earthquake Microzonation Conference, Proceedings*. Vol. 2. June 28–July 1, 1982.

Zadeh, Lotfi. *Fuzzy Sets and Their Applications to Cognitive and Decision Pro-*

cesses. New York: Academic Press, 1975.

Zadeh, Lotfi. "Fuzzy Sets as a Basis for a Theory of Possibility." *Fuzzy Sets and Systems*. Amsterdam: North-Holland, 1978.

Zeigler, Donald J., James H. Johnson, Jr., and Stanley D. Brunn. *Technological Hazards*. Washington, D.C.: Association of American Geographers, 1983.

Ziegler, Philip. *The Black Death: A Study of the Plague in Fourteenth-Century Europe*. New York: Day, 1969.

Zimmerman, Rae. "The Relationship of Emergency Management to Governmental Policies on Man-Made Technological Disasters." *Public Administrative Review* 45, special issue (January 1985): 29–39.

Index

Contributors

Louise K. Comfort is Associate Professor of Public and International Affairs at the University of Pittsburgh, Pittsburgh, Pennsylvania.

Charles F. Bonser is Dean of the School of Public and Environmental Affairs, Indiana University, Bloomington, Indiana.

Anthony G. Cahill is Assistant Professor of Public Administration at the Institute of Public Administration, Pennsylvania State University, University Park, Pennsylvania.

Beverly A. Cigler is Associate Professor of Political Science and Public Administration at North Carolina State University, Raleigh, North Carolina.

Yehezkel Dror is Professor of Political Science and Wolfson Professor of Public Administration at the Hebrew University of Jerusalem, Israel.

Richard F. Elmore is Professor at the College of Education, Michigan State University, East Lansing, Michigan.

Richard L. Ender is Professor of Public Policy and Administration at the School of Business and Public Affairs, University of Alaska, Anchorage, Alaska.

William J. Kelley is Associate Professor of Urban and Regional Planning at Eastern Washington University, Cheney, Washington.

Jack D. Kartez is Associate Professor of Environmental Science and Regional Planning at Washington State University, Pullman, Washington.

John Choon K. Kim is Professor and Chairman of the Department of Public Policy and Administration at the School of Business and Public Affairs, University of Alaska, Anchorage, Alaska.

Josephine M. LaPlante is Assistant Professor of Public Policy and Management at the University of Southern Maine, Portland, Maine.

Ralph G. Lewis is Associate Professor and Director of the Department of Public Administration, Florida International University, Bay Vista Campus, North Miami, Florida.

Peter J. May is Associate Professor of Political Science and Public Affairs at the University of Washington, Seattle, Washington.

Jeffrey G. Mitchell is Assistant Professor of Emergency Health Services at the University of Maryland, Baltimore County, Catonsville, Maryland.

Elliott Mittler is Assistant Professor of Systems Management at the University of Southern California, Los Angeles, California.

Richard Stuart Olson is Associate Professor of Political Science and Director of International Prog. ms at Arizona State University, Tempe, Arizona.

Ernest Partridge is a Research Fellow in the Department of Philosophy at California State University, San Bernardino, California.

Thomas J. Pavlak is Associate Professor of Public and International Affairs at the University of Pittsburgh, Pittsburgh, Pennsylvania.

Bruno Podesta is Professor and Director of the Grupo de Estudios para el Desarrollo (GREDES) at the Universidad del Pacifico in Lima, Peru.

Uriel Rosenthal is Professor of Public Administration at the University of Leiden, Leiden, the Netherlands.

Leonard I. Ruchelman is Eminent Professor of Urban Studies and Public Administration at Old Dominion University, Norfolk, Virginia.

Richard T. Sylves is Associate Professor of Political Science at the University of Delaware, Newark, Delaware.

William L. Waugh, Jr., is Associate Professor of Public Administration at the Institute of Public Administration, Georgia State University in Atlanta, Georgia.